LOUIS NAPOLEON

AND

THE RECOVERY OF FRANCE

NAPOLEON III

From a lithograph at the British Museum, after the painting by Alfred de Dreux

LOUIS NAPOLEON & THE RECOVERY OF FRANCE

BY

F. A. SIMPSON
FELLOW OF TRINITY COLLEGE, CAMBRIDGE

GREENWOOD PRESS, PUBLISHERS
WESTPORT, CONNECTICUT

Library of Congress Cataloging in Publication Data

Simpson, Frederick Arthur, 1883-
    Louis Napoleon & the recovery of France.

    Reprint of the 1965 issue of the 3d ed. first
published in 1951 by Longmans, Green, London, New York.
    Bibliography: p.
    Includes index.
    1. Napoléon III, Emperor of the French, 1808-1873.
2. France--History--Second Empire, 1852-1870.
3. France--Politics and government--1852-1870.
I. Title.
DC276.S62 1975   944.07   75-8490
ISBN 0-8371-8153-4

944.07

This edition first published in 1951 by Longmans, London.
New impression 1965

Reprinted with the permission of Mr. W. F. Ewbank

Reprinted in 1975 by Greenwood Press,
a division of Williamhouse-Regency Inc.

Library of Congress Catalog Card Number 75-8490

ISBN 0-8371-8153-4

Printed in the United States of America

NOTE TO THE 1960 IMPRESSION

When this volume was first published, unsigned condemnations of it from the same pen appeared in the two most authoritative journals in the language. And during the thirty years' silence on their part which followed, the author was given some reason to suppose that, in the interests of consistency, similar treatment would await any continuation of his work; continuation which the various consequences of disparagement so sponsored tended in any case to make difficult. In the last few years, however, their condemnation has in both journals been tardily, but most handsomely, retracted. Had this kindness come sooner, the present reissue might have been not of two volumes only, but of the four volumes originally designed. But glad though the author is to have lived long enough to receive it, he lacks strength now to rekindle a flame which he ought perhaps never to have suffered to be snuffed out.

CAMBRIDGE, 1959.

PREFACE TO THE THIRD EDITION

A FEW corroborative details have been added both to the text and to the notes of the present edition ; and a new appendix has been inserted, dealing with the only three points on which the writer has been challenged on any statement in this book. In two instances he has been charged with a judgment unduly hostile to Louis Napoleon : in one, with an attitude unduly favourable towards him. It will be seen from this appendix that he admits the truth of one charge out of the three : fresh evidence, as a note prefixed to the last edition of this volume explained, has shown that the casualties of the *coup d'état* were only about half of his original estimate. On the other hand, he believes himself to have refuted alike the excuse for the *coup* which would make it a mere anticipation of an Orleanist *attentat*, and also an attempt to shift the major burden of responsibility for the Crimean War from the shoulders of Stratford Canning.

In the author's original intention, his two books *The Rise of Louis Napoleon* and *Louis Napoleon and the Recovery of France* were to have been followed by two others, on *Louis Napoleon and the Liberation of Italy*, and *The Fall of Louis Napoleon*. Some portion of these later volumes was actually written. But several causes combined to discourage or delay the prosecution of a design perhaps in any case over-ambitious. And delay gave place to abandonment when, in 1940, the entire stock of the existing volumes was destroyed, in circumstances which made immediate replacement impossible, and even eventual republication improbable. The author is all the more grateful to his publishers for their willingness to reissue, even as a fragment, a work which he must regretfully recognise that he can now no longer hope to complete.

CAMBRIDGE, 1951.

vii

FROM THE PREFACE TO THE FIRST EDITION

THE extraordinary concentration of historic interest which the dominating figure of Napoleon has drawn to the First Empire has had for accompaniment—and possibly in part for consequence—a hardly less extraordinary neglect of the Second. The personal appeal of the first Napoleon sufficed to secure the prompt investigation as it became available of every kind of documentary evidence bearing upon his reign ; and his imperious sway has kept historians toiling indefatigably upon his domain long after the Law of Diminishing Returns was beginning to illustrate itself in the results of their labours.

No such commanding figure exists to summon their services to the Second Empire, which has hitherto formed the theme of only one real history at all. For Ollivier, who might at first sight seem to dispute with M. de La Gorce the title of its sole historian, was engaged upon an apologetic too purely personal to produce more than a contribution to the material of history. Valuable as that material is on the closing years of the Empire, it must even there be utilised with caution ; while of the Emperor's earlier and more vigorous years it supplies but a cursory introductory sketch.

La Gorce's finely written history shares with the work of Ollivier the disadvantage of being practically undocumented ; but on the whole it gains more from its author's remoteness from his subject than does Ollivier's from his proximity to the events which he described. On the other hand, as compared with Ollivier, La Gorce laboured under one grave disadvantage. He disliked and distrusted in its entirety Napoleon III's Italian policy : throughout it remains to this zealous Catholic a thing alien, mischievous, and incomprehensible. Such an attitude constitutes an overwhelming disability to any complete understanding of Louis Napoleon ; and though his liberal premier exaggerated the foresight and tenacity of the Emperor's methods in the pursuit of his schemes for Italy, yet his general sympathy with those schemes did enable him more nearly than La Gorce to approach what was after all the heart of Louis Napoleon's foreign policy.

The two works are thus in some sort complementary, and that of La Gorce especially is possessed of distinguished and enduring merit. But it remains impossible to compare the minute and numerous histories of the First Empire with either these or any minor studies of the Second, without being struck by a sense of disproportion. For personal issues apart, from the standpoint of European and universal history the First Empire, as compared with the Second, was an episode. Both its victories and its defeats were, by the side of its successor's, sterile ; and colossal as were its commotions they were as a whole singularly barren of proportionate and permanent result. For in general they evoked reactions strong enough, but only strong enough, to overwhelm them. Hence the whole affair ended at Vienna in an order which was as nearly a

successful 'As you were' as any which has ever been
issued in History.

Wholly different were the consequences of the Second
Empire. Its triumphs too were transitory : but its transit
left both the map and the moral order of Europe revolu-
tionised. The Europe of 1815 and the Europe of 1789
were neither in ponderables nor imponderables so far apart
as the Europe which contained and the Europe which
lacked the new Italy, the new Germany, and the temporal
power of the Pope. It remains of course possible to trace
back to the Napoleonic era almost any subsequent change
which is not already hypothecated to the age of Louis XIV.
Directly or indirectly Napoleon has been credited with
giving an impetus to any nationalist movement which
later in the nineteenth century succeeded, just as he would
have been pronounced to have rendered inevitable the
success of Poland, had she not failed. Such deductions
have their interest, and even in a measure their value. But
they involve processes so attractive to writers of history
that it would be well if they were accepted somewhat
cautiously by readers of it. For the remoter that are his
historic causes the finer fellow the historian feels himself.
Anybody can attribute a deed to the doer of it : it takes
an historian to trace it back to its opponents of some
previous generation. Yet even for historians the time is
approaching when it will be permissible to recognise, that
the most fruitful act after all of the First Empire was the
begetting of posthumous issue in the Second. For the
Second Empire itself is nearly remote enough now to seem
a respectable spiritual ancestor ; and the first régime to
take seriously the idea of self-determination has by this
time a large and turbulent offspring of its own. It is
moreover increasingly clear that without the unexpected
aid of one sincere friend at court the struggling and un-

orthodox cause of nationality could not have achieved its unexpected triumphs : and to have presented such a cause with such an ally is the historic function of the Second Empire.

But even on purely personal grounds its mournful and enigmatic ruler presents a challenging figure to posterity. And more than the neglect of French historians entitles him to the attention of historians other than French. No ruler of France—none perhaps of any European country— was so cosmopolitan in his training and outlook as Napoleon III. None certainly was less French. Essentially he was an international figure : too good a citizen perhaps of Europe to be the ultimately successful ruler of any one country in it. The dreams and broodings of South Germany, the sleepy dignity of the Dutch, the slow speech and kindliness of England, the secretiveness and fatalism of the Italy he so loved—these were his, and a compassion for the people and a humanitarian idealism that were not peculiarly French. In particular he had a dream that after they had combined in war to overthrow a despotism which they believed to threaten civilisation, the two great Western Powers should co-operate in peace to heal the wounds of a distracted Europe. ' The eyes of all who suffer,' he said, ' turn instinctively to the West.' [1] It was a speech in which he described himself as ' the interpreter of France.'

The generation which has passed since the appearance of the earlier volumes of Ollivier and La Gorce has added materially even to the published sources which formed for this portion of their work almost their sole source of information. As a result the present study can claim on some portion of the period it covers to be based on a wider survey of available evidence than any hitherto essayed.

[1] *Infra*, pp. 293, 294.

For the rest it owes to the comparatively virgin soil which
it turns a harvest which has at least rewarded beyond
his expectation the labour which the author has expended in gathering it. Of the printed sources consulted
by the writer of this volume a sufficient indication
will be found in the annotated bibliography at its close.
A word may perhaps be added in this place as to the unpublished material which has been drawn upon. The
French government still declines to permit the examination of its diplomatic correspondence after 1848 ; and the
Archives du Ministère des Affaires Étrangères cease in consequence to be accessible almost from the exact point at
which this volume begins. The writer of it is in no way
entitled to complain of a refusal most courteous in form
and universal in application. But it is impossible not to
regret the imposition of a close time so far exceeding, even
after a dynasty has disappeared, that found necessary in
a country where no such breach of continuity has occurred
to facilitate the incorporation of a past epoch into history.

The English Foreign Office Papers at the Record Office
—always, owing to the frankness with which they are displayed, the most valuable single source in existence for
recent diplomatic history—are however for the period of
the Second Empire of quite especial interest and importance. Not only did the Anglo-French alliance in its early
years render the diplomatic relations of the two countries
unusually intimate, but in the person of Lord Cowley
England possessed an ambassador at Paris who for a time
enjoyed in an unique degree the confidence of the sovereign
to whom he was accredited. For this reason he was on
occasion better informed even on the foreign policy of
France than was the French Minister of Foreign Affairs. I
have examined as well as the Paris Congress Papers the
whole correspondence with this embassy for the period

covered by this volume ; and on particular points de-spatches to and from all the major European capitals, as well as the Scandinavian, Italian, and Iberian embassies or legations. I have endeavoured not to obtrude the technical minutiæ of these investigations into the text : but where in my opinion new facts of general interest emerge or old theories of long standing are rendered untenable the claim to their establishment or refutation is made explicitly. Vague praise in prefaces of important or neglected documents is in the historian an empty form of self-laudation, unless he ventures also to indicate what new facts his researches in them have discovered.

Other manuscript sources to which I have had access are the English Home Office Papers, and the far fuller records of French public opinion contained in the political reports of the *procureurs généraux* at the Archives Nationales. I have also made use of the now numerous and voluminous collections of correspondence bearing on the period which have by this time become accessible both among the Additional MSS. at the British Museum and the Nouvelles Acquisitions françaises at the Bibliothèque Nationale.

CAMBRIDGE, 1922

The process employed in the present issue, while it allows of the removal of verbal misprints, precludes the possibility of real revision. But for this fact I should have rewritten pages 172 and 173 below, in view of the important new document from the Flahault papers published in 1924 in Lord Kerry's volume, *The Secret of the Coup d'Etat*, p. 156. I have already (*Times Literary Supplement*, 14 Aug., 1924) given reasons for my complete acceptance of the authenticity and veracity of this document; and in the light of it I should now accept the official version of six hundred as an approximately correct estimate of the total casualties of the coup d'état.

CAMBRIDGE, 1930.

NOTE TO THE 1965 IMPRESSION

Held up to ridicule in *The Times* on the morning of its publication, and shorn in consequence of sales and of reviews, this volume survived precariously until it eventually received praise which to its author seemed excessive. But he allows himself to hope that such praise may more nearly accord with the judgement of posterity than the treatment which originally denied completion to his work.

CAMBRIDGE, 1965.

CONTENTS

LIST OF PLATES

LOUIS NAPOLEON

AND

THE RECOVERY OF FRANCE

CHAPTER I

FALSE DAWN

Hail, Dawn of the Day !
How many things shalt thou quicken, how many shalt thou slay !
How many things shalt thou waken, how many lull to sleep !
How many things shalt thou scatter, how many gather and keep !
WILLIAM MORRIS.

ἤδη μυρί᾽ ἐσεῖδον ὀνείρατα, κοὐδέπω ἀώς.
THEOCRITUS.

ON the 21st of December 1848 the sun rose full and clear over Europe, dawning as he did so on the shortest day in the strangest year of memorable history. For it had been a year—this year of grace 1848—set for the ruin and resurrection of many things in Europe. Many courts had been dispersed, many potentates deposed, since that year began. Metternich was in exile ; and from one end of Europe to the other his authority was in abeyance. Guizot was gone, and in France his system had perished with him. The King of Bavaria, the Emperor of Austria, the King of the French, had abdicated lest worse should befall them ; from Berlin, Vienna, and from Rome itself reigning monarchs had for a season, and for a reason, retired. In their dominions, and those of half a dozen lesser sovereigns, constitutions innumerable, unworkable, and well-nigh unintelligible, had been published and applauded : some the handiwork of well-meaning assemblies, others the gifts of dissembling kings ; but all alike calculated, with

1

scarcely an exception, to make the very name of constitution a contempt.

But the year which was now expiring had more to its credit than this. Names in that year had taken to themselves men, and lived. Over stagnant peoples and into decadent bodies a breath of new life had passed. Strange half-forgotten flags fluttered in that breeze : German tricolor of black, white, and gold flaunting itself fitfully at Frankfort ; Italian tricolor of red, white, and green making a somewhat braver show of it in Lombardy. Eastwards the spirit passed, and still at its approach smouldering embers burst into flame, that diplomats had imagined quenched for ever. Venice blazed out a republic once more, and Hungary found herself again a nation. Everywhere there was a coming together of dry bones, not without noise and shaking.

Indeed to all appearance the European liberals were now on the point of realising the hopes which they had entertained a generation ago, on the morrow of Napoleon's downfall. At that time they had looked forward to a general restoration of civic liberties and national independence. But disillusion had followed swiftly ; by 1818 they were made to realise that they had cast off Napoleon's despotism only to fall under the even more galling oppression of Metternich. The feverish energy of Napoleon had forced weak men to body-wearing activities : the sullen lassitude of Metternich condemned strong men to soul-destroying sloth. In urgent pursuance of his frantic schemes Napoleon had laid heavy burdens on men's backs, but at least he had done so with the clearly-expressed intention that the men should move the burdens. Metternich's burdens seemed to be imposed with no other object than that the dead-weight of them should prevent men from moving at all. Beneath that senseless incubus an exhausted Europe had indeed found peace. But such a peace brought no golden age in its train ; only to an age of iron had succeeded an age of lead.

But now at last Metternich was fallen, and his ' system ' laid in ruins. Not since the fall of the Bastille, sixty

years earlier, had any sound struck so joyfully the ears of
nations.   It is true that at the time of his collapse Metternich, like the Bastille, was an outworn institution.   But
in either case the name had become the symbol of a
system ; and this fall too was hailed as the ruin of an edifice
that had existed, loathed and long, for the oppression
of mankind.   With Vienna in revolution and Metternich
in exile men felt that the very citadel of reaction was
stormed.

Yet liberal Europe was mistaken in assuming that the
fall of Metternich would suffice to ensure the final dissipa-
tion of his power.   A generation earlier his downfall might
indeed have prevented the erection of the system at all.
For at the time of Napoleon's overthrow, Alexander of
Russia, the most powerful ruler in Europe, was still a
liberal ; it was only after three anxious years that Metternich had succeeded in banishing from the mind of this
royal mystic his golden dreams of a new age which he was
destined to inaugurate, and substituting for them a dark
nightmare of international anarchy which it must be his
task at all costs to repress.

But in 1848 the Czar needed no conversion.   Since 1826
Russia had been ruled by Nicholas I.   Alexander was
by nature a generous and benevolent enthusiast ; it was
only as a disillusioned idealist that he had succumbed to
Metternich's suggestions, lending himself wearily at the
last to a policy not his own.   But his successor brought to
the task of repression not only a stern and ruthless energy,
but all a young man's ardour for his first political convictions.   Alexander in his prime had abolished as abomin-
able the Russian secret police, and even in his decadence
had not repented that decision : Nicholas on his accession
solemnly restored them to all their powers for the un-
restricted arrest, imprisonment, or deportation of any of
his suspect subjects.   Under his direction the censorship
was revived and carried to such a pitch as not merely to
render newspapers newsless but to make manuscript once
more a main means for the circulation of literature.   Spies
and delations abounded ;   the indiscretion of a word or

gesture might suffice to secure a man free passage to Siberia.

Nor was it in his internal government alone that Nicholas had applied and exceeded the methods which Europe had learnt to associate with the name of Metternich. At the time of the revolutionary outbreak of 1830 he had not only crushed the rising of the Poles in his own dominions, and abolished their constitution, but he had offered to come to the aid of Austria in suppressing the revolution in Italy. Three years later he had concerted with Austria and Prussia a secret agreement, by which the ruler of each power held himself in readiness to intervene to assist any brother monarch who should find himself in difficulties with rebellious subjects ; thus forming a sort of mutual insurance company for legitimate sovereigns against the ravages of revolution. Since this company was admirably designed to secure the perpetuation of his system, Metternich had gladly taken out a policy in favour of his own half-imbecile master, the Emperor Ferdinand. But though he had smiled on its formation, and still took a benevolent interest in its operations, he himself by 1848 had subsided into the position of little more than a sleeping partner in the concern. He was still generally regarded as the founder of the firm ; his name still symbolised the system which it existed to maintain ; but the real direction of affairs had passed out of his grasp into the more active hands of Nicholas.

It was this fact which the liberals of Europe ignored when they hailed Metternich's fall as the final fulfilment of their hopes. Alone among the great continental powers Russia remained unresponsive to the revolutionary spirit of 1848. But Russia alone, as directed by Nicholas, was able to insure the failure of the revolution throughout Europe. For the Czar was not content to repel the movement from his own frontiers ; in all good faith he conceived it to be his highest duty to aid in casting out the spirit of revolution wherever it should make its appearance. And if the, onrush of revolution among the nations had been sudden, spontaneous, enthusiastic, the exertions of Nicholas to repress it were devoted, ubiquitous, indefatigable. Everywhere he was at the service of stricken authority ; encouraging terrified monarchs to resistance, dissuading wavering ministers from concession, rebuking such princes as showed a momentary tendency to accept the new order, promising to those who held fast the true faith the ultimate succour of his own still servile serfs. It was the final fulfilment of that promise which was to give its *coup de grâce* to the revolution, when in the summer of 1849 two hundred thousand Cossacks poured across the Carpathians to crush the last resistance of Hungary, and hand over the prostrate country to the vengeance of its legitimate oppressors. And for the rest of his reign, as even the cold pages of the *Annual Register* take fire to testify, ' dread of his power alone kept half the sovereigns of Europe upon their thrones.' [1]

Hence neither in what it had raised up nor in what it had put down did the work of 1848 seem destined to endure. Already the spirit of that year appeared to be waning with its waning months ; having shared its spring and summer it was now visibly subsiding into its autumn. ' Summer is flying fast from earth and man's heart,' wrote Bulwer-Lytton to a friend, ' and with the fall of the leaf Kossuth may be what Mazzini is.' [2] That indeed was six months later still, when the lingering hopes of the liberals were giving place to an ultimate despair. But even now such nations as had not already fallen by the close of 1848 were for the most part clearly lapsing towards foregone failure in 1849.

And for liberal Europe failure in 1849 was forlorn indeed. For a whole generation the system of peaceful repression, of blank opposition to all change, had been maintained with practically unbroken success. Time and again since Napoleon's fall men's hopes had shot up, only to be extinguished by the machinations of ministers and the counsel of consenting kings. But now this last and greatest con-

---

[1] *Register*: 1855. 258.
[2] *Lytton*, ii. 119. The whole letter is typical of the prostration of liberal hopes. ' The world goes on in its iniquities. . . . More and more do we see that our only realm of liberty and improvement is in our own individual natures. *Hoc regnum sibi quisque dat.*'

flagration of all, which was to have fused and welded freed
peoples into nations, was expiring like the lesser flames
before it.   And with it hope itself seemed to flicker out as
well.   Doubtless the continental liberals exaggerated the
evils of their position ; the triumphs of new and militant
nationalism, when against hope they were finally attained,
were not destined to prove an unmixed benefit to mankind.
The older cosmopolitanism of Europe had at least contributed to European peace ; and that peace, sordid and
uninspired as it was in motive, was yet productive of
material, and tolerant even of moral progress.   The policy
of letting sleeping dogs lie was inglorious enough ; but
while they slept some ugly passions slept with them.
Those who watched for their awakening as for the dawn did
not live to see the pack in full cry, or the state to which
they have reduced their kennels since.   Else some of those
expectant watchers might have looked back on the regime
of Metternich much as Mme. de Staal looked back on her
imprisonment in that very Bastille of which his downfall
had reminded them ; with a sigh of regret for ' the happy
hours when we were so miserable.'   Perhaps it was well
that they did not foresee through quite what a wilderness
their promised land was to be sought ; or that it was not
the fleshpots only of Egypt that must be left behind on the
journey.

Happily men lack, to reconcile them to the sorrows they
have, the knowledge of greater sorrows to come.   And in
default of such consolation the European nationalists on the
morrow of 1848 allowed themselves to be very miserable
indeed.   It was not strange that hope so long deferred
should have sickened their hearts and jaundiced their
outlook on the world.   Their causes for grief were palpable
and patent.   It was bad enough that they should have
watched and waited so long, risen and striven so often, and
yet failed to free themselves from the system of Metternich.
But it was far worse to realise, as after 1848 they were
forced to realise, that the system was no longer dependent
on its founder ; that in Metternich's old age a new champion
had arisen to perpetuate his work ; and that this champion

was none other than the most powerful sovereign in
Europe. For the defeat of the Revolution of 1848 was the
victory of Nicholas ; a monarch still in the prime of life,
whose reign had been a series of unbroken triumphs, whose
practice and declared purpose it was to maintain existing
authority inviolate, and to beat down the spirit of revolution under his feet.

The continental liberals then, after the failure of their
efforts in 1848, had cause enough for despondency, excuse
almost for despair. Certainly their fears were better
founded than were the hopes of their fathers a generation
before. Yet their fears, no less than their fathers' hopes,
were destined to be falsified. And the two events were
curiously connected. It was the falsification of one
generation's hopes which rendered possible the rise of Louis
Napoleon.[1] It was in turn the rise of Louis Napoleon
which rendered possible the falsification of a second
generation's fears. For the revolution of 1848, that had
strengthened so ominously the already powerful position of
Nicholas, had served one other permanent purpose besides.
It had introduced a new man into the company of European
rulers : a man who was to raise up some at least of the
ruins of 1848, to fight and to defeat the invincible reactionary of Russia ; a man in whom the fallen cause of
European nationalities was to find first a willing apostle
and finally an unwitting martyr. Among the names that
had taken to themselves men in the year 1848 was the name
Napoleon.

And of all the resurrections of that year, none had been
stranger, or fraught with more momentous consequences to
Europe, than this. Three and thirty years ago, in the
Palace of the Elysée, Napoleon had signed his formal
abdication of Empire. That was on a midsummer day in
1815 ; amid high hopes of a great future on the part of the
peoples whose uprising had contributed to his downfall.
And now, on the shortest day of 1848, deep in the winter
of men's discontent, the sun shone in to that same
palace of the Elysee—to awaken Napoleon's heir from

[1] *Simpson*, 10–19.

his first night's sleep in any palace since his uncle's abdication.

For Louis Napoleon, no less than for liberal Europe, the interval had been a period of watching and waiting and hope deferred ; broken only by occasional and apparently futile attempts at insurrection. Indeed, as their fathers had discovered a counterpart to their own sufferings in the martyrdom at St Helena which followed on Napoleon's fall, so with more reason might the present generation of European liberals have sympathised with those of Louis Napoleon which had contributed to his rise. Had they dared and suffered for their convictions ? So had he : in exile and captivity, in homelessness and friendlessness, in journeyings and disguises, in transportation, perpetual imprisonment, trial for his life ; dreaming, brooding, studying, and for his dream's sake forgoing fortune, despising danger, contemning contempt ; incurring, as became a prophet, the ridicule even of his relatives ; and that whether he were heading hopeless insurrection in Italy, raising diplomatic imbroglio in Switzerland, flinging himself at a French garrison town from Germany, or invading a nation in an English pleasure boat, with fifty men and a name for all his army.[1]

And the dreams of Louis Napoleon, if not actually identical with those of the continental nationalists, were yet closely allied to them by virtue of a common descent. The liberal tenets of the revolutionaries in 1848 were logical developments of the liberal ideals of their fathers in 1815. But the liberal ideals of 1815 had been annexed bodily by Napoleon at St Helena, and incorporated into the Napoleonic legend. For in order to attach the liberals of his own generation to his cause, Napoleon had posed at St Helena not as a death-bed convert to their doctrines, but as their life-long, though hitherto grievously misunderstood disciple. And this pose had succeeded in deceiving not liberal Europe only, but Louis Napoleon as well. Hence the championship of nationalities, to Napoleon a

---

[1] The story has been told by the present writer in a volume entitled *The Rise of Louis Napoleon.*

pose, to Nicholas anathema, to the liberals a dream and
a despair, was by Louis accepted in all sincerity as an
essential portion of his inheritance.

Not without reason therefore might the continental
nationalists have regarded with interest akin to hope the
advent of Louis Napoleon to the Elysée. That such was
not their immediate attitude towards him was due to the
circumstances of his attainment of power. It was not as
President but as Emperor, not from the Elysée but from
the Tuileries, that Louis Napoleon could alone render them
effectual service. But his progress from the Elysée to the
Tuileries was so conducted as to make any alliance between
him and the liberals seem improbable to a degree. Not
merely did the fact of the progress, by absorbing for four
years all his energies, serve to postpone the alliance for
the present ; but the method of it, by alienating liberal
opinion in Europe, seemed to render it impossible for the
future. For the President's internal policy culminated in
an act of illegal violence which liberal Europe naturally
denounced as criminal ; while his one notable excursion
into foreign politics had the appearance—though as we
shall see the unwarranted appearance—of a deliberate
betrayal of the nationalist ideal.

Yet it was indeed to this strange champion strangely
raised up to her service that liberal Europe, fast-bound by
Metternich and Nicholas, was to owe the final overthrow
of that ill-omened combination ; by the successive isolation
and defeat at the hands of Louis Napoleon of both the
autocratic empires of the East. It was only the second of
those victories—that which struck down Austria—which
rendered possible Louis Napoleon's greatest work, the
liberation of Italy. But as the defeat of Austria was an
essential preliminary to the liberation of Italy, so was the
defeat of Russia an essential preliminary to the defeat of
Austria. In the generation which preceded 1848 Austria
had placed an apparently unlimited reserve of reactionary
force at the disposition of any petty German despot or
Italian Grand Duke whose repressions had otherwise
brought him into immediate and unsuccessful conflict with

his own subjects. The years which followed 1848 served
to show that behind Austria herself lay the inexhaustible
resources of Russia. But even to the conquest of Russia
there was another necessary preliminary. Louis Napoleon
could never have succeeded in the overthrow of Nicholas,
unless he had first placed his own power in France on
a less precarious basis than that assigned to it by the
constitution of 1848. To say this is by no means to accept
the wholly unwarrantable contention that these two
preliminary contests were undertaken by Louis for no
other end than to pave the way to his Italian exploit. It
is merely to insist on the fact that whatever his motives in
either struggle, neither can be dismissed as a mere barren
victory of reaction.

It was a matter not immaterial or barren of result, that
for fifteen momentous years the hegemony of Europe
should be transferred from Russia to France, from Nicholas
to Napoleon III. Alike during the Great Reaction which
followed the downfall of the First Empire, and the Armed
Peace which succeeded upon the overthrow of the Second,
the control of European politics was in the hands of men to
whom the fact that a given condition of affairs existed was
strong if not all-sufficient reason that it should continue so
to exist. Whether by an inviolable international agreement
in the past, or by a precarious balance of power in the
present ; whether based upon theoretical principle before
Louis Napoleon's rise or maintained by practical expedience
after his fall, the whole official diplomacy of Europe tended
in either period to the maintenance of existing frontiers
because they existed. But between these two periods
there intervened another strangely different : wherein
Europe was dominated by a man in whose case all ordinary
rules of diplomacy were not merely suspended but reversed.
The ordinary monarch, born on the footsteps of the throne,
comes somewhat easily by the conclusion that what is, is
right : half a lifetime's exile and proscription had engendered in the mind of this particular ruler a fixed idea that
what was, was wrong. And for other and more concrete
reasons the *status quo*, to the conventional diplomatist

little less than a fetish, was to Louis Napoleon a thing positively repellent. To Louis Napoleon, as to his opponents, the *status quo* spelt the Congress of Vienna ; but to him that Congress stood for the downfall of his dynasty and the humiliation of his country. Hence to him there was always an initial presumption not against but in favour of change : since any change would be so far welcome that it would tend to set the treaty law of Europe upon a new basis.

But to these natural incentives inclining Louis Napoleon to supersede the Congress of Vienna other and more disinterested motives were added. Whatever service the Congress of Vienna had rendered to Europe in the past by the establishment of a lasting order and peace, that order was now visibly outworn. Many of its provisions had from the first been imposed upon unwilling peoples ; and the increasing hardship inflicted on them by the rigid maintenance of an obsolete system had produced in the complex and brooding mind of Louis Napoleon a genuine sympathy, coupled with a real desire to compass such changes as would better their condition. For thirty years he had gazed at the sullen surface of European politics, pent and dammed by Metternich and his system into one stagnant and unruffled pond. And as he gazed he had become possessed with the desire at all costs to stir up its leaden depths : partly from the proverbial desire for troubled waters of a certain class of fisherman ; but partly also from a sincere belief that the troubling of the waters would be for the healing of the nations. Interested and disinterested motives here propelled him in the same direction. With an adventurer's natural detestation of routine, a wanderer's inherent appetite for change, Louis Napoleon stood by instinct, interest, and conviction for the precise antithesis of all the cherished changelessness of the preceding age.

Hence for the failures of 1848 no compensation was to prove so valuable as the success of Louis Napoleon in the two struggles recounted in this volume. By making himself supreme in France, and France once more ascendant in Europe, he was to secure for Europe a period in which the

shackles of diplomatic order and routine were so far loosened
as to allow of much that in the generation before or after
had been impossible. So long and so long only as a crowned
adventurer held sway in Paris, were adventures to be permitted in the sphere of international politics all Europe
over. During the reign of this imperial dreamer, and
during it alone, did the conditions of nineteenth-century
diplomacy allow dreamers to translate their dreams into
action. This fact, naturally hidden from contemporary
observation, suffices to give permanent importance to the
conflicts by means of which Louis Napoleon won first a
fleeting supremacy for himself in France, and then a
supremacy as fleeting for France in Europe. In any case
the history of those struggles could now command restate-
ment in the light of documents formerly unavailable. But
it is due to this larger light upon their significance, that
what they can command, they deserve. For they emerge
now, not as the purposeless reactions for which on their
morrow they were dismissed ; but as events fraught with
consequences of supreme importance to Europe. They
served no less a purpose than to render possible a period in
which all things were possible : a period into which enterprises of great pith and moment must pack themselves,
or lose the name of action ; a period into which was in fact
compressed almost whatever of vital change the century had
witnessed since Waterloo.

It was on this theme that Liszt is credited with not the
least brilliant of his extemporisations, and Louis Napoleon
with the most extravagant compliment which he ever
received. It was towards the end of his reign, and the
Emperor had been indulging in political retrospect.
' *Quand je pense*,' he concluded, ' *à tout ce qui s'est déjà
accompli pendant mon règne, je crois avoir cent ans.*'
' *Sire*,' came the reply, ' *vous les avez : car vous êtes le
Siècle.*' [1]

[1] *Ebeling*, 72.

CHAPTER II

THE GORDIAN KNOT

Bonum animum habe : unus tibi nodus, sed Herculaneus restat.

SENECA.

A State without the means of some change is without the means of its conservation.

EDMUND BURKE.

THE position to which Louis Napoleon awoke on the morning of December 21, 1848, was one which at first sight might well seem to afford him ground for legitimate satisfaction. After three and thirty years of exile, imprisonment, and failure he had at length won his way to a place among European rulers. Now at last he was the official head of the French nation ; elected to that position, it is true, for four years only, but elected to it without official pressure by a majority more overwhelming than official pressure had succeeded in securing for the vote that conferred the Empire on his uncle.

Louis Napoleon's election to the presidency in December 1848 was indeed of its kind the freest vote in French history. Such pressure as the republican government had been able to apply had been employed on behalf of the official republican candidate, Cavaignac ; but circumstances had combined to render this pressure practically ineffective [1] Hence his election to the presidency by a vote exceeding the combined total of his five competitors by over three and a half millions, was for Louis not only an unparalleled personal triumph, but a political portent of good omen for the future.

None the less, great as was the prestige conferred upon

[1] *Simpson*, 313, 317.

13

him by this spontaneous ebullition of popular good-will, the newly-elected President was confronted with difficulties which might well tax all his resources. A stranger in his own land he lacked the friendship of any prominent Frenchman ;[1] for this lack the good wishes of some distinguished foreigners[2] were but poor compensation. His education had given him a wider range of sympathy and experience than could be claimed by any contemporary sovereign ; but its many uncommon advantages could not atone for some perfectly commonplace omissions. A cosmopolitan idealist, he was ill-qualified to rule the most insular and realist of European races. Swiss by upbringing, and later to be Spanish by marriage, he had already lived long enough in Italy, Germany, and England to converse fluently in the languages of all three countries. But the price of these accomplishments was a heavy one. For he spoke German like a Swiss[3] and all his other languages like a German. Even in his French he had still to be on his guard against some German proclivities. By uttering his words slowly he could pronounce them perfectly ; but to speak French slowly was itself the mark of a foreigner. Any real excitement or acceleration in his speech at this time gave his v's and d's and b's a chance of trying once more to harden themselves into f's and t's and p's.[4] This need of minding his p's and b's gave to the Prince's manner an appearance not only of deliberation but of reticence. The sense of deliberation and the ordinarily impenetrable aspect of his eyes were in fact the two things which most struck strangers at first sight of him ; an impression

---

[1] He bewailed this fact to Malmesbury on 30 March 49, and again in April of the following year. ' The friends I have I don't know, and they don't know me even by sight. Although a Frenchman not fifty of them had ever seen me when I came over from England. . . . I stand perfectly alone, but the army and the people are with me, and I don't despair.' *Malmesbury*, i. 244, 259.

[2] *E.g.* on 9 Jan. 49, Walter Savage Landor writes : ' I feel a great interest, a great anxiety, for the welfare of Louis Napoleon. I told him if he were ever again in a prison I would visit him there, but never if he were upon a throne would I come near him. He is the only man living who would adorn one, but thrones are my aversion and abhorrence.' *Blessington*, ii. 394.

[3] *Roon*, i. 251.

[4] *Englishman*, 239. Cf. *Melun*, ii. 29 ; *Du Casse : Souvenirs*, 247.

generally followed by a surprised recognition of a really engaging frankness and an indefinable charm penetrating his unprepossessing exterior. ' When Prince Louis Napoleon held out his hand and I looked in his face,' observed an Englishman who first met him in 1848, ' I felt almost tempted to put him down as an opium eater. Ten minutes afterwards I felt convinced that he himself was the drug, and that everyone with whom he came in contact was bound to yield to its influence.' [1]

For the moment Louis' sole source of strength was the immense popularity of his name among the mass of the people with whom as yet he had come into no personal contact at all. Yet even this one great asset contained on reflection some cause for anxiety ; for in France popularity is a thing more easily won than retained. The fate of Lamartine and Cavaignac offered recent and striking testimony to this fact. Even the magnitude of his victory did but increase this danger for Louis Napoleon. His vast majority proved that the people hoped great things from his election ; there was a corresponding danger of a great revulsion of popular feeling should he fail to make good the vague hopes on which his election was based.

The ardent support which he had recently received from the people, though it entailed some cause for anxiety, was at any rate a real fund of strength to the new President. It was otherwise with another class of his adherents. In the closing months of 1848 many distinguished French politicians had given their adhesion to his candidature. Not only had such lesser political lights as Jules Favre, Montalembert, and Victor Hugo ranged themselves on his side, but even Molé, Guizot, and Thiers themselves had given his cause their grudging benediction. [2] At first sight it might well seem that such patronage would prove only less useful to Louis after his election than his own overwhelming triumph at the polls. Nothing could be further from the truth. The majority of the conservative leaders had in fact been driven to espouse Louis' cause by a

[1] *Englishman*, 239. Cf. *Morley: Cobden*, ii. 249.
[2] *Pierre*, i. 523. *Greville*, 15 Nov. 48.

process of deduction more cogent than satisfactory. Had they come forward as candidates for the presidency themselves, they would have shared the fate of Lamartine, Changarnier, or Ledru-Rollin ; they would have suffered a defeat so overwhelming as to be damaging to their future political careers. Recognising this fact they were faced with the further alternative of complete abstention, or the transference of their support to one or other of the only two really serious candidates.

But in a political crisis of any importance no action is so lowering to the prestige of a politician as complete inaction : to do nothing on such an occasion is to be for this, and possibly for all future occasions a nonentity. The question resolved itself therefore into one final alternative, that of supporting Cavaignac or Louis Napoleon. This last choice was the easiest of all. The majority of these diplomatic politicians shared the opinion of the great mass of the country, in disliking Cavaignac's uncompromising republicanism : they did not at all share the country's opinion of Louis Napoleon. But that they did not was for them only the greater reason for voting for him. ' They thought he would be a tool, and a tool that they could break,' observed de Tocqueville two years later ; ' the folly of clever men is wonderful ' was his comment.[1] But there was at least this much of wisdom in their folly ; that Louis Napoleon was obviously going to win. Now to support the winning candidate was to be able afterwards to claim a share in the credit and perhaps also in the spoils of victory. To support Cavaignac, on the other hand, was at best to stamp one's personal following as the mere fraction of a beaten cause ; at worst it was to be upbraided afterwards as a contributory factor in an inglorious defeat.

---

[1] *Tocqueville : Correspondence*, i. 195. The mistake was not quite universal, even before his election. *Cf.* Montalembert's entry in his journal of 30 Oct. 48, the day of his first interview with Louis Napoleon : ' I cannot conceive how he comes by his reputation for incapacity.' *Lecanuet*, ii. 417. In general the politicians seem to have considered him too young at forty. ' Notre jeune homme ' was Thiers' patronising periphrasis. *Lireux*, 363. His first premier, Barrot, though referring to Louis as the ' Prince-Président ' when he was vexed, spoke of him when things went well as ' cet excellent jeune homme.' *Falloux*, i. 114.

It was to this necessity on the part of the monarchical leaders of maintaining their own political importance intact, that Louis Napoleon owed their original declarations in his favour. Some of them however would have been willing to continue to support him as President, if he had been willing to become dependent on their support. But any sign of personal initiative, any act of political self-reliance, would suffice to alienate men who were only ready to support their own dependants.[1]

Here then at the outset of his term of office Louis Napoleon was confronted with a dangerous dilemma. The millions who had voted for him expected great things at his hands ; yet having once elected him they could not strengthen his hands to any task. For once elected the President was constitutionally cut off from them, and deprived of any legal means of invoking their aid : an isolation from his sole real basis of power of which he was himself acutely conscious. On the other hand the distinguished Royalists who had lent his cause their nominal support intended that Louis should only do small things ; that he should in fact serve as a mere warming-pan, until the way was clear for one or the other of their kings to take his place. And these nominal supporters had what his real supporters had not, a very present means of making their wishes effective. Experienced parliamentary tacticians, they were able to hamper the President's movements at every turn by opposing him in the Assembly. And persistent opposition in the Assembly could at any time produce a deadlock, which the President was constitutionally powerless to overcome.

This brings us to the sum and substance of all Louis Napoleon's difficulties as President,—the constitution under which he was expected to govern France.[2] The French constitution of 1848 does not err in the direction of lucidity :

---

[1] 'Another curious thing is to observe how all men of note have laboured to place L. N. in his present position ; and then when they have put him there all refuse to stand by him. They probably think to pull the strings and not to be responsible for the way their puppet dances.' Clarendon to *Reeve*, i. 204.

[2] The most accessible work in which this constitution is published verbatim (not translated) is *Normanby*, ii. 389–410.

but some effort to comprehend it is a necessary preliminary to any real understanding of events during the years in which it was in force. No single cause has done so much to obscure the history of the Second Republic as the failure of historians to read its constitution.

In any case this constitution, voted in the autumn of 1848, would merit a moment's examination. To a lengthy preamble, in which much excellent advice was lavished upon an inattentive world,[1] succeeded a comparatively concise epitome of the whole rights of man, if he chanced to be a French citizen. These introductory maxims served to usher in the constitution itself : a document comprising clauses culled with admirable impartiality from almost every previous paper constitution in French history. Such homage rendered to native invention did not preclude a tribute to foreign experience as well : several ingenious provisions were incorporated from the constitution of the United States, designed to ensure an exact balance between the executive and the legislative powers. For ' the separation of powers is the first condition of a free people.'[2]   In defiance however of the American precedent, the legislative power was vested in a single chamber[3] of seven hundred and fifty members.[4] Like the President, this chamber was to be elected by universal suffrage ; but whereas the former was elected for four years, the latter sat only for three. Two compensations were given to the Assembly to make up for the year[5] by which the President's term of office would exceed its own. Its members were normally allowed to seek immediate re-election, from which not only the President himself but all his relations within six degrees, were automatically disqualified.[6] Further, they were covered by the parliamentary privilege of being inviolable : while the President was expressly declared responsible,[7] and

---

[1] *E.g.* Preliminary Maxim VII., 'Citizens ought to love their country,' etc., v. *Pierre*, i. 480.
[2] Art. 19.   [3] *Ibid.*, 20.   [4] *Ibid.*, 21.
[5] But by a special arrangement, the *first* president's term (*i.e.* Louis Napoleon's) was to last for only three years and a quarter, for his successor was to be elected in the middle of May 52 (Art. 46).
[6] Art. 45.   [7] *Ibid.*, 68.

provision was made for his possible impeachment. Here
the framers of the constitution, at the very moment when
they believed themselves to be tying the President's
hands, were in point of fact adding to his importance.
So completely did they misunderstand the maxim ' The
King can do no wrong,' that they seem to have imagined
that in making the head of the state responsible they were
actually decreasing his powers for mischief.[1]

What was to happen in the event of a quarrel between
two powers poised in such deliberate opposition was a
question which the Constituent Assembly did not stay to
answer.   But it was careful to rule out the obvious solution
of an appeal to the country.   Save for certain definite
legal offences the chamber could not dismiss the President :
on no pretext at all could the President dissolve or even
prorogue the Assembly [2]; even the Assembly itself could
not dissolve itself ; three years it must continue, neither
more nor less.[3]

So much for the actual constitution : a constitution as
to which later experience only confirmed the judgment
which the British ambassador recorded in his journal on
the day of its adoption as law.[4]   ' I think any impartial
examination must lead to the conclusion that it is the very
worst that ever reached that finishing stage of manufacture.   With no one original idea, it is so confused in its
expressions, and contradictory in its provisions, as to be
unintelligible to many of its authors, and undoubtedly
impracticable in execution.'   Thirty years later, the first
premier to serve under the constitution pronounced this
verdict, severe as it was, to be ' only too just.' [5]

But it is only when we turn from the constitution itself to
the arrangements for its revision that we can understand the
more poignant phrases of French contemporary criticism.[6]

---

[1] On this, see *Barrot*, iii. 84.   [2] Art. 51.   [3] Arts. 51–52.
[4] 6 Nov. 48.   *Normanby*, ii. 280.   [5] *Barrot*, ii. 479.
[6] *E.g.* the Duc de Broglie's dictum :   ' C'est un œuvre qui a reculé les
limites de la stupidité humaine ' : *Normanby*, ii. 281.   Thiers described it
as ' la plus sotte, la plus absurde, la plus impracticable de toutes celles
qui ont régi la France ' : adding ' Tout son esprit est dans sa perfidie,
dans les conditions exigées pour sa revision et qui rendent cette revision
impossible.'   *Ollivier*, ii. 278.

For having first framed a constitution which invited a deadlock, and then provided it with no legal issue,[1] the Constituent Assembly proceeded to preclude the one way out remaining, by rendering impossible any change in the constitution itself. The President, quite rightly, had no power to change it at any time. But during the first two years of its session—during that is to say two-thirds of its total life—a unanimous vote of the entire Assembly was powerless to alter a syllable of the constitution.[2]

The newly-elected Constituent Assembly had at once composed an entire constitution, with no other light than nature and a committee of its leading members could furnish. But it was not so rash as to assume any similar endowments in its successors ; these last must make up by experience for what they would presumably lack in ability ; they must therefore be denied all opportunity of revising the constitution until they should have served a two years' apprenticehood in political life. Unfortunately such experience had to be bought at a price : for the effect of this precaution was to prevent any subsequent Assembly from embarking on the most important task which could confront it until by the passage of time it had itself ceased to be completely representative of the feeling of the country. The Constituent Assembly had devoted to the proposition, public discussion, revision, and final passage of the entire constitution something under two months of its time. But such speed must not be attempted by succeeding Assemblies ; should they persist in their hardy desire to revise the handiwork of their great original they must only do so after three consecutive debates, separated each from the other—lest aught should be done in haste—by intervals of at least a month. Further, repentance to be effective, must be not only leisurely, but thorough. For if on any one of the three occasions there was a majority of less than three to one in favour of change, the entire revisionist movement was doomed. To obtain

---

[1] Such as is provided in every existing constitution by e.g. dissolution, referendum, joint session, or creation of peers.
[2] Art. 111.

a change three-quarters [1] of the members voting must say
yes three times over : to avert it one-quarter had only to
say no once. And of the house that quarter need not even
be a quarter : a quarter of the votes cast, though cast
by only a sixth of the whole house, sufficed. By an
ingenious additional precaution abstentions were given
the virtual effect of negative votes : if on any one of the
three occasions less than five hundred members actually
voted then the vote for change even if unanimous was void.
Nor was it merely void, but it would suffice to invalidate
even two previously sufficient affirmative votes. To be
valid as a total the three valid affirmations must be consecutive : a hitch in any one of them meant that the whole
business must start all over again from the beginning. At
best in point of fact it was only a beginning that had been
effected. But the later complications which were to follow
even the surmounting of these preliminary obstacles we
need not stay to examine ; for the preliminary obstacles
were, and were intended to be, insurmountable. Somewhere beyond them however were vague vistas of an
especial Assembly of Revision, nominated for three months
only, capable of no other revision than that for which it was
convoked. [2]

In effect then, for the space of two years no power
could alter a syllable of the constitution : at the end of
two years, in an Assembly no longer representative of the
existing condition of popular opinion, one-quarter of the
members actually voting could again make all change
impossible for at least three further years to come. A
dissolution which nothing could either advance or retard
rendered difficult any definite appeal to the country on
any particular question. But on this the most important
political question of all, such appeal was not merely difficult
but impossible. For a dissolution when it did automatically
occur automatically precluded the newly elected assembly
from dealing with the constitutional issue for another two

[1] Not two-thirds, as stated by Professor Alison Phillips. *Modern
Europe*, 334.
[2] Art. 111.

years ; until it too in its turn had ceased to represent the existing condition of public opinion in the country. It was thus to the mere fraction of an outworn Assembly that the Republicans of 1848 deliberately assigned the right to veto any change of any portion of their handiwork ; without the assent of this fraction, France must remain in its own despite fast-bound to the rigid and ridiculous constitution of 1848. That the country might grow restless under the restraint, might come to question the right even of the Constituent Assembly to tie its hands in this way for all future time, might actually welcome as a deliverer the man who would cut the cords that could not legally be loosened,—this was a contingency against which even the Constituent Assembly could not provide. But it could prevent the voice of France from being heard at the time. One deputy had the temerity to propose that before this unalterable constitution was riveted upon the people, the people should be given a chance of ratifying or condemning it : [1] only forty-four votes were cast in favour of the proposal ; the republican Assembly decided that whether or no France should hereafter hold her peace at least she should not speak now. For they had made the constitution what it was while they knew, and because they knew, that the country was not republican.

That, to do them justice, was the method in their madness. Republicans themselves they knew that the country desired to be rid of the Republic ; that it would elect an anti-republican President to begin with, and as soon afterwards as it could an anti-republican chamber as well. A twofold remedy was devised to meet the twofold evil. First the office of President must be minimised. Under the Third Republic the President is re-eligible, and is armed with the right of dissolving parliament. Both these privileges were withheld from the anti-republican President of the Second Republic. It was not quite such a simple matter for the Constituent Assembly to render powerless for mischief

---

[1] As, for example, the constitution of the United States had been submitted to the legislature of each state : or even the Code Napoléon to the local parlements. v. *Pierre*, i. 479.

its own successor. Merely to decrease the power of the anti-republican legislature would only serve to increase the relative power of an anti-republican executive. The solution lay elsewhere. Even the new chamber must contain a republican minority, which might reasonably be expected to form a quarter of its entire strength : this republican minority must be armed with dictatorial powers to see to it that the republic took no harm. Their use of their veto to prevent all constitutional change would, it was true, produce a deadlock ; but even a deadlock was better than a defeat : where victory is clearly impossible, it is something to get oneself stalemated.

We have been forced at the outset to a somewhat detailed consideration of this carefully prepared constitutional entanglement of 1848, because it formed the chief source of all Louis Napoleon's difficulties during his term of office. His attempts to unravel that entanglement mark the chief interest of the internal history of France during the next two years : his final resolution to cut through it resulted in the *coup d'état* of December 1851.

It is interesting to observe that a question which so underlies the whole history of the Second Republic as to have escaped the notice of the majority of its historians was yet posed most precisely in advance by a shrewd foreign observer in 1848. In that year the ablest radical journalist in England, editor of that remarkable newspaper *The Examiner*, had written : ' It will be a curious problem now to see how a government repugnant to a people resolves itself into some form suitable to them, as a misshapen shoe with wear acquires an awkward kind of adjustment to the foot. Which will first be forthcoming, the people of Republicans, now the one thing wanting to the Republic, or an acceptable monarch, the one thing wanting for the restoration of monarchy ? ' [1] That in fact was the exact alternative : either the shoe must be altered to fit the foot, or the foot must be crushed into fitting the shoe. The second alternative pleased the shoemaker ; and to secure its adoption he praised his

[1] *Fonblanque*, 396.

handiwork ecstatically as the latest fashion and a perfect
fit, but proceeded so to strap and tightlace it that except
by bursting it altogether there was no way of getting out
of it at all.

For the moment Louis was saddled not only with the
shoe but with the shoemaker. The constitution was
published perfect and complete; but the Constituent
Assembly refused to disperse. Its republican majority,
more honest or less cautious than the Royalists, had
strenuously supported the republican candidate General
Cavaignac, in the recent presidential election; his overwhelming defeat was therefore implicit but unmistakable
notice to it to quit. Further the Constituent Assembly
had been elected to frame a constitution; this done its
occupation was gone. But in its constitution it had
omitted to set any term to its own activities, and had
declined to give to either President or people any power
of enforcing its dissolution.

This dissolution it proceeded on the morrow of
Cavaignac's defeat to postpone indefinitely; by a decree in
which it announced its intention of considering and passing
before it separated ten Organic Laws, covering the entire
field of French political life. Electoral Reform, Poor Relief,
Education, the Reform of the Judicature—these and half
a dozen other questions of equal variety and importance
the devoted Assembly felt bound in duty to deal with
before it died. No new chamber, even though it might
more faithfully represent the fleeting current of popular
opinion,[1] could safely be left to pass these laws; laws
which the Constituent Assembly described, in a periphrasis
designed to justify its own unique capacity for their discussion, as 'laws fundamentally necessary to the constitution.' Contemporary popular opinion in revenge
misconstrued the motives of the Assembly; inclining some-

---

[1] On 27 Nov. 48, Normanby told Cavaignac that the most effective
step he could take to improve his prospects of election would be to dissipate
' the belief that it was his intention to prolong indefinitely the existence
of an Assembly which the country thought had accomplished the purpose
for which it was chosen.' ' The general's only answer was that new elections
for some time to come would destroy the Republic.' *Normanby*, ii. 329.

what clamorously to the conclusion that this devouring zeal
for duty was nothing better than a vulgar dread of death.
For the whole of the newly-elected President's term of
office would scarcely have sufficed to enable the moribund
Assembly to set its house so scrupulously in order.

Confronted with a hostile Assembly,[1] surrounded by
experienced politicians whose hopes were based upon his
own political inexperience, Louis soon discovered that the
mere formation of a ministry—the first duty incumbent on
him—would be no easy task.   Since the majority of the still
existing Constituent Assembly were moderate Republicans,
supporters of Cavaignac, republican writers [2] have blamed
the President for not choosing a purely republican ministry
from this majority.   In reality such action was doubly
impossible for him.   Cavaignac, and with him his more
notable followers, would certainly have refused to serve
under his successful rival ; [3] nor could Louis well have
availed himself of such services even had they been available.   For his own election to the presidency had constituted a recent and overwhelming repudiation by the
country at large of Cavaignac and his orthodox republican
following : and it was already notorious that only by
avoiding a dissolution at all costs could this majority
maintain its power even in the Assembly.

In point of fact Louis did attempt to induce Lamartine
himself, the very personification of French idealist republicanism, to become his first premier.   The scene and

---

[1] To a simple request of a purely formal nature bearing Louis' ordinary
signature 'Louis Napoléon B.,' its President had replied on 11 Oct. 48 :
' Le Président de l'assemblée nationale ne peut admettre une demande
signée d'une initiale. Si comme il le croit cette initiale est celle du nom
de représentant Louis Napoléon Bonaparte il est invité à formuler une
nouvelle demande et à la signer de son nom tout entier.'   B.N. Nouv.
Acq. Fr. 22,740, f. 14.

[2] E.g. *Bourgeois, C.M.H.*, 118.

[3] Witness this incident in the Chamber at the close of Louis Napoleon's
inaugural speech as President on Dec. 20 : ' When Louis Napoleon, after
descending from the tribune, walked up to the back bench, where the
General had retired, and in the most becoming manner held out his hand
to him, Cavaignac took it, but never got up, and turned away his head
to his next neighbour. . . . There was much gentle kindness and no
ostentation in the way in which the Prince approached Cavaignac, which
contrasted favourably with the rudeness of the other.'   *Normanby*, ii. 375.
See also on this incident, *Fleury*, i. 78 ; *Barrot*, iii. 29 ; *Maupas*, i. 45.

manner of their interview were entirely typical of the
prince's methods.   He had spent the first day after his
election in unsuccessful attempts to form a ministry of
all the talents and had met with a series of rebuffs.   At
the close of a long day of formal and fruitless negotiation,
he lost patience and resolved upon a direct personal appeal
to Lamartine.   'Without warning me,' wrote Lamartine
in his memoirs, 'the Prince flung himself upon his horse
at nightfall and galloped towards my house in the Bois
de Boulogne,' accompanied only by one friend.   Halting
himself 'in a dark pine alley in the neighbourhood,' he
sent forward the single friend who accompanied him to
urge Lamartine to meet him there at once for a secret
interview.   'I had just sat down to dinner when Duclerc
arrived and sent for me : he told me in two words that
the Prince was there . . . I immediately ordered my
horse to be saddled and rode off with him to meet the
Prince as if by chance.   It was night, and there was no
longer another horseman but ourselves in the wood. . . .
I entered the pine alley where the Prince awaited me :
Duclerc presented me and withdrew.'

And so in the heart of that desolate place—for it was
Louis Napoleon himself who was later to convert this
wilderness into a garden—the President and Lamartine
were left to their interview ; for all the world like a couple of
highwaymen plotting nocturnal assault upon some opulent
wayfarer.   Their actual business was honest and respectable enough ; but it pleased Louis even when he was not
conspiring to have the *mise en scène* of a conspiracy : night,
and a secret assignation under the most sombre tree that
grows ; black pines towering into a stark December sky.   It
formed indeed an entirely characteristic conclusion to his
first day's work as ruler of France, this sudden refreshing
plunge from the routine of office, which though new was
already tedious, into the old childish delight of mysterious
adventure :   none the less characteristic that the deed
done in the dark might just as well have been done by day ;
none the less characteristic that the nocturnal interview
ended without solid result.   For Lamartine, though clearly

gratified, excused himself on the ground of his present unpopularity ; and proceeded to an eloquent exposition of the causes of such an unnatural requital by the country of his services. Instead of protesting, Louis somewhat tactlessly assented to this statement : " ' But as to popularity,' he added with a smile, ' you need not trouble yourself on that score : *I have enough for two.*' " [1]

Lamartine however would only consent to take office if no other premier could be found. The whole incident is the more remarkable when it is remembered that in 1848, throughout the most critical months of Louis Napoleon's career, Lamartine had strenuously opposed his return to France, repeatedly endeavouring to prolong his exile and even to cancel his election to the Constituent Assembly.[2] Nor did these facts prevent him as Emperor from twice offering to rescue Lamartine from the financial embarrassments of his declining years, by paying from his privy purse the author's debts of some two million francs.[3] The offer was in each case most properly declined, for Lamartine could not be so beholden to a ruler whom after the *coup d'état* he held in abhorrence. None the less, when in 1860 his affairs had come to a desperate pass, it was to the carefully concealed action of the Emperor that Lamartine was to owe the provision by the Municipal Council of Paris of a chalet situated at the outskirts of the same Bois de Boulogne which had been the scene of this early interview with the President.[4]

Since the interview itself proved ineffective, Louis now turned finally to the old dynastic opposition of the last reign ; a party which while free from that republicanism which the nation had just so overwhelmingly repudiated, was not composed of uncompromising supporters of either of the exiled kings ; which had moreover the advantage of being in some sort the centre party of the existing chamber.[5]

---

[1] *Lamartine,* iv. 57–59.   [2] *Whitehouse,* ii. 379–386.
[3] *Lamartine,* iv. 67.   [4] *Whitehouse,* ii. 456.
[5] Two years later Louis himself described to Cassagnac the process of exhaustion which thus led him to choose his first ministry from the parliamentary opposition to Louis Philippe. *Cassagnac,* i. 40.

As premier of a cabinet formed in the main from this
party Louis chose the only distinguished member of it
with whom he had had personal relations during his
exile ; M. Odilon Barrot, who had extended to him a somewhat condescending patronage during his imprisonment
at Ham.[1]   Barrot was an upright and respected politician,
and a more than respectable orator ; somewhat lacking
in ideas, but by compensation almost without enemies.
' No man in the whole world,' remarked one of his
friends, ' thinks so deeply about nothing ' : but it is fair
to set beside this judgment Cobden's verdict that born
in England his eloquence would have made him a second
Bright.[2]

A week or so earlier, when his own election to
the Presidency seemed certain, Louis had interviewed
Barrot on the subject of his possible acceptance of the
Premiership.   In the course of the interview he had re-
curred to his old communist schemes.   Had M. Barrot
read his book on *The Extinction of Pauperism* ?[3]   And
did he not think it possible that something might really
be done on the lines it suggested ; the state purchase from
the communes of land now lying idle ; and its colonisation
by the surplus and starving populations of the large towns ?
Barrot at once pointed out difficulties manifold and insurmountable ; only half convinced, Louis had replied
after a moment's silence, ' Perhaps you are right.   But
when a man with my name is called to power he ought to
do *great things*.'   To which Barrot replied by arguing
that such *coups de théâtre* were not the really great
things.   And this stern mentor considered that his advice
had really been accepted by Louis Napoleon, when on
December 20 the latter closed his inaugural speech as
President with the words, ' God helping us, we will at least
do good, even if we cannot do great things.'[4]   Satisfied
with his reading of this utterance, Barrot now accepted
the office which Louis again pressed on him.   But his
reading of it was wrong.   In reality Louis was still un-

[1] *Barrot*, iii. 33, 34.   [2] *Walpole*: *Studies*, 264.
[3] v. *Simpson*, 214.   [4] *Barrot*, iii. 37, 38, 39.

reconciled to the trite and trodden path. And his saying
showed it.[1]

Hardly was the new ministry appointed than an event
occurred which threatened to dissolve it. Either from
curiosity, or from a desire to see whether the late government had in its possession information which might compromise his friends, the President requested Malleville,
his Minister of the Interior, to send him the dossiers
relating to his own youthful insurrections at Strasburg
and Boulogne. Malleville refused, and as he was entirely
within his rights in so doing, Louis with an ill grace
acquiesced in his refusal. But a few days later he
learnt that the same minister was withholding from him
despatches and reports which he was undoubtedly entitled
to see. 'They are trying,' he exclaimed, 'to make me
the Prince Albert of the Republic,'[2] and forthwith he wrote
to Malleville, forbidding him for the future to withhold
despatches from the President which it had been customary
to communicate to Louis Philippe, explaining that he had
no more intention than Napoleon of submitting to a Sieyès
constitution, and reiterating—this time in peremptory
terms—his demand for the official papers connected with
his own attempts on Strasburg and Boulogne. Malleville
naturally resigned ; in this he was very properly followed
by the entire Cabinet. Louis at once begged his ministers
to reconsider their steps, even writing to Malleville expressing his regret at the peremptory form of his request.
The Cabinet, content with this apology, withdrew its
resignation ; Malleville, with one personal friend, alone
persisted in retiring.[3]

This apparently trifling incident at the outset of Louis'
official life is worthy of narration, not only as his first step
forward in his advance towards supreme power, but also
because it is typical of his entire method of progress as

---

[1] Five days later, on Christmas Day, to an emissary from Manin, he
complained that he was hampered by details, and what was much worse,
by ' les hommes de détail.' Manin, ii. 64.

[2] Hugo : Choses Vues, 517.

[3] Barrot, iii. 52 sq. ; Falloux, i. 411 sq.

President. At first sight he appeared to have provoked an altercation with his Cabinet, only to be forced to ' climb down ' in somewhat humiliating fashion. In reality he had gained his point. He had declined at the outset the rôle of *roi fainéant* ; he had asserted his right—never afterwards contested—to the personal perusal of his cabinet's despatches ; and incidentally in his phrase about a Sieyès constitution he had thrown out a reminder to the people [1] of a possible further parallel between his own career and his uncle's. If in return for all this his ministers had secured a personal apology, no one had better reason to be satisfied with the exchange than Louis Napoleon. The fact was that Louis as President fully realised the wisdom of the national adage, bidding a man draw back in order the better to leap forward. But he interpreted the saying in a manner of his own. He formed the habit of drawing back for his second leap directly after taking the first, and frequently remained pondering in this attitude of recoil until men had forgotten that he was ever going to leap again at all. It was a method of progression as deceptive as it was ungainly. To the casual observer Louis appeared not to be drawing back in order to leap forward, but to be leaping forward only to draw back. Throughout his presidency his opponents had constantly the laugh over an adversary whose every advance was followed by precipitate retreat : yet they were perpetually amazed and irritated to find that despite his uncouth procedure the President was making real and constant advance towards his goal. As well might they have denied the progress of an incoming tide, because its every several wave is no sooner shot forward than sucked back into the parent ocean.

This passage of arms between Louis Napoleon and his Cabinet was followed almost immediately by an encounter between his ministers and the Assembly. At the end of December a conservative member [2] had brought forward in the Assembly a proposal by which the Constituent Assembly

---

[1] The letter was published in the *Moniteur*. v. *Giraudeau*, 130.
[2] Dec. 28, M. Rateau.

was to dissolve itself, and allow the country to elect a successor to it in the ensuing March. After a long and stormy debate Barrot at last intervened, asking the Assembly to fix a date for its own dissolution : [1] as a result, the Assembly which had at first seemed disinclined even to discuss the question, finally decided by a majority of four in a house of eight hundred to take it into consideration.[2] Consideration in this case could only lead to one conclusion : petitions pouring in from the country besought the Assembly to end its honoured life : [3] the vote was in effect a decisive victory for the presidential government.

There remained however a more serious conflict, before Louis could consider himself securely seated in his new position. During the troubled existence of the Second Republic it was unusual for any party to receive a decisive defeat at the hands of the electorate, without making some attempt to recover by armed insurrection in the streets of Paris what it had lost by the ballot of the country. The present occasion proved no exception. In the autumn of 1848 the Red Republicans had formed an association—the *Solidarité Républicaine*—to forward the candidature of their champion, M. Ledru-Rollin. After his crushing defeat at the presidential election, this association did not dissolve, but on the contrary multiplied its organisations, openly with a view to a conflict at an early date. So threatening did its preparations become that on January 26 M. Faucher, Louis Napoleon's new Minister of the Interior, asked the Assembly to pass a law immediately for the suppression of such Clubs. The Assembly refused ; conscious of their unpopularity, its members had been forced to yield in the matter of their own dissolution : they now gladly took the opportunity of an early revenge, by throwing out the first contentious measure proposed by Louis Napoleon's ministers. These last at once offered to resign if the President wished : Louis however told them quite truly that public opinion was entirely in their favour,

[1] *Barrot*, iii. 69.   [2] Jan. 12, v. *Pierre*, ii. 11.
[3] *Castellane*, iv. 129.

and against the Assembly ; that under a normal constitution they could confidently have appealed to the country with the certainty of a verdict in their favour ; that since this the proper solution was forbidden, they should hold themselves responsible to the real will of the country rather than to a fractious and fictitious parliamentary majority.[1] And on the following morning, he inserted in the *Moniteur* an official notice that the President saw no reason to modify his policy, and that the Cabinet could count on his firm and persistent support.[2] Naturally the ministers were grateful, and in their gratitude failed to see that they had allowed Louis to establish a precedent which no single one of them desired to see established : to wit, that when the executive backed by popular opinion found its way barred by a legislative veto from which the existing constitution allowed no legal appeal, then the executive was morally justified in ignoring such parliamentary veto.

Of the ultimate price at which they had thus bought the President's support his ministers were not however conscious ; of its immediate value they were at once apprised. On January 27, Ledru-Rollin formally demanded their impeachment. On the afternoon of the following day some hundred and fifty of the *garde mobile* marched to the Elysée to demand an interview with the President : the request was refused, and in the evening slight demonstrations took place in the streets. But to Louis Napoleon trifles were seldom trivial ; in this instance his attention to them was justified ; for during the last year demonstrations no less trivial had been followed by revolts, rebellions, revolutions. On this occasion none followed : Paris awoke on Monday the 29th to find every strategic position occupied in overwhelming force by regular soldiers.[3] For such a demonstration the agitators were wholly unprepared ; a single colonel of the National Guard, with three legions, offered to protect the Assembly against a show of military force which he professed to believe was

---

[1] *Barrot*, iii. 83.   [2] *Moniteur*, 29 Jan. 49.
[3] *Pierre*, ii. 18.

directed against them ; but he was arrested without trouble. In the afternoon Louis Napoleon reviewed the troops, who received him with enthusiastic greetings, the cry *Vive Napoléon* everywhere drowning the counter-cry *Vive la République* ; [1] before evening order was restored without bloodshed. After this, Ledru-Rollin's motion for the impeachment of the Ministry fell to the ground ; it was left to Republicans within and without the Assembly to contrast the magnitude of the forces employed to keep order on January 29, with the feebleness of the attempts to disturb it ; and to proclaim as the inference from this disparity, that the whole trouble was trumped up by Louis Napoleon, as an excuse for a *coup d'état* of his own.

The contention will hardly bear examination even on *a priori* grounds. Time and again in 1848 efforts to disturb order had proved serious or successful, because the forces employed to maintain order had been ludicrously inadequate. Louis Napoleon and his military commander Changarnier preferred that in 1849 efforts to disturb order should be rendered ludicrous by the display of overwhelming force in its defence. It is true no doubt that a third course was open to them. By somewhat decreasing the number of troops mobilised, and so in all probability somewhat augmenting the number of agitators who would attack them, they might have found a moderate use of force sufficient to quell a moderate sized rebellion. But it has not generally been held the duty of a government to bring about, by nice calculations of this sort, an exact equipoise between supporters and assailants of public order. And though it was only natural that after their experience of 1848 the Republicans should feel that their latest attempt at revolt had hardly been given fair play, yet a later generation can scarcely admit the cogency of the assumption which underlies their complaints—the assumption that it is the part of any well-conducted government to allow to revolutionaries at least a sporting chance of success.

Further, though it was easy for the Republicans to assert that Louis Napoleon had designed a *coup d'état*, it was far

[1] *Barrot*, iii. 87.

from easy for them to explain why in that case he had failed to carry out his intention. No effective obstacle to such a design was then in existence. Both the national guard and the regular troops in Paris were under the command of General Changarnier, who at this time seems still to have been desirous of a *coup d'état*,[1] believing that it must in the end prove favourable to a restoration of the monarchy. The President had his unprecedented triumph at the polls fresh upon him ; his only opponent, the exhausted Constituent Assembly, was almost as discredited in the country as had been the Rump of the Long Parliament in England : in this case too it is doubtful whether a second Cromwell clearing the chamber of its deputies would have heard ' a dog that barked at their going.'

Were any further refutation of the charge necessary, it would be forthcoming in the despatches of the British ambassador at this time. Lord Normanby, who could not sufficiently condemn the actual *coup d'état* when it took place two years later, has only praise for Louis Napoleon's conduct on the present occasion. On January 28 he writes that persons lately arriving from the provinces report them ' in a state of extreme excitement against the Assembly, and express their astonishment at the calm with which Paris tolerates their usurpation.' [2] ' Disgusted as the country is with all that has occurred since February, and dreading the return to power of those who have brought them to the brink of ruin,' he considered that it would welcome a presidential *coup d'état*, a step which would therefore probably be successful, if it were attempted. Next day he added that his former opinion of the President's firmness and energy had been ' confirmed to me on all hands by the reports of his conduct yesterday. Several of the ministers told me that their opinion of him had been very much raised by the resources he seemed to possess in moments of difficulty.' [3] ' I have reason to believe,' he

---

[1] *Viel-Castel*, ii. 103. *Senior: Thiers*, i. 45. But cf. *Senior: Empire*, i. 59 *sq.*
[2] F.O. France, Normanby to Palmerston, 28 Jan. 49.
[3] *Ibid.*, 29 Jan. 49.

continues, ' that the ultra-republican plot was more extensive and more completely organised than will ever be known
now its outbreak has been averted, as if the government
were to disclose their actual sources of information they
might not again be forewarned.' The funds rose when
it was known ' that the President was riding through
the streets attended only by his staff, inspecting the
different stations of troops and surrounded by an immense
crowd, by whom he was received with much enthusiasm.
This disregard of personal danger at the moment when
threatened assassination was the prevalent source of alarm
certainly produced a favourable impression . . . it would
however be desirable that such occasions of unnecessary
exposure should not at present be too frequently repeated.' [1]
Three years later Faucher, Louis' Minister of the Interior,
described his conduct on this occasion in almost identical
terms.[2] ' His indifference to personal danger amounts to
rashness ' was his comment.   In any case Lord Normanby's
despatches would seem to show that the President's activity
was in no way misdirected : and that so far from seeking
an occasion for a *coup d'état*, he abstained from attempting
one at a time when the attempt might have been made
with every prospect of success.

Despite his firmness in public, when faced by actual
insurrection, Louis Napoleon during this very period was
privately but persistently struggling to induce his ministers
to concede a complete amnesty to the several thousands of
political offenders who were still suffering punishment for
their share in the June days of 1848.   Thrice during the

[1] F.O. France, Normanby to Palmerston, 31 Jan. 49.   A few weeks later
Admiral Cécile, the new French ambassador to England, told Queen Victoria
that ' the President had risen amazingly in the opinion of everyone by his
firmness, courage, and determination, which he had shown in those critical
days a fortnight or three weeks ago ; in these two months he had acquired
"une grande aptitude pour les affaires ; tout le monde est étonné parce que
personne ne s'y attendait." '   *Q.V.L.*, ii. 214.   Cécile was a strong Orleanist.
' When the Embassy was offered him he told the President that he had
always been attached to Louis Philippe, and that if he were to be made
the instrument of doing anything disagreeable to him he could not accept
it.   The President said he might be perfectly easy on that score, and
that he might go and pay his respects at Claremont as soon as he arrived
if he pleased.'   *Greville*, 11 Feb. 49.
[2] *Senior : Italy*, ii. 283.

first six months of his presidency he urged this step upon
his Cabinet : thrice their unanimous and vehement protestations bore him down.[1] To this theme he returned in
season and out of season. Thus a fortnight after his first
proposal of it had been quashed, a Cabinet meeting was held
to discuss the financial schemes of his Chancellor of the
Exchequer. With the optimism common to his class,
M. Passy concluded his statement by a prediction that all
difficulties would disappear in natural course, granted only
the restoration of public confidence in the government.
Louis as usual sat silent at the head of the table : not
infrequently during the lengthy arguments of his ministers
he appeared like some inattentive schoolboy to be entirely
engrossed in making small paper toys or drawing figures
on his blotting-pad.[2] But his customary silence—irritating
in its presumption that he was not listening—was broken by
occasional utterance, more irritating in its proof that he
was. So now he cut in on the word ' confidence.' ' Quite
right,' he interjected, ' everything depends on public
confidence ; and it is only to a strong government that
confidence is given. The best proof of strength would be
the amnesty. We ought to couple a vote for that with the
vote for the budget.'[3] But again a threat of resignation
brought the President to what his advisers considered
reason.

Meanwhile the complete collapse in Paris of this the
solitary demonstration in favour of its continued session,
together with a distant but ominous rumble of provincial
disapproval, served at last to convince the Constituent
Assembly of the inexpediency of its attempt to perpetuate
its own existence : by a majority of five it now regretfully
declined the invitation of those who bade it live for ever,
and consented to the common lot of parliaments. It still
secured to itself however a decent interval in which to

[1] *Falloux*, i. 417–419. In March 1849 he vainly supported the one
minister who opposed the first resort by the new Republic to the guillotine.
Hugo: Choses Vues, 484. ' Despite the best intentions in the world, and
a very visible quantity of intelligence and aptitude, I fear he will find his
task too much for him.' *Ibid.*, 522.
[2] *Hugo: Napoléon-le-Petit*, 34.
[3] *Falloux*, i. 418.

wind up its affairs; it was not until May 13 that the elections to the new Assembly took place.

In these elections the Bonapartists co-operated with the leaders of the Orleanist and Legitimist parties; a common electoral association put forward candidates pledged to the maintenance of order and the protection of society. The coalition was successful in its general object; its candidates secured five hundred of the seven hundred seats in the new Assembly. But since he contributed the personal popularity and the Royalists the political machinery, the President had naturally the worst of the bargain. Somehow it was always the Bonapartist candidate who was found to have retired, when the common cause demanded the withdrawal of one or other of the anti-Republican candidates. Louis Napoleon watched this sacrifice of his proclaimed and personal followers with an equanimity which to some of them was exceedingly provoking.[1] The fact was that he still clung to the belief, to which the letters of his exile bear frequent testimony,[2] that the possession by a ruler of an organised party of personal adherents was a confession of weakness rather than a source of strength. As a result he found himself landed with a parliament far more reactionary than he really wished. For in his vague and opportunist fashion the man was still a liberal at heart.

Much the most dramatic result of the election was the practical annihilation of the old majority of parliamentary Republicans. In the new house a bare tenth of them survived; among their more notable losses was the defeat of Lamartine, who even more closely than Cavaignac himself was associated with the origin of the Second Republic. On the other hand, Ledru-Rollin's small following of Socialists and Red Republicans had received a slight increase in numbers, and a considerable increase in prestige, from some striking victories at the polls;[3] in the new chamber they decidedly outnumbered the remnant of orthodox Republicans. Of the Conservative majority,

---

[1] E.g. *Persigny*, 23.   [2] *Simpson*, 337, 345.
[3] *Lebey*, 297.

some two hundred were Legitimists, the remainder mainly
Orleanists.   Among the new members was Louis Napoleon's
devoted adherent, Persigny, who at once took his place at
the head of a small group which had had no precedent in
the Constituent Assembly ; a parliamentary Bonapartist
party.   Though this group owed little to Louis Napoleon's
patronage in the first instance it received ever-increasing
attention from him and rendered him ever more valuable
support as he slowly realised the impracticability of his old
non-party ideal.   Indeed, for the next two years, the chief
interest of the internal development of the new chamber
consists in the gradual growth of this group—soon to be
known   as   the   *Parti d'Elysée*—from   an   insignificant
minority into a compact party, possessed of a casting vote
in the chamber.

The Constituent Assembly, to which this newly-elected
chamber formed the successor, has in the history of
representative institutions one melancholy distinction all
its own.   It succeeded in devising a completely new method
of bringing parliamentary government into disrepute ;
a method which has remained not only without precedent,
but even without imitators.   It declined to dissolve itself
until its successor had been elected : and after painfully
keeping itself alive for the express purpose of seeing its
heir, it so little liked his appearance when it did see him as
to feel bound in duty to keep alive a little longer still.   It
accordingly announced its intention of sitting up to the
very eve of the date fixed for the first meeting of the new
Assembly : even declining to grant to the harassed officials
responsible for the fabric the three days interval considered
necessary for even the most summary of spring cleanings.
The days thus snatched from the grave by the Constituent
Assembly were spent in a pitiful succession of bickerings
and recriminations, in which mournful headshakings over
the approaching ruin of the Republic were enlivened by
occasional outbursts of hysterical indignation, what time
some conservative deputy, serene in his personal re-election
to the new chamber, made bold to remind the Assembly
of its own hourly approaching demise.

The end so much protested against came at last.　On May 27 the Constituent Assembly was dissolved ; and its disappearance marked a definite stage in Louis Napoleon's advance towards supreme power in France.　In these opening months of his official career he had displayed what was to the professional politicians a totally unexpected resourcefulness of expedient and tenacity of purpose.　He had scored thereby a threefold success.　He had asserted his personal position in his own cabinet ; he had secured the dissolution of a hostile chamber, that threatened to constitute itself into a sort of Long Parliament ; and by a timely display of vigour he had quelled without bloodshed a potential rising in the streets of Paris, the first that had been promptly and effectively suppressed since that to which the Second Republic owed its existence.　Two other trifling acts of self-assertion on Louis' part at this time pained his political advisers.　Before his election Thiers had asked him to dinner, and invited Molé to meet him, in order that their joint eloquence might induce him to shave off his moustache.　The request was prefaced by a lengthy discourse on the essentially civilian character of modern institutions, and softened by an undertaking on the part of his two advisers to remain clean-shaven themselves.[1]　Louis not only refused, but proceeded immediately after his election still further to scandalise his would-be successors by assuming the costume of a general of the national guard.[2]　Again Thiers protested, in the name of civilian institutions ; adding ruefully, "Besides, what is your successor to do ? "[3]　It was a question which Louis did not feel bound to answer.

The practical achievements of the opening months of Louis Napoleon's official life were obvious alike to his countrymen and to foreign observers of his career.　It was far otherwise with two notable attempts made by the

---

[1] This story Cassagnac professes to have had from Louis himself a few years later.　*Cassagnac*, i. 53.

[2] Blue tunic and trousers with red stripes, three-corner hat and feather.

[3] *Merruau*, 395.　And see *Barrot*, iii. 101.

new President during these same months to give effect to
the grandiose dreams of his long political exile. Both
attempts failed, through lack of English co-operation :
both might conceivably have produced results beneficial
to Europe, had they been translated into action : one at
least of them has remained in absolute oblivion until the
present day.

It is a matter of common knowledge that in the last
year of his reign Louis Napoleon's government endeavoured
to concert some scheme for the limitation of armaments
with Prussia, the only military rival of France. But it
has hitherto escaped the notice of historians that in the
first month of his official life Louis himself was the author
of the most drastic proposal for the limitation of naval
armaments ever put forward by the head of any nation.
At this time, and for forty years to come, France was the
only country in existence whose fleet in any way approxi-
mated to that of Great Britain : the naval armaments
of the other powers were inconsiderable. On January 17,
Louis Napoleon caused his newly appointed Minister for
Foreign Affairs, Drouyn de Lhuys, to propose to Normanby,
the British ambassador, that the two Western Powers
should take common action in regard to the limitation of
their navies. The French Government would, said Drouyn,
' be prepared to make almost any reduction we might
suggest, provided we were disposed to do so upon somewhat
the same relative scale ' ; [1] adding ' that so long as England
and France thoroughly understood each other their reduced fleets would be quite sufficient to ensure the respect
of the rest of the world.' Louis Napoleon himself formally
repeated the offer to Normanby in a subsequent interview
with him.[1]

Palmerston was apparently somewhat at a loss as to
how to deal with such an unprecedented proposal : he
expressed himself as gratified by the proof of friendly
feeling shown by the President in his overture ; but stated
that it was impossible for England with its world-wide

[1] F.O. France, Normanby to Palmerston, 17 Jan. 49. ' Secret and
confidential.'

possessions to make its fleet dependent on the size of the
fleet maintained by any one Power.[1]	Thus the door was
politely closed upon a proposal which might have produced
beneficent results for both nations, had it received a some-
what different treatment.	For the rivalry in ship-building
which it was designed to avert did in fact take place
between the two nations in the later years of the Second
Empire.	Yet on Louis' part the proposal was no mere
passing whim : six years later, in the course of the Crimean
War, his conversations with Cowley show the persistence
of the same idea.[2]	On the present occasion, in spite of
England's refusal to co-operate, the President resolved that
France should make on her own account a beginning at
any rate in the process of disarmament : in the teeth of
considerable opposition he succeeded in effecting large
reductions both in men and material in the naval and
military budget of 1849.[3]

Some six weeks later Palmerston quashed remorselessly
a second of Louis Napoleon's visionary suggestions.	On
the 5th of March 1849, the President proposed to the
British ambassador that the two governments should
issue a united invitation to the powers for a general congress to deal with all questions which threatened to disturb
the peace of Europe.	Louis proposed the scheme in a
confidential interview, and without any previous con-
sultation of his cabinet.	At present, he said, the only
hope of maintaining order was based on appeals to the
treaties of 1815 : but these treaties had been violated over
and over again by almost every one of the contracting
powers : attempts to patch up peace in every part of
Europe upon such an outworn basis could hardly be
expected to prove successful.	Among other advantages
of the scheme Louis Napoleon urged, that in any such new
congress for the modification of the treaties of 1815, France
would be able to co-operate on equal terms with the other

---

[1] F.O. draft, Palmerston to Normanby, 25 Jan. 49. ' Secret and
confidential.'
[2] See p. 272 below.
[3] For details see D'Orsay to Fonblanque, 26 Jan. 49.	*Fonblanque*, 57.

Powers : naturally she had always regarded the original Congress of Vienna with some aversion, but after sharing on equal terms in such a congress as Louis now proposed she would be able to give her whole-hearted support to the cause of order based on treaties she had herself assisted in revising.[1] The suggestion of ' modification ' of these several treaties evidently served however to arouse Palmerston's suspicions, and he had little difficulty, with every appearance of goodwill, in crushing the project. Political questions which could be debated at congresses, he pointed out,[2] were of two kinds ; international and internal. Now the policy of non-intervention, to which both England and France were committed, held that the former alone were fit subjects for debate in congress. But none of the questions which at present threatened to disturb the peace of Europe were of this class ; they did not turn on questions of political boundaries, and so form the legitimate subject of a European congress : they were internal questions, which France and England were precluded by their past principles from urging the competence of any congress to discuss.[3]

Here again it seems open to question whether Palmerston might not have done well to give Louis Napoleon's scheme somewhat less cavalier treatment. Such a congress as Louis suggested, could it have been convoked at the time he suggested, by the two moderate liberal Powers of the west, might possibly have served to rescue some considerable fragments of national liberties for the not yet desperate revolutionaries of the Continent. In taking up the attitude that the European disturbances of 1848 and 1849 were purely internal questions, Palmerston was in fact denying the right of such provinces as the Italian dominions of Austria to receive any external assistance in their struggle

---

[1] F.O. France, 4 Mar. 49, Normanby to Palmerston. ' Secret.'
[2] F.O. draft, Palmerston to Normanby, 5 Mar. 49. ' Secret.'
[3] Thus rebuffed by the English government, Louis, at the end of the same month, sounded his friend Lord Malmesbury as to the possibility of a different attitude on the part of the opposition in the event of its obtaining office : saying that ' France and England together could remodel everything.' *Malmesbury*, i. 244.

for liberty, so long as their legitimate overlord could hold them under control.   It was without doubt the condition of affairs in Italy that Louis Napoleon primarily desired to submit to the examination of an international tribunal. It was in Italy, eighteen eventful years ago, that he had first drawn sword as a political adventurer.   It was in Italy, though to all appearance in a very different rôle, that he now made his first excursion into foreign politics as the head of the French nation.

CHAPTER III

THE ROAD TO ROME

The sun, which was just setting behind the distant hills, shone with dazzling splendour for a moment upon the towers and spires of the city across the placid water. Behind this fair vision were dark rain clouds, before which gloomy background it stood in fairy radiance and light. For a moment it seemed a glorious city, bathed in life and hope, full of happy people who thronged its streets and bridge, and the margin of its gentle stream. But it was 'breve gaudium.' Then the sunset faded, and the ethereal vision vanished, and the landscape lay dark and chill.

'The sun is set,' Mr Inglesant said cheerfully, 'but it will rise again. Let us go home.'

JOSEPH HENRY SHORTHOUSE.

OF all the revolutionary movements of 1848 none has made a stronger claim upon the sympathies of posterity than that which for five fantastic months made Rome a republic, with Mazzini as its head and Garibaldi for its right arm. The hour, the place, the men ; a scene that was in itself a consecration, for a drama that needed no adventitious aid ; odds that would argue any conflict heroic, and heroism that in fact was no mere matter of inference ; these must in any case have made the defence of Rome memorable, even had it lacked ultimate success to prove it statesmanlike, immediate failure to stamp it as sublime.

Valuable as was to prove the mere fact of its early death to the memory of the Roman Republic, the pathos of that appeal was immensely enhanced by the actual circumstances of its extinction. Of all European Powers that which might first have been expected to sustain a republic in distress was the mother of republics, France. Of all

European rulers he who might most have been expected
to oppose a papal restoration was the ruler of France,
Louis Napoleon. The preamble to the new French constitution contained a clause affirming that France respected
foreign nationalities, and that her might should never be
used against the liberty of any people : [1] the new French
President had himself borne arms against the Pope at the
time of the last serious attempt to free the States of the
Church from papal misgovernment. Yet it was by the
act of that very country and ruler that the Roman Republic appeared to be barbarously done to death in the
spring of 1849 : perishing by a fratricidal blow from the
one hand that might have been expected to be raised in
its defence. It is with the causes of a betrayal, apparently
so inexplicable and inexcusable, that we have now to deal.

Eighteen years ago Louis Napoleon had risked his life,
and his elder brother had died, in leading an armed insurrection in the Papal States. But in those eighteen
years much had happened to change men's attitude towards
the Papacy. The last eight of those years—the period
immediately preceding the great uprising of '48 — had
formed the very climax of the European reaction. To
the east Russia stayed still and Poland lay crushed under
the iron heel of Nicholas. In Italy and Germany Metternich's system of organised repression seemed only a degree
less triumphant than in Austria itself. After its quarrel
with England in 1846 even France, the one power on the
Continent which was still nominally liberal in its sympathies,
had been drawn into reactionary alliance with the policy
of Metternich. In the years which followed strange
champions arose to defend the expiring liberties of Europe,
and strange dreams were dreamed because of them. After
the revolution was over, when continental Europe was
relapsing into the bondage from which for a moment it
had raised itself, it was Turkey which offered a secure
retreat to the beaten revolutionaries of Hungary and
Poland.[2] And in France and England for that reason

---

[1] Clause 5.   [2] v. p. 219 below.

men were found to believe in the possibility of a reformed
Ottoman Empire, wherein the only gentleman of the east
should govern his unruly peninsula with all the adjuncts
of western constitutionalism.

But before the revolution had broken out, there had
arisen another and stranger champion of liberty and reform. In the summer of 1846 died Gregory XVI ; a pope
whose chief political legacy to his successor consisted in
the memory of fifteen years of mediæval misgovernment.
In his stead was elected a comparatively young and unknown bishop, destined to the longest and well-nigh the
most momentous reign in papal history. He was proclaimed as Pius IX. And never had the venerable formula
in which that proclamation was cast found speedier justification in the events of the new reign : it was ' a great joy '
that had been announced from the balcony of the Quirinal
to the populace beneath ; a joy that was to go rippling
outwards from Rome to Italy, from Italy to the world.
For within a year men had learnt to believe that there was
but one liberal sovereign on earth ; and that one, the Pope.

That a rumour so incredible should have found general
and even passionate acceptance was due in part to the
extraordinary psychological condition of Europe in 1847.
But it would be unfair to forget that in part also it was
based upon the actual and authentic achievement of the
pope ; an achievement of which the daring and sincerity
was scarcely more unduly exaggerated by its contemporaries than it has since been unduly disparaged by
historians. In its judgment of its own contemporaries the
whole world is not easily in entire error, even for a day.

Handsome, debonair, and for his office, young ; possessed of a personal charm which none who met him
could ignore, the new Pope had every accidental aid to
popularity. And if any better foil had been conceivable
for his political debut than the reign which he actually
succeeded, it would have been that of the retrograde and
absolutist archbishop whose triumph his election had
averted. But even his initial advantages were neither
wholly negative nor wholly accidental. By birth the

member of a consistently liberal family,[1] he had as bishop, both at Spoleto and Imola, honourably distinguished himself for his humane and tolerant administration ; after 1831 he had been summoned to Rome and officially rebuked by his predecessor for his clemency towards the insurgents in that very rising in which Louis Napoleon had acted as leader. He had in fact provided Louis, when he was in imminent risk of capture by the Austrians, both with guides and with a large gift in money : to which timely succour the prince possibly owed his successful escape.[2]

Within a few weeks the Pope proceeded by definite acts of reform to give substance to the vague hopes occasioned by his accession. The military tribunals of the last reign were abolished.[3] A liberal Cardinal was appointed Secretary of State. A complete amnesty was proclaimed to all political offenders.[4] A new commercial tariff was published, by which import duties were reduced on many articles of popular consumption : [5] and in the following year the Pope eagerly supported a scheme for the formation of an Italian Zollverein.[6] The censorship was greatly relaxed,[7] and a relative freedom allowed of speech and press. A municipal charter was granted to the city. Judicial reforms were set in hand, and in Rome itself a National Guard was created.[8] A Council of Ministers was instituted, which though purely consultative in the first ·instance received within six months the right to discuss all important decisions of state before they could be submitted to the Pope for his approval.[9] Education received a tardy measure of state encouragement and endowment : and money was voted for the erection of

[1] *Johnston*, 31 ; *King*, i. 171.
[2] *Grabinski*, 34, 35, whose unnamed informants had these details from Pius IX himself. Cf. *Blount*, 37. Personal gratitude to Pio Nono may well have had its share in Louis' refusal to have him robbed of Rome : were he to die, Louis told Arese in 1861, and to be succeeded by a reactionary with no such personal claims upon him, he would recall his troops. *Bonfadini*, 282. On the other hand Metternich told Loftus in 1859 that it was he who had allowed Louis to escape in deference to Hortense. *Loftus*, i. 57.
[3] *Johnston*, 37.
[4] For text, see *Thayer*: *Italy*, ii. 19, 20.
[5] *Register*: 1846, 289.
[6] *King*: *Italy*, i. 187.
[7] *Johnston*, 72.
[8] *Register*: 1847, 396.
[9] *Ibid.*, 1847, 396 ; 1848, 329.

labourers' houses.[1] Railways for the first time were admitted into the Papal States : for the last pope, like the English Universities, had kept them at arm's length as a demoralising innovation.[2]

These various reforms of Pio Nono in the first year of his reign were largely the outcome of a somewhat nebulous benevolence : for the new pope, with all the goodwill in the world, had no great administrative experience. But statesmanlike or the reverse, his reforms at this stage seemed spontaneous and sincere. Hence it is small wonder that in 1847 Pius IX was the most idolised sovereign in Europe. For at a time when every considerable monarchy on the Continent was sinking deeper and deeper into the reactionary policy of the age, he was seen to be offering his subjects a series of concessions and reforms : reforms far from inconsiderable in themselves, and naturally hailed with rapture when coming at such an hour from such a source. For it was in the wilderness that these waters had broken forth ; and men fainting for thirst are poor critics of their drink.

On December 30, 1847, still anticipating the European revolution of which more than any other man he was the author, Pius proceeded to make his ministers severally responsible for the entire administration of their respective departments, assigning to them the appointment of all public officers and functionaries, reserving to himself only the nomination of nuncios and cardinals. Attached to the council was a body of auditors half of whom were laymen.[3] In March 1848 the Pope became for the first time the follower of his own imitators in other states : but a follower still with a free hand and a good grace. ' Our neighbours,' he wrote in a proclamation of March 14, ' have decided that the people are already ripe for the benefits of a representative system of government, not

---

[1] *King*: *Italy*, i. 208.
[2] Pio Nono the Second reverted to this opinion. In 1851 the sacred college refused to allow a line joining Venice and Leghorn to cross the Romagna, on the ground that 'railways produce commerce, and commerce produces sin.' *Senior*: *Italy*, ii. 165.
[3] *Register*: 1848, 329.

merely consultative but deliberative. We are unwilling
to think less worthily of our own subjects, or to repose
less faith in their gratitude not only towards our own
humble person, for which we desire none, but towards the
church and this Apostolic See.' A complicated constitution was appended : and a new ministry was announced
which included a number of capable and liberal laymen.

But by this time the Pope was no longer master of the
forces which he had set in motion. Three days after the
promulgation of their constitution, the Roman citizens
learned that Vienna itself had risen in revolution, and that
Metternich was fallen and a fugitive. At the news a
wilder hope took possession of them ; the Pope should be
headed into heading not merely a liberal but a nationalist
movement, whereby the whole soil of Italy should be freed
from Austrian oppression for ever.

The conception at that time was just not wholly incredible. In general it has been at once the weakness and the
strength of the Papacy, that its claims are cosmopolitan.
Overriding all frontiers, admitting of no boundaries ;
claiming to amalgamate because claiming to include all
peoples of the earth, the influence of the Roman Catholic
Church has logically been non-national even where it has
not in practice proved anti-national. But nowhere had
the grip of that religion proved stronger than in those few
countries where in its own despite as it were, the cause of
Catholicism had been identified with the cause of nationality. Upon that strange amalgam had been built
securely the two uttermost buttresses of European Catholicism : for the like lamentable conditions had made Faith
and Fatherland a cry to conjure with in Ireland and in
Poland.

Already during the later years of the First Empire, in
countries so different as Spain and the Tyrol, the new and
sterner cosmopolitanism of Napoleon had thrust upon
Catholicism the occasional championship of a national
cause. But after his fall the Congress of Vienna proceeded
to prepare the way for other and more permanent coalitions
between these two forces in the future. By ratifying an

unnatural partition, it perpetuated such an alliance in Poland ; by forcing an unnatural union it created such an alliance in Belgium. For it was thought necessary, for the greater inconvenience of France, to reconstitute a kingdom of the United Netherlands ; whose Catholic provinces were subjected to the Protestant domination of the Dutch. Unlike the existing coalitions of Catholicism and Nationalism this new alliance was situated not in the confines of Europe, but at its heart ; unlike them also it was destined not to long failure but to swift success. Hence the achievement of national independence by Belgium in 1830 gave a startling advertisement to a co-operation, which now for the first time men were beginning to regard as natural and right.

This same European revolution of 1830, which had crowned with triumph the alliance of Catholicism and Nationalism in Belgium, had served to inaugurate a hardly less wonderful alliance between Catholicism and Liberalism in France. For in that country the long and sordid reign of Louis Philippe, by showing that it was possible to be reactionary without being religious, to be at once anticlerical and undemocratic, called into existence a new school of Catholic apologetic ; whose members dreamed of a great liberal Catholicism of the future, essentially popular and progressive. And while on this side of the Alps such ideas found eloquent exponents in Montalembert and Lamennais, beyond the mountains Gioberti had enunciated an even fonder dream—a restored Italy, a revived Papacy, a regenerate people confederate under the hegemony of a truly paternal pope. These ideas were still fresh in men's minds when the election of Pio Nono and the *annus mirabilis* at Rome seemed to give them startling corroboration, and even to promise them speedy fulfilment. Men remembered the gentle sufferings of Pius VII : they saw the generous actions of Pius IX : for the second time within the memory of living men they were confronted with the spectacle of a good and wise pope. And at that sight the admiration of the faithful, setting in full flood towards the see of Peter, was augmented by a stream of wistful wonder welling up from the heart of many a half-envious heretic ; wonder whether the new vision could indeed be destined to prove a waking dream.

But while a liberal Pope was an awkward and uncomfortable possibility, a nationalist Pope was a contradiction in terms.   Even the misty good nature of Pio Nono was clearer than his admirers on this point ; at no time was he really converted to the belief that the leadership of an aggressive nationalism could be for one in his position either possible or right.   He had it was true in 1847 protested energetically and successfully against Austria's aggressive and reactionary occupation of Ferrara ; denouncing the Pope for a Freemason and a Carbonaro, Metternich had been forced to beat an unaccustomed diplomatic retreat. But because he had outfaced Austria in 1847 when she was aggressive and apparently all-powerful, Italian nationalists expected that Pio Nono would be ready to take the aggressive against Austria in 1848 when she was stricken and apparently helpless.   In this they were mistaken : and to do the Pope justice, so long as he had effective control of events he never failed to reiterate his refusal as the head of Catholic Christendom to take up arms against a Catholic Power which had done him no wrong.   A league of Italian states to which Austria should somehow be persuaded pacifically to assent he genuinely desired ; but this was probably the extreme limit of Pio Nono's nationalism.[1]   Even the celebrated ' God bless Italy ' of his allocution on February 10 meant to its utterer no more than this ; both then, and on the following day when he repeated the words from the balcony of the Quirinal, he accompanied them with an explicit repudiation of any papal war on Austria.[2]   But his audience heard only what they wished to hear ; and still hoped to force their reluctant monarch to declare war on Austria, much as Louis XVI

[1] This too seems to have been Louis Napoleon's own hope at this period. Two years later at any rate he explained to the English ambassador in a confidential interview that he was meditating a project to establish at Rome ' a sort of confederation of the Italian powers.'   F.O. France, Normanby to Palmerston, 28 Apr. 51

[2] *Masi* : *C.M.H.*, xi. 81.

had been forced to a similar declaration at a similar stage
of the French Revolution.   In this they were unsuccessful,
but without a formal declaration of war the papal troops
crossed the frontier to take part in military operations
against Austria.   Bitter therefore was their disillusion [1]
and disappointment when at the end of April, in response
to a specific request from his ministry for his views, the
Pope proceeded to declare that a war with Austria was
wholly abhorrent from the counsels of one, who as Pope
' regarded with equal affection all peoples, races, and
nations.'   ' He wished,' he said, ' the extension of Christ's
kingdom, not of the temporal dominions of the Holy See :
and how should he be the wager of war, who was the
unworthy servant of the Author of Peace.'   Italian
nationalists never forgave the Pope his allocution of
April 1848 in which he thus refused a kingdom of this
world or to let his servants fight.   After all, his predecessors had fought before now in worse causes ;   and
though he would not fight to extend the papal dominions,
Pio Nono was soon to show himself quite ready to fight in
their defence. [2]   Meanwhile it was in vain that he endeavoured, by an autograph letter to the Austrian Emperor
urging the peaceful cession of his Italian possessions, [3] to
atone for his failure to eject him from them by force ;
in vain that he placarded the walls of Rome with the
very words of the Reproaches : *O my people, what have
I done unto thee, or wherein have I wearied thee ?   Answer
me.*   Appeal and question were unheard.

The Pope's refusal of armed support to the Italian
nationalists was but one of many contributory causes to
their failure in 1848.   But it was so much the most dramatic
defection which their cause had yet sustained as almost

---

[1] For the measure of it contrast e.g. *Ossoli*, iii, 155 and 171 ; the ' real
great heart, the generous man ' of 20 Dec. 47 had become on 30 Apr. 48
the man whom ' those who loved can no longer defend,' to whose blessing
' none can now attach any value.'

[2] Cf. *Story*, 2 May 47.   ' Here is a man who refused to aid by his word
a war for the liberation of Italy because of the blood by which it must be
purchased, and who less than a year after sheds, indirectly, the blood of
his people to regain his temporal power.'   *Story*, i. 156.

[3] *Buffoni*, 272.   For a moment he even intended to proceed to Milan
and attempt a mediation in person.   *Pasolini*, 70.

to appear to the Italians the sole source of all their disasters. Upon the head of the unfortunate Pope, therefore, his recent admirers proceeded to heap denunciations which were not only unmerciful but in many ways unfair. None the less the popular instinct was right which seized on Pio Nono's April allocution as the great refusal. In effect it was his announcement to the Italian people that he was the Pope, and could not be their leader. In any nationalist uprising the two rôles were in reality incompatible ; and it was not the tardy recognition of the fact but the failure to recognise it sooner which was truly deplorable in either side. It was a correct though a belated instinct which finally forbade the Pope to exchange his cosmopolitan dominion for the leadership of any nation, even the Italian. But just so certainly correct was the deduction of the Italian people, which bade them henceforth seek national leadership elsewhere. Each side eventually was greatly the gainer from a discernment which for the moment brought bitterness to both. A secular temporal government gave to the new kingdom guarantees for its liberties impossible under the auspices of even the most benevolent pope. And both Italy and the world were gainers that the Papacy did not become a national institution. Of all the triumphs of nineteenth-century nationalism none was fraught with less admixture of evil or attended by a clearer balance of gain than that of the Italian risorgimento. But the new and noisy nationalisms in general stood in urgent need of every sane corrective available. Everywhere that they might become better than themselves nations were encouraged to believe that they were better than their neighbours. The hypnotic process did not lack success : and by means of it unsuspected reserves of energy were unlocked. But exactly in proportion to its success was this process conducive also to a quarrelsome megalomania. Never was it more necessary to Europe than in the years which followed that its religion also should not be national. National churches with each a Judaic Jehovah of its own could not restrain but only reinforce the evils as well as the benefits of nationalism.

The non-national Papacy—feeble and time-serving as in moments of crisis its policy might appear—did at least and did alone preserve in Christian Europe an uneasy sense that its wars were civil wars, and that where one part of the body suffered the whole in some sort suffered with it.

But though their final and legitimate decision to go their several ways redounded to the eventual gain both of Pope and people it involved an immediate injury to both. Because the Pope had at last rejected a part he had not the right to play the Romans in turn rejected at his hands the benefits which he could and still would legitimately have conferred on them. With what appeared to Pio Nono a black ingratitude they would have none of him as a liberal reformer if they could not have him also as a nationalist leader. This tragic consequence of his position and theirs the Pope had not the discernment to perceive. In September 1848 he took what would otherwise have been the most hopeful step forward in all his liberal career, by calling to office an honest, able, and essentially practical reformer, Count Rossi, ' the man whose illustrious life was to be the price of the last desperate effort to maintain the union between Pius IX and his people.' [1] Rossi's wife was a Protestant, and some of his own writings, as he himself reminded the Pope, had been placed on the Index. ' " That is of no consequence," answered Pius IX,' [2] and insisted on making him prime minister. ' With marvellous judgment and knowledge Rossi flung himself into the task of curbing the all-prevailing anarchy, and of infusing fresh life into an administration which was already in dissolution. He met the hatred of both clericals and demagogues in the open, concealed none of his proposals, never retreated, put his hand to everything.' [3] It profited him nothing.

Scorning all precautions as to his personal safety—' If they want my life,' he said, ' you may be sure they will get it one way or another ' [4]—he proceeded in spite of warnings and without protection to open the new session of the

---

[1] *Masi*: *C.M.H.*, 89. [2] *Pasolini*, 84.
[3] *Masi*: *C.M.H.*, 89. [4] *Agresti*, 37.

Council of Deputies : according to plan he was set upon
and assassinated, on the threshold of the parliament house.
Within, the Representatives not daring to condemn the
deed affected for a while to discuss their own minutes,
and then slunk off to their homes : without, a select
assortment of the people they represented proceeded to
put a fitting end to the day by serenading Rossi's widow
with hymns in praise of his assassin. On the morrow
Pius received delegates from a threatening mob ; bullets
penetrated the Pope's ante-chamber, and his private
secretary was shot dead. For three hours this desultory
firing continued, during which time the Pope repeatedly
refused to accept the advice of his entourage, and submit.
The Swiss guard protested their willingness to die to a man
around him, but there were less than a hundred of them all
told.[1]

Finally the insurgents ' brought cannon to force the
gates of this unfortunate Pope, who is mildness itself. . . .
The Pope during the entire period showed much coolness
and courage, but it was impossible to resist, and as he
desired less than anybody to cause blood to be shed he was
consequently compelled to submit.' [2] Protesting to the
diplomatic body that he submitted only to force and must
consider void and invalid the results of his submission [3] he
accepted a new ministry composed of approvers of
yesterday's assassination. Its first act was to replace his
trusty Swiss guard by hostile troops in whose hands he was
virtually a prisoner. The fate of Louis XVI seemed fast
to be closing in upon him, when a week later he avoided
its final culmination by a successful version of the flight
to Varennes. England [4] as well as France and Spain had
ships on the coast waiting to convey him to some haven
of refuge in their dominions ; but Pius chose the easy road
that led to Gaëta. Thither messages of sympathy and
condolence flowed in upon him from the chief Protestant

[1] *Farini*, ii. 418–420.
[2] Harcourt to Bastide. The French ambassador was an eyewitness :
to protect the Pope he had taken up his residence at the Quirinal.
Register : 1848, 331.
[3] *Farini*, ii. 420.   [4] *Key*, 170, 175.

as well as from all the Catholic powers ; that of Queen
Victoria was the first letter despatched to any Pope by
any English sovereign since the Reformation.[1]

Such was the situation which confronted Louis Napoleon
on the morrow of his election. On the eve of it both he
and his only formidable rival Cavaignac had been forced
by the all but universal sympathy of the electors with the
Pope to make pronouncements in his favour. Both
probably were reluctant suitors for the Catholic vote,
but Louis Napoleon had the appearance of being the more
reluctant of the two. It was Cavaignac's [2] government
which at the end of November 1848 proposed the despatch
of three frigates and over three thousand men to Civita
Vecchia to protect the Pope. On this motion Louis refrained from voting. There was nothing strange in that :
it was his settled policy at this time to withdraw himself,
as future President, from the discussions and divisions
of the Assembly. But this particular division was on
a burning question, and this particular abstention was
at once made the occasion of a strong electoral attack.
Somewhat surprisingly, Louis stood his ground. ' Knowing,' he wrote to the *Constitutionnel* on December 2, ' that
my absence on the occasion of the vote for the Civita
Vecchia expedition has given rise to remark, I feel it my
duty to declare that although resolved to support all
measures really calculated to guarantee the liberty and
authority of the Sovereign Pontiff, I could not give the
approval of my vote to a military demonstration which
seemed to me a danger even to the sacred interests it was
intended to defend, as well as a menace to the peace of
Europe.' Renewed electioneering attacks followed : and
the advocates of Cavaignac proceeded to cast in Louis'
teeth the extravagant republicanism of his cousin the
Prince of Canino in Rome.[3] Upon this, under pressure
from Thiers and Molé,[4] he wrote to the Papal Nuncio ;

---

[1] *Q.V.L.*, i. 209, 210.
[2] On Cavaignac's lack of sympathy with the Italian cause, *v.* Cavour to
Bastide 25 Apr. 58. *Bastide*, 11.
[3] *Normanby*, ii. 355, 356. [4] *Manin*, ii. 57 ; *Lagrange*, i. 468.

stating that for a long while he had had no dealings with his cousin, and regretting that Prince's entire inability to understand ' how intimately the temporal sovereignty of the Pope was bound up not only with the prestige of Catholicism but also with the liberty and independence of Italy.' The Prince of Canino had in fact many worse things to reproach himself with than his failure to reconcile contradictory propositions : but it was ominous that Louis after a momentary stand for his own convictions should have felt forced to take refuge in ambiguities of this kind. In this matter his conduct as candidate was only too apt an epitome of his conduct as President ; tangled in word before his election he suffered himself after it to become tangled in deed.

From this entanglement however there seemed a momentary means of escape. The Pope's flight, and his choice of Neapolitan territory for his refuge, deprived Cavaignac's expedition of its object of existence ; this fact might well have served Louis Napoleon as an excuse for withdrawing entirely from a project of which he had already at some risk expressed his disapproval. Unfortunately he allowed his instinctive dislike of the intervention to be overborne eventually by arguments which though not overwhelming were yet more cogent than has sometimes been admitted.

The Roman Republic proclaimed in February 1849 had at no time a hold on contemporary sympathy at all approaching its appeal to posterity. It is the fashion of an age which knows them to have failed to write down Pio Nono's reforms as altogether fumbling, feeble, and inadequate. Englishmen at the time did not so regard them. They had seen the Romans presented in two years with as large a measure of constitutional progress as they had themselves won arduously in two centuries. For this reason they may be forgiven perhaps for thinking that the pace was not so bad, especially for a Pope. The fact is that historians contemplating this early struggle between Garibaldi and Pio Nono are inevitably influenced in their judgment of the conflict by their knowledge of the later careers of its protagonists. Now it is the historian's legitimate

privilege to utilise the light of later events in forming his
own final judgments.   But only by remembering that his
position is privileged will his use of that privilege remain
legitimate.   He is not entitled to condemn contemporaries
for failing to use a light they had not got and could not have.
If he would judge their judgments he must condescend to
their disabilities ; voluntarily for a moment himself forgoing all knowledge that was necessarily hidden from them.
In the winter of 1849 Garibaldi's laurels were all in front
of him, Pio Nono's all behind.   But observers could no
more know that then, than historians can help knowing
it now.   In contemporaries it is an error at least excusable,
to judge men not by their future but by their past.   So
seen the two sides had not their now traditional aspects.
The exiled Pope was not yet Pio Nono the Second : he
was merely the most lenient of living monarchs.   No
contemporary king had treated his subjects so well, none
to all appearance had been requited by them so ill.   Here
if ever in history was seen ' a prince, the acts of whose
whole reign was a series of concessions to his subjects, who
was willing to relax his authority, to remit his prerogatives,
to call his people to a share of freedom not known, perhaps
not desired, by their ancestors.'

The chief doubt about Pio Nono then seemed whether
he was not too weakly good-natured to be effective even
as a constitutional monarch.   The chief doubt about his
subjects [1] seemed to be whether even constitutional
monarchy was not a bigger stride forward than they were
yet prepared to make good.   A generation later all the
experience and sanity of the Northern Italian was taxed
to the utmost to save even a limited monarchy from being
swamped by the corruption and constitutional backward-
ness of the long servile South.   Rossi had sought and
failed to give the institutions of Orleanist France or of
contemporary England to a people whose treatment of
him is best defended by the plea that their civilisation in

---

[1] Key, an English officer who was in Rome at the time of the Pope's
flight, attributes it to ' the ingratitude of a cowardly and short-sighted
people to a liberal-minded but weak prince.'   *Key*, 176, 1 Dec. 48.

some ways was ' at very much the same stage of evolution
in 1848 as English civilisation two hundred and twenty
years before.' [1] Palmerston and his England need not be
too severely blamed for supposing that some apprenticehood in institutions approximating to their own might
really be better for central Italy than a further plunge
forward into the paraphernalia of a Spanish-American
republic.

This plunge was actually made early in February 1849 :
and the Pope appealed formally to the Catholic powers
to undertake his restoration. Once that appeal was made
the only question in doubt was not whether, but by whom
the task should be performed. Austria, Spain, and the
Two Sicilies were all eager to restore the Pope ; and to
restore him in frankly reactionary fashion. No single
Power was prepared to defend the new republic. France
as a whole was more eager now to be rid of her own republic
than to support republics elsewhere : already by an overwhelming majority she had rejected a republican President ;
and she was on the eve of electing—and but for the reluctance of the Republicans to face their constituents would
already have elected—a strongly anti-republican Assembly.
Even the republican minority itself contained a liberal
Catholic element not yet disillusioned with the idea of
a liberal Pope. For in France the revolution of 1848
had been largely welcomed by the clergy : even in Paris
the symbols of religion were treated by the revolutionaries with a deference wholly absent in the rising of
1830 ; the liberal Catholic movement had succeeded in
establishing for some a momentary harmony between the
Marseillaise and the Magnificat. To be a Republican in
France in 1849 was to belong to a small political minority ;
but even this did not necessarily involve dissent from the
general national sympathy with Pius. To pit France
single-handed, in the early ardour of her Catholic revival,
against the most popular of modern popes, at a time when
he seemed to lie in the depths of most undeserved misfortune—to do this and in doing it to embroil her with all

[1] *Trevelyan: Garibaldi*, 82.

Catholic Europe and not improbably Russia as well : [1] this
was a course which but to state was to condemn. True,
a few extreme Republicans did demand such a step : regarding as automatically democratic any war on behalf of
a republic though undertaken against the will of almost
the whole people who were to wage it. But democratic
or not the thing could not be done : it would have been as
easy to make England fight to maintain the Temporal
Power as to make France fight to suppress it.

The alternatives which faced Louis Napoleon were therefore not three but two. He could stand aside and leave
the Romans to their fate : allowing the inevitable restoration to be effected by powers whose every interest was to
promote absolutism and reaction. Or he could seek to fore-
stall and frustrate Habsburg and Bourbon by effecting the
restoration himself. So doing he could not indeed demand
formal constitutional guarantees from the Pope : a demand
unnecessary if Pius remained a liberal, and impossible if he
had ceased to be one ; for in the latter case the difficulty
would be to persuade him to acquiesce in the choice of a
liberal Power for his restoration at all. But what could be
done was to attempt to surround the restoration with an
atmosphere as far removed as possible from absolutism :
nursing and keeping alive whatever liberalism was left as
assiduously as rival restorers would have quenched its
final spark. For Austria and Naples would have taken no
risks : not from this chimney for a second time should
neighbours' houses be set on fire.

For taking the matter out of such neighbours' hands,
French history offered recent and respectable precedent.
In 1832 Louis Philippe had anticipated and prevented a
reactionary Austrian intervention in the Legations by
himself despatching an expedition to Ancona ; in this

---

[1] The trouble was, Louis Napoleon told Tommaseo on Christmas Day
1848, that it would require a European war to deprive the Pope of his
temporal power. Tommaseo to *Manin*, ii. 64, 25 Dec. 48.   The whole
interview is significant : speaking in Italian, Louis agreed that the twofold objects of his own Italian policy should be ' to augment the spiritual
by decreasing the temporal power of the Pope,' and ' to repair Campo-
Formio.'   His pro-Italian sentiments were pronounced 'without the
theatrical warmth of some Republicans, but with much firmness.' *Ibid.*

action he had been supported by Palmerston and the
liberal Government of England. On the other hand there
was no lack of technical justification in the present instance
for standing aside. The Pope's refusal of France as a
refuge would have excused it diplomatically : the fact that
the Constituent Assembly with its obsolete republican
majority was still undissolved would have excused it
constitutionally. The spectacle of France remaining
passive while Austria restored the Pope would have been
unpopular it is true in the country at large ; and on the
face of it a papal restoration under such auspices would
have been the worst fate that could have befallen the
Pope's own subjects. Still Louis' position in adopting an
attitude of non-intervention would have been technically
unassailable ; and in the light of later events it is easy to
see that by washing his hands of the whole business he
would have been spared an infinity of embarrassment.

For a moment he sought a way out which might enable
him to combine the advantages of both courses and escape
the penalties of either. The only country except France
which could essay the task of a liberal restoration in Rome
was the only state besides France which was at once
liberal and catholic. A week before Louis Napoleon
became President of France, Gioberti—the only-begetter
of the liberal Pope—became premier of Piedmont. Through
the mediation of Louis' old Italian friend Count Arese,
negotiations were promptly set afoot between them, with
a view to a purely Italian restoration. Arese himself
arrived in Paris on the morning of Christmas Day 1848 ;
the same day on which Louis gave such an encouraging
reception to Manin's secret envoy from Venice. The
welcome which awaited Arese was if anything warmer
still. He found himself 'received with open arms' and
pressed to come and dine that very evening at the Elysée.[1]
It is possible that both Tommaseo and Arese found their
way smoothed for them by an interview which Louis had
already given on Christmas Eve to his old friend Madame
Cornu,[2] who had waited upon him at the request of the

---

[1] *Grabinski*, 105.   [2] v. *Simpson*, 225.

Italians resident in Paris to ask what he could do for
Italy. ' " Tell them," he said, " that my name is Bonaparte, and that I feel the responsibilities which that name
implies.   Italy is dear to me, as dear almost as France,
but my duties to France ' passent avant tout.' I must
watch for an opportunity. For the present I am controlled by the Assembly, which will not give me money and
men for a war of sentiment, in which France has no direct
immediate interest. But tell them that my feelings are
now what they were in 1830, and repeat to them that my
name is Bonaparte." ' [1]

In any case Arese was now charged with a scheme which
had it succeeded would have prevented an Austrian
intervention without entailing the intervention of France ;
and Louis Napoleon hoped that the association of Naples
with Piedmont might render the project just palatable
enough for the Pope to swallow.   But even so gilded Pio
Nono refused the pill, and showed himself aggrieved at
France for prescribing it.   His appeal to the Catholic
Powers in February 1849 pointedly ignored Piedmont.
By this time his most trusted adviser in such matters was in
fact Cardinal Antonelli : and Antonelli's medicine was
undiluted Austria.

At this juncture Charles Albert of Piedmont took a mad
decision which later helped as much to give Italy her king,
as a no less mad decision of Garibaldi's helped eventually
to give her her capital.   Beaten by Austria in the summer
of 1848, Charles Albert had concluded an armistice by
which he retired to his own dominions, leaving Lombardy
and Venice to their fate.   This armistice he now denounced.   Alone, and against the advice of his only conceivable ally, he took the field against Austria once more ;
and was once more decisively beaten.   The news of his
defeat at Novara reached Louis Napoleon on March 27.
Before the event, feeling himself powerless within a few
weeks of his own election to plunge his country into war,
he had endeavoured to avert a disaster otherwise in-

---

[1] Mme. Cornu to Senior, 8 May 59. *Senior*: *Thiers*, ii. 263.

evitable by causing the most explicit assurances to be conveyed to the Sardinian government, that if it restarted the war it must look for no help from France.[1] But now he all but broke his promise. It was one thing to say that he would not help when by saying so he might prevent a hopeless enterprise. But not to help her now seemed to him at first impossible. It was evening when the news of the disaster reached him ; and in it he found occasion for another of his nocturnal interviews. He sent an aide-de-camp for Thiers, bidding him come at once to the Elysée.

' I found him,' said that hater of Italy, ' gloomy and excited. " You see," he said, " the result of your pacific policy. . . . We must immediately send an army across the Alps." ' For two hours Thiers argued with him. ' " You may destroy the throne of your friend the King of Sardinia, and occasion his kingdom to be partitioned," he urged ; adding " a war with Austria is a war with Russia, and probably with England." . . . " Are we then," he said, " quietly to see the Austrians seize Turin, and crush Piedmont by a requisition of 220,000,000 ? " ' Thiers replied that this might be averted without war. And so, though it was now midnight, he proceeded at once to interview Hübner, the Austrian chargé d'affaires, whom he found naturally as much elated by the day's news as the President had been cast down by it. ' " We shall now," said the Austrian, " revenge ourselves on Piedmont for the treachery and baseness of her attack. We shall give those Republicans a lesson from which they will not recover for a century." " Charles Albert," he continued, " has destroyed in a week the kingdom which it took his ancestors three centuries to collect " ; adding that his country would prefer war to any interference between it and the object of its " just resentment." ' At this Thiers turned on him abruptly. Were war his wish, ' " You will find us perfectly prepared for it. I have passed the whole night with the President striving to prevent his instantly declaring it. The decrees calling up 250,000 additional conscripts, and providing

[1] On this see his speech to the Legislative Assembly. *Register* : 1849, 253.

250,000,000 for their equipment, are already drawn up. If I merely repeat to him your last words, they will be presented to the Assembly to-morrow." He cooled as if I had thrown over him a pail of cold water. "God forbid," he said : ' [1] and in the event the indemnity was cut down from 230 to 75 million lire : [2] and Piedmont was suffered to retain her territories and her constitution intact. In the general wreckage of her hopes the salvage of this fragment was not the least service which even Louis Napoleon was to render to Italy.[3] Had he not been Piedmont's shield in 1849 he could not in 1859 have been her sword. For Austria, twice wantonly attacked and twice victorious, had every excuse for seeing to it that Piedmont was left in no condition to give her trouble again.

His arguments to the President in his cabinet Thiers repeated more vigorously to the Republicans in the chamber ; adding now to his arguments a taunt. Why, he asked, did they cry out for Italy now when it was too late, when her cause was plainly lost, and France if she intervened must face alone a coalition of all Europe ? Why had they not lifted a little finger for her in the spring of 1848, when no European Power could have opposed French aid to Italy and even without it she had almost attained success ? [4] This shrewd thrust at the Assembly left the President untouched, for when the tide was at the flood he was still a private citizen in exile. But he too had been forced to admit that the time for action was not now ; though to his advisers' loud ' too late ' he might answer *sotto voce* ' too soon.' [5] For the moment, though still

---

[1] *Senior : Thiers*, i 48–51. Thiers always exaggerated his own importance, and doubtless does so here : but the same story which he told Senior in March 1852 he repeated to Hohenlohe in July 1874. *Hohenlohe*, ii. 120.

[2] *King : Italy*, i. 356, 357.

[3] A service handsomely acknowledged by Azeglio in his letter of 21 Aug. 49 to the French Government : v. *Gaillard*, 127. *Cf.* Farini to Lord John Russell, 20 Feb. 59 : ' We can never forget that the President of the Republic wanted to come to the aid of Piedmont.' *Ibid.*, 140, 141 *n.*

[4] *Barrot*, iii. 154.

[5] ' I love Italy,' he said to General Della Rocca in Feb. 1858. ' Had I occupied the place I now fill in 1849, I should certainly have gone to the aid of Charles Albert.' *Della Rocca*, 131.

determined to employ force if necessary should Austria persist in her original terms,[1] he was content with the modification of them actually obtained ; French pressure also succeeded in extracting from Austria in August a fairly complete amnesty for her Italian subjects.

Though the corner was safely turned the emotional effects of the crisis on the President were important, and the ablest and most clerical of his ministers exploited them with extreme dexterity. With naïve satisfaction Falloux explains in his memoirs the method of his triumph. ' I let a few days pass,' he wrote, ' till the first emotion had subsided at the Elysée. Then I went and asked the President if he were going to leave Austria to absorb the pontifical states and " depopularise " Pius IX, by placing him hopelessly under the power of a state so utterly anti-Italian. " Now at last you are right," he answered, " France cannot remain an unmoved spectator any longer. Now that Austria's flag flies in triumph all Italy will welcome ours." And from this moment the President urged and desired the dispatch of the troops already collected by Cavaignac on the French coast.' [2] Before Novara it was already true that only a French or Piedmontese restoration of the Pope could avert a restoration of him by Habsburgs or Bourbons. But after Novara the President supposed that that truth would at once be obvious even to the Romans themselves. Piedmont was now out of the running, and the advocates of reaction—thanks in part to Louis' own reluctance to enter France on such a race [3]—had already a long start.

Already the victorious Austrians were at Florence, at Bologna, at Ferrara. Already Bomba's troops had earned their sovereign his new name at Messina, and their business in Sicily finished would soon be free for fresh exploits on the mainland. Even Spain had its own reactionary expedition under way. And ever at the Pope's elbow was Antonelli, whispering that here to his hand were loyal and

[1] *King: Italy*, i. 357 ; v. *Gaillard*, 140–141.
[2] *Falloux*, i. 444, 445.
[3] On the President's steadfast opposition to the expedition until after Novara, v. *Gaillard*, 109, 110.

devoted servants, true sons of the Church [1] who would
ask no questions and impose no conditions, but do the job
thoroughly and for the joy of it.   Why should his Holiness
wait longer for the half-hearted intervention of France, a
country with no aptitude for this kind of service, itself
in name a Republic, its President a Buonaparte at best,
a cousin of that Prince of Canino's ; at bottom probably
no better than a Freemason and Carbonaro, certainly an
old leader himself of armed insurrection in the Papal
States.   Even supposing that such a man—such a country
—should eventually condescend to some kind of patronising
restoration, who knew that he would not seek to insinuate
conditions for his service, conditions derogatory to that
liberty which the Supreme Pontiff should ever enjoy in
his own dominions ?

Mistakenly as the event proved, but not altogether unnaturally, Louis Napoleon imagined that the disaster of
Novara would render French intervention if less palatable
to the Pope, at least more palatable to the Romans.   As
naturally and perhaps less mistakenly, he conceived that
it had made such intervention now imperative in Italy's
own interests.   While Piedmont still stood the mere
presence of Austrians in Ancona had seemed intolerable
even to Louis Philippe : with Piedmont prostrate how
should Louis Napoleon stand by and see Austria take
possession not merely of Ancona but of Rome ?   Such
an occupation now would mean the absolute supremacy
over the entire peninsula—north and centre and south
alike—of the worst enemy of Italian liberties.   So entrenched, with Russia behind her and all Italy under her,
the position of Austria might well become impregnable.[2]

That his convert was animated not by love of the Pope but
by hatred of Austria Falloux himself was perfectly aware.[3]

[1] Bomba had just gazetted Ignatius Loyola as an honorary field-marshal
of his army. *King: Mazzini*, 135.
[2] To this day it is not easy to see what Louis could have attempted,
except what he did attempt.   At least it is noteworthy, that of the innumerable historians who have condemned him for doing what he ought
not to have done on this occasion, not one has ventured to suggest what
he ought to have done, or how he could conceivably have done it.
[3] *Falloux*, ii. 129. So also was Barrot. *Barrot*, iii. 193.

Still the great thing was to have him converted at all, especially by an argument which required not only action but haste. Haste was now of the essence of the expedition, as Louis understood it ; if the absolutists were to be forestalled there was no time to be lost. And so he who had urged delay now urged speed ; not for a second time should his advisers be able to shake their heads and say, ' too late.'

With all speed some seven thousand men were mustered at Marseilles ; hardly an army, but since no fighting was expected this scarcely mattered. In command of them was placed a son of Marshal Oudinot, no general as the event proved,[1] but this fact also was as yet unknown. On April 16 the necessary vote of credit was carried by a two to one majority in the Assembly : on the 21st the expedition set sail, and on the 24th Civita Vecchia was occupied without any show of resistance. A leisurely progress followed over the forty miles which divided the seaport from Rome ; on the evening of the 29th the expedition bivouacked a dozen miles from the city. Next Oudinot advanced upon it without observing the most elementary military precautions : [2] to his utter astonishment he was decisively repulsed.

The rôle of deliverer is at all times congenial to French troops on foreign soil ; and in this case both army and country had persuaded themselves that the expedition would be received if not with rapture at least without resistance. They believed that the Romans themselves were by this time apathetic about the future of their

---

[1] Marshal Bugeaud, the French commander-in-chief, had the poorest opinion of him. B.N. Nouv. Acq. Fr. 20,617, f. 427 *sq.* And Louis Napoleon himself so disliked the appointment as to make it the occasion of a private remonstrance to his cabinet on their habit of presenting him with accomplished facts. ' For example, I regard it as an irregularity that General Oudinot should have been spoken to about the possibility of giving him the command of the Civita Vecchia expedition, before we had even decided the circumstances in which the expedition should be dispatched. What I wish to avoid is the almost daily inconvenience of being left to learn through the public press of decisions on which I have not been consulted.' Barrot admits that the President's protest was ' not entirely devoid of foundation.' *Barrot,* iii. 366.

[2] *Garibaldi,* ii. 3.

Republic, and apprehensive of the evils which an Austrian or Neapolitan restoration would entail.

This belief was not wholly ungrounded.[1] Contemporary opinion was indeed deceived in its denunciations of misgovernment and discontent within the walls of Rome. Mazzini was nothing if not high-minded ; and his brief rule was characterised by a magnanimity and moderation most rare in the annals of threatened republics. So natural and almost excusable would have been a reign of terror in the circumstances, that a belief in its actual existence was itself neither unnatural nor wholly inexcusable. The belief was in fact unfounded, and though held by many in good faith it must have been propagated in bad faith by a few : the clericals had little to learn in the arts of propaganda. Only victims of that propaganda could have expected to be hailed as deliverers ; but there were solid and all but justified reasons for expecting no resistance. For their reforms hitherto the Romans had done nothing but the shouting ; all Italy knew by this time in what manner Austria and Naples restored legitimate authority ; and from such restoration a French occupation was the only safeguard. Left to themselves the Romans would not in fact have resisted it. But they were not left to themselves. Those who counted on an unopposed occupation had forgotten Garibaldi, or rather had yet to learn him. His timely arrival with his Legion on April 27, followed by that of a Lombard contingent on April 29, alone enabled the city to be defended. Had Oudinot reached Rome but three days earlier he might have entered it unopposed.[2]

[1] ' Altogether, I incline to think the Roman population *has* shown a good deal of " apathy," ' is Clough's conclusion of the whole matter in his last letter from Rome, 3 July 49. ' The Lombards are fine fellows, and the Bolognese too,' he adds ; ' the only pity is there were not more of them.' *Clough*, i. 156. His entire correspondence however disproves the charges current outside Rome of terrorism or misgovernment within it.

[2] Cf. *Senior: Italy*, ii. 134 : ' I afterwards called on Dr Nicholl. He was in Rome when the French made their first attack, and related to me some of its details. " I was returning," he said, " from a ride, when I found a crowd at one of the gates. Garibaldi was on the outside, and the government was debating whether to let him in. The general wish among the Romans was to exclude him. They had no serious intention of resisting the French, and feared with truth that his presence might

The news that Rome had resisted his expedition, and resisted it successfully, at once placed Louis Napoleon in a most awkward predicament. His own assent to the expedition had been dependent on a belief that the dispatch of it was in the best interests of the Romans. But the republican Assembly's assent to it had been based on a further belief that the Romans themselves would recognise that this was so. True, the majority had been a large one, and it had included also all the conservative advocates of a papal restoration. Further, it was highly probable that France as a whole, and any new Assembly which could now be elected from it, would yield an overwhelming majority in favour of a French unconditional restoration of the Pope. But the moribund Assembly with its obsolete republican majority was still in session : and the knowledge that they would shortly be succeeded by a conservative chamber only rendered the Republicans more frantic that they themselves should have been tricked into anticipating the actions of their successors. They therefore passed a vote urging the government ' to take immediate steps to prevent the expedition from being used for any but its original purpose ' ; a somewhat ambiguous resolution since the ' original purpose ' of the expedition still lacked clear definition ; but none the less an implied vote of censure on the government. As in January so in May his ministers at once tendered their resignation to the President : now as then he refused to accept it, and inserted

force on them useless sacrifices. Mazzini's influence however prevailed. He and his followers were let in, but very coldly received. The next day, the French marched up the Porta Cavalleggieri, expecting to find it open. They were received by a fire from the neighbouring bastion, and Garibaldi made a sortie and brought in some prisoners who had exposed themselves incautiously. From that instant the feelings of the people were changed." ' This conversation was recorded in Rome on 7 April 51. *Cf.* Story's diary, 27 April 49 : ' Here nothing is in right earnest. . . . I understand from Vincenzo Bassanelli that the Guardia are nearly unanimous in desiring the return of the Pope and the abolition of the Republic, and that they will not fight.' But on May 1, *ibid.* : ' The Romans are all elated and surprised even at themselves.' *Story*, 152, 154. A sudden stiffening was in fact apparent on the eve of the attack, of which Dandolo writes : ' Whoever could have had a glimpse of Rome that night would not have recognised the city which he had seen in the morning ; and we rejoiced in having reason to change the opinion which had so depressed us on our first arrival.' *Dandolo*, 196.

a note in the *Moniteur* announcing that his cabinet retained his confidence and that he did not propose to change it. This time the parliamentary vote which Louis Napoleon disregarded was within a week of decisive reversal by the country at a general election ; but this time he emphasized his independence of it by writing and publishing a letter to Oudinot assuring him of immediate reinforcements. ' I hoped, as you know,' he wrote, ' that the Romans would face the facts and welcome an army whose mission towards them was entirely benevolent and disinterested. This hope has been falsified. Our soldiers have been received as enemies ; our military honour is engaged ; I will not allow it to suffer any injury. You shall have no lack of reinforcements.'

But although he dispatched reinforcements ostentatiously and at once, Louis Napoleon could not rid himself of the idea that it was some mere misunderstanding that led to their necessity. French intervention was so manifestly to the interest of the Romans that if they could only be made to see the facts they must surely desist from any opposition to it. Accordingly he entrusted his letter to Oudinot to a special emissary, M. de Lesseps, instructing him to discover whether there were not some removable misunderstanding, and if so to do his best to remove it. In handing him the letter the President bade him remind the Romans that he himself had fought for them, that his elder brother had lost his life in their last insurrection against the Pope.[1] What really worried him, he said, was what the French troops were to do if the Austrian or Neapolitan expeditions overtook them. ' At all costs,' he added, ' we must prevent our action from being confounded with theirs.'[2] A second letter to Oudinot from Louis' Minister of Foreign Affairs, of which also Lesseps was the bearer, was even more explicit on this point. ' You should be at particular pains,' it ran, ' to keep your action distinct from that of the Austrians and Neapolitans, and

---

[1] *Clermont*, 60. It was Louis who had persuaded his elder brother into joining the insurrection, *v.* article in the *Revue des Deux Mondes* of 1 Nov. 48 |by Feuillet de Conches].

[2] *Lesseps : Mission*, 21.

not to lend the slighest colour to any confusion between them.' [1] At the same time Lesseps was expressly charged by the government ' to abstain carefully from any step which would seem to resemble explicit or implicit recognition of the Roman Republic.' [2]

Armed with these vague instructions, an optimistic temperament, and a natural desire to magnify his office, M. de Lesseps arrived at Rome on May 15. There he found a general atmosphere not unfavourable to his hopes. The Romans, anxious alike to conciliate possible friends and to concentrate against their obviously implacable foes from Spain and Naples and Austria, had fêted their French prisoners, and let them go free : Oudinot, though quite secure from attack,[3] was momentarily powerless

---

[1] *Lesseps : Mission*, 61. [2] *Barrot*, iii. 218.

[3] All recent historians have regarded the Lesseps negotiations as a mere blind, designed to save the French from attack until they could be secretly reinforced ; meanwhile concealing their real intentions from the Romans. The contention ignores dates and facts.

(1) Lesseps in Paris was not even sounded as to his willingness to undertake the mission until May 8. *Clermont*, 55. On the morning of May 9, Key, an English officer sent to report officially to his government on the state of Oudinot's army, found it already augmented ' to about 15,000 men ; including 1500 cavalry, 26 field guns, and 6 heavy siege pieces.' *Key*, 199. Now Mazzini's own outside estimate of the forces defending Rome was ' 14,000 men, a young army without traditions, and improvised under the very fire of the enemy.' *Mazzini*, v. 299 : elsewhere he puts the figure lower still. *English Family*, i. 124. The actual armistice moreover was only signed on May 17 : by which time Key's estimate of the French army is ' upwards of 20,000 men : and the perfect arrangement of every branch cannot be surpassed.' *Key* (May 18), 206. The French army therefore was in a position of complete security from attack during the entire period of the negotiations : and it was simply immaterial to it whether the period of military stalemate was utilised for negotiations or not.

(2) Throughout the month reinforcements were landing without any attempt whatever at concealment : and a week before the arrival of Lesseps, Louis Napoleon had published his letter to Oudinot announcing their dispatch in terms so strident as to secure its insertion in every newspaper in Europe. Louis' hope of making the Romans see reason was in fact dependent on their realisation that the odds against them would be overwhelming. Mazzini's hope of making them follow a possibly higher thing was not quite independent of an effort to conceal from them how desperate those odds would be.

(3) The tables, such as they are, can be turned : both on military and political grounds it is arguable that Mazzini had more to gain from the negotiations than the French. See below, pp. 74 *n.*, 85 *n.*

for offence. The French envoy proposed to the Romans
that they should formally request the protection of the
French Republic and admit French troops to occupy and
protect Rome conjointly with their own ; remaining free
to choose their own form of government and retaining their
local administration. On May 17 an armistice was concluded for the consideration of this proposal.

In making such an offer at all Lesseps had virtually
recognised the *de facto* government in Rome, and thereby
exceeded his original instructions ; which in his rosy
imagination were already receding into a distant and
nebulous background. But of rosy dreams and nebulous
backgrounds Lesseps had no monopoly. The fact was
that illusions were fully as rife in Rome on the state of
public opinion in France, as they were in France on the
state of public opinion in Rome : and in Rome as in Paris
genuine error was assisted by propaganda on the part
of some who had means of knowing that their propaganda
was delusive. Lesseps had left France on the eve of
a general election : extreme Republicans there affected
a blind confidence of success : emissaries from them had
imbued Mazzini, a willing victim, with the like mistaken
hopes. And now, was not this very offer a confirmation
of them ? On May 19, with the unanimous assent of the
Roman Assembly, Mazzini rejected the overture ; basing
his refusal primarily on its avoidance of all mention of the
Roman Republic.[1]

A week later M. de Lesseps made fresh proposals : his
lively enthusiasm had generated by this time a still more
gorgeous fog, behind which his original instructions had
receded into a yet more remote horizon. Let his present
terms be but accepted, and the French would undertake
to defend any portion of Roman territory they should
occupy from any Austrian invasion whatsoever. This was
' distinguishing French action from the Austrian ' with
a vengeance. But once more optimist met optimist, and
dreamer answered to dreamer. It mattered not to Mazzini
that the ground of yesterday's hopes had crumbled beneath

[1] *Mazzini*, v. 389.

his feet ; that the French general election of May 13,
which was to have seen the triumph of his sympathisers,
had produced instead an Assembly which could not claim
a quarter of its members as republican. New castles as
immaterial reared themselves at once on the ruins of the
old : France had defeated her Republicans by ballot ; no
matter : all might yet be recovered by republican bullets
in the streets of Paris. May 13 had been a failure :
June 13 remained untried. So once again Mazzini
counselled refusal ; this time he made counter-proposals,
but the last French offer had been cast in the form of
an ultimatum, requiring definite acceptance by noon of
May 30 ; counter-proposals were therefore tantamount to
rejection.

But though the result of the French elections thus lacked
effect in Rome, they had naturally an immediate reaction
on the diplomacy of France. This reaction, coupled with
the impression that Lesseps was fast outstriding his instructions, led to the dispatch to him from Paris first of
a telegram bidding him to return to the line of conduct
those instructions prescribed,[1] then, since the telegram
seemed to lack effect, of a final letter of recall. The letter
reached him on the evening of May 31, the very day on
which he had finally succeeded by dint of forgetting his
instructions altogether in concluding an agreement with
the Roman triumvirs. Regardless of the fact that on the
lapse of his ultimatum Oudinot on the night of May 29
had resumed hostilities, the French envoy had pursued a
personal negotiation of his own ; he had indeed, by a last
instinct of diplomatic propriety, made its validity dependent
on the ratification of the French government ; but this
he had persuaded himself that he could persuade that
government to accord. Instead he found waiting for him
his letter of recall. Disillusioned at last he returned to
Paris ; the required ratification was never of course forthcoming.

On the following day the Roman commander applied
to Oudinot for a fortnight's armistice ; this would give

[1] *D'Harcourt*, 53.

time for the expected rising in Paris to take effect ;[1] and
Oudinot naturally declined the proposal. But to leave
time, he said, for French citizens to withdraw from Rome,
he would not attack the place before Monday, June 4.
Nor did he, but by a highly discreditable piece of sharp
practice[2] he took possession on Sunday of ground commanding the Janiculum ; then, as two thousand years before,
the key to Rome.

The last faint hope of the defenders consisted now in
the successful issue of the republican rising which, as they
knew, was to be attempted in Paris on June 13. That
attempt was duly made on the promised date. Two days
earlier, as a sort of parliamentary preliminary to it, Ledru-
Rollin rose in the new Assembly and demanded that it
should impeach the President and his ministers ; the
attack on the Roman Republic was also a breach of the
French constitution : ' We will defend it by all means
possible, even by arms.' It was not the first time that
Rollin had demanded the President's impeachment ; but
what a republican Assembly had refused to his persuasions
it was not likely that a conservative Assembly would grant
to his threats. On the 12th it rejected his motion ; on the
13th the walls of Paris were covered with revolutionary
placards ; crowds collected to read them in the streets ;
a few representatives attempted to organise them in openly

---

[1] Besides, Mazzini had as much to hope from Generals June and July
as the Czar had later from Generals January and February. ' The malarial
fever has already made its appearance in the French army, and the season
is now close at hand when their position will be untenable.' *Key*,
202, 1 June 49.

[2] The plain purpose of Oudinot's letter was to deceive ; and it would
have been more respectable in him to have broken his word and been
done with it than to have sheltered it behind a technically correct use of
the word ' *place*.' But it is perhaps worth while to point out that the
ambiguity of that word, in the language of France and of diplomacy,
has been a frequent source of controversy in good faith. An example
may be found without going further afield than that same Austrian occupation of Ferrara in 1847 already alluded to in this chapter. The Treaty
of Vienna gave Austria the right to garrison ' the place ' : the Pope put
the narrowest interpretation on the word, limiting it to the citadel ;
Metternich the broadest, extending it to the whole city and all outlying
military positions. For documents see *Amigues*, 93–118. Here as usual
it was the narrow interpretation which was eventually justified. Incidentally it is worthy of note that even in the Austrian army there were
some who condemned Oudinot's act. v. *Ellesmere*, 323.

rebellious demonstration. A year earlier the attempt
might conceivably have been successful. But the government of France was in very different hands in June 1849
from those which controlled it in June 1848. On the eve of
this rising troops had been summoned by telegraph from
the suburbs : on the morning of it Changarnier dispersed
without bloodshed a nondescript insurrectionary procession in the Rue de la Paix. During the afternoon Ledru-
Rollin himself with some two hundred artillerymen of
the National Guard took possession of the Conservatoire
des Arts et Metiers, whence he deposed the President,
announced a provisional government, and gave orders for
the erection of barricades. But the incipient barricades
were destroyed before they were well built ; Ledru-
Rollin's followers were dispersed, his temporary citadel
was surrounded, and several of his fellow-members were
arrested. He himself escaped precipitately through a
broken window and fled to London in disguise. There
he devoted his leisure to a study on the *Decadence of
England*.[1]

The attempted insurrection in Paris had been in fact a
complete fiasco. Even the workmen's quarters had shown
themselves actively hostile or coldly indifferent to the
rising : [2] all the demonstrations of popular enthusiasm
which were forthcoming on that day were reserved for
Louis Napoleon himself, who with a small escort rode
round the city in the evening. ' Many of the bystanders
among the blouses repeated exclamations of " There's a
man who's not afraid to show himself." ' [3]

Of this fact the President had just given proof of another
kind. Paris at this time was stricken with a severe outbreak of cholera : to which three days before the rising
Marshal Bugeaud, the conqueror of Algeria, one of the last

---

[1] For his own account of the rising, see *Ledru-Rollin*, ii. 365–395 : and
for a sympathetic study of the author, *Vermorel*: 1848, 146–186.

[2] *Clermont*, 191.

[3] F.O. France, Normanby to Palmerston, 14 June 49. *Cf.* Lanjuinais—
a member of the Barrot cabinet—to Senior, 21 Apr. 54 : ' His courage
is perfect. In June 1849 when we expected a dangerous insurrection he
was quite unmoved ; not depressed as some were, or excited as was the
case with Changarnier.' *Senior: Thiers*, i. 351.

survivors of Napoleon's marshals, succumbed. Louis visited him shortly before his death, and received his dying salute as the future saviour of France : [1] but he did not neglect the humbler victims of the epidemic, who were dying at this time at the rate of some two hundred a day. With Falloux he drove to the hospital where the outbreak had first occurred ; [2] he spent more than two hours among the sick, gave away all the money he had on him and then borrowed more from his friend. On his entry he was literally mobbed by enthusiastic inmates trying to touch his hand or at least a portion of his raiment : those who could not get near enough for that kissing their hands to him and shouting, ' Vive mon petit Napoléon,' and the like. And on his exit crowds caught up the cry following his carriage as long as they could keep pace with it.

Possibly the President may have been impelled to this visit and the tour of the Parisian cholera-wards by which it was followed, by some reminiscence of Napoleon's oft-depicted visit to the hospitals at Jaffa. Even so, the risk of infection was far from negligible ; [3] during a similar epidemic in 1832 a single visit to the cholera wards had cost Louis Philippe's Premier, Casimir Périer, his life. This well-remembered fact greatly enhanced the effect [4] of Louis' lengthy and repeated tours of them. Moreover, whatever the motive which first led him to visit the sick, when he was once inside the hospitals there could be no question of his genuine sympathy with any suffering

[1] *Thirria*, ii. 97.

[2] Of the 1859 cholera patients in this hospital, 1402 died. *Merruau*, 200.

[3] To demonstrate that the risk was exaggerated was in itself a real service to the State. Competent observers attributed the absence in 1849 of the panic, which had so gravely aggravated the last outbreak of the disease in Paris, largely to the effect of the President's series of long visits to the civil and military cholera wards. *Merruau*, 204.

[4] Not enough however to save later anti-imperialist writers from the somewhat impudent assertion that Louis Napoleon fled from Paris on the mere rumour of the approach of cholera; *e.g.* M. P. Jacobi, *Putnam's Monthly*, Dec. 1868. In point of fact when cholera broke out in Paris in Oct. 1865, while the Emperor and Empress were at Biarritz, they promptly returned to the capital and visited the six chief cholera hospitals in it. v. *Giraudeau*, 296. Even now a serious American historian can describe Louis Napoleon as ' carefully screened from contact with suffering.' *Thayer*, ii. 88.

he saw.[1] Nurses and patients alike were impressed by it ;
on one of the former, with a few words in commendation
of the humble heroism of her calling, Louis conferred for
the first time since its institution the cross of the Legion of
Honour.

Although in Paris itself the rising of June 13 was quelled
easily and without bloodshed, a more serious insurrection organised in conjunction with it at Lyons was only suppressed after considerable loss of life. Accordingly Louis
Napoleon followed up his triumphant passage through Paris
with a proclamation somewhat sterner than his wont. ' A
few factious citizens have dared once more to raise the
standard of revolt against a government which is legitimate, since it is the outcome of universal suffrage. They
accuse me of having violated the constitution ; me, when
for six months I have endured unmoved their insults,
slander, and provocations. . . . This systematic agitation
prolongs unsettlement and mistrust, and consequent
misery, in the country. It must cease. It is time that
good citizens should be reassured and the ill-disposed made
afraid. The Republic has no more deadly enemies than
those who force us by perpetual disorder to turn France
into one great camp, and divert our plans for progress and
reform into preparations for strife and defence. Elected
by the nation, the cause I defend is yours, your families',
and your properties' : the cause of poor as well as rich :
the cause of our common civilisation. I will stay at
nothing to make that cause triumphant.'

At Rome the news that the rising of June 13 had
ignominiously collapsed deprived the garrison of its one
minute chance of a successful defence. By falsifying his
news from Paris,[2] as he had already falsified his news from
London,[3] Mazzini might prolong vain hopes among his

---

[1] 'Je dois ajouter qu'en visitant les malades, le président se montra
très simplement et très sincèrement compatissant, et joignit à sa libéralité
des paroles qui partaient vraiment du cœur.' *Falloux*, iii. 455.

[2] *Johnston*, 305, 306.

[3] In May 1849 Palmerston had vehemently urged the chief Roman
emissary in England to counsel his government to treat frankly and
immediately with France, on the basis of a conditional restoration of the
Pope, with guarantees for a constitution, the freedom of the Press, and the

followers ; but neither false news nor most authentic
valour could long delay the inevitable capitulation. On
July 3 the French made their entry into the city : on
the 14th the restoration of the papal authority was formally
announced. But the Pope instead of returning in person
sent a commission of three cardinals to take over the
business of government. This ' red triumvirate ' which
arrived in Rome at the end of July proceeded without a
word of thanks to the French army to restore in its presence
the Inquisition, to suppress the municipal councils, to deny
freedom of the press, and to institute elaborate and vin-
dictive preparations for the punishment of all officials
concerned in the recent troubles.[1] The Pope himself
formally thanked ' the Catholic Powers ' for his restoration,
and allowed an inscription in honour of Oudinot to be set
up in the Capitol ;[2] but he refused to mention France
singly or by name : he showed himself in fact more grateful to those who had even wished to restore him as an
absolutist, than to the country which had actually and
painfully effected the restoration but had tried to reconcile
that restoration with liberalism.

For many weeks Louis had watched the progress of the
ill-fated expedition with a sort of helpless fatalism ; a
mood to which his private correspondence bore witness as
early as the beginning of June.[3] As the summer advanced,
and the new dispositions of the Pope became more evident,

secularisation of the government: offering England's good offices and
speaking not only in his private capacity but ' as the Minister of the Queen
and of the British nation.' Mazzini not only suppressed his envoy's
report, but gave out that ' England, about to recognise the Roman
Republic, advised a desperate resistance.' *Farini*, iv. 145–146. Throughout, Mazzini's concern was to make the best possible fight, not to get the
best peace possible. From the point of view of the future of Italy the
best peace possible was not worth having ; but this fact alone rendered
negotiations hopeless. Neither Palmerston nor Louis Napoleon realised it.
[1] Fortunately most of the prospective victims escaped, largely through
a lavish issue of passports by the English consul Freeborn. *Johnston*,
314 *n.*, does less than justice to Palmerston here. Though at first inclined
to disapprove, F.O. Rome 14 Aug. 49 shows him vigorously defending
his agent, on the ground that events had already justified him. ' It moreover appears that Freeborn was requested by the French officers to do so
in many cases.' *Ibid.*   [2] *Lushington*, 199.
[3] *E.g.* 4 June, to Vieillard, quoted by *Jerrold*, iii. 82.

he allowed his disillusion and disappointment to become
manifest to more than his familiars. ' *Ah, M. Molé,*' he
exclaimed, ' *dans quelle galère m'avez-vous mis là !* ' [1] He
was distracted by the memories of old friends, and quite
other comrades-in-arms in that last uprising against the
Papacy in 1831. On the eve of his dispatch of M. de
Corcelles to succeed the discredited M. de Lesseps he had
advised his new emissary to get into touch with some of
his old Italian friends. ' Ah, but my friends,' he had added
with a sudden smile and afterthought, ' my friends are no
doubt among the besieged.' [2] It is never an entirely
pleasant discovery for a man of one and forty to find himself
faced by the sword he bore himself at twenty-three. For
when in such case the boy is found fighting against the
man there is always the awkward possibility that the boy
was right. And though Louis had allowed himself in this
instance to be led by the old men, he could never quite
forget the voices of the young men whom he had failed,
nor entirely forgive the counsellors whom he had followed
for their success. ' Not once since I have been here has
that door opened,' he exclaimed, pointing to the door of
his cabinet at the Elysée, ' except to admit men who
cried at me " To Rome ! " M. de Montalembert, M.
Thiers, M. Berryer, have repeated those two words at me
incessantly. The advocates of the expedition increased
daily : in the end there was a flood of them.' So, in
language scarcely compact of gratitude, Louis spoke of
his advisers to one of the old republican ministers of '48 :
indicating by a helpless gesture of his hands above his
head that the flood had borne him down. [3] His more
intimate friends had long known and shared his discontent.
Dr Conneau, his companion at Ham, complained that he
would rather they were back in prison again ; better the
cholera itself than to see French and Italians fighting. But
in the midst of his complaints he writes : ' Amongst all
this swarm of selfishness and corruption I see only one
man I can love and honour : our Prince. Oh, if he had

[1] *Gaillard*, 301.   [2] *La Gorce : République*, ii. 222.
[3] *Delord*, i. 142.

the power, what changes there would be for France and our Italy.' [1]

But it was only at the end of August, when reaction was flaunting itself shameless and unabashed at Rome, that Louis determined to make public proclamation of his displeasure. A fortnight earlier he had given expression to his indignation in a strongly-worded letter to Colonel Ney, a son of the Marshal and a personal friend of his own, who was serving with the expedition at Rome. This letter he had originally dispatched with the intention that it should be brought unofficially for their warning before the eyes of the Pope's reactionary deputies in Rome. Since nothing came of it, Louis proceeded early in September to publish the letter in the *Moniteur*. ' The French Republic,' he wrote, ' has sent an army to Rome not to stifle Italian liberty, but to regulate it by preserving it against its own excesses ; and to give it a solid basis by restoring to the pontifical throne the prince who was the first to place himself boldly at the head of every kind of useful reform. It grieves me to learn that the good intentions of the Holy Father, together with our own action, lack result, owing to the presence of hostile passions and influences. There is a desire to make proscription and tyranny the basis of the Pope's return. Tell General Rostolan from me to permit no act to be done under the shadow of the tricolor which might falsify the character of our intervention.' Louis went on to propound as the proper bases of the papal restoration a general amnesty, a secular administration, the Code Napoléon, and a liberal government : adding a sentence of mere bravado in conclusion. ' When our armies made the tour of Europe, they left everywhere, as token of their passage, the destruction of feudal abuses and the germs of liberty ; it shall not be said that in 1849 a French army could act otherwise or leave other results.' These were brave words enough, and in their way sincere ; for it is probably true that by this time Louis ' hated the whole business from the bottom of his soul.' [2]

---

[1] Conneau to Arese. *Grabinski*, 109–112.
[2] *Martinengo Cesaresco*, 185.

But they were words which showed an entire misunderstanding of the relative positions of Pope and President.
From the first Louis had been powerless to exact conditions
from Pius for his restoration, since he was only one of a
competing crowd of papal champions, and of them all the
one whom the papal advisers were least anxious to employ.
But if anything he was more powerless still, now that the
restoration had actually been effected.   Pio Nono showed
his true appreciation of the position by launching, five
days later, his famous *Motu proprio* from Naples ;   a
document placarded in Rome on September 20.   In it
he promised to his well-beloved subjects certain exiguous
semblances of political rights, capping the proclamation
with an amnesty which was little better than a general
proscription.

The reassembly of the conservative Chamber at the
beginning of October did but emphasize the impotence of
Louis' position.   ' The President of the Republic alone was
not satisfied, because the terms of the *Motu proprio* differed
too widely from those of his letter ;   he therefore desired
that the Ministry should form its plans on his letter and not
on the *Motu proprio* :   and that it should signify to the
Assembly the intention of the government.' [1]   He insisted
also that they should demand from the Vatican a definite
amendment of the pontifical brief, by which at any rate the
voting of supplies would have been formally secured to an
elective assembly in Rome. [2]   He tried to transfer the
command of the ' Army of Italy ' to the Protestant General
Randon. [3]   But his cabinet as a whole had no real desire
to give effect to his wishes in this matter.   On October 15
a debate took place in the Chamber upon a vote of credit
for the expenses of the Roman expedition, ' in which Barrot
played the part of a puppet of Montalembert rather than

---

[1] *Farini*, iv. 294.
[2] *Bourgeois, C.M.H.*, xi. 128.
[3] ' He was good enough to say to me,' wrote *Randon*, i. 30, ' that I
had no reason to make known my religious creed, and that he did not
regard it as an obstacle serious enough to prevent my acceptance of a
post in which I could render services to my country.'   But Randon rightly
replied that such a choice would make dealings with the Pope more
difficult than ever.

of a minister of Bonaparte.' [1]   Anxious to commend themselves to the parliamentary majority the cabinet put up
Thiers to open the debate ; in doing so he spent his eloquence
in a laudatory and optimistic version of the *Motu proprio*
and passed over the letter to Ney in damaging silence.
Louis was indignant :   ' It is perhaps the only time I have
seen him moved by something resembling passion,' wrote
his premier.[2]   He wrote Barrot a letter, which he asked
him to read to the Assembly ;   he had defended the
expedition, he said, against republican opposition when
it had suffered a military check :   he must equally have it
defended against resistance ' of another nature ' which
threatened now the political honour of the expedition.

Unwilling however to throw down the gauntlet to the
Catholic majority Barrot, by agreement with his colleagues [3] and in spite of the repeated requests of the
President, contrived to avoid reading this new letter : [4]
the most he would do was to rise and defend both the
letter to Ney and the *Motu proprio* alike :   the one as the
ultimate aim of France, the other as a first step towards
it already conceded and attained.   For parliamentary purposes, this mediating attitude was successful ; the Assembly
voted the credit by a three to one majority.   But Barrot
recognised that it was a success unwelcome to ' the secret
thoughts ' of the President.[5]   Louis Napoleon disliked
the pretence that the *Motu proprio* was satisfactory even
as a starting-point ;   and he resented the general attitude
of half-apologetic tutelage adopted towards him by his
cabinet in the entire debate.   Further he regarded the
final vote, though a victory for his cabinet, as a victory
at his expense :   for in effect it approved not only all
the former actions of the expeditionary corps, but also
its maintenance at Rome at the Pope's service with no
further conditions as to reform than those vaguely adum-
brated in the papal brief.   Louis resolved that victories
won at his expense should involve the penalties of defeat :

[1] *Farini*, iv. 295.   [2] *Barrot*, iii. 443.
[3] *Bourgeois* : *France*, i. 378.   [4] *Barrot*, iii. 446, 447
[5] *Barrot*, iii. 471.

at any rate that they should not be won by the same cabinet twice.

Once more he made Edgar Ney his postman. On the last day of October Barrot received a visit from the Colonel, who produced a new letter from Louis Napoleon. This time it was a demand for the resignation of his ministry. He had come to the conclusion, he said, that he must dominate all parties by forming a ministry representative of none. He wrote also on the same day announcing his decision to the President of the Assembly, informing him that France had need of ministers who 'realised the necessity of a single and firm lead and of a clearly defined policy ; men who will not compromise the Government by irresolution, who will be as careful of my responsibility as of their own, as ready in action as in utterance.' His attempt at uniting men of different opinions had not produced the good effects he expected. 'Instead of obtaining a fusion of thought I got only a neutralisation of forces. France, uneasy for lack of a clear lead, seeks the hand and the will of the elect of December 10. . . . Let us build up authority without disturbing true liberty ; let us calm fears by a bold suppression of evil passions and by opening a useful channel to all noble instincts ; let us fortify religion without any surrender of the conquests of the Revolution, and we shall save the country in spite of the parties and in spite of any defects in our existing institutions.'

Pious aspirations such as these seemed harmless enough ; nor was there anything particularly startling in the President's tardy discovery of the inconveniences of a coalition ministry. Technically too he was within his rights ; the constitution reserved to the President alone the power of appointing and dismissing ministers.[1] No doubt he was making somewhat high-handed use of his powers ; but on the whole his cabinet found, and perhaps deserved, little sympathy in their misfortune. After all they were only paying now the logical price of the President's previous support. Twice already he had continued them in office after parliamentary defeat, on

[1] Art. 64.

each occasion publicly explaining that in spite of that defeat they retained his confidence. Now after a parliamentary victory he had dismissed them, with a no less public intimation that in spite of that victory they had lost the one thing that mattered. By consenting to remain in office in January and May, they had forfeited the right to complain of their dismissal from it in October. In any case their departure was unwept. 'The change,' wrote Normanby, 'could hardly be for the worse as far as the conduct of their departments was concerned': and of the President's action in dismissing them, he adds, 'Affairs had arrived at a point where, unless he meant to accept the character of a cypher, a bold stroke was before long his only resource.' [1]

The new cabinet, with which the outgoing one was replaced on the following day, brought to Louis Napoleon a threefold advantage. It contained no men who were not his personal supporters ; it contained no names which could even for an instant eclipse his own ; and it contained no prime minister at all. That office for the future Louis reserved to himself. Further he had henceforth in his dealings with his ministers a small source of prestige which he had hitherto lacked : in his future political life he could count himself a few months older than his ministers. For the rest the new cabinet was noteworthy as introducing into political life several men who were to become prominent in the administration of the Second Empire. Among them were Rouher the new Minister of Justice, and Fould the new Minister of Finance ; while a quaint link between the new cabinet and the old was provided in the person of a brother of the late premier, who now became Minister of the Interior, and received for his act of political fratricide the sobriquet of ' Cain ' Barrot.

It was a simple matter to change a ministry : to change a policy was not so easy. To show resentment at it was one thing, to effect a reversal of it another. This, the President soon discovered. The Assembly could not be dissolved, and it was impossible to pursue a foreign policy

[1] F.O. France, Normanby to Palmerston, 5 Nov. 49.

to which three-quarters of its members were heartily opposed ; the more so that even if a dissolution had been possible there was no reason to suppose that the country would on this point have reversed the vote of the Assembly. The general election of May 1849 had in point of fact occurred at one of those most rare moments in history, which admit of the direct consultation of a nation on a question of foreign policy before its action has been hopelessly prejudged. For the negotiations which Louis Napoleon had instituted in that month did just keep the door of diplomacy open, until France had had an opportunity of declaring whether she wished it opened further or closed.[1] Had the nation's verdict been different the President's action would have been different too : with the country behind him nothing would have pleased him better than an attempt to translate what in fact remained a futile protest, into a genuine ultimatum to the Pope. For allowing his action to be affected by the clearly-expressed will of the electorate, for submitting, even restively and with a bad grace, to the democratic control of his foreign policy, all good democrats have denounced him for an opportunist and worse. Superficially the charge does not lack curiosity, but it admits in any case of an extenuation. Until he became a despot Louis *could* not be despotic. And at least the opportunist was biding his opportunity.[2] Once

---

[1] The mission of De Lesseps is far more truly obnoxious to the charge of political than of military opportunism; though here too attention to dates is desirable. De Lesseps reached Rome on May 15 : the elections had actually taken place on May 13 and 14. Still, since he was approached on the subject on May 8, it may be conceded that the French government in sending him was playing for time. But so also, it must be remembered, was Mazzini. ' We were bound to gain sufficient time to enable us to appeal from France deceived to France better informed.' Mazzini to De Lesseps, 25 May 49. *Mazzini*, v. 395. And more generally to Mazzini every way and every day that the Republic could be kept in being, was gain. Something might turn up somewhere—Palmerston, Paris, anything —who knew ? Or if not, that the Republic might even become a memory, the little longer was still gain.

[2] The friends of his youth were generally sure of it, even in 1849 ; *e.g.* the Princess *Belgiojoso*, 194. The Princess, who acted as a hospital nurse in Rome during the siege, had been a visitor of Louis Napoleon's both in his prison at Ham, and in London directly after his escape. On the latter occasion, in 1846, Louis had taken her two hands in his and said : ' Princess, give me time first to get things to rights in France, and then we will see what we can do for Italy.' *Ibid.*, 147. Sooner or later she was

he was Emperor, though failing to treat his subjects with quite the contempt demanded by his critics, he did yet strain their loyalty repeatedly by the extent of his services to Italy.[1]

At present he was forced to treat them still not as subjects but as citizens ; and his second intervention in Italian affairs ended therefore like his first in failure. Like it however it had important consequences on his own career. His brother's death in his first venture in arms for Italy had been the starting-point of Louis Napoleon's political life, by leaving him for the first time head of his own house. The fall of the Barrot cabinet, which resulted from his present unhappy excursion into Italian affairs, inaugurated the period of his personal rule, though not yet of his personal supremacy, in France. For Italy, little ground as there seemed at the moment for suspecting it, every stage in Louis' onward career towards that supremacy was in reality a matter for congratulation. Her one hope of deliverance in fact consisted in his attainment of a power so absolute in France as to enable him to engage his country on a policy contrary alike to its national traditions and to all its obvious immediate interests. For it must be remembered that it was as much the traditional policy of France that no great power should flank her on the Mediterranean, as it was the traditional policy of England that no great power should face her in the Netherlands. In the fifties and sixties there was nothing that England relished more, or France less, than a whack at the Pope. In the interests of the balance of power a new potential rival to the French navy was a clear gain to England, a less apparent advantage to France. In fine, as the union of Italy administered to every obvious interest of England [2]

sure that he would keep this promise. *Ibid.*, 194, 233. So too were Arese and Conneau; v. *Grabinski*, 106, 109–112. But Landor sent him back his book on Artillery. *Wheeler*, 175 *n.*

[1] ' Il n'y a que *moi seul* ici qui suis dévoué à la cause italienne.' Napoleon III to Arese, 4 Oct. 59. *Grabinski*, 180.

[2] The true analogy to England's feeling for Italy, was France's feeling for Poland. In the former case especially there was a strong strain of idealism in the sympathy. But the union of Poland would have gratified every religious instinct and served every political interest of France, exactly as the union of Italy incidentally gratified the instincts and served

so did it run counter to every selfish interest of France.
It is possible that it might have been England that delivered
Italy, had England in the fifties become a democracy :
it is certain that it could not have been France, unless
France in the fifties had become a despotism.

Meanwhile her intervention had done Italy more harm
than good. It had saved the subjects of the Pope from the
horror of a Neapolitan or Austrian restoration, and was
still somewhat to alleviate the political consequences of
their revolt. But the moral position of a Pope restored
by France was stronger than that of a Pope restored by
Austria ; and present alleviations were dearly purchased at
a price which seemed to perpetuate essential evils. It is
small wonder that in their despair Italian refugees should
have denounced the rôle of France as criminal.

Historians who have adopted this verdict have commonly
gone on to make it the vehicle of one of the moral warnings
of history. Almost without exception they have allowed
themselves the satisfaction of pointing out that by a signal
instance of poetic justice this crime was destined to lead
its author eventually to Sedan. An allusion to Sedan in
this connexion has in fact become a *cliché* without which
no reference to the expedition is complete. The contention
underlying it has been widely accepted, but in its usual
form it will not bear serious examination. It must be
dealt with more fully elsewhere, but even in this place a
caveat may be entered against the customary unquestion-
ing acceptance of it in advance. It is true that in the
last years of the Second Empire the surest, though by no
means the only, defence of France against Prussia would
have been the actual materialisation of the projected
triple alliance between France and Italy and Austria.
It is true that the alliance failed of accomplishment because

the interests of England. Had Louis Napoleon made Poland and not
Italy the first charge on his knight-errantry, he would have had a united
nation behind him. His services to Italy can only be appreciated by
remembering that in rendering them he lacked, for perfectly intelligible
reasons, the support of the majority of Frenchmen. For he was strengthening his next-door neighbour, not weakening him by strengthening his
next-door neighbour but one.

Italy most reasonably insisted on her price : either an
Austrian surrender of Trent and Trieste, or preferably a
French surrender of Rome.   Each of Italy's potential
allies hoped by manœuvre and delay to make the other
foot the inevitable bill.   But the alliance was throughout
a luxury for Austria ; and eventually, through the throwing
away of other safeguards, very nearly a necessity for
France.   Hence it was France for whom the delay was
fatal, and France who, without delay, should have brought
herself to pay the price.   But that is not to say that it
was to the disadvantage of France that in the last resort she
had the wherewithal for payment.   On the contrary the
fact that Rome was still hers to give or to refuse was the
last strong diplomatic card which Napoleon III retained.
Thanks to his possession of it, at any moment, could he
but bring himself to play it, he had the power of making the triple alliance a reality.   Without it, had Italy
already been in possession of Rome, there is not the faintest
reason to believe that she could have been induced out of
gratitude for merely past favours to take part in 1870 in
a European war.   Italian gratitude is a genuine and warm-
hearted emotion enough.   But to be effective in the sacred
egoism of international politics it must needs be reinforced
by the solid expectation of favours to come.   Napoleon III
in 1869 would have been not in a stronger but in a
weaker position towards Italy had all his potential gifts
been given already.   In that case the sole chance of the
triple alliance would have been that Austria should have
been induced to pay the bill.   France would have had
nothing to pay it with, but Austria had no sufficient
reason for paying it at all.   It was thanks only to the
French occupation of Rome that the same country which
had the need to pay had the means to pay, for a service
which quite certainly would not have been rendered
gratuitously.   All this does nothing to excuse the French
occupation, and only renders the more inexcusable Louis
Napoleon's failure to make timely use of his ill-gotten
gains.   But the fact remains that at the last they could
so have been used as both to reconcile Italy finally to

France, and to safeguard France effectively against Prussia.
It is a specious but wholly spurious fatalism which is invoked in the suggestion, that already in 1849 Louis had
suffered himself to be caught in a trap from which there
was no issue but Sedan.

This suggestion has in turn reacted upon men's verdicts
on 1849. For once they have discovered an example of
historic retribution, few historians can resist the impulse
to make the crime fit the punishment ; satisfying thereby
alike their own sense of justice and the general conviction of a moral order in the universe. It is an impulse
capable in this instance of quite innocent gratification.
Only if history must needs be teased into a vindication
of poetic justice, the moral must here be extracted in
somewhat more attenuated form. Louis Napoleon did ill
for Italy in 1849, but even in 1849 he meant her well. In
his position a worse man or a wiser would have stood
aside and left the Romans to their fate. His true fault
was his failure to foresee how little his intervention could
mitigate that fate, or how less than little the mere mitigation of it mattered. His true punishment was that as
in 1849 he had blundered into a position which actually
strengthened his country diplomatically, so by a worse
blunder in 1869 he failed to make use of the advantage
which he had undeservedly won. The first blunder in
no way necessitated the second, and the second only threw
away advantages accruing—most unfairly—from the first.
A legend has been created in order to point a moral ; but
short of a moral the mere facts admit of a reflection which
is both soothing and incidentally true. Crimes and even
blunders sometimes pay : but the payment of them is
sometimes wasted.

CHAPTER IV

ATTEMPTED UNRAVELMENT

Sagt, wo soll das enden ?   Wer
Den Knäul entwirren, der sich endlos selbst
Vermehrend wächst—Er muss zerhauen werden.
Ich fühl's, dass ich der Mann des Schicksals bin,
Und hoff's mit eurer Hülfe zu vollführen.

SCHILLER.

ALTHOUGH the appointment of Louis Napoleon's new ministry marked a definite stage in his advance towards personal power it was far from indicating a final breach between him and the Assembly. Indeed his relations with his parliament were seldom smoother than during the nine months of the ensuing session. But this parliamentary truce was dearly purchased at the price of a series of concessions on Louis' part to the reactionary tendencies of his chamber, culminating in his almost fatal capitulation in the passage of the famous May Law. The chief obstacle to the realisation of the Royalists' hopes was the principle of universal suffrage ; that principle was also the sole source of Louis' constitutional strength. Yet he carried complaisance to the parliamentary majority so far as finally to allow a grave infringement of that principle ; an infringement which threatened to cut him off from the soil that was his strength.

At the outset this complaisance was probably due to Louis Napoleon's habitual practice—a compound of caution and generosity—of going out of his way to conciliate an antagonist over whom he had achieved a success that

sufficed for his immediate purpose. His ministry out of
deference to the Catholic majority in the Assembly had
failed to support his anti-papal attitude ; to its astonishment it had been promptly dismissed. But having scored
his point at their expense Louis characteristically proved
more deferential than usual to his recent opponents. The
chief business of the session concerned education ; and
here executive and legislature soon found material for
compromise and co-operation. In January Louis' minister
of education secured the passage of a bill placing the school
teachers under the control of the prefects of their departments ; in March his ministry assented to an act long
vainly desired by the Catholics, securing to them and to
their religious orders liberty of instruction in primary and
secondary State schools. Professedly a deduction from
that liberty of the citizen which was regarded as a natural
right, Falloux' Act was in reality one which granted to the
religious communities facilities for ousting secular instruction from the State schools altogether. The increase in
the powers of the prefect effected by the first act was indirectly an increase in the powers of the President. But
the advantages accruing to the Catholics from the second
were out of all proportion to the price they paid for them.

From this legislative co-operation for a mutual benefit
President and Assembly passed easily to administrative
activity against a common foe. In this alliance too Louis
Napoleon had the worst of the bargain. For the foe in
question was the socialist party ; a party whose principles
were genuinely and fundamentally opposed to those of the
Catholic Royalists, but by no means so totally divergent
from the medley of humanitarian projects which floated
before the mind of Louis Napoleon. It was in fact a
recurring charge of both Orleanist and Legitimist against
Louis Napoleon that he was little better than a Socialist
himself ; and this charge they were to bring against him
as freely, and in some respects as truly, after the *coup d'état*
as before it.[1]

In the winter of 1850 there ensued administrative action

[1] *Cf. e.g.* Circourt to Reeve, 12 Mar. 52. B.M. Add. MS. 37423, f. 83.

not yet actively repressive, but symptomatic already of a desire to undo the Republic. Thiers in February denounced the days of February as *funestes* ; and observance of them as fête-days was forbidden. In the first days of the republic ' trees of liberty ' had been planted conspicuously in every open space of public resort. But whether from the inclement season of their planting or the amateur conduct of the operation the trees tended to languish ; and the presence of a stunted poplar of a bare year's growth at every cross-road was neither exhilarating as a spectacle nor commodious to traffic. On the plea that they were cumbering the ground, the prefect of police now had large numbers of them cut down ; but he carried out his task with a zest which made it clear to the Republicans that if their planting of the trees had been a sacrament, so also was his cutting of them down. These short-lived trees of liberty, hurriedly transplanted from their natural soil, cut down before they were well grown up, formed indeed only too apt a symbol of the brief and chequered career of the Second Republic.

Measures of this kind, trivial, tactless, and provocative, had naturally the effect of exasperating rather than intimidating those against whom they were directed ; moderate Republicans under the impact of them began to see red.[1] Moderation is in any case a virtue not easily afforded by a minority, driven naturally to atone by the intensity of its convictions for the paucity of its adherents. And the general election had already proved Republicans of all kinds to be a definite minority in France. But now it began to look as though the only real alternative to the White flag was the Red. At this juncture, in March 1850, elections were held in thirty constituencies, to replace as many members condemned for their participation in the attempted rising during the preceding June. Of these thirty seats only ten were captured by the party of order ; two-thirds of the constituencies concerned again returned socialist or advanced republican candidates. On the heels

---

[1] On the resentment caused by the tree-cutting especially, see *Siboutie*, 330.

of this miniature general election followed a bye-election in Paris itself ; at the end of April the constituency concerned elected as its new member Eugène Sue, a popular and wealthy novelist who had only become richer and more popular than ever since his recent conversion to socialism.

The election of this literary Socialist was followed by a wholly unnecessary panic. Funds fell : foreigners fled the capital : it was assumed that once more, as in the two preceding years, June would bring its June Days. In the event if it failed of this consequence, the election had an only less sinister result. For in 1850 May brought the May Law—*la Loi du* 31 *Mai*.

On the first of May a Commission was announced to prepare a reform of the electoral law ; for the panic-stricken party of order imagined that the only way of reducing the Socialists to impotence lay in some method of restricting universal suffrage. The Commission appointed included some of the best known of the royalist leaders—among them, Thiers, Molé, Montalembert, Berryer, and M. de Broglie : in a week's time it produced its draft of a bill for ' rectifying ' universal suffrage. In the course of the month the bill was revised, discussed, and passed in all its stages ; becoming law on May 31st. The Conservatives deemed it necessary to exclude from the suffrage the vagabond classes—the ' vile multitude,' as Thiers designated them—who were particularly open to allurement by socialist emissaries. But at first sight such exclusion seemed impossible. For the constitution was based upon universal suffrage, and the Assembly, being not yet two years old, was still prohibited by the constitution from even debating any change in the constitution. But luckily for the Royalists the constitution comprised a good deal of loose writing as well as of loose thinking. It had plainly intended to establish universal suffrage ; and had definitely ordained that there was to be no property qualification, no double election, and no higher age limit than twenty-one for entitling a citizen to vote. But without technically infringing any of these vetoes, it proved possible to abate or even to abolish universal suffrage. For while forbidding any qualification of residence even for deputies, who had to be twenty-five years old,[1] the constitution had forgotten to do so in the case of voters, who need only be twenty-one.[2] Clearly there was the strongest *a fortiori* presumption against any intention to permit a higher qualification for a lower function. But the presumption was implicit only, and the May Law proceeded to ignore it with a vengeance. Not merely did it require in a voter a three years' period of residence, but it accepted as proof of that residence only such evidence as practically proved also the possession of some slight property qualification. Of some ten million possible voters under universal suffrage three million were thus deprived of their political rights, contrary to the clear intention of the constitution. But technically the constitution remained intact.[3] The Monarchists might well congratulate themselves on their achievement; they had not merely swallowed the camel, but were still free to strain at the gnat. Where it was fundamentally opposed to the realisation of their hopes, they had altered the very foundation of the constitution : yet—and herein lay the beauty of it—they had not touched a syllable of the constitution, and could defend its last letter against any later modification in favour of the President.

But every consideration which explained the jubilation of the Royalists seemed to render inexplicable the acquiescence of Louis Napoleon in the law. For Universal Suffrage, to the Republicans a doubtful ally, to the Royalists a certain foe, was to him the very source of his political life. It was universal suffrage which when he was without money, without a press and without administrative support, had given him in the teeth of official pressure an overwhelming triumph over rivals who enjoyed all these advantages. It might well seem that any tampering with that principle on his part was a sheer act of political suicide.

---

[1] Art. 26.   [2] Art. 25.

[3] One member of the majority more scrupulous than the rest would not vote for the bill until he had privately asked the Speaker, a lawyer, for an assurance that it did not violate the constitution. 'Non, il ne la viole pas, mais il la trousse aussi haut que possible !' was Dupin's characteristic reply. *Hugo : Choses Vues*, 501.

So obvious was this fact that at the time all France believed that the Royalists had tricked the President. Only later did it occur to anyone that it might be a case of the biter bit. Certainly the Monarchists themselves after their defeat suspected the President of a single and far-sighted Machiavellianism in the matter. They credited him after the event with an uncanny prevision of it ; supposing him to have foreseen the exact course by which their apparent triumph was to facilitate their final overthrow. His motives in point of fact were probably mixed and almost certainly mistaken. His own statement, in his message to the Assembly a year and a half later asking for the repeal of the measure, was that the operation of the law had altogether exceeded its intended object. ' No one foresaw the suppression of three million electors—two-thirds of them peaceable country citizens.' [1] So far as Louis himself was concerned this simple confession was probably true. Foresight is a merit so rare in history, and the discovery of it a process so flattering to historians, that it should be a first canon in their training to attribute as little of it as possible to anyone. Few of them would in fact be the worse for learning to believe six accidents a day before breakfast.

None the less it is clearly true that neither Louis nor his advisers could have failed to see at the time that the May Law must result in some infringement of universal suffrage. It is possible that even so the President was not sorry to see any change effected in any manner in the immutable constitution. Conceivably he may have discerned advantage to his office in becoming for the first time the sole exponent of universal suffrage ; a sanction hitherto shared by him with the co-ordinate Assembly. Without doubt his chief motive was the hope that by his very substantial concession to the monarchical majority now, he was establishing a heavy claim upon it for co-operation in a legal extension of his own term of office, when next year such revision of the constitution should become legally possible. But at this time and throughout the following year all the evidence goes to show that Louis

[1] Message of 4 Nov. 51.

still believed in the possibility of legal revision ; and it is unlikely therefore that his acquiescence in the May Law had the deeper design which the Royalists later attributed to it. His subsequent demand for the repeal of this unconstitutional act certainly strengthened his position in his subsequent conflict with the Assembly : but it would be to attribute to him an unnecessary degree of foresight to suppose that he foresaw alike the unpopularity of the act, the failure of his alliance with the Conservatives, and the utility of the one as a possible weapon against the other.

The two months which remained after the passage of the May Law before the close of the session tended still further to depress the President's prestige. Administrative measures, now not merely exasperating but oppressive, were multiplied against the Republicans : their press was harried, their meetings watched, or their societies broken up,[1] and a regular purge of their sympathisers effected from the ranks of minor officialdom. A law was passed raising the caution money required from newspapers and requiring all press articles to be signed. At the same time the President asked and after some demur received from the Assembly a large augmentation of his civil list. Originally fixed at £24,000 a year, it had already once been doubled : it was now, though for one year only, doubled again. Any advantage the President might hope to attain by dint of more lavish expenditure was dearly bought at the price of such a grant at such a time. For it exposed him to the suspicion that his assent to monarchical reaction had been merely bought. Nor did even this increase suffice for his expenditure : penniless at the time of his election to the presidency, and already £60,000 in debt by the autumn of 1849,[2] he owed by the end of 1851 some half a million pounds.[3]

From the 11th of August to the 11th of November the Assembly was prorogued ; in accordance with the constitu-

---

[1] On the government's treatment of ' secret ' societies and its results, v. *Tchernoff : Associations.*

[2] *Barante*, vii. 479.

[3] F.O. France, Jerningham to Granville, 24 Jan. 52.

LOUIS NAPOLEON RIDING THROUGH THE BOULEVARDS
JUNE 13, 1849

From a contemporary French print at the British Museum

PREMIÉRE APPLICATION DE LA NOUVELLE LOI ÉLECTORALE DITE DES BURGRAVES.

—Pardon citoyen Prince-Président . . . . . vous ne pouvez pas voter ! . . . . vous n'avez
pas trois ans de domicile à Paris !

Montalembert
Thiers

From the Charivari, 23rd May, 1850

tion it nominated a permanent commission to represent it in Paris during the interval. But in its use of this privilege it took the opportunity of displaying its feelings towards the President by nominating commissioners uniformly hostile to his person and policy.

The vacation was marked by events of considerable importance. For during these three months every party in France began to display unreservedly its designs for the future. The advanced Republicans it is true ostentatiously did nothing. From leaders of this party already in exile for previous rebellions—Louis Blanc for his rising in May 1848, Ledru-Rollin for the June insurrection of 1849 —letters or pronouncements were indeed forthcoming urging another attempt at revolution in 1850. Nor could it be denied that the passage of the unconstitutional May Law was a far better justification for such a rising than either Louis Blanc or Ledru-Rollin had possessed for his earlier insurrection ; which had in each case been a mere protest against the legal election of conservative legislators by a misguided country. But the home Republicans had learnt by this time that Louis Napoleon did not give such attempts at revolution a fair chance of success ; hence June-1850 saw no succession to the risings of the two previous years. Making a virtue of necessity, Republicans announced that for the present they would do nothing ; they would not even vote at bye-elections, since all voting under the May Law was unconstitutional and void. But in revenge they were loud in their explanations of what they would do at the general election of 1852. In the spring of that year a new President and a new chamber had to be installed practically simultaneously ; Louis Napoleon would be gone ; everything could be done and should be done then. The three million voters who had been deprived of their votes should be provided then with a different occupation. France as a whole was considerably impressed by the fact that the Republicans were saving up their revolution for a year : the absence of the annual insurrection was felt to be more ominous than its occurrence : the action of the party had ceased to terrify ; its inaction seemed portentous.

And the country at large misread the portent ; imagining
that the Socialists had postponed their rising not from the
certainty of failure in 1850, but from the certainty of
success in 1852. In all this the Republicans were playing
straight into the hands of Louis Napoleon ; for in effect
they were prophesying after him, the deluge. And as
Louis had an ark of his own to launch, the prediction was
exactly what he needed ; for in such case a single un-
solicited testimonial as to the genuineness of the flood is
worth a thousand dissertations as to the elegance and
commodiousness of the ark. The prime need of a Saviour
of Society is something to save it from.

Scarcely less useful to the President than this menace
of the Socialists were the activities of the Royalists during
this same summer. Both Orleanist and Legitimist leaders
proceeded openly to prepare for the return of their respective sovereigns. Thiers, Molé, and Broglie visited Louis
Philippe at Claremont ; and on his death at the end of
August General Changarnier had a regal requiem celebrated
at the palace of the Tuileries itself. Meanwhile the
Legitimists were even more ostentatious in their preparations for a coming change. Berryer, de la Rochejaquelein,
and others of their leaders visited Henri V. at Wiesbaden ;
whither they were followed by organised deputations
inviting the king to remount his throne. The royal
answer was replete with that leisurely dignity so dear to
the heart and fatal to the cause of the French Legitimist ;
it amounted in fact to a public and sporting declaration
on the king's part that ' he was going to begin.' For the
conference resulted in the issue of a circular dated August
30th, in which the Legitimists were told to hold themselves
in readiness to take advantage of impending events ;
they were informed that their king reserved to himself
the direction of the political situation which would ensue
upon those events, but that he had nominated delegates in
France to act for him in case of any sudden emergencies.
Coupled with this information was a formal condemnation
of any appeal to the country on the question ; the divine
right of kings must not even seem to owe its divinity to

the voice of the people. The document was intended only for private circulation ; but through some indiscretion it found its way into the public press, which published it with comments for the most part far from favourable. Though less serviceable to Louis Napoleon than the threats of the Republicans, this patent assumption by the Monarchists of the coming triumph of their cause was not without its uses to him. For it accustomed men's minds to the belief that change of some sort was inevitable ; with the result that at the very moment when the Royalists were boasting that they had made the President their warming-pan,[1] they were in fact themselves serving that very function for the Empire.

Meantime, while Royalists and Republicans alike were unconsciously fortifying the President's position by the ineptitude of their attempts to strengthen their own, Louis was himself both testing and increasing his hold on the country by a method of his own devising. So soon as the Assembly was prorogued he left Paris and proceeded to tour the provinces. This tour was no mere public function, but a studied appeal from the capital to the country, from parliament to the people. Such appeal from Paris to the provinces was an essential and recurrent feature in Louis Napoleon's government of France. Every other regime in the history of modern France had been imposed by Paris on the provinces ; under the Second Empire alone, in the person of Louis Napoleon, the provinces imposed a ruler upon Paris. This fact throughout his reign the provinces never forgot, and Paris never forgave. The memory of it, and the general excellence of his internal administration, preserved to Louis Napoleon the unabated loyalty of the provinces down to the very close of his reign, despite every vacillation and disaster in his foreign diplomacy. The consciousness of the same fact rendered Paris far from enthusiastic for the Empire even in the hey-day of its early triumphs. Not all the embellishments of her

---

[1] ' Il fait le lit du roi,' was the remark of a legitimist leader on Louis Napoleon on the eve of the coup d'état. F.O. France, Normanby to Palmerston, 11 Dec. 51.

buildings, the completion of her palaces, her thoroughfares thronged with traffic, her royal residences too few by far for her royal visitors—not congresses that made her the crisis of diplomacy, nor exhibitions that were the wonder of the world—neither these nor her brave new boulevards, nor the fresh victories from which they were named, could ever quite reconcile Paris to the rule of Napoleon III. All these things he was to give her, but at the cost of a supremacy which she coveted more than them all. For though, thanks to Louis Napoleon, Paris became for a season the capital of Europe, yet thanks to him also she ceased for a while to be mistress of France. And for Paris this was to have gained the whole world, and lost her own soul.

The interest of Louis Napoleon's present voyage was augmented by the fact that he chose for the scene of his expedition precisely those towns and departments of France which were known to be most hostile to his rule. At no time had that rule been so resented by the Socialists as immediately after his acquiescence in the May Law, and in the reactionary administrative measures which followed it. In no part of France were the Socialists so strong as in the great towns of Burgundy, the Franche-Comté, and Alsace. It was exactly at that time and to those towns that Louis now directed his almost provocative visit. The hardihood of the venture redeemed it from the monotony of the ordinary royal progress. Such hardihood was scarcely a matter of physical courage ; for though occasionally in momentary danger of rough handling,[1] the President rightly ridiculed all risks of assassination. The real hazard was a moral one : unlike the ordinary monarch he could not count upon the suppression by the press of any untoward incident that might occur to mar the success of his voyage. Throughout, he was attended not only by friendly witnesses, but by correspondents of every variety of hostile journal,[2] ready

---

[1] *E.g.*, v. *Castellane*, iv. 269.

[2] For copious quotations from the French press on the journey, in papers both friendly and hostile to the President, v. *Thirria*, ii. 277–304. Both owing to their full utilisation there, and to the inevitable bias in one direction or the other of all contemporary French journals, I have preferred the very full reports of the English *Times*, which detailed a special correspondent to observe the journey.

to note and magnify whatever might render him ridiculous. It was this risk which led his advisers to dissuade him from the experiment. But the advice was vain and, as the event proved, mistaken. For not merely was the President's reception far more favourable than either friend or foe had expected, but such opposition as was forthcoming proved curiously unable to survive the mere presence of its object. ' I have observed nearly the same thing here,' wrote the *Times*' correspondent from Metz, ' as in the other towns through which the President has passed, where it was believed that an unfriendly population existed : that is that he has been received either coldly or hostilely for the first few hours, or the first day, and afterwards with a very kindly feeling.' [1]

Between the 12th of August, when Louis left Paris, and the 28th, the date of his return, he had shown himself at some fifty towns and villages ; travelling sometimes by boat, generally by carriage, hardly at all by train : spending a night at the important towns, and sometimes two at a few of the very largest, he was yet careful to stop his carriage or pass in slow procession through any large village or small market-town that lay on his route. Even here there was generally some improvised affability, a local wedding to be attended, an old soldier to be decorated— and handsomely tipped into the bargain—or at least there were bows to be made, bouquets to be received, *maires* to be treated as though they bulked as large in the Prince's eyes as in their own. At the big cities there were cathedrals at which to hear Mass, bishops and archbishops to be visited at their palaces, troops to be reviewed, banquets to be eaten—above all speeches to be made. A bare recital of his doings on one day may suffice to illustrate the Prince's activities during his entire journey. The most important city to be visited on this tour was Lyons, the largest and most turbulent of French provincial towns. For this reason Louis chose the date of his entry with especial care, so arranging his route as to reach it on the morning of August 15. For August 15 is the Feast of the Assump-

[1] *Times*, 30 Aug. 50, p. 5, c. 3.

tion, and on that day the peasants of Burgundy and
Provence were wont to assemble at this cathedral city of
their primate, prefacing by brief devotions their ancient
provincial games. But the same day was also the birthday
of Napoleon, the Fête de St Napoléon : his nephew could
therefore have selected no more auspicious occasion for
making his entry into the second city of France. The
concourse which the double event assembled at Lyons on
the morning of the Prince's arrival was the largest that had
yet been seen in its streets : every possible place of accom-
modation was crowded to the utmost : hundreds of peasants
from a distance slept in the surrounding fields, in order to
witness the President's entry.[1]

This took place a little after ten in the morning ; hardly
too soon to enable the president to hear Mass, even *des
paresseux* : for what was ordinarily a quarter of an hour's
walk needed this morning, by reason of the crowd, some
six times that period,[2] at any rate for the mere man in the
street. To arrive thus early, Louis had been forced to leave
Mâcon, his last resting-place, at half-past five in the morning ; even so saluted by a considerable gathering on his
departure. The fifty miles between Mâcon and Lyons
he had traversed by boat, sailing slowly down the Saône,
greeted at intervals by crowds on either bank who cheered
him on his passage and fired salutes from the river edge.
In the early morning he disembarked at half a dozen
villages or petty towns : sometimes greeted officially by
the *maire*, at others merely landing to speak informally to
some chance gathering of workmen on the bank. All this
however was but the prelude to the real business of the
day. From the last halting-place to Lyons both banks
of the river were lined by a continuous crowd, such as
hardly the boat-race itself could have assembled in England.
On landing Louis at once mounted a magnificent white
charger which was waiting for him by arrangement. For
he rode well, and on horseback his length of body still gave
him a commanding presence. In no way could he better
display himself on that brilliant summer morning to the

[1] *Times*, 20 Aug. 50, p. 5, c. 1.   [2] *Ibid.*

three hundred thousand spectators who crowded every
cranny of pavement, window, or balcony along the line of
his approach. Received first by the municipal council,
he repaired next to the cathedral. Mass heard, he reviewed
a company of Napoleonic veterans ; a body still numerous
enough to be mustered over a thousand strong for such an
occasion as this, yet already small enough to savour of that
rareness which is the essence of all solemnity. Many were
in the very uniforms they had worn in Napoleon's service ;
some had visibly donned them now for their last parade.
And who should blame them if, bowed shoulders braced
again for the instant and tattered tunics taut, they should
throw out once more the old raucous battle-cry—*Vive
Napoléon! Vive l'Empereur!* Not surely his nephew ;
though to him the salutation was no pathetic echo of the
past, but a dramatic challenge for the future.

The brief military pomp was followed by the tamer
business of civil activities, excursions to hospitals, alms-
houses and the like ; capped by a call on the Archbishop,
from the balcony of whose palace Louis showed himself
again to the still clamorous crowd. After another appearance for the benefit of another crowd, from the balcony of
the *Hôtel de Ville*, came the inevitable banquet to which all
these long days rang at last ; and after the dinner an after-
dinner speech. ' Believe me,' said Louis, ' I have not come
here, to the countries where the Emperor my uncle has
left such profound traces, merely to receive ovations or to
hold reviews. The object of my journey is by my presence
to encourage the good, to lead back spirits that have
strayed, to judge in my own person the feelings and needs
of the country. For that I need your co-operation ; and
to gain it I owe you a frank explanation of what I am and
what I want. I am the representative not of a party but
of the two great national manifestations which in 1804
as in 1848 intended to secure by order the great principles
of the French Revolution. Proud of my origin and of my
flag, I shall remain faithful to them ; I shall be entirely
at the country's service, no matter which alternative it
demands of me, sacrifice or perseverance.' It was the

President's first open hint of the possibility of a prolonging of his powers ; and it was followed by a claim that he too, not less than the Assembly, stood for the people's voice. ' I do not admit that anyone has a greater right than I to call himself the Representative of the People.' But he ended by thanking his hearers for refusing to believe rumours of a *coup d'état* : ' the elect of six million,' cried Louis magnificently, ' does not betray the will of the people : he executes it.' Speech and banquet were followed by a ball, which ended a day typical of the President's activities during his tour of the provinces.

But though his days were always long, and his course everywhere crowded, the crowd was not quite invariably friendly ; during the next stage of his journey, as he turned eastwards towards the frontier, signs were not wanting of a real element of disaffection. Once he was roughly handled, and more than once he was made the object of heckling on the part of individuals which only some ready repartee or dignified rebuke prevented from becoming the occasion of an awkward demonstration.[1] Such incidents, everywhere exceptional, only became noteworthy as the President approached Strasburg : at that city itself the town council refused to take any part in the reception, or to vote any grant in connexion with it. Fearing that even if he escaped personal violence he would be the object of a demonstration injurious to his prestige, and prejudicial to the success he had already won, Louis' advisers redoubled their efforts to induce him to curtail his programme and omit Strasburg from his tour.[2] But he insisted on going forward, and was rewarded by receiving an unexpectedly friendly welcome ; while at the banquet boycotted by municipal authority he took his audience into his confidence. ' Before I started attempts were made to dissuade me from my journey in Alsace ; they kept on telling me, " You will be badly received there." . . . But I, I said to myself, " Wherever there are dangerous illusions to dispel or good citizens to confirm, there I ought to go." Alsace was libelled, and I was right.'

Strasburg was the turning-point of the expedition ; the journey back through Lorraine and Champagne was an unbroken triumph. Not a village or hamlet did Louis pass but bore unmistakable signs of joy at his presence ; not merely the largest but the smallest [1] houses testified to the feelings of their occupants by some attempt at decoration by day or illumination by night. Working men would subscribe their coppers to build some archway in his honour ; in one case, hearing that a socialist raid on their erection was threatened, they took turns to guard it till the Prince had passed beneath it.[2] Towns at his passage doubled and more than doubled [3] their population : for twenty miles on either side of his route the countryside was emptied and the roads were filled by a throng of peasants trudging on foot, farmers moving sedately on slow-going horses, or more often driving in carts with their wives and children : [4] displaying always at their journey's end an enthusiasm surpassing even that of the townsmen.[5]

During the last week of the tour the weather broke, and semi-tropical rain took the place of a semi-tropical sun. But the opposition journalists of Paris, who had they prayed at all had prayed this last fortnight for a republican rain, found little to console them in the issue : no downpour could damp the popular enthusiasm. Peasants in crowds still trudged their twenty miles through mire and water, and then cheerfully waited fo hours in the pelting rain [6] to see the President pass: hundreds of the National Guard, in every variety of antiquated uniform, armed some of them with no more destructive weapons than cudgels, still marched as far to the President's line of route, and refused to return until they had been reviewed by the ' Prince.' [7] Occasionally the enthusiasm of some veteran took embarrassing form. ' One old man went up to him yesterday at Sarrebourg, and fell on his knees as he kissed his hand. The President raised him at once, and said, " *Mon ami, il ne faut*

---

[1] *Times*, 30 Aug., p. 5, c. 3.   [2] *Ibid.*, 29 Aug., p. 5, c. 6.
[3] E.g. Besançon, from 33,000 to 73,000 ; *Times*, 23 Aug., p. 6, c. 2.
[4] *Times*, 30 Aug., p. 5, c. 3, and 16 Aug., p. 6, c. 1.
[5] *Ibid.*, 22 Aug., p. 6, c. 1.   [6] *Ibid.*, 29 Aug., p. 5, c. 6.
[7] *Ibid.*, 30 Aug., p. 5, c. 3.

jamais s'agenouiller qu'au bon Dieu." '[1] As it was in the large towns, so it was also in the small villages, save that at these the festivities were more primitive, and the President's stay necessarily shorter. Thus at Dieuze, one of the several villages at which Louis halted in this way on August 24, he took his midday meal in company with five hundred men employed in the chalk-works of that place : the foreman of the works sat next to him, but all the workmen, and many members of the peasant invasion were introduced to him as well. ' Afterwards the President mixed among the workmen, and the country people, and went about unaccompanied by any escort ; not even by a single *gendarme*. He was covered up to the face with mud, and got wet through to the skin, yet he never seemed to enjoy himself more.'[2]

Louis' own impressions of his journey are well shown by his brief after-dinner speech made at Rheims, the last large town at which he tarried on his return journey. ' Our fair country,' he began, ' has no other wish than order, religion and a wise liberty. Everywhere, and I speak from what I have seen, the number of agitators is infinitely small, the number of good citizens is infinitely great. God grant that these last be not divided against themselves. For this reason, on finding myself once more to-day in this ancient city of Rheims, where the kings came to get them crowned, kings who, they too, stood for the large interests of the nation, for this reason I prayed that *we* might be enabled to crown here no mere man but an idea : the noble ideal of union and conciliation. To pray for the peace of France is to pray for the prosperity of Rheims.' The speech was not read, but ' quite extempore ' :[3] short as it was it was prolonged by frequent outbursts of applause.

Even the opposition press in Paris was constrained to admit that the President had greatly strengthened his position by his tour. ' Politics apart,' wrote the *National* on August 28, the day of Louis' return to Paris, ' politics apart we render justice to the personal qualities of the

---

[1] *Times*, 30 Aug., p. 5, c. 3.   [2] *Ibid.*, 29 Aug., p. 5, c. 6.
[3] *Ibid.*, 23 Aug., p. 5, c. 1.

President. We know that he is brave ; and even if the
two enterprises of Boulogne and Strasburg had not proved
clearly enough already that he knows how to "face the
music," we should regard his voyage through the midst of
populations of whom the greater part are Socialists as an
undeniable proof of his firmness of character and decision
of spirit.' And to foreign observers the magnitude of
the Prince's achievement was even more unmistakable :
the *Times* for example dwelt upon the obvious political
significance of ' the enthusiasm with which all classes of the
provincial population have thrown themselves upon the
track of Louis Napoleon.' [1]

Least of all was the significance of his achievement
hidden from Louis Napoleon himself. He told Normanby
that he had returned from his tour with a much stronger
impression of the hold he had on the people than he had
before entertained.[2] And the British ambassador reported
that the truth of the President's impression was confirmed
to him by an interview he had with General de la Hitte,
who stated that he had never seen such signs of enthusiasm
when accompanying the progresses of the elder Bourbons.[3]

This was in September, at the conclusion of Louis'
second tour. For on September 3, after a bare week's
sojourn at the Elysée, he started forth on a second mission-
ary journey ; following his arduous passage through the
socialist east by an easy triumph through the royalist west.
Here in the leisured heart of Normandy were no excited
crowds of artisans to be appeased, no fiery interruptions
to be quenched, no mutinous manifestations to be quelled :
only in the very home and season of fruitfulness, long days
of placid driving under triumphal arches, down the still-
narrow streets of cathedral towns, out into the country
through lines of peasants in holiday attire, who had flocked
peaceably from their habitations to see Napoleon's heir; on
whom as he passed they pressed flowers and bouquets until
his very carriage became one garland of flowers.

---

[1] *Times*, 21 Aug., p. 4, cc. 3 and 4.
[2] F.O. France, Normanby to Palmerston, 16 Sept. 50.
[3] *Ibid.*

Louis profited by this unbroken series of ovations to make more explicit references in his after-dinner speeches to the possible prolongation of his powers. ' What the people acclaim in me,' he said at Caen, ' is the representative of order and of a better future. As I pass through your people I rejoice to hear them say, " The bad times are over : we wait for better things." He would be blameworthy indeed who at the very moment when prosperity seems everywhere to be reviving should attempt to check its growth by a change of existing institutions, however imperfect these may be. None the less, should dark days come and the people desire to impose new burdens on the head of the government, he in turn would be most worthy of blame did he desert his high mission.' Both here and at Cherbourg Louis' speeches amounted to a direct endorsement of a series of petitions in favour of a revision of the constitution, which had just been received from fifty-two out of the eighty-five *conseils généraux* of France.

Meanwhile the permanent commission had watched with ill-concealed dismay these fresh proofs of the President's popularity. But even the constitution of 1848 contained no proviso forbidding the President to travel in the provinces ; and the committee felt powerless to intervene. Its opportunity came with Louis' next step. Early in October he proceeded to hold a series of military reviews. Military manœuvres at this time of the year were regular enough ; nor was it unnatural for the President, as head of the state, to be present on such occasions. But it was distinctly irregular that he should allow himself to be hailed by the troops with cries of *Vive Napoléon!* or even *Vive l'Empereur!* And though some precedent could be alleged for the practice, it was clearly in the highest degree improper that at the close of the reviews officers and men should be fêted at his personal expense. The parliamentary commission had here a legitimate grievance which it might well have pressed home against Louis Napoleon so effectively as in some degree to counteract his access of prestige from the provinces. But this very access of prestige prevented the commission from striking at all : mistrusting the issue of any conflict which it should provoke against so provedly popular a power, it contented itself with passing, two days after the last of these reviews, a vote of censure which it did not venture to publish.

Unfortunately for the cause which they were appointed to defend, the commissioners, who had thus lost a favourable opportunity of action, proceeded almost immediately to forfeit the sole compensation for inaction, the dignity of a contemptuous calm and an unbroken reserve. The commission had in its employment secret agents who were instructed to keep close watch on all Bonapartist propaganda.   On October 30 one of these agents furnished M. Yon, the commissioner who had charge of this particular branch of the parliamentary defence, with a full and particular account of a plot hatched in his presence on the preceding evening for the assassination of General Changarnier and of the president of the commission itself. The murder of the latter, M. Dupin, had been assigned to the spy Allais himself by the witless conspirators. Such, stripped of details and adornments, was the plot which filled the ears of Paris in November 1850. The chief parliamentary organ—the *Journal des Débats*—published the story of the entire conspiracy ; the commissioners sent a solemn embassage to Louis Napoleon's Minister of the Interior, asking why they had not been warned of this plot against their leader's life ; irritated by his contemptuous assurance that their lives had never been in danger, they appointed a judicial committee to investigate the affair for themselves. Too late they learned that the room in which the conspirators were alleged to have met was not large enough to have held half their number ; that the conspirators themselves had no difficulty in proving alibis : finally the unfortunate agent confessed that the whole story was an invention ; and the parliamentary commission, instead of avenging an attempt on its president's life, found that it had only succeeded in securing a year's imprisonment for one of its own paid spies. Worse than that, by its indirect and abortive action now, the com-

mission showed that it had taken no steps against the
President after the reviews not because it had not deigned
but because it had not dared to attack him openly.   To
Louis the exploded plot rendered the same kind of service
which the forgery fiasco conferred on Parnell a generation
later :   more fortunate than Parnell, he received the help
when it was timed to retrieve a past indiscretion rather
than to be cancelled by a future one.

On the balance therefore the vacation ended with the
advantage clearly to Louis in his now hardly hidden
conflict with the Assembly.   Secure perhaps in the sense of
this advantage he adopted an unusually conciliatory
attitude towards it when it reassembled.   Five days
before the meeting of the chamber he dissolved the *Société
du Dix-Décembre.*   This was the most militant organisation
of Bonapartist propaganda ;   and its ardour had led it to
favour indiscreet popular demonstrations in favour of the
Empire.   Its dissolution at this time amounted to a public
disavowal by Louis of those of his followers who desired an
immediate, and therefore an illegal, overthrow of the
Republic ;   for the moment he desired to concentrate his
endeavours upon an agreed prolongation of his powers.

The message with which he greeted the chamber on
December 12 at the beginning of its new session was
calculated to enhance the impression produced by this act
of conciliation.   ' France before all things desires repose,'
said the President ;   ' I have often declared that I should
consider as gravely to blame those who, through personal
ambition, should compromise the little stability which the
constitution affords us.'   This was quite in Louis' best
manner ;   at once to profess his loyalty to the constitution
and his contempt for it.   He continued in the same strain
to explain the provincial tours and the military reviews :   it
had been his mere duty as chief magistrate to put himself
into closer relations with different classes and sections of
the French people ;   and as for the army :   ' If my name no
less than my efforts has contributed to strengthen the
loyalty of the army, of which according to the terms of the
constitution I have the sole disposition, in that case I

venture to say that this seems to me a service rendered to the country. For I have ever used my personal influence in the interest of order.' Again an admirable instance of Louis Napoleon's facile gift of combining two conflicting sentiments in one seemingly consistent sentence. In the act of denying any sinister designs in the army, he had contrived to assert his exclusive constitutional right of disposing of it ; and to allude openly to the fact that behind his constitutional right lay his personal popularity, and behind his personal popularity, his name. But the close of the message, in which he alluded to the proposed revision of the constitution, seemed to leave equivocation behind. ' To-day,' he concluded, ' it is permitted to every one—except myself—to wish to hasten the revision of the constitution. A great number of the *conseils généraux* have expressed such a wish. . . . Uncertainty as to the future gives rise, I am assured, to many fears, just because it gives rise to many hopes. Let us all know how to sacrifice these hopes to the country, thinking of its interests only. Rest assured that what most concerns me is not to know who will govern France in 1852, but so to spend the time at my command as to insure that the transition, whatever it be, may be effected without tumult and without trouble.'

So conciliatory a message did not lack effect,[1] and seemed to augur a more harmonious session than the last ; but the truce was almost immediately broken by a legacy from the episode of the reviews. At the last and largest of these the cavalry had raised the now customary cry of *Vive l' Empereur!* as they passed the President : but the infantry marched past in dead silence. Their general—a personal friend of Changarnier, the commander-in-chief—had issued orders that no acclamations were permissible from troops under review. The general was promptly promoted, to a post in the provinces. Changarnier supported the conduct of the subordinate who had thus in effect been disgraced : on January 3 he took an opportunity afforded by a debate in the Assembly to display his hostility to the President : two days later he was dismissed from his post.

---

[1] Cf. *Daudan*, ii. 218.

No act of Louis Napoleon since his election, not even his dismissal of the Barrot cabinet, created such a sensation as this. For General Changarnier was, with the exception of the President himself, the most outstanding man in France. It was to Louis Napoleon on the morrow of his election that Changarnier owed his extraordinary official position, as commander at once of the National Guard and of the regular army round Paris. A Royalist at heart, he had worked in willing alliance with the President in the cause of order ; rendering prompt and effective service in suppressing the attempted risings of January and June in 1849. But towards the new monarchical Assembly he was much more favourably inclined than to its republican predecessor ; in fact he had now a parliament to whom he could be General Essex as well as a variety of kings to whom he could be General Monk. But he was in no hurry for a *dénouement* ; he enjoyed the position of the strong silent man, maintaining a sphinx-like attitude with the greater ease that he was probably uncertain of his own exact moment and method of striking. Meanwhile the deference which all parties were bound to pay to so important a potential ally was grateful to him, and he was careful for all their attentions not to give any binding pledge to any of his suitors. In his hands were the destinies of the future : all in good time he would enlighten the country as to its fate : till then his business was primarily to conserve and to enhance his own political prestige.

For some months past at his dinner-parties at the Tuileries Changarnier had permitted himself to make openly contemptuous references to the President, not merely in conversation with his junior officers, but without even waiting until the servants had retired.[1] In December 1850 an officer present at one of these dinners informed the Princess Mathilde that Changarnier had actually discussed with his guests methods of putting the President under arrest and imprisoning him at Vincennes.[2] The Princess took her informant straight to the Elysée, where

---

[1] Witness a guest present on such an occasion, *Canrobert*, i. 499.
[2] *Ibid.*, 507, 508.

LOUIS NAPOLEON, PRESIDENT OF THE REPUBLIC

From a contemporary French lithograph at the British Museum

THE EMPRESS OF THE FRENCH

From an engraving by D. J. Pound

he repeated his story to Louis Napoleon ; since it confirmed information already to his hand, the President seized the occasion of Changarnier's speech a few days later to effect his dismissal.

In spite of previous unguarded utterances [1] this speech was in fact the first formal and public sign of hostility evinced by the General to Louis Napoleon ; as recently as the close of the previous session he had actually supported the increase of the President's salary. But Louis' triumphant tour of the provinces seems for the first time to have opened the General's eyes to the fact that here there existed another and a formidable claimant to the rôle of necessary man. Upon that discovery a breach became inevitable. For of two would-be necessary men each is bound to find the other very unnecessary indeed.

But no one expected that the President would strike so soon or strike so hard. His constitutional power to do so was undoubted ; but the General seemed already so strongly entrenched in his double command that the cabinet boggled at the prospect of attacking it. Louis insisted, dismissed his old ministry, and appointed a new one.[2] Even his personal well-wishers thought him rash : but he refused to be deterred, and summoned the leading politicians of the Assembly to meet him : nominally to ask their advice, really to acquaint them with his decision. The scene has been described by Montalembert, one of the representatives so summoned. ' Each of us,' he said, ' made a speech ; and not a short one. We were full of the sacredness of the constitution and of the omnipotence of the Assembly. . . . He listened with the utmost patience, but when he said to Thiers, " Do you ask me to retain as my commander-in-chief the man who boasted that he would drag me to Vincennes ? " his eye, habitually so cold and dead, flashed.'[3] With that the interview ended : and

---

[1] v. *Cassagnac*, i. 59 ; *Richard*, 152.
[2] *Bourgeois* : *France*, i. 388.
[3] *Senior* : *Thiers*, i. 363, 364. It was ' the only time when I saw him moved,' commented Montalembert ; ' he has a self-command which I never saw in any other human being. He is never angry, never excited, never depressed, never impatient.' *Ibid*. And *cf.* the contemporary entry in his *Journal* (4 Jan. 51), quoted by *Lecanuet*, iii. 15.

it only remained for the conservative leaders to attempt
by measures in the Assembly to avenge the disgrace of
their champion. On January 10 they carried a vote
appointing a commission to prepare such measures as
circumstances should necessitate,—a commission which,
as they were careful to explain, might easily be developed
on provocation into a sort of committee of public safety.
But the internal divisions of the Assembly rendered it
powerless to fulfil its threat. The Republicans gladly
joined in blaming Louis Napoleon, but they refused to
praise their old enemy Changarnier : the moderate Conservatives were anxious to testify to their devotion to
Changarnier, but hesitated to censure the President, lest
an open breach with him should risk the entire cause of
the party of order.

Hence after long debates the Monarchists only succeeded
in carrying a vote of censure not on the President, but on
his cabinet ; and to win even this small success they had
to buy the co-operation of the Socialists by forgoing any
expression of sympathy with Changarnier.   This inglorious
termination of a conflict on which the Assembly had
embarked with such high boasts on such great provocation
was a clear victory for Louis Napoleon.   For in spite of all
its threats the Assembly had proved unable either to
censure the President or to commend Changarnier ; still
less to restore him to his command.   Henceforth the
Royalists, deprived of their military champion and discredited in the country, were unable even in the chamber
to defeat the *Parti d'Élysée,* except by the aid of their old
enemies the Republicans.   And though the presence of a
common danger could render possible temporary coalitions
between these incongruous allies, the memory of past
struggles recently embittered sufficed to prevent any
cordial co-operation.

The motion of censure on the President's ministry had
been carried by 417 to 286 : but both majority and minority
were composite votes ; the majority including the Republicans and the unreconciled Royalists, the minority the
Bonapartists and the Monarchists who had rallied to the

President. The last combination was numerically just about equal either to the Republicans or to the Monarchists opposed to the Elysée. Henceforth there was in fact no clear coalition majority in the Assembly at all ; but any two of the groups could at any time unite to defeat the third—which in turn tended to avenge itself on the first opportunity by combining with one half to defeat the other half of the lately victorious combination.

Louis Napoleon took advantage of the vote of censure to form a new cabinet composed of even more devoted personal adherents ; to it he gave the name of a ' ministry of transition,' since it was to serve until some permanent majority had emerged in the chamber. Meanwhile he declared it useless to attempt to form ministries to reflect every chance and changing coalition that the business of the day might produce. But save for the ' rubbing in ' in this way of the weakness of his opponents' position, by demonstrating that he could as easily govern without a parliamentary cabinet as with one, Louis was on the whole characteristically conciliatory in the months which followed Changarnier's dismissal. He had pounced, and as usual the pounce was followed by a pause.

One slight diversion he did indeed permit himself. Napoleon had varied his finer dramatic conceptions at St Helena with an occasional appeal to the gallery pure and simple. None of these more primitive *coups de théâtre* had achieved greater success than his complaint that he was deprived of common comforts or necessities, followed by the sale of portions of his plate. This device, or a variation of it, Louis Napoleon now repeated. He caused his ministers to ask for an extra million and three-quarters of francs for his State expenses. The Assembly as was natural met the request with an emphatic refusal. At once the Bonapartist press announced a subscription on the President's behalf ; Louis Napoleon magnificently waved it aside.[1] Instead, though he did not reduce his subscriptions, he dismissed servants, sold horses and carriages, and ostentatiously economised in his domestic expenditure.

[1] *Véron*, vi. 102.

Incidentally the episode served to increase the divisions of the old monarchical majority. For Montalembert—next to Berryer the most eloquent of the legitimist leaders —made the Assembly's refusal of the request the occasion of an impassioned defence of the President's conduct ; a defence which practically marked the defection of the Catholic party from the Legitimist to the Napoleonic cause. Another debate at the beginning of the following month still further emphasised the divisions of the Royalists. On March 1 a proposal was discussed which would have allowed the return to France of princes of both branches of the royal house. Such a proposal might at first sight have been expected to command the united support of all the Monarchists, who at this time were eagerly discussing schemes for pooling their resources by a ' fusion ' of their rival claims. But the revocation of the edict of exile was a boon quite valueless to the Bourbon though of extreme importance to the Orleanist pretender. For whatever his legal rights, Henri V could never set foot in France save as its acknowledged and legitimate king. But the heir of Louis Philippe had no false pride, and might eventually have returned as a private citizen, presented himself as a candidate for the presidency, and so attempted to attain at last a well-earned crown. The legitimist members saw that they had everything to lose and nothing to gain by giving a dynastic rival a start of this kind ; they therefore joined the Republicans to defeat the proposal. The result was to throw back all prospects of an arrangement by which the childless King of France should adopt the would-be King of the French, and ' the union of foolscap and blotting-paper ' [1] was once more postponed.

It was while the chamber was in this state of internal division that Louis Napoleon prepared to make his bid for a legal prolongation of his powers. Since the Assembly alone was empowered to alter the constitution, he was bound to approach it with somewhat greater deference to its sus-

---

[1] This curiously felicitous description of the ' fusion ' occurs in a letter of Walter Savage Landor to the *Examiner* of 17 Dec. 53.

ceptibilities than he had recently troubled to display.
After lengthy negotiations he succeeded in forming a
parliamentary ministry under M. Léon Faucher : the
President promised his loyal support to his new cabinet,
on condition that they would do everything in their power
to win the chamber's assent to a legal prolongation of his
presidency.

It was only on the 28th of May, the second anniversary
of its meeting, that the Assembly became constitutionally
competent to revise the constitution. In the country at
large the question had already been much canvassed. As
far back as the spring of 1850 it had been discussed by the
departmental assemblies of France : of the eighty-five
departments only two had desired to maintain the constitution unaltered, while fifty-two had formally expressed
themselves as in favour of revision. In the winter of 1851
petitions were circulated in favour of the prolongation of
the President's powers, and more than a million signatures
were obtained. The value of these petitions as an indication of popular opinion may well be questioned. For
though there is no evidence to show that they were less
spontaneous than such things usually are, yet they were
undoubtedly viewed with benevolence by authority. On
the whole the executive seem to have been content to
remain favourable spectators : unfeignedly pleased that
petitions should be signed, but careful,[1] if only from
motives of policy, to avoid any such show of official
pressure as would neutralise the effect of the petitions in
the eyes of the country.

On May 31 a petition in favour of revision was handed
in signed by 233 of the representatives themselves. Even
in the chamber it was only from the Orleanists and the
Republicans that opposition was now certain. The former
hoped that in default of Louis Napoleon an Orleanist
president might be elected in his place : the latter, with a
few exceptions,[2] regarded an extension of the President's

---

[1] v. e.g. *Moniteur*, 17 May 51.

[2] Notably Lamartine, who vainly urged that the surest way to make the
Republic detestable and destructible was to baulk the will of the nation
in its name. v. *Lamartine : Orateur*, 360–366.

term of office as fatal to the Republic. Moderate Republicans derided, and extreme Republicans desired the crisis of 1852. This crisis depended for its existence on the fact that as things stood a new Assembly and a new President were to be elected almost simultaneously at the beginning of May 1852 ; so that for a moment France would lack any effective government either legislative or executive. If however the constitution were revised the crisis would be conjured away, and all exploitation of it rendered impossible.

The Red Republicans were therefore quite logical in their opposition to any revision. Equally consistent was the opposition of even the more moderate Republicans to an extension of Louis' term of office. They had opposed his election in the first instance, because they regarded it, rightly, as a repudiation of republicanism by France. Foreseeing that their opposition must for that very reason fail, they had inserted into the constitution a provision which had the effect of reducing the first president's term of office from four years to three and a half.[1] The intention of this provision was merely to shorten the regime of Louis Napoleon : its effect was to create an interregnum in which France would be left without either President or Assembly. The more moderate Republicans had not indeed any desire for an interregnum for its own sake. But they still preferred the risk of anarchy ensuing on an interregnum to the risk of a dictatorship ensuing on a prolongation of Louis Napoleon's power.

Even in the present Assembly the advocates of a legal revision were known to be in a decided majority. But the constitution of 1848 empowered a quarter of the members voting to veto any constitutional revision. The only chance of securing revision lay therefore in driving a wedge between the Royalist and the Republican elements in the minority. It was perhaps in the hope of doing this that the President at the beginning of June deplored in a speech at Dijon the reactionary tendencies of the Assembly. ' If my government,' he said, ' has not been able to realise

[1] Art. 46.

all the reforms which it has had in view, you must make
allowance for the paralysing effects which party manœuvres
may produce even on those assemblies and governments
most devoted to the public good. For three years past,'
he continued, ' I have noticed that I can always count on
the backing of the Assembly when there is any question of
combating disorder by means of repression. But whenever
I have tried to do good, to ameliorate the conditions of the
people, I have found apathy and inertia.' In reality this
was an unwise statement, even if it were true : since
whatever its intention, its effect was to conciliate opinion
in the country which was already overwhelmingly in
Louis' favour, at the price of losing votes in the chamber,
where alone opinion legally mattered. The conclusion of
the speech was still more impolitic. ' If France recognises
that no one has the right to dispose of her future without
her consent, France has only to say so ; my energy and
courage will not fail her. Be sure of this, gentlemen :
France will not perish in my hands.' These words
were deleted from the official account of the speech
in the *Moniteur*, and the speech itself was followed
by others more conciliatory in other provincial towns :
but the effect of it in the chamber could not entirely be
neutralised.

Even so on July 19 the motion in favour of revision
was carried in the Assembly by 446 to 278. The minority,
which for the purpose in hand counted as a majority,
included not only Republicans, but Orleanists hoping for an
Orleanist president, and even a few Legitimists. No
positive bond united it, but only a common distrust of
Louis Napoleon. Three weeks later the Assembly prorogued itself for three months.

During the vacation the Departmental Councils proceeded
by a majority of 79 to 6 to repeat their petitions in favour
of the revision which the minority in the chamber had just
refused. In form the vote was but a reiteration by a larger
majority of similar petitions from the same source a year
ago. In fact what had then been a recommendation to a
particular course of action had now become a vote of

censure on its refusal. Indeed, since there was now no
further prospect of legal revision, the vote was capable of
being interpreted as an invitation from the people to the
President to cut his cords and theirs.

To cut them Louis Napoleon now determined. Instead
of his usual summer tour he shut himself up at St Cloud,
gathering round him the men who were to be his instruments
when the time for action had arrived. Many thought the
time ripe for it already ; the Assembly was dispersed, and
the issue clear. But Louis insisted on a new session, and
at its opening on November 4 he asked for the abrogation
of the May Law. He based his request on grounds both of
expediency and equity ; but he was careful to build a
bridge for the Assembly which would allow them to repeal
the law without any too open avowal of inconsistency,
and to associate himself with such inconsistency as could
not be explained away entirely. The law, he said, had
been well intended ; it had had for the time salutary
effects ; and in any case he had no wish to deny that he
had himself given his approval to its passage. But its
utility had been of the nature of a measure of public
safety ; and it was of the essence of such measures that
their operation should be but temporary. Further the
operation of the law had been far wider than the intentions
of its devisers ; no one had foreseen that it would lead to
the suppression of three million votes. Besides there was
this crisis of 1852 ; and ' to re-establish universal suffrage
would be to deprive civil war of its flag.' To these arguments the President added another based on the equilibrium of the constitution. By the constitution unless the
President received two million votes the right of election
was to pass from the country to the Assembly. But the
constitution had contemplated ten million electors ; so
that the new President was only to be appointed by the
Assembly if the country gave no candidate one-fifth of its
votes. Now, with only seven million voters, practically
a third of the voters must agree to render their vote
effectual : as things stood therefore the people stood in

danger of being robbed of another right which the con-
situtution had intended to confer on them.

A stormy debate followed, terminating in a close division ;
but by a majority of six votes the President's proposition
was refused. For although the Republicans rallied to the
Bonapartists in its favour, both branches of the monarchical
majority found themselves united in their distrust of
universal suffrage. The result was disastrous for the
Assembly. Already by a minority vote it had refused to
allow the country to have the new constitution which it
desired. Now by the barest possible majority it had
refused to restore the one feature in the old constitution
which was really popular.

So manifestly did the rejection of his proposal strengthen
the President's position and weaken that of the Assembly,
that it has generally been held that Louis Napoleon desired
and designed its rejection himself. Even those who do
not accuse him of passing the May Law in the first instance
with the express object of demanding its repeal later, are
yet inclined to assume that when later he did demand its
repeal he hoped for the rejection of his own demand. The
belief leaves out of account two facts : first that the proposal was made in a most conciliatory form, and secondly
that it was thrown out by a most minute majority. Had
Louis' attitude been a mere pose designed to put the
Assembly in the wrong by their rejection of a popular
measure, nothing would have been easier for him than to
have imported elements of provocation into his introductory message which would have secured the rejection
of anything for which it asked. Instead he had gone out
of his way to shoulder a share of the responsibility for the
passage of the May Law, and to extend to the Assembly
the excuse which he pleaded for himself : failure to foresee
the full consequences of the Act. Even more cogent is
the argument from the size of the majority. Even under
the most stable of parliamentary conditions, where only
two organised parties confront one another on lines of
traditional cleavage, the most expert whip with the best-
disciplined of followings cannot safely reckon on a single-

figure majority ; the accidents of illness or social engage-
ments are too great, or even the chance of some stray
member being affected by argument in debate. It is to
carry the credulity of scepticism a little far, to suppose
that into the wild welter of the Legislative Assembly,
where no two majorities had recently been composed even
of the same combination of parliamentary groups, Louis
Napoleon could have cast a measure cutting across such
vague lines of party division as existed in it, and staked his
future on a correct prediction of a majority of six in a
house of seven hundred and fifty.

But though hostile criticism has been in error in asserting
that Louis expected and intended the rejection of his
appeal, no less erroneous is the plea of his chief apologist [1]
that the passage of the law might have averted any
irregular or illegal step at all. ' I dined yesterday with the
President at St Cloud,' wrote the English ambassador on
the eve of the session.[2] ' After dinner the Prince took me
aside into another room.' There Normanby urged on him
a compromise : why not propose to modify the May Law,
instead of to annul it ? ' " No," he replied, " no modification
would answer my purpose. I must have absolute repeal,
and I shall have it." ' Normanby asked would not the
Assembly reject the proposition ? ' " No," he thought they
would be obliged to adopt it. . . . " Then, sir, you will have
a triumphant re-election and a red Assembly." " No," he
said, " not a red Assembly. Matters will not proceed in
quite such a regular train." ' Unfortunately at this point,
feeling himself on the verge of perilous confidences, Normanby changed the subject.

Whatever the intention of the President, there can be no
doubt of the folly of the Assembly's action. Indeed its
members seem belatedly to have recognised themselves
how much they had facilitated a possible *coup d'état*. The
Monarchists to whom was due the refusal of the repeal now
demanded that the Assembly should safeguard itself by
passing a bill empowering its own chairman to claim and

---

[1] *Ollivier*, ii. 438.
[2] F.O. France, Normanby to Palmerston. ' Most secret.' 26 Oct. 51.

dispose of the military power of the country. But the Republicans, furious at the defeat of universal suffrage, united with the *Parti d'Élysée* to oppose the measure ; 'they were not going,' they said, 'to arm the Law of May 31.' They accused the Royalists of plotting a *coup d'état* of their own, and desiring to acquire control of the army in order to facilitate it ; as for the Assembly itself it was in no danger : 'let it trust in its invisible sentinel, the people.'

The folly of that phrase has commonly been imputed also to the vote which followed ; by which on November 17 the Assembly threw out by a majority of over a hundred the proposal that it should demand for itself some more palpable protection. The defeat of this demand was due to the opposition of the republican deputies : an action later denounced by republican as well as royalist historians as a crowning mercy for Louis Napoleon, and a supreme and suicidal folly on the part of his opponents. The censure is of doubtful justice. Article 50 of the constitution definitely assigned the disposal of the armed forces to the President of the Republic. True, another article [1] admitted of a contrary sense. But the matter was ambiguous at best, and the present proposal if carried would have been denounced as a breach of the constitution. The breach—if breach it were—would have been voted only, not accomplished ; for the executors of the *coup d'état* were standing by, ready to deliver their blow the instant that this the best excuse for it conceivable was forthcoming. Already the Assembly had baulked France of its known desire for a legal revision of the constitution. Already it had refused to repeal a law most unpopular in itself and almost certainly unconstitutional in its consequences. To have capped such a record by what would plausibly have been represented as a second breach of the constitution—and that not in response to a popular demand but apparently in preparation for a royalist *coup d'état* of their own—this might well have made the President's success even more easy

[1] Art. 32.

and overwhelming than it was. As it was, Assembly and
constitution were alike discredited : such a vote would
have enabled Louis to turn these two most feeble foes
against each other. In the name of the constitution he
could have broken the Assembly, and a constitution which
had twice been broken by the Assembly without popular
support none could have blamed him for breaking a third
time with it.[1]

It was not in fact the failure of this eleventh hour
attempt to clutch at armed support which was fatal to the
Assembly. Its doom was earlier sealed ; when by much
baulking of the popular will it had hopelessly alienated
' its invisible sentinel, the people.' To hide the fact of
that estrangement from posterity and from themselves
both royalist and republican historians have assumed that
at the critical moment the sentinel slept at his post. The
mischief lay deeper. When the Assembly was struck down
the ' invisible sentinel ' was not caught napping : he
merely watched—and laughed.

---

[1] *Cf.* Proudhon, writing 19 Dec. 51. ' Tout ce qu'on a dit à ce sujet
est dénué de sens politique. Si le 17 novembre, la gauche s'était unie à
la droite pour requérir les troupes et décréter le Président, vous auriez eu
le 18 novembre ce que vous avez eu le 2 décembre, et avec le même succès.
Les mesures étaient prises à l'Élysée, et toutes les apparences en sa faveur.
L'opinion lui aurait même encore moins fait défaut.   Devant un décret qui
violait, quoi qu'on en ait dit, la Constitution, devant une coalition entre la
gauche et la droite contre l'homme qui représentait à la fois le suffrage
universel, l'ordre, et même la révolution, la masse qui, le 2 décembre, dans
un cas bien moins favorable à l'Élysée, n'a soufflé mot, aurait couru à son
aide.' *Proudhon*, iv. 147–148. But for a denial of both these contentions,
v. *Chambolle*, 289, 291.

CHAPTER V

CUTTING THE CORDS

Quidam putant captum imperii consuetudine, pensitatisque suis et inimicorum viribus, usum occasione rapiendæ dominationis quam ætate prima concupisset. Quod existimasse videbatur et Cicero, scribens semper Cæsarem in ore habuisse Euripidis versus, quos sic ipse convertit :

nam si violandum est ius regnandi gratia
violandum est : aliis rebus pietatem colas.

SUETONIUS.

ON the 1st of December 1851 Louis Napoleon gave a small dinner-party, followed by his usual Monday evening reception, at the Elysée. During the opening months of his presidency these receptions had been informal to a degree : few men of note had graced the half-furnished salons of this upstart official.[1] But latterly, with the growing importance of the President's position, the social attractions of the Elysée had increased ; on this occasion the Prince's reception-rooms were thronged[2] by a brilliant assemblage of officers, diplomats, deputies, French and foreign nobility with their ladies attendant. Louis Napoleon received his guests with his customary quiet courtesy ; and his manner gave no hint to his guests that anything unusual was afoot. To one of them, a municipal councillor of Paris,[3] he spoke at some length of his plans for the rebuilding and embellishment of the capital :[4]

---

[1] *Evans,* i. 6 ; *Delord,* i. 283.   [2] *Times,* 3 Dec. 51, p. 5.
[3] M. Merruau. *Merruau,* 457.
[4] Haussmann, his actual instrument in hacking his ways through Paris, was also a chance guest at this reception : at which Louis charged him to proceed next morning to Bordeaux as prefect, first calling—' if possible before daybreak '—at the Ministry of the Interior for important instructions. This Haussmann did at 5 a.m., to find a new minister in possession, and himself a willing co-operator in the *coup d'état. Haussmann,* i. 474.

with others he discussed a bye-election which had taken place in Paris on the previous day. This election, of which the result was announced in the actual course of the evening, was the occasion of a new and notable act of co-operation between the *Parti d'Élysée* and the Republicans. For at it the Bonapartists no less than the Republicans refused to vote ; thus testifying that in their eyes also the May Law was now unconstitutional, and elections held under it of no effect.

When no other topic distracted it, conversation turned at times, outside of the President's immediate circle, to rumours of a *coup d'état* : [1] but languidly and without interest, for as a theme of conversation the subject had long lost all edge of freshness. Paris had grown used to the idea of it, and was becoming a little incredulous, and more than a little wearied, of the incessant rumours of the still unaccomplished coup. A score of times it had been predicted, and as often it had falsified its prophets. Time and again before now zealous members of parliament had sat up all night on some report of its impending occurrence, only to be laughed at for their pains next morning in the Bonapartist press. Perhaps a certain disgusted deputy [2] was right, who after receiving a midnight summons and sharing one of these November vigils came to the conclusion that the real source of these false alarms was the Elysée itself. Other rumours as useful to their purpose were almost certainly fabricated at this time by the authors of the *coup d'état*. Of these the most serviceable was that of an imminent royalist *coup d'état* ; it had been the real object of the Questor's Proposition, said the Bonapartists, to facilitate such a stroke ; a stroke which the defeat of that proposal had only momentarily postponed.[3] The beauty of such rumours was that they served the President's turn almost equally well whether they were believed or not : an atmosphere was produced of general uncertainty in the one case or general incredulity in the other ; and from

---

[1] *Maupas*, i. 298 ; *Cassagnac*, ii. 398.   [2] M. *Joigneaux*, ii. 72, 73.
[3] For a detailed but unconvincing contention that this plot was genuine and its execution imminent, *v.* Palmerston's memorandum in *Ashley*, ii. 200–202. See also Appendix B, p. 390, below.

hearing of *coups d'état* everywhere men passed easily into disbelieving in them anywhere.

Even those who stopped short of final scepticism had ceased to expect any immediate action now that December was come. ' We have at least a clear month ahead of us,' said General Changarnier : [1] a *coup d'état* could hardly do less than observe the amenities of a general election, by avoiding a date gratuitously inconvenient to the Christmas trade. No one surely would be more anxious than the President not to annoy the small shopkeepers of Paris.

This impression Louis himself had been careful to confirm. Two days ago he had addressed a calculated indiscretion to a deputy entirely attached to his cause, but given, as he had discovered from previous experience, to the habit of circulating widely among his acquaintances any semi-confidences with which the President might honour him. To this devoted busybody Louis had re-marked expansively after dinner on Saturday evening, ' that there was nothing for it now but to wait patiently : that the Assembly were determined not to furnish him with any occasions, and therefore nothing could be done but to show moderation.' Big and bursting with his secret the deputy had hurried away ; among the many to whom the remark had been repeated within an hour of its utterance was the British ambassador, Lord Normanby.[2]

A close observer at this later reception on Monday evening might have noticed that in the course of it the President withdrew for a few minutes about eight o'clock and again at nine, to the room of his private secretary, M. Mocquard. Permitted to accompany Louis to this sanctum, he would doubtless have applauded the secretary's zeal, on discovering him engaged in methodically sorting and docketing packets of papers ; but he would perhaps have wondered why the President, before returning to his guests, stayed to endorse one such package in pencil with the word ' Rubicon.' [3]

[1] *Barrot*, iv. 213.
[2] F.O. France, Normanby to Palmerston, 3 Dec. 51.
[3] *Véron*, vi. 171, and see v. 247 ; *Ténot: Paris*, 107.

Later in the evening the same intelligent spectator, had
he been present, might have found food for thought in
another little scene, transacted this time in the reception
room itself.   Louis was back among his guests, leaning
against the mantelpiece ; a young officer was passing by,
the most notable Bonapartist commander in the most
notable anti-Bonapartist force in Paris—Colonel Vieyra,
recently and inexplicably promoted to a high command
in the Second Battalion of the Paris National Guards.   To
him Louis beckoned lightly, and then—fearing the French
habit of gesticulation so alien to his own manner—' Colonel,'
he said in a low voice, ' can you keep a calm face if you
hear important news ? ' [1]   The Colonel thought he could.
' Well then, it is for to-night.   Can you make certain that
the call to arms will not be sounded to-morrow ? '   The
Colonel was sure he could ; given men enough to carry out
certain necessary measures that had already been resolved
upon.   And next morning the National Guard discovered
that all their drums were burst [2] and all their powder was
wet : whence the more intelligent of them divined that the
coup d'etat was upon them at last.

Shortly after ten the President took leave of his guests,
and withdrew finally to join his secretary in his study.
From the walls a portrait of Hortense looked down on both
her sons.   For Louis was accompanied by his half-brother,[3]
M. de Morny, one of the latest arrivals at the public
reception that evening.   That night had seen the first
performance of a new play at the Opéra Comique ; and the
Count had been present in his box at the earlier acts,
very much in evidence.   Rumour had already assigned
him a prominent rôle in the coming *coup d'etat* ; hence his
presence at such a function tended to lull suspicion.   A few
minutes later the trio were joined by Saint-Arnaud [4] and
Maupas, who had just bidden the President good-night and
passed out by the main entrance of the reception hall ; only
to make their way back at once by a side door and private

---

[1] *Mayer*, 47.   [2] *Pierre*, ii. 641.
[3] ' If you believe the people in the Salons, the President is not the son
of his father, and everybody else is the son of his mother.'   *Bagehot*, i. 112.
[4] On Saint-Arnaud's antecedents, see *Fleury*, i. 129–153.

passage to Louis Napoleon's study. One other arrival
completed the party : somewhat to the annoyance of his
later allies, Louis had insisted that Persigny, the accomplice
of his youthful adventures at Strasburg and Boulogne,
should have a share in this last and most desperate coup
of all.

So soon as the five other conspirators were all present,
the President unfastened his packet labelled Rubicon, and
read out to them his written proclamation to the French
army and people. Persigny as he listened to the rolling
phrases must have felt that this was indeed like old times :
on this occasion however there was no need of Dr Conneau
and his hand-press : [1] the national printing-house, with
certain preliminary precautions, could be entrusted with
the task of translating these latest manifestoes into type.
Once more, as at that last nocturnal meeting on the eve of
the Strasburg insurrection, each conspirator rehearsed the
part he was to play in the coming adventure, recapitulating
the various measures for which each was severally responsible ; reassuring one another and themselves that no
hitch was possible. Shortly after eleven the meeting broke
up. Morny, whose rôle as Minister of the Interior only
devolved on him at five the next morning, returned to his
calculated round of gaieties ; a rubber of whist at the
Jockey Club formed a pleasant and effective finale to his
evening's obvious amusements. Louis Napoleon went to
bed, first ordering his valet to call him at five o'clock on the
morrow ; an hour not so much in advance of his usual time
of rising as to occasion any surprise to his servants. They
were among the last in fact to hear the news of the *coup
d'état*, only learning the truth of the report from the servants
of the British embassy when all was over.[2]

Saint-Arnaud and Maupas did not go to bed. The latter
on leaving the Elysée took with him in his carriage an aide-
de-camp of Louis Napoleon's, Colonel Béville, who had
been summoned to the council just before its close at
half-past eleven.[3] Together they drove to the *Imprimerie*

---

[1] See *Simpson*, 172 *n.*   [2] *Gronow*, ii. 162.
[3] *Cassagnac*, i. 216

Nationale, where Béville was deposited with the manuscript of the proclamations. In the courtyard he found a company of armed police which had just arrived, ignorant of the nature of its errand, but captained by a devoted adherent of the Prince's. The greater part of this force the colonel disposed as a cordon round the building ; entering at the head of the remainder he stationed sentinels at every door and window with instructions to shoot anyone who attempted to escape. The director of the establishment had already received orders to have a special staff of compositors ready for an important piece of night work ; the order had given rise to no suspicion, since the Government had made a point of having some entirely innocent printing done by night on several previous occasions. It was close on midnight when the printers, hermetically sealed in their printing-house, began to put Louis Napoleon's proclamations into type. The work proceeded slowly ; for by an almost superfluous refinement of caution, no single workman was allowed to handle more than a few fragmentary sentences of the proclamations ; [1] thus the very printers were supposed to be prevented from fully understanding the nature of their task. It was not until five o'clock that Béville was able to deliver the proclamations to Maupas at the *préfecture de police* ; gangs of bill-stickers were already waiting there for them, in conveyances ready to carry them at once to every quarter of Paris ; by half-past seven the whole city was placarded, and an hour later the bill-stickers had done their work in the uttermost suburbs.

But the posting of the proclamations was but one among many details which Maupas had to supervise during the night of December 1. It was thought necessary to the success of the *coup d'état* that some eighty persons, capable of becoming centres of resistance to it, should be placed under arrest for a few days. It was only with some difficulty that the President's assent had been won to this measure : it would be better to arrest no one, he urged : a mere appeal to the nation would suffice. But De Morny

[1] *Delord,* i. 287.

overbore him : in effect on the grounds that the arrests would 'save time and prevent argument.'[1] Besides 'made judiciously' they might avert civil war.[2] The secret and simultaneous arrest of eighty prominent citizens residing in fifty different parts of Paris was however a somewhat ticklish matter. A single attempted capture bungled would suffice to give the alarm. Eight hundred police had to be put in motion at dead of night without any previous preparation for their errand. For the success of the *coup d'état* could not safely be made to depend on the keeping of a secret shared by eight hundred policemen.

But Maupas had made his preparations carefully. Several times during the last few weeks he had called out large bodies of police at night, on the pretext of guarding against some socialist conspiracy. The day before the *coup d'état* he circulated a rumour that Ledru-Rollin and some other red Republicans from London were meditating a midnight appearance in Paris on the night of December 1. His request that eight hundred men should hold themselves at his absolute disposal during that night occasioned therefore no surprise. Between three o'clock and half-past four in the morning of December 2, De Maupas interviewed in turn and by appointment some sixty sergeants of police.[3] Each was furnished with the name and address of the general or deputy whom he was to apprehend ; each was told the exact spot at which he would find a posse of police waiting to execute his orders ; and each was despatched on his individual errand before the arrival of his successor, so that he might remain in ignorance of the fact that any other arrest was being effected that night at all. Here, as in the printing of the proclamations, Louis Napoleon's agents realised the advantages of division of labour. For the rest, each sergeant was to forgather with his subordinates by the doorway of his victim at five minutes past six : at a quarter past precisely he was to make his entry. And as each officer before he left had set his watch by M. Maupas' clock,[4] there was little room for

---

[1] 'On n'a plus à sévir contre des gens en prison.' *Véron*, vi. 162.
[2] *Ibid.*   [3] *Maupas*, i. 310.   [4] *Cassagnac*, i. 220.

miscarriage, None at any rate occurred : before seven
o'clock in the morning, without violence and without
noise, eight-and-seventy deputies, demagogues, generals,
and journalists had been quietly conveyed to the fortress
of Mazas.

Meanwhile the new Minister of War had not been idle.
At three o'clock Saint-Arnaud sent for General Magnan,
Commander of the Army of Paris, and informed him that
the time for action was come. Magnan, when sounded as
to his conduct in the event of a *coup d'état*, had already
promised his aid, stipulating however that he should only
be told what was required of him at the last moment.
Since at 3 a.m. on December 2 Saint-Arnaud was already
Minister of War, the military conscience of Magnan was
satisfied that in obeying him he would merely be obeying
orders transmitted in regular course from a superior in
command. Now, in the small hours of December 2, he
received the expected summons ; and obeyed it with an
alacrity and absence of scruple which throws some light
on his probable course of action had Louis Napoleon
scored an initial success at Boulogne in 1840. Under
Magnan's direction the Palais Bourbon, the meeting-place
of the Assembly, was seized by troops ; the strategical
positions in the city were occupied in force, and the
garrisons of Versailles and St Germain were summoned to
the city.

At half-past six the night's work was completed by the
instalment of Morny as Minister of the Interior. His first
care was to telegraph to the provinces glowing accounts of
the enthusiastic reception with which Paris had welcomed
the President's action ; an enthusiasm which, it was
implied, the recipient of the telegram was expected to
share. Fortunately the provincial prefect is not accustomed
to criticise the official communications of central authority.
A fastidious critic might have quarrelled both with the
manner and the matter of Morny's telegrams. For if
there were a worse epistolary *gaucherie* conceivable than
the phrase ' Thanking you in anticipation ' it would surely
be ' Anticipating your thanks.' Moreover the news itself

was a slight though perhaps an intelligent anticipation of
events. In point of fact when the telegrams were dispatched, Paris had not yet had an opportunity of expressing its gratitude for what it had received.

For the Parisian is not in general addicted to the habit
of early rising ; nor does a raw December morning offer any
particular temptation to the practice. It was not until
half-past seven that small bodies of working men, setting
out towards their morning labour, began to collect in groups
round the President's newly-posted proclamations, con-
spicuous upon the walls alike by their size and colour.[1]
Generally the most expert reader was deputed to read them
aloud to his fellows ; who expressed their opinions of each
clause as they heard it, with oaths or laughter or applause.
Usually the last predominated,[2] for the manifestoes were
cleverly written. First there was a decree. The Assembly
—that discredited reactionary Assembly—was dissolved.
The May Law,—the law which had stolen the people's
votes—was repealed. Universal suffrage—the bedrock of
popular sovereignty—was restored. The Republic, thanks
to Louis Napoleon's present stroke against monarchical
conspiracy, was maintained. And the People, whose
voice would be law, the People would vote Yes or No to
those things a fortnight hence. The decree was flanked
with proclamations to the Army and People of France.
' I count on you,' wrote Louis to the Army, ' not to violate
the law, but to make respected the first law of the land, the
sovereignty of the nation, of which I am the legitimate
representative. The Assembly tried to attenuate the
authority which I held from the nation as a whole : it has
ceased to exist. . . . Soldiers, your history is mine. In
the past we have tasted glory and disaster together : the
future holds for us a common devotion to the repose and
grandeur of France.'[3] The proclamation to the people
began by denouncing the Assembly as a centre of intrigue,
a source of disturbance, a mere nursery of monarchical

[1] Since 1848, only government placards were allowed to be printed on
white paper. *Gronow*, ii. 165.
[2] *Hugo* : ' *Histoire*,' 164.
[3] For the proclamations in full, v. *Times*, 3 Dec. 51, p. 5.

civil war : this Assembly 'I have dissolved : I call the people to judge between it and me.' Against the constitution, in so far as it was expressly composed to restrict the power which the people had determined to confer on him—against this constitution their six million votes cast for him in 1848 had already been an implied protest : yet even thus protested against he had faithfully observed it hitherto. 'But to-day when the fundamental compact is thrown to the winds by the very men who have incessantly invoked it : when men who have already lost two monarchies wish to tie my hands in order that they may destroy the Republic also, to-day it becomes my duty to save the Republic and the country by appealing to the solemn judgment of the people—the sole sovereign I recognise in France.' Convinced that the feebleness of the executive together with the single-chamber system were permanent occasions of the present discontents, Louis propounded for the people's acceptance the outlines of a constitution : a responsible head of the State elected for ten years, with ministers dependent on him ; a Council of State, a Senate, a legislative body and other institutions resembling those of the Consulate of 1799. If the people did not ratify his proposal, he would at once convoke a new Assembly and resign his power into their hands ; but if they still believed in the cause of which his name was the symbol—France regenerated by the revolution and organised by the Emperor—then they would proclaim their opinion by ratifying his authority with their vote. In any case, for the first time since 1804 they would have an opportunity of voting with their eyes open, really knowing *pour qui et pourquoi.*

These proclamations were admirably calculated to conciliate the classes who would be the first to read them ; at first sight they had all the appearance of a bold vindication of democratic rights in the face of reactionary opposition. Moreover there was an air and gusto about the President's language, a hardihood and adroitness in his sudden action, that appealed to the sporting instincts of the working man. *C'est bien joué, bien touche* ; were

among the commonest exclamations of the first readers of
the manifestoes : followed not infrequently by the spoken
reflection ' Now we can vote again.' [1] Even the rumour
of the arrests was hailed by the workmen with a little
spiteful pleasure. Thiers, author of that famous phrase
' the vile multitude,' Thiers and his royalist friends had
talked at large about the impending impeachment and
imprisonment of the President : and here they were,
prettily clapped in prison themselves. He had been more
than a match for them, then, this Louis Napoleon ! And
without more ado the workman moved on to his work :
whilst the concierges and domestic servants who had more
recently joined the groups, hastened back to wake their
masters with the news. These in their turn hurried down
into the streets to read the proclamations for themselves.
Shop-keepers and small business men, whom no mirror
delayed in the dressing, were the first to arrive ; they too
read the proclamations, less complacently indeed than the
workmen, but without visible protest. The workman had
not resented because he had not realised the theft of his
political liberties. The shop-keeper saw through the cun-
ningly devised phrases, but consoled himself easily for the
loss of his parliamentary representatives by the prospect
of better business and securer markets.

It was left to citizens who were something more than shop-
keepers to read the proclamations with discernment and
pure anger.[2] These were generally among the latest to
arrive, Parisians of more aristocratic deportment, gentlemen
whose appearance in the boulevards must be preceded by
a leisurely toilet though Paris itself were in the throes of a
revolution. Sympathisers for the most part with the mon-

---

[1] ' The general remark of the operatives was " Ma foi, il a bien fait :
maintenant nous voterons puisqu'il a rétabli le suffrage universel." ' *Times*,
3 Dec. 51, p. 5, c. 3.

[2] The only sign of disturbance Victor Hugo could discover in the working-
class districts of Paris on Tuesday was the spectacle of two men quarrelling
in an argument for and against the *coup d'etat* : ' celui qui était pour avait
un blouse, celui qui était contre avait un habit.' *Hugo* : ' *Histoire*,' 158. And
even on Wednesday an English correspondent wrote : ' The workmen and
artisans are calm, and do not seem by any means so much enraged as the
bourgeoisie and the upper classes.' *Morning Chronicle*, 5 Dec. 51, p. 5,
c. 6 (written on Dec. 3). So too, *Limet*, 189.

archical majority of the dissolved Assembly, they both saw
and hated the meaning of the proclamations. But even of
this small minority, the clearer-minded perceived that there
was just enough of truth in Napoleon's charges to render
resistance all but hopeless of success. It was true that the
people cared little for the constitution, which with all its
cast-iron safeguards against revision had been riveted upon
them without their ratification. The President could
safely vilify an Assembly whose members, however unjustly,
were considered more careful of their salaries than of the
prosperity of France ; he could attack with impunity a body
whose crowning repudiation of universal suffrage had left
it destitute of popular support. And not discernment only,
but a certain innate fastidiousness served to deter these
royalist spectators from any rough resistance of the *coup
d'état*. The President's act could not now be reversed unless
the gentlemen who saw and hated deigned to enlighten the
workmen who might have hated if they had seen. But to do
this the aristocrat must sink his dignity and soil his clothes ;
must condescend to the common crowd, must mingle with
unwashen workmen and assist at all manner of unsavoury
details ; first helping to build barricades, and then perhaps
dying messily in the midst of them. It was a dirty deed,
but actual opposition to it would be dirty too : a sneer, an
epigram, a washing of the hands, these were the limits of
aristocratic opposition in such a case. Meanwhile it was
early to be out in the streets ; the morning was still raw,
and all these things could be done more comfortably in
one's club, in the company of one's peers. And to his
hotel or club or café the gentleman of Paris proceeded
gracefully, while without the vulgar quarrel should settle
itself as best it might.

As a result, acquiescence—eager, complacent, or indifferent—was the general attitude of the capital on the
morning of the *coup d'état*. 'I have walked through the
principal thoroughfares of Paris from seven o'clock this
morning until 12 o'clock, the moment at which I am
writing,' reported a *Times* correspondent, on December 2,
uninformed as yet of the policy of his proprietors, ' I have

entered into conversation with the *Blouses* reading the President's decree, and I have not heard one word of disapprobation by anybody at the President's *coup d'état.*' [1] And another correspondent, writing four hours later, could only echo in the afternoon what his colleague had said in the morning. ' All my accounts from the faubourgs are unanimous in declaring that the people are well pleased at what has been done.' [2]

This latter report was based on observation of a testing of popular opinion by Louis Napoleon himself. A little before ten, clad in General's uniform, he descended into the courtyard of the Elysée, whither a considerable body of his well-wishers, political and military, had already forgathered. His favourite English charger was led up : Louis vaulted into the saddle amid enthusiastic cries of ' *Vive Napoléon* ' from the assembled troops. Brandished swords and waving handkerchiefs gave the cavalcade a tumultuous send-off as it passed out into the street towards the Place de la Concorde. Of the impression produced by the ride a stray testimony survives in the reminiscences of an English officer, Captain Gronow of the Grenadier Guards. Still something of a dandy, though a veteran of the Peninsula campaign, he had dropped in to a barber's on Louis' line of route to get shaved. The operation was protracted, for the barber ' was in a state of great excitement, expatiating on the many virtues of Prince Louis Napoleon ; with which he had become acquainted from having on two occasions dressed the hair of the chambermaid whose duty it was to lay the fire over-night in the cabinet of the President, which he himself generally lighted at an early hour in the morning. The excellent *soubrette* could never speak in sufficiently high terms of the gentleness and amiable temper of her master, and the worthy barber had caught the infection.' Other customers, waiting to have their beards trimmed, began to grow impatient : interjections of dis-

---

[1] *Times,* 3 Dec. 51, p. 5, c. 3. Of the same morning, he wrote two days later : ' To a stranger the scene bore the semblance of a carnival, and the passage of the military a pageant which excited the cheers and applause of the populace.' *Ibid.,* 6 Dec. 51, p. 5, c. 3.
[2] *Ibid.*

agreement became frequent ; Republicans were fast in the making ; when suddenly a cry arose that the Prince himself was passing by. ' Away everyone rushed out to see the passing show, and upon their return there was a universal opinion expressed, that the Prince-President looked like a noble soldier, and " every inch a king " : his gallant bearing had evidently produced a strong impression upon the spectators, the majority of whom from that moment were evidently in favour of the changes that had taken place.' [1]

Spectators of the Prince in any case had no difficulty in seeing him. For though an advance guard of mounted cavalry went in front to clear the way, Louis Napoleon followed behind alone upon his war-horse ; [2] not flanked, as is the manner of majesty even when carriage-driven among peaceful citizens, by bands of outriders whose ever-changing pace should distract the aim of any disloyal pistol. To right and left, a little behind, followed Jerome [3] and Saint-Arnaud ; Magnan with a number of officers brought up the rear. ' I met the President of the Republic at eleven o'clock,' wrote a *Times* correspondent, ' crossing the Pont Royal. He bowed right and left and raised his cocked hat to the crowds. Most of the men raised their hats in return and there was some cheering, but no enthusiasm. He was followed by an immense mob shouting *Vive la République!* [4] which they were permitted to do in full liberty. Everyone was suffered to express himself as he wished without molestation.' [5] On the whole Louis had no reason to be dissatisfied with the result of his

---

[1] *Gronow*, ii. 167, 168.

[2] *Sonolet*, i. 46. ' Louis Napoleon does not conceal himself, and his open confidence in the people elicits favourable cries.' Tuesday, 4 p.m. Correspondent of *Morning Herald*, 3 Dec. 51, p. 5, c. 1.

[3] Like his son, Jerome was careful to have a foot in both camps until the success of the *coup d'état* was assured ; on the following day Prince Napoleon actually attended a meeting of the Republican Committee of Resistance. *Beslay*, 241. See also on his action on this occasion, *Ollivier*, ii. 466, *Maupas*, i. 236, *Rochefort*, i. 132 and *Du Casse* : *Coup d'état*, passim. It was Du Casse who induced Jerome to join his nephew in the ride. *Ibid.* 86.

[4] To a *Morning Herald* correspondent (3 Dec. 51, p. 5, c. 1) one of the utterers of this cry explained that as a matter of course it was intended as a cheer for Louis Napoleon, ' because he has declared for the Republic and has restored universal suffrage.'

[5] *Times*, 3 Dec. 51, p. 5, c. 3.

excursion ; on his return to the Elysée he received a number
of generals, ministers and ambassadors : those of Austria,
Russia, and Spain were profuse in their congratulations on
his deed.   In the evening Turgot, his new Minister of
Foreign Affairs, gave an official dinner party, at which
the varied demeanours of the guests reflected the attitudes
of their different countries to the *coup d'état* : Normanby
sombre, the Belgian minister anxious and perturbed,
Austria's obviously cheerful, and the representative of
King Bomba most cock-a-hoop of all.[1]

Yet there was present that night another minister
who had greater right by far to jubilation than the
ambassador of Austria or of Naples.   On the morrow of the
coup d'état the Sardinian minister at Paris called on the
President at the Elysée to offer his congratulations.   ' I
found the Prince,' he wrote, ' a man transfigured.   *Lui
naguère si sombre vint à moi tout souriant, et me dit en propres
termes : "A présent que je puis faire ce que je veux, je ferai
quelque chose pour l'Italie.   Vous pouvez le mander à votre
gouvernement."* ' [2]   This interview, besides its intrinsic importance, is incidentally of interest on other grounds.   For it
occurred on one of the two days of this week—Dec. 3 and 4
—on which Louis stayed indoors.   Of this fact the equally
invisible [3] Victor Hugo made the most, as did his disciple
Kinglake.   ' In an inner room,' wrote the English author,
' with his back to the daylight, they say he sat bent over a
fireplace for hours and hours together, resting his elbows on
his knees, and burying his face in his hands.' [4]   During those
two days in fact the President gave audiences as usual : and
all accounts of those who saw him describe him as serene and
confident.   But he was clearly ill-advised in not again
appearing in the streets.   How desirable it was that he
should do so he had himself the sense to see ; urging that

[1] *Hübner*, i. 35.   [2] *Reiset*, i. 465.
[3] On the purely fanciful character of all that portion of Hugo's ' *Histoire* '
which describes its author as ' in imminent peril of his life, tracked by
Bonapartist spies and only just escaping by the skin of his teeth,' v.
Davidson, 210.   ' In reality, the game of hide-and-seek seems to have been
one in which it was all hide and no seek.'
[4] *Kinglake*, i. 258.   On the characteristic *on dit*, see Bibliography, p. 382
below.

the danger if there were any was but reason the more for his going. But his protests were overborne by the united pressure of his fellow-conspirators : if any stray bullet were to strike him, insisted Magnan, all who had risked their lives for him would lose them. To this last argument Louis yielded.[1]

For the moment the chance of even a stray bullet seemed remote. For Paris remained quiet : on the day of the *coup d'état* the only notable protest against the President's action in dissolving the Assembly came from members of the dissolved Assembly itself. In taking possession of the Palais Bourbon, the troops had accidentally omitted to guard a small side door of the Assembly house ; through this door, at ten o'clock on the morning of December 2, some fifty deputies had entered the Chamber, whither they summoned M. Dupin, the President of the Assembly, to meet them. But despite his office it had been the crowning cleverness of the authors of the *coup d'état*, when in the small hours of the morning they had locked up the sixteen deputies from whom alone they feared real resistance, to leave M. Dupin to sleep in peace. For the man did not exist better qualified to bungle any business, to belittle a great occasion, to damp the ardour of his own followers, enervating their resistance and dissipating their courage—than M. Dupin.[2]

He was now huddled [3] into his official robes, and conducted to the Assembly room. The deputies rose to greet their President, prepared for some heroic scene in the presence of the already advancing soldiers. Instead they were soused with a short speech. ' Gentlemen,' said M. Dupin, ' it is evident that the constitution is being violated. Right is with us, but might is with them : I can only invite you to retire.' [4] Then as a few indignant colleagues

---

[1] *Canrobert*, i. 534, 535.   *Fleury*, i. 174.   ' According to what has been told me on good authority about his behaviour on Dec. 2 he possesses a personal courage far excelling that of his uncle.'   *Ernest*, ii. 77.

[2] *Barrot*, iv. 217.

[3] According to *Hugo* : ' *Histoire*,' 74, he was forced by other deputies both into them and into the Chamber.

[4] *Jerrold*, iii. 249.   *Schoelcher* : ' *Crimes*,' 91.   *Lefranc*, 165.

expostulated and gesticulated their disagreement, ' Gentlemen, gentlemen,' he cried, ' you are making more noise
than all these soldiers put together.' [1] And with this
entirely true but not very helpful remark the President
withdrew, and was seen no more that day ; leaving these
same commendably silent soldiers to hustle the disgusted
deputies out of the house.

An hour later they reassembled in far larger numbers
at a neighbouring town-hall ; some two hundred and
twenty members succeeded in effecting a meeting in the
Mairie of the 10th arrondissement. Here, in the article
of its dissolution, the Assembly took on a melancholy
dignity long alien to its debates. Dignified and legal
protest against an illegal usurpation was all that it could
hope to effect ; for of the members so assembled the great
majority were Royalists, less anxious to preserve the
Republic than to avoid the Empire. At this supreme
hour of their corporate existence a leader emerged from their
ranks who was all that Dupin was not. Berryer, the great
legitimist orator, the advocate whose eloquence had
defended Louis Napoleon when he was tried for his life
after Boulogne—Berryer it was who dominated the last
legal resistance of France.[2] A clear lead of some kind was
much needed. The room was badly ventilated and
stiflingly hot.[3] Moreover it was crowded. For besides
the actual deputies there were present on the floor of the
house a number of enthusiastic strangers. ' But in an
hour's time we may have given our lives for you ' protested
one of them, when it was proposed that they should be
asked to leave the house. And in the applause which
greeted the remark the motion was lost.[4] Other proposals
followed thick and fast ; in fact half the members wished to
speak at once, and would have done so had not Berryer
reminded them that they could count on barely a quarter
of an hour in which to die. And in that quarter of an hour,
above the confused noise of deputies suggesting good things,[5]

---

[1] *Barrot,* iv. 224.   [2] *Falloux,* ii. 137.
[3] *Chambolle,* 305.   [4] *Ibid.,* 306.
[5] For a verbatim report of the debate, see *L'Indépendance Belge,* 16 Dec.
51. Probably however it is very much ' touched up.'   v. *Belouino,* 109.

passing resolutions—that last infirmity of the irresolute—
boomed ever and anon the great voice of Berryer : dictating decrees, deposing the President, transferring to General
Oudinot [1] the command of the army : an impotent but
not unwarlike fusillade, less the last broadside of a beaten
battleship than the forlorn echoes of some great minute
gun, vainly summoning help to the sinking ship.

For no help came. A large number of spectators it is
true had by this time collected in the street. But when
Berryer by way of appealing to the country strode to the
window—the room was on the first floor—and began to
harangue the crowd outside, the limitations of his eloquence
were soon visible. ' It was easy to see,' wrote one of the
deputies [2] sadly, ' that we were not popular enough to rouse
the people.' For while there were not many cries for
Napoleon there were far fewer still for the Assembly : most
of the crowd ' merely laughed, and seemed to look on the
whole affair as a game in which we were taken as rats in
a trap.' [3]

Meanwhile soldiers were arriving : few in number at
first and civil in their bearing ; for most of the assembled
deputies were Royalists, with whom Louis Napoleon had
not the least desire to quarrel. Later, as the Chamber
continued in session, more troops arrived ; still very
civilly, but intolerant of further eloquence, they conducted
the docile deputies to a neighbouring barracks. By twenty
past three they were all under lock and key ; between six
and seven they were served from a neighbouring restaurant
with an excellent dinner,[4] and afterwards—save for a few
who said that their people would be getting anxious about

---

[1] Leaving him loose had been another cleverness of the conspirators :
of proved incompetence he was also odious to the Republicans as the
personification of the Roman Expedition.

[2] *Melun*, ii. 92.

[3] *Ibid.*, 91. *Cf.* Proudhon to Edmond, 19 Dec. 51. ' La masse, sur
laquelle on comptait, a trouvé l'affaire tout à fait réjouissante ; des
représentants à vingt-cinq francs jetés à la porte, cela lui a semblé drole.'
Proudhon, iv. 148. On the circumstances which made Proudhon a
spectator of the events of Dec. 2 in Paris, see *Ranc*, 80–82 ; *Proudhon*,
iv. 160.

[4] *Barrot*, iv. 229. *Quentin-Bauchart*, i. 437. But at their own expense,
complains *Chambolle*, 306. All three were among the prisoners.

them—comfortably interned for the night. Other occupants
were forthcoming for the places of those who went home
owing to the delicate health of their wives. For several
royalist deputies who had only reached the Town Hall
after the Assembly had been dissolved, managed to find
their way on to the barracks : there they insisted that
they also had the right to be made prisoners ; it was not
their fault that they had been late ; after some parley the
soldiers consented to humour them.[1] Once arrested, the
conservative deputies had all the glory of political martyrdom, with none of the risks incidental to the manning
of barricades. Early next morning they were driven out
in omnibuses from the barracks to join their colleagues at
Mazas and Vincennes. There they at least showed signs
of resistance when the government attempted to set them
at liberty. For when two days later their prison doors
were opened a number of them sturdily refused to leave
the fortress. So eagerly did they hug their chains that
their gaolers were driven to liberate them by guile. A line
of carriages was drawn up outside the fortress, destined,
so the deputies were told, to take them to some more
distant prison. In this belief the deputies entered 'the
carriages without demur, hoping for a better martyrdom.
Instead they were driven half-way to Paris, and then
informed that they were free to walk home.[2] If they
persisted in remaining in their carriages, they could stay
there in the arid plain that lay at that time between
Paris and Vincennes. But in that case they must
excuse their gaolers if before leaving them they first took
out the horses, for use on their own homeward journey.
Realising that further imprisonment was now impossible,
the deputies bowed to the inevitable and resumed their
liberty.

So ended the resistance of the royalist deputies to the
coup d'état, a resistance which throughout had been

[1] *v.* an unsigned letter by Alexis de Tocqueville, *Times*, 11 Dec. 51, p. 5.
Among the deputies who insisted on being arrested, very elegantly dressed,
was Eugène Sue, the harmless occasion of the May Law. *Canrobert*, i. 535.
Hugo : ' *Histoire*,' 72.
[2] *Barrot*, iv. 233.

histrionic rather than heroic.[1] Many of them in a few weeks, some in a few days, were openly to rally to the President's cause.

Meanwhile their protest had at any rate been a shade less feeble than the only other which occurred on the day of the *coup d'état*. By the terms of the constitution [2] any infringement of it by the President was to be dealt with in the first instance by the High Court of Justice. The members of the court, under pain of forfeiting their office, were bound to meet instantly on the news of a *coup d'état*, and decree the deposition of its perpetrator. They did in fact meet at a little after eleven, and began very leisurely to prepare the necessary decree. Anxious above all things not to sign it they were forced by the negligence of the government to spin out their proceedings unmercifully ; at last however, at about one o'clock, the tardy troops arrived ; with scarcely concealed relief the judges dispersed to their homes, leaving their unsigned document behind them.[3] Save for these faint semblances of legal protest no opposition whatever was forthcoming to the *coup d'état* on the day which followed its occurrence. Paris remained to all appearance unconcerned.[4] Except in the boulevards people ' seemed to be at work as usual.' [5] While it was day the shops did not put up their shutters, the Law Courts did not adjourn, the restaurants remained open,[6] banks and warehouses transacted their business as usual. And in the evening the theatres produced their plays before full houses,[7] and the cafés afterwards closed if anything later than their usual hour.

---

[1] A fact which its republican opponents were not careful to disguise : e.g. *Schoelcher* : ' *Crimes*,' 118–120. *Vermorel* : 1851, 368–374.

[2] Art. 68.

[3] *Hugo* : ' *Histoire*,' 80–94. *Vermorel* : 1851, 373. *Schoelcher* : ' *Crimes*,' 143. *Mayer*, 91. *Cassagnac*, 39.

[4] ' Il y avait du monde sur les boulevards : partout ailleurs, pas la moindre apparence d'agitation ' was George Sand's impression on 2 Dec. ; *v.* her diary of this week published in *La Revue de Paris*, June 1904, pp. 673–690.

[5] *Globe*, 3 Dec. 51, p. 1, c. 6. Throughout the entire *coup d'état* ' scarcely any large manufactory stopped work for more than one day.' *Times*, 17 Dec. 51, p. 5, c. 1.

[6] *Delord*, i. 334. *Times*, 6 Dec. 51, p. 5, c. 3.

[7] *Ibid*. *Véron*, vi. 185. *Hugo* : ' *Histoire*,' 157.

The first faint signs of real resistance were forthcoming from another quarter on the following day. About nine o'clock in the morning of December 3, some half-dozen republican deputies in the full insignia of their office marched down the Faubourg Saint-Antoine, that historic centre of revolution in the past, and endeavoured to rouse its populace to resistance. Usually the workmen of Saint-Antoine were as eager for any pretext of street-fighting as ever the old London apprentices. But now they stood sullenly on their door-steps, and refused the fray : [1] what was the reactionary Assembly to them, that they should fight for it ?   The majority of its members were men who had approved and openly applauded the drastic suppression of their own last effort at civil war.   With the events of the June days of 1848 in their minds—their streets stricken with bullets, their barricades laid level by cannon shot—with the memory of their own wounds and their brothers' deaths still fresh before them, were they now to fight for the very men whom they regarded as the authors of their recent wrongs ?   Both directly and in-directly the June days discouraged resistance to the *coup d'état*.   To some extent they had emptied Paris of the old barricade-builders, and terrorised their incipient disciples. But the deterrent effect of all those thousands of deaths and deportations was not their sole result.   For the odium of them lay to the door not of the President but of the Republic ; Louis Napoleon had been still an exile while the constitution-makers were mowing down the people ; since his election he had notoriously done everything in his power to amnesty the surviving victims.   Never were June and December more ironically linked.

Earlier that very morning, escorted only by a handful of lancers, the imprisoned deputies had been driven on their way to Vincennes down that very street : it was then the hour when the working men were just setting out to their day's work : yet from this democratic place and throng, these constitutional martyrs had been greeted only with signs of ridicule and contempt.[2]   '*À bas les vingt-cinq*

[1] *Times*, 9 Dec. 51, p. 5, c. 1.   [2] v. *Canrobert*, i. 531.

francs!' had been the first cry that greeted them yesterday, when they emerged as prisoners from their temporary parliament-house.[1] On Wednesday morning on their own showing their reception was no whit more friendly.[2]

On the other hand the same workmen alleged as a reason for not fighting now that they had offered to fight earlier in the morning, and that their offer had been refused. They had been ready they said to stop the slow-moving buses containing the deputies, and to overpower their trivial escort : but the deputies themselves had begged them to desist.[3] It was in fact true that at one point in their passage through the Faubourg Saint-Antoine an attempt had been made to rescue the captive deputies by one of their republican colleagues. M. Malardier, assisted by a few vigorous supporters, had seized the horses' heads and so stopped the first omnibus ; the door of the bus was actually opened, yet its inmates declined to get out. But the workmen had in reality taken no part in the scene, of which they had merely been the amused spectators.[4] Still it is possible that if the deputies had consented to get out the workmen would have stopped laughing and lent them a helping hand. As it was it was scarcely to be wondered at that later canvassers of insurrection in the same street found recruits rare and excuses plentiful : scarcely a hundred men from all that fighting Faubourg were out for battle that day.

But even with a hundred men something may be done. Two small pickets of police were overpowered, and their thirty muskets appropriated.[5] Thus armed the insurgents held up the four first vehicles that came their way. A milkman and a baker contributed all unwillingly, each the van in which he was plying his morning trade.[6] A passing market cart was annexed ; an omnibus lumbering up the street was arrested in mid-career and laid upon its side. For such things are the raw material of barricades. This particular barricade was still in embryo : the four vehicles

---

[1] *Hugo* : '*Histoire*,' 117.   [2] E.g. *Barrot*, iv. 231.
[3] *Weill* : *Parti Républicain*, 357.
[4] *Delord*, i. 335, 336.   *Vermorel* : 1851, 376.
[5] *Schoelcher* : '*Crimes*,' 132.   [6] *Ibid. Durrieu*, 21.

placed alongside did not obstruct the entire breadth of the
Faubourg ; another omnibus at least was needed, and some
of the flags with which the side-walks were paved must be
dug up and added to the structure ere it could be pronounced complete of its kind. But at this moment a boy
ran up the street shouting ' *La Troupe !* ' And close behind
him three companies of soldiers were seen advancing at the
double. At the sight of them the hundred insurrectionary
recruits bethought them that their fellow-workmen, passive
on their door-steps, had chosen the better part of valour :
by the time the troops came within hail of the barricade its
hundred defenders had shrunk again into the original
handful of fifteen. But of these fifteen eight were deputies,
and of the eight one was Baudin.

' Why should we risk our lives for your twenty-five
francs ? ' said the vanishing hundred ; recurring to a taunt
with which many of their wiser brethren had refused to
assist the deputies in the first instance. For with their
occupation was gone also the deputies' salary of twenty-
five francs a day. ' Stay here,' Baudin is said to have
replied, ' and you shall see how a man dies for twenty-five
francs.' [1] And a few minutes later he was dead behind his
barricade. The troops had been ordered to avoid violence
if possible, and only to shoot if fired upon themselves.[2]
Hoping to overawe them the deputies advanced and bade
them halt in the name of the constitution. For a few
minutes civilians and soldiers stood facing each other, the
one side pleading the law, the other its orders. One deputy,
more urgent than the rest, was repelled by a soldier at last
with the point of his bayonet ; no wound was inflicted or
intended ; [3] the soldier wished merely to free himself from
the too-pressing advances of his *vis-a-vis*. But his action
was fatally misunderstood by the defenders of the barricade
behind. Thinking that their representative was being
attacked, they let fire ; a young soldier fell mortally
wounded, the troops without waiting for a command [4]

---

[1] *Schoelcher:* '*Crimes*,' 137. Schoelcher was present, but *Seignobos:*
France, 207, dismisses the remark—perhaps rightly—as a fabrication.
[2] *Times*, 5 Dec. 51, p. 5, c. 1. [3] *Hugo:* '*Histoire*,' 217.
[4] *Canrobert*, i. 530.

replied with a volley, and Baudin with one of his followers was killed. The rest fled,[1] the barricade was at once demolished ; and the soldiers passed on without further opposition through the silent street.

In later years Baudin was justly honoured as a martyr of the Second Republic : the first, and of his kind the last ; for no other deputy was killed or even wounded in opposing the *coup d'état*. But at the moment his death produced in Paris no such wave of indignation as swept Louis Philippe from his throne after the massacre outside the Foreign Office in February 1848. Although these three deaths, one military and two civilian, had at last stained the *coup d'état* with blood, they produced at the time no visible effect on public opinion at all.[2] The workmen, as the very deputy whose supposed assault occasioned the firing testifies, still replied that the fate of the Assembly was no concern of theirs.[3] Vainly in their robes of office Baudin's survivors trudged the weary streets : another hour of marching and speech-making had not brought the number of their adherents back to its previous high-water mark of a hundred : ' we could only recognise that the people did not wish to move : its choice was made.'[4]

None the less that Wednesday afternoon did witness the first signs of not quite isolated disapproval of the President's act. True, the working men of the East End still obstinately refused to take up arms : but west and south, along the stately boulevards, well-dressed citizens gathered to demonstrate their disaffection for the *coup d'état*. ' I assisted in the evening,' wrote Walter Bagehot to his father two days later,[5]

' at a great gathering in the Boulevards, and a man whose name I could not learn read a paper announcing the *déchéance* of the President, but the appearance of a very few soldiers sent the swarm in all directions, for they were

---

[1] *Mauduit*, 160.   [2] *Seignobos : France*, 207.
[3] *Schoelcher : ' Crimes,'* 138. 'Malheureux peuple, comme ils se trompaient,' was his comment. ' Les ouvriers du célèbre faubourg jouent au billard (historique) alors que Paris est en émoi et disent que cela ne les regarde pas,' wrote Proudhon on 9 Dec. 51. *Proudhon*, iv. 131.
[4] *Schoelcher : ' Crimes,'* 139.   [5] *Bagehot : Life*, 193.

mere peaceful citizens or curious foreigners, and had no
fighting aptitude. Altogether the characteristic of that
day was exactly what Lord Byron in some letter calls
" *quiet inquietude.*"

' Yesterday, Thursday . . . was much more disturbed . . .
and a formidable notice was affixed to all the walls informing all persons that the " enemies of order " had begun
their operations. Being curious to see their tactics, I
immediately hied to the Boulevard St Martin, which I
fancied would be the centre of operations ; for it is in the
narrow streets leading out of that great thoroughfare that
the most " exalted " of the *ouvriers* are said to reside. I
had not been misinformed, for as soon as I got on the ground
the preparations for barricades were immediately visible.
It is a simple process, though there being no paving stones
on the Boulevards was a difficulty, but the stones of a half-
built house supplied the place excellently well for the one
where I was. These with palings, iron rails, planks, etc.,
and three overturned omnibuses and two upset cabs
completed the bulwark. It took about half an hour to
make mine, as the Boulevards are about there very wide ;
but others, especially in the side streets, were run up much
more rapidly. The people making them were of two very
unlike sorts. Immensely the greater number were mere
boys or lads, *gamins* is the technical word, the lower sort
of shopboys and sons of the better artisans, not bad-
looking young fellows at all, liking the fair, and in general
quite unarmed. Besides these and directing them were a
few old stagers who have been at it these twenty years—
men whose faces I do not like to *think* of—yellow, sour,
angry, fanatical, who would rather shoot you than not.
Each barricade that I saw was constructed under the eye
of one or two, not more, of such fellows. . . . I . . . found
that they thought that all the troops were out of Paris,
that the provinces—Lyons especially—were rising, and that
all the military would be wanted to prevent their march on
the capital. . . . Why the troops did not come I do not
know, but for I suppose a couple of hours the barricade-
people had it all their own way, and erected I think five

in that part of the Boulevards, one after another, with
about a hundred yards between them. I scrambled over
two and got as far as I dared towards the centre. The
silence was curious . . . all as quiet as the grave. . . . I tried
hard to hire a window to see the capture of the fortress as
well as its erection but this was not to be, for everybody
said they meant to shut their windows, and indeed it would
not have been very safe to look on them firing. I therefore
retired, though not too quickly. It is a bad habit to run
in a Revolution, somebody may think you are the " other
side " and shoot at you, but if you go calmly and look
English, there is no particular danger. As I retired I met
the troops at some distance, slowly and cautiously hemming
in the insurgents. Anybody might go out who would,
but no one come in.' [1]

The explanation of the events which this letter describes
is to be found in the deliberate plans alike of the republican
and of the military leaders. The Republicans on Wednesday had formed a ' Committee of Resistance ' of which
Schoelcher, Victor Hugo, and Jules Favre [2] were the
principal members. Though their following was small
their plans were well-laid. The combat was to be prolonged, the area of disturbance widened, barricades were to
be multiplied, the troops were to be wearied. Wednesday
morning had been discouraging enough it was true, but
none the less it had been a beginning. Could such incidents
be repeated, sooner or later the sluggish citizens might be

---

[1] *Bagehot : Life*, 194, 195. ' I shall not,' he adds reassuringly, ' go again
into the citadel of operation. In no other part is there any danger for a
decently careful person. To-day is much quieter.' How much quieter
another chance English observer may testify. ' On the fourth night after
the *coup d'état*,' wrote Gronow, ' my daughter and myself were present at
a ball given by the Duchess of Hamilton in honour of the Prince-President
at the Hôtel Bristol, Place Vendôme.' At midnight the Prince's carriage
was announced ' whereupon the Duke of Hamilton, taking two wax candles,
conducted his imperial guest downstairs and handed him into his plain
brougham. On the return of the Duke to the ballroom he observed :
" How extraordinary ! There were neither military nor police in the
courtyard of the hotel, to protect the President in case of danger." In
fact the Prince returned at midnight, without an escort, to the Elysée, in a
one-horse brougham.' *Gronow*, ii. 185.
[2] On the latter's share in the resistance, v. Reclus: *Favre*, 174-186.

aroused.[1] Proclamations, written or even possibly printed,
could be placarded and distributed ; in Victor Hugo the
committee possessed an admirable composer of such
documents.

In some respects proclamation and counter-proclama-
tion were remarkably alike. The republican manifestoes, like the President's, abrogated the May Law : they
too convoked the people to vote on December 21,[2] but
for a parliamentary and not a presidential election. So
detested was the May Law, so contemned the existing
Assembly, that the Republicans felt forced to rid themselves of such an incubus even at the cost of a virtual
ratification of this part of the President's act. But for the
rest no charge of plagiarism was possible. In virtue of the
unsigned document prepared for the High Court of Justice,
one decree placed the President under arrest : his prisoners
were liberated by a second, his state of siege raised by a
third. Bluff was a necessary part of the business at
present ; with any luck however it might yet be translated
into good earnest. To attain such an end the prescribed
tactical method was the avoidance of any single or final
conflict. Instead by countless skirmishes the handful of
resisters were to baffle the soldiers, to dissipate their
energies, to win over stragglers, and finally to raise up the
entire city against Louis Napoleon. Paris had acquiesced
in a *fait accompli* : but could it once be induced to believe
that the end was not yet, that the revolution was still in
the making, it might eventually pronounce that it would
not have it made at all. Moreover this policy of multiplying barricades and avoiding fighting at close quarters
coincided admirably with the temper of such insurgents as
were at present forthcoming. For while many were
willing to build barricades, it was doubtful whether in all
Paris there were a hundred men ready to fight behind them
when they were built.[3]

---

[1] ' On the morning of Wednesday, and up till 2 o'clock in the afternoon,
there was nothing to indicate that Paris was on the brink of a crisis. In the
cafés there was a universal game of dominoes.' *Times*, 6 Dec. 51, p. 5,
c. 3. The dominoes were due to the lack of newspapers.

[2] *Schoelcher*, 145.   [3] See *Merruau*, 466.

Given the conditions and the desired result, there could be no possible doubt as to the wisdom of the course advised by the Republican Committee. Unfortunately their reasoning was only too transparently correct. General Magnan, desiring from the same conditions to induce a precisely contrary result, had merely to reverse the revolutionary procedure. Because they wished his troops scattered, he would concentrate them : because they wished them wearied, he would refresh them : because they desired the conflict to be long, doubtful, and indecisive he would have it short, certain, and conclusive.[1] The insurgents might raise rumours and build barricades to their hearts' content on Wednesday evening and Thursday morning : by sundown on Thursday all doubts should be determined, all ambiguities resolved.

Accordingly on Thursday morning Paris had awoken to a new surprise : its streets, which yesterday had bristled with bayonets, were suddenly freed of troops. Not a uniform was to be seen. Was the *coup* cancelled ? Had the provincial Republicans really freed Paris while it slept ? But then there would not be this new proclamation by the side of the now familiar manifestoes. Paris was placed in a state of siege, peaceable citizens were warned a trifle grimly that to-day they would be safer indoors. Magnan meanwhile had recalled all his troops, and given them a good night's rest in barracks ; the next day would see the end of their labours. As it had been decreed, so it was done. Between two and five on December 4 all real resistance was crushed.[2] But in the conflict it was not only the combatants who fell.[3] In certain boulevards, occupied themselves by curious and hostile spectators, the troops were fired upon, or imagined themselves to have been fired upon,[4] from windows of houses. In one

---

[1] *Maupas*, i. 447. [2] *Jerrold*, iii. 289.
[3] Admitted even by e.g. *Mauduit*, 218, 219.
[4] As always in such cases, the evidence is conflicting ; the one side alleging and the other denying, the firing from houses. The balance of evidence seems somewhat to favour the contention of the former. v. *Canrobert*, i. 539-541, an eyewitness. *Pierre*, ii. 657, 660.

instance [1] at least the soldiers, exasperated or panic-stricken, replied by indiscriminate firing, which continued for nearly a quarter of an hour ; directed by the troops not merely against their invisible assailants, but in blind panic and anger against the fugitive crowd in the street.

It is not perhaps strictly accurate, even of this massacre, to describe the victims as totally unwarned. ' I think it right to warn you,' wrote the *Times* correspondent on Saturday in regard to it, ' against the exaggerated rumours that will no doubt reach England of barbarities on the part of the troops. There is no doubt that deplorable accidents occurred in which many innocent and inoffensive persons perished. But the fault is not with the army. An order had previously been posted up in all Paris, and published in the papers, warning all idle spectators from the streets.' [2] Even on Thursday, the same correspondent adds, the real working-class districts did not stir. [3] None the less, it was this ruthless repression of Thursday afternoon which provides the history of the *coup d'état* with its least pardonable page. It remains the more inexcusable that even for the success of the *coup* itself it was entirely unnecessary. Of the days which immediately followed upon that *coup*, Tuesday as we have seen had passed in complete tranquillity : and as late as Wednesday evening only three deaths lay to its door. But for two totally gratuitous blunders on the part of the government, which took effect both of them on Wednesday afternoon, those three lives, or a dozen more at most, might have formed the entire casualties of the *coup d'état* in the capital.

Of these blunders the first and smaller was political. In the original proclamations announcing the *coup d'état* the most attractive feature to their readers had been the restoration of universal suffrage. A supplementary decree written on Tuesday, but only generally published on Wednesday,

---

[1] The Boulevard Bonne-Nouvelle. For republican accounts of this undoubted massacre, see *Hugo* : ' *Histoire*,' ii. 56 *sq.*　N. le *Petit*, 83 *sq.* *Ténot* : *Paris*, 163 *sq.*　*Schoelcher* : ' *Crimes*,' 163 *sq.*

[2] *Times*, 8 Dec. 51, p. 5, c. 5.　In regard to the *coup d'état* the *Times* was the most hostile representative of the English Press, as the English Press itself was the most hostile in Europe.

[3] *Times*, 9 Dec. 51, p. 5, c. 1.

now made it clear that on the occasion of the first use of
the restored suffrage—the coming plebiscite by which the
people was to vote its approval or disapproval of the *coup
d'état*—the vote was to be an open one. Since hitherto
every plebiscite in history had been public,[1] Louis Napoleon
was merely following a universal precedent, from which
it had not occurred to him to deviate. But the manhood
suffrage established in March 1848 had been protected by
the secrecy of the ballot. Now the workmen of Paris were
by no means so entirely unintelligent as republican historians, for their lack of Republicanism, have felt bound
to portray them. They were in fact quite capable of
realising the difference between an open vote and a vote
by ballot. If the vote were open they were being robbed
of the remnant of universal suffrage by the very act which
affected to restore it in its integrity. The percolation of
this news on Wednesday afternoon created for the first time
the elements of real popular resentment, though hardly
yet of effective popular resistance, to the *coup d'état*.

' Your second proclamation dealing with the plebiscite,'
wrote King Jerome to his nephew next day, ' is badly
received by the people, who do not consider it a real re-
establishment of universal suffrage. The time has come to
complete a material by a moral victory: what a government
cannot do when beaten it ought to do when victorious.'[2]
Louis at once replied that his uncle's advice had only
anticipated his own decision :[3] and early on Friday morning,
after all resistance had been crushed and all pressing need
of conciliation had disappeared, he issued another proclamation. In it he explained that though his first proposal
had only followed previous precedent yet ' considering that
the essential object was to obtain the free and sincere
expression of the will of the people ' and that the ballot
was a ' better guarantee ' of this, the plebiscite would be by
secret ballot.[4] A proclamation of De Morny's, issued the

---

[1] As well as many after it—*e.g.* all those which ratified the Union of Italy.
[2] For text in full, v. *Hugo: N. le Petit*, 91, 92.
[3] *Du Casse: Coup d'état*, 223-228. Du Casse conveyed both the letter
and the reply.
[4] *Times*, 8 Dec. 51, p. 5, cc. 5 and 6.

same day, was still more emphatic. ' The President of
the Republic desires that all the electors shall be completely
at liberty in the expression of their votes, whether they
exercise public functions or not, and whether they belong
to the civil professions or the army. Absolute independence, complete liberty of voting, is what Louis Napoleon
desires to see established.' [1]

On the same day Louis wrote himself to his Minister of
War ; since the army voting first had largely voted publicly
already, it was especially important he said that soldiers
who had given a negative vote should be assured that their
careers would in no way be affected [2] : ' be good enough
therefore at once to make it known that I wish to be
ignorant of the names of those who have voted against me.'
For the better securing of this result, he ordered that in
the case of the army so soon as the taking of the votes had
been terminated and verified, the records of them should
be burnt. So far as the fighting on Thursday was concerned however the concession came too late. Generosity
on the morrow of victory is all very well, but justice on
the eve of it is sometimes a great deal better. For it
sometimes renders victory itself unnecessary.

Far graver however than this political blunder was a
military miscalculation by which it was followed. General
Magnan's action in concentrating and resting his troops
because his opponents wished to have them scattered and
wearied was logically correct, and at a cost it was completely
successful. That cost was the street fighting of Thursday
afternoon. *Il faut en finir* was the general's dictum : but
in order to make an end of the resistance he allowed it
to make a beginning. Opposition was permitted to come
to a head and then crushed ; barricades to be built and
then taken by storm. But it was only the temporary with-

---

[1] *Times*, 8 Dec., p. 6, c. 1. On Dec. 18 he caused a letter to be addressed
to the President of the Chamber of Printers of Paris, denying ' a rumour that
it was forbidden to print voting papers bearing the word No.' ' Be kind
enough to transmit to the printers of Paris the notice that they may in all
liberty print as many negative bulletins as they please.' *Times*, 22 Dec.
51, p. 5, c. 2. But see p. 162 below.

[2] On the strictness with which Napoleon III observed this promise,
v. *Du Barail*, i. 439, iii. 349.

drawal of the troops which allowed resistance to come to a head or barricades to be built at all. To denude Paris of troops on Wednesday evening was asking for trouble, and asking for it just when for the first time trouble was to be had for the asking. No sooner had the political blunder given cause for barricade-building, than the military blunder gave opportunity for it. And not opportunity only but encouragement ; for the withdrawal of every soldier from the streets of Paris rendered credible and even inevitable the rumour of a serious provincial insurrection. By no other hypothesis could even hard-headed citizens account for an occurrence so unprecedented in Parisian revolution.

In point of fact a desire to break with precedent had been one main motive in dictating the withdrawal : witness Morny's [1] comments on his own instructions to Magnan on Wednesday that all the troops should be recalled to barracks, given hot soup and a good night's rest. All revolutions he said accomplished themselves in three days : look at February, look at July. And the reason was clear : on the first day the troops promenaded the streets ; on the second they grew tired ; on the third they became de-moralised and fraternised with the people. To-morrow would be the third day : well, there should be no fraternisa-tion to-morrow. Such an argument was not immune perhaps from that touch of superstition to which all con-spirators are prone. But it was a reasoned process none the less, and one which needed nerve for its execution. Yet in spite of its success the result of the decision was deplorable. A few days more of the ' quiet inquietude ' of Tuesday or even Wednesday would have been a small price to pay for the avoidance of the bloodshed of Thursday. Paris had shown itself on the whole surpris-ingly ready to excuse ' the crime ' of December 2.[2] For

---

[1] In the presence of *Véron*, vi. 209. On his insistence on adequate arrangements for the feeding of the troops, v. *Du Casse* : *Coup d'état*, 71.

[2] On Dec. 10 Mrs Browning, present in Paris throughout the *coup d'état*, wrote, ' We have suffered neither fear nor danger. . . . Thursday was the only day on which there was fighting of any serious kind. There has been *no resistance* on the part of the real people. . . . To judge from our own tradespeople ' il a bien fait ! c'est le vrai neveu de son oncle.' *Lubbock*, 283.

that very reason the blunders that produced December 4
were inexcusable.

Excusable or not, the heavy repression of December 4
did serve its professed purpose of making an end of all
resistance in Paris. In the event, the armed opposition
of the Republicans on the 4th had proved only a degree
more formidable than the academic opposition of the Conservatives on December 2.

For the ease with which he had overcome these two
attempts at resistance, Louis Napoleon was indebted in
part to the essential antagonism of his two opponents, in
part to the extraordinary inversion of their accustomed
rôles inflicted on either of them by his own successful
usurpation of administrative power. The old party of
order—the monarchical majority in the recent conservative
Assembly—found themselves thrust into the position of
opponents of public order, should they attempt any effective
opposition of the illegality of their own dissolution. Awak-
ing on the morning of December 2 to find Louis Napoleon
already in actual and present occupation of administrative
power, they were from the outset debarred by their inherent
reverence for any *de facto* government that was pledged to
maintain order, from all but a half-hearted and hesitating
resistance. Armed resistance to armed force, mob violence
opposed to administrative violence, barricades reared
against breakers of the constitution, soldiers disabled from
obedience to their officers because officers had been dissuaded from their allegiance to the Republic—such were the
methods by which alone the *coup d'état* could now be encountered with any hope of success. But against such
methods were ranged all the instinctive and inherited antipa-
thies of the Conservatives ;[1] and even had they consented to
adopt such methods, the party of order could count on little
support for their first amateurish attempts at insurrection
from the ranks of the veteran republican barricade-builders,
the experienced and professional exponents of the art of

---

[1] 'La résistance populaire armée, même au nom de la loi, leur semblait
sédition. . . . Au fond, ces membres de la droite avaient raison. Qu'eussent-
ils fait du peuple ? Et qu'eût fait le peuple d'eux ?' *Hugo* : '*Histoire*,' 107.

street-fighting in Paris. For the latter had neither forgotten
nor forgiven the stern suppression by this same party of
order of their own great revolutionary effort in June 1848,
or of the half-dozen lesser socialist insurrections since then.
Hence of the Conservatives, even the boldest, finding
themselves in their own despite insurgents for the nonce,
were left to flounder helplessly in the stream of revolution.
Like unwilling bathers they had eyed its chilly waters on
that December morning ; some, after shivering awhile on
the brink of action, had finally refused to make the plunge
at all ; others had decorously and dutifully damped themselves ; few indeed were really sorry to find themselves
after a brief and unpleasant immersion unceremoniously
hauled to land—if not to the sacred shore of the monarchy,
at least to the *terra firma* of the Empire.

If the party of order had proved but shy and awkward
revolutionaries, the old socialist insurrectionaries were no
less out of their element as champions of the *status quo*,
legal supporters of an existing constitution. Accustomed
to disport themselves among the frothy phrases of Socialism,
the agents of secret societies found themselves based in this
conflict on the solid rock of the constitution : a position in
which the typical disciple of Ledru-Rollin could not but
feel himself something of a fish out of water. With a sense
of unwonted virtue the revolutionary leaders found themselves repeating the old watchwords of the defenders of
the existing order : but even for their own followers such
legal watchwords had not quite the zest of the irresponsible
war-cries of the past, while in the ears of the Conservatives
they could not succeed in effacing the memory of these
earlier and more natural hostilities. Royalists and Republicans nursed against each other at heart an older and
deeper hate than either had yet learned for Louis Napoleon.
Republicans would as soon have him as a king : Royalists
would rather have him than a republic. Even in their
prisons the conservative deputies could hardly disguise the
satisfaction with which they learned the news of Louis
Napoleon's heavy-handed but successful suppression of
the republican opposition in Paris and of its socialist

offshoots in the provinces. ' I was so pleased,' remarked
Falloux, ' that I could hardly manage only to seem
resigned.' [1]

In the greater part of France the report of the *coup
d'état* had been received with acquiescence, almost with
approval. Only in the south-east did the news occasion
serious disorder.

From the time of Cæsar onwards the turbid torrent of
the Rhone has reflected not inaptly the character of the
people on its banks. On this occasion no great city rose in
revolt : Lyons and Marseilles, the two most turbulent of
French provincial towns, remained quiet ; for strong
garrisons were soothing them. But in the smaller towns
and villages occurred a number of isolated attempts at
insurrection. In almost every case these risings collapsed
at the mere approach of the first handful of soldiers that
could be directed against them. But meanwhile in
country districts still distant from the rare and recent
railways, scattered bodies of insurgents had remained all-
powerful for several days, and nights,[2] before these soldiers
were forthcoming. And, in the interval, things had
happened in remote market-towns and inaccessible villages
by the side of which the wildest extravagance of Paris
seemed Attic and urbane.

Years earlier, in the factories of the Faubourg Saint-
Marceau, Heine had found writings written ' which had as it
were an odour of blood,' and ' heard songs sung which
seemed to have been composed in hell.' [3] But of late such
propaganda had been spreading in ever cruder form from
the artisans of the great towns to the peasantry of the rural
provinces. Now for some years agents of the socialist
societies had been circulating secretly among the vine-
dressers of Burgundy and the fishermen of Provence :
fraternising with the woodmen of Auvergne, penetrating
the remote sub-Alpine valleys whose scanty tilth furnished
a precarious subsistence to the peasants and shepherds of

[1] *Hugo* : '*Histoire*,' 121.   [2] *Viel-Castel*, i. 238.
[3] *Heine* : *Lutèce*, 29, and see *Weill*, 211. *Dickinson*, 151.

the Dauphiné. To every man these emissaries promised the removal of his besetting grievance, the righting of his individual wrong. For months past in many a small town or country village the labourer had eyed his victim; consoling himself, as he turned to execute an order which he dared not yet disobey, with a muttered reference to the great and terrible crisis of 1852.[1] For though Socialism as preached to the peasants comprised the removal of all public wrongs, it included also the consummation of many private vendettas. True the conscript would escape his term of military service, the poacher would be freed of his game laws, the village innkeeper eased of his excise duties, the tenant liberated from the irksome necessity of paying rent. The peasant proprietor would indeed find his holding doubled, the debtor his debts remitted, the working-man the need of working done away for ever. But all were agreed that a Red Sea divided them as yet from the Promised Land. Some were only reconciled to the unpleasantness of the journey by the delights of the destination. But others made no secret of the fact that the journey itself would be delightful, and that the vindication of social justice would be enhanced by the incidental accompaniment of individual revenge. All the ancient animosities of the countryside were to find, in the treasured crisis of 1852, their complement and satisfaction.

It was on ground thus prepared that the news of Louis Napoleon's successful *coup d'état* fell suddenly, four months before the crisis was due. To those who feared that crisis the news was a source of overwhelming relief:[2] to those whose every hope for two years past had been based upon it, the same news came naturally as a disastrous shock. The immediate effect of the announcement was to precipi-tate in the disaffected regions a series of premature and abortive insurrections. Predatory bands roved over the country, and bore away locally for several days. Registers of taxes were burned; castles were looted and their

---

[1] *La Gorce*: *République*, ii. 557.
[2] Cf. *Guizot*, 329.

owners arrested as hostages ; prisoners were set free and
their cells filled with prefects, maires, and magistrates.
Nor were occasional violences, more brutish and besotted,
lacking to lend terror to the threats with which these lesser
illegalities were accompanied. A curé had offended some
of his parishioners ; now he could be put to torture. The
local schoolmaster was disliked ; this was the time to murder·
him. A policeman was unpopular ; a recently released
criminal superintended at the leisurely putting of him to
death.[1]

Such was the news which came back to Paris from the
provinces in the days which followed the *coup d'état*. The
narrative lost nothing of its horror in the columns of the
conservative journals, which alone were left to tell the tale ;
and its effect upon public opinion was wholly favourable to
the cause of Louis Napoleon. He was well served by his
newspapers. The ready acceptance of the *coup d'état* by
the bulk of the provinces had in the first instance been
assisted by official telegrams assuring them that Paris had
hailed the deed with delight. Now the nature of the
opposition forthcoming from a section of the provinces
helped to reconcile Paris itself to a saviour of society. A
year ago, in a despatch predicting and approving the
coup d'état, Normanby had written : ' France is at present
in the state of a sick man, who feels relieved and is pronounced better, but has the certain consciousness that
his perfect recovery must be preceded by an inevitable and
dangerous operation of which it is as yet impossible to fix
the time or foresee the result.' [2] Louis Napoleon had not
quite succeeded in persuading the world that the patient
had enjoyed the operation ; but thanks to exaggerated
accounts of these provincial saturnalia he had at least
been successful in convincing the patient that the disease
would have been worse than the remedy.

To this conviction France bore witness in the plebiscite
of December 20. Nearly seven and a half millions of

---

[1] At Clamecy, v. *La Gorce : République*, 552 ; *Gazette des Tribunaux*,
27 and 28 Feb. 52. On the rising generally at this town, see *Millelot*.
Also on the entire provincial movement, *Ténot : La Province*.
[2] F.O. France, Normanby to Palmerston, Paris, 24 Jan. 50.

votes were cast in Louis Napoleon's favour ; less than
six hundred and fifty thousand were recorded against the
maintenance of his power. The actual figures are now
generally admitted to be authentic.[1] But no less in-
disputable is the effect on them of official pressure. The
vote was technically by ballot : but while there was
everywhere an abundance of printed *Ouis* it was generally
necessary for the *Nons* to be written. For though at the
last moment negative forms were also printed, they were
forthcoming too late to be of general use.[2] A comparison
of the vote at the presidential election of December 1848
with the plebiscite of December of 1851 goes far however
to show that official pressure did not create but merely
exaggerated Louis Napoleon's majority on the latter
occasion. In the former year, for reasons which we have
considered elsewhere,[3] the popular vote was practically
uninfluenced by administrative pressure ; but such pressure
as could then be applied was definitely hostile to Louis
Napoleon. The result had been an absolutely unchallenge-
able [4] vote of five and a half millions in his favour against
less than two million votes secured by his opponents. The
two million votes—representing the turnover of a million
voters—by which his majority was now augmented forms
the maximum area of probably effective pressure brought
to bear upon the plebiscite of 1851. At the time, save for a
handful of literary exiles, even those who were most disgusted with the result admitted that its least pleasing
feature was its truth. In this admission Royalists and
Socialists concurred. 'The people has the government
it prefers,' sneered Broglie, 'and the *bourgeoisie* the
government it deserves.' A year later Proudhon quoted
this very dictum only to confirm it. ' *Tout ce qu'impriment
vos proscrits pour infirmer cette vérité,*' he wrote to one of

[1] The counting took place publicly, in presence of the electors. ' The
tables on which this is to be done are to be arranged in such a way that
electors may walk round them.' For this and other detailed precautions,
v. Morny's circular to prefects of departments, *Times*, 10 Dec. 51, p. 4, c. 6.
[2] F.O. France, Normanby to Palmerston, 21 Dec. 51. Cf. *Times*, 24
Dec. 51, p. 4, c. 6.
[3] *Simpson*, 306.
[4] On this, v. *Cobden : Speeches*, ii. 538.

them, ' *est faux, archifaux. Napoléon III est l'expression
légitime, authentique, des masses bourgeoises et prolétaires.
S'il n'est pas précisément le produit de la* volonté *nationale, à
coup sûr il l'est de la* permission *nationale.*' [1] And thence the
writer proceeded not to praise Cæsar but to pour scorn upon
the people ; inveighing against them with a deeper and
more aristocratic disdain than any which in the nature of
things a Royalist could use or understand. For better or
worse the people had made the act their own ; and though
in doing so they could not absolve Louis of his offence they
had yet put it out of their own power later to don with
dignity the robe of Cato. The plea of official pressure has
its limitations : one cannot intimidate an entire nation.
If the *coup d'état* was a crime France was less its victim.
than its accomplice.

The official verdict of contemporary Europe was only
a degree less unanimous than the verdict of contemporary France. Austria, Prussia, and the minor monarchies
were loud in their felicitations. Nicholas himself deigned
to approve ; not unnaturally, he imagined that Louis
Napoleon's present recourse to repressive measures argued
a permanent inclination to his own reactionary ideals.
Only he warned Louis to be content with the substance of
power, and not to seek the Empire also.

In one quarter alone was the chorus of praise broken.
Public opinion in England declared itself vehemently in
condemnation of Louis' deed ; Palmerston's indiscreet
approbation of it cost him his seat in the Cabinet. A
common dislike of Austria and the Orleanists made Palmerston and the President natural allies ; this alliance the
English Foreign Minister now cemented by expressing his
complete approval of the *coup d'état* to Walewski, the
French ambassador in London ; Walewski's despatch
embodying Palmerston's views was read by the French
Minister of Foreign Affairs to the ambassadors of the other
Powers in Paris [2] as an indication of the real opinion of the
British government. Now when the first news of the *coup*

---

[1] *Proudhon*, v. 110.   [2] Normanby to Palmerston, 6 Dec. 51.

d'état reached England, the Queen had very sensibly ordered
that Normanby should be instructed to remain entirely
passive, since ' any word from him might be misconstrued
at such a moment.' [1] Normanby was an Orleanist, and
much as he disliked the Republic he disliked the Empire
more ; his own suggestion had been that he should suspend
his diplomatic functions.[1] Thus even instructions to
express no opinions came to him as something of a disappointment. Instead therefore of contenting himself with
expressing none he informed the French government that
he was ordered to express none, which was not quite the
same thing ; by calculated delay and a glacial demeanour
he indicated that no opinion was emphatically a bad
opinion, and that it was not to be expressed diplomatically
because diplomatic expression of it was impossible. It had
therefore been peculiarly galling to him to find his ominous
communication received with a cheery reassurance that
the delay had not mattered in the least, since the French
government had been apprised two days ago through its
ambassador in London of Palmerston's entire approval.
To have one's carefully rehearsed effects spoiled in this
way without warning was intolerable ; and if the Foreign
Secretary was allowed to bless the *coup d'état* why should
the ambassador be denied the satisfaction of cursing it ?
The thing was manifestly unfair : and Normanby could
only relieve his feelings by writing to Palmerston all that
he would have liked to say to Turgot, and writing to the
Prime Minister [2] all that he would have liked to say to
Palmerston.

The protests of the outraged ambassador achieved a
result which exceeded his wildest hopes. Palmerston's
honest hatred of Austrian tyranny had led him into a series
of diplomatic indiscretions [3] which were not only embarrassing to his ministerial colleagues but in the highest degree
displeasing to his sovereign and her husband. These

---

[1] *Martin*, ii. 411.   [2] *Greville*, 25 Dec. 51.
[3] But in 1850 with no such excuse he had exposed the good name of
England and risked a breach with France by using the fleet to bully Greece
on behalf of a fraudulent Portuguese Jew Pacifico ; technically, as ill-luck
would have it, a British subject.

indiscretions had just culminated in certain incidents connected with the visit of Kossuth ; a born orator who spoke Shakespeare's English as no Englishman for two centuries had spoken it, turning the full hose of Elizabethan invective on Czar and Emperor to the envy and delight of audiences who had forgotten how inexhaustible were the resources of their native tongue.

Hitherto the trouble about Palmerston's indiscretions had been that they had always contrived to be popular in the country just in proportion as they had been unpalatable to crowned heads. But now at last they had caught him tripping ; this time he had been at once indiscreet and undemocratic ; and so could safely be sent about his business.[1] In consequence the *coup d'état* was a piece of tyranny which might be denounced in the highest circles : even the poet laureate risked an ode in condemnation of it.[2] Respectable politicians of late had been sadly conscious that all the best words were being left to the radicals : here was heaven-sent opportunity of mouthing them themselves. The *Times* and the whole pro-Austrian press took up the tale ; beating the big drum of democratic indignation with the delighted knowledge that in reality they were drumming out of office the one democrat in England of whom they were afraid.

It has been necessary to dwell a little on the story of this quarrel because its significance in moulding English public opinion on the *coup d'état* has not been adequately appreciated. The fact that Normanby was done out of his snub to Turgot led him in his subsequent despatches to Palmerston to put the worst complexion on the *coup d'état* : the fact that Palmerston was dismissed led to the publication of his charges : the true reason of that dismissal made a megaphone for them not only of the few English newspapers which genuinely disliked continental tyranny but also of the many which secretly supported it. The result was an

---

[1] The well-informed pro-Austrian anti-Palmerston *Greville* writes on 23 Dec. 51 : ' Though this was the pretext, the *causa causans* was without any doubt the Islington speech and deputations.'

[2] Under the pseudonym of Merlin.

apparent [1] unanimity of condemnation which impressed contemporaries and imposed upon posterity.

One other minor feature of the quarrel deserves a publicity which it has hitherto lacked. When taxed by Normanby with his approval of the *coup d'état* Palmerston had no better defence than to essay a reasoned vindication of the measure. This he did vigorously enough ; but a defence on these lines, as the Premier pointed out,[2] was really entirely beside the point. To his hand, had Palmerston but known it, lay a far more crushing and conclusive retort. Normanby himself in his own unpublished despatches had repeatedly and eagerly predicted a *coup d'état*, praising it as the sole salvation of France.[3] The ambassador doubtless owed his escape to the portentous length of his communications ; not all of which deserve even Palmerston's faint praise of one of them, that ' it would have made a good article in the *Times* a fortnight ago.' [4] How excusable it was in him

---

[1] Walewski reported that the Premier himself on Dec. 6 had expressed to him opinions ' if anything stronger ' in favour of the *coup d'état* than those which Palmerston was dismissed for having employed on Dec. 3. *Ashley*, ii. 217, 224. For the most part however English disapproval was both sincere and fine : unfortunately it was based on a very imperfect apprehension of the facts. What Englishmen condemn is almost always worthy of condemnation—if only it has happened.

[2] *Martin*, ii. 415.

[3] *Cf.* p. 161 above for a typical expression of his opinion in 1850. As early as 1849, in his ' Secret and confidential ' despatch of 23 July, he had reported that the middle classes of Paris felt ' that it would be impossible for the social system to stand the shock prepared for it by the constitution in electing another President (for the same is ineligible) and a new Assembly also by universal suffrage in three years' time. . . . And yet clumsy as the constitution is in its own operation, all the little skill exerted in its invention went to prevent the possibility of any beneficial change taking place without an evident illegality, and therefore without passing through a " coup d'état." . . . All classes are convinced that sooner or later this state of things will have to be saved by extra-constitutional means. . . . Prince L. Napoleon has very much conciliated the good opinion of all public men who have approached him by the personal qualities he has displayed in emergencies.' Normanby went on to predict as the most prudent and probable means of restoring public confidence the extension of the present President's tenure of office for ten years with power of re-election, with possibly a power of dissolution and veto. This might satisfy Paris itself ; but not the rest of France or the troops, which want an Empire. Moreover the working classes of Paris themselves want it. ' They are sick of the name of socialism and republic, which has failed to give them work : they now believe a monarchic government alone will restore confidence to their masters and so orders for work to themselves : this they associate with settled government and luxurious habits.'

[4] *Ashley*, i. 293.

to skip or skim them the task of reading them entire best testifies; but his failure to read them attentively did in fact disarm Palmerston at the crisis of his affairs; nor did any of his biographers manage to make good the omission. Contemporary opinion outside of England, where it was largely influenced by the results of this quarrel, had thus declared itself overwhelmingly in favour of the President's action. There remains the verdict of History, before whose tribunal Louis Napoleon stands arraigned on three several counts: a broken oath, a violated constitution, and a massacre in the streets of Paris. Of these three charges the second, though far from little, is by far the least. To us, and to all well-governed citizens, to call an act unconstitutional is to condemn the act. But that is because we have learned to hold in honour the abstraction that serves us for constitution, regarding it as the gradual growth of ages, the unconscious creation of mature experience in the past, almost applying to it the great apostrophe,

'Thou still unravished bride of Quietness,
Thou foster child of Silence and slow Time':

holding at any rate the constitution so far sacred as to hold the violation of it in abhorrence. It does not follow that by the bare process of being christened a constitution any new-fangled bundle of bad laws becomes entitled automatically to the same respect. Most writers on the subject do unconsciously believe in a sort of baptismal regeneration at this stage, investing with mystical grace and virtue what they would otherwise recognise for the palpable offspring of hysteria and haste. Against this high sacramentarian view Palmerston protested at the time in plain prose. 'As to respect for the law and Constitution,' he wrote, 'that respect belongs to just and equitable laws framed under a Constitution founded upon reason, consecrated by its antiquity and by the memory of long years of happiness which the nation has enjoyed under it: it is scarcely a proper application of those feelings to require them to be directed to the day-before-yesterday tomfoolery which the scatterbrained heads of Marrast and Tocqueville invented for the torment and perplexity of the French nation ; and I must say that the Constitution was more honoured by the breach than by the observance.' [1]

The constitution of 1848 was in fact the ninth which France had scrapped since 1792. Whether it was really so bad that it could only be preserved by the breach of other allegiances, those especially who have not read it may well be permitted to doubt. But it is not doubtful that such collisions of allegiance are conceivable. In the realm of civic duty there exist virtues perpetual, such as patriotism or equity, and virtues temporal, such as loyalty or legality. It is the mark of a well-ordered state that in it these two classes of virtues coincide, confirming and completing one another. It is the tragedy of a nation misgoverned that the two goods are brought into conflict ; and in so far as the republican authors of the constitution of 1848 had deliberately made their handiwork incapable of legal revision, to that extent they had given colour to Louis Napoleon's own excuse for the *coup d'état* :—'*Je n'étais sorti de la légalité que pour rentrer dans le droit.*' [2] It is the final and perhaps the fitting fate of a too rigid constitution that in seeking to make itself legally immortal it succeeds in condoning the illegal stroke that alone can end it. The authors of the Republican Constitution of 1848 had in fact succeeded in effecting for it what Achilles' mother accomplished for her son. They had made their offspring immortal save for the heel. They had forgotten that one cannot confer such exceptional immunities on one's champion, and at the same time postulate for him the ordinary rule of the ring—that there shall be no hitting below the belt. They had forgotten too that any despotism, otherwise altogether intemperate, will in the end be tempered by assassination ; worse, that in such cases assassination will not lack excuse or even applause. Few facts in connexion with the *coup d'état* stand more in need of emphasis than this : that on the morrow of it Louis

---

[1] Palmerston to Normanby, 3 Dec. 51 : in *Ashley*, i. 291.
[2] Louis Napoleon to *M.* Billault, 31 Dec. 51, in answer to the official communication to him of the result of the plebiscite.

Napoleon appealed to the French people not as a tyrant, but as a tyrannicide.

On the constitutional [1] count of the indictment, then, Louis Napoleon escapes conclusive condemnation. If his reign·rested on an illegality, almost every other dynasty or regime in French history is open eventually to a similar charge. France as usual was called upon tó approve a change already accomplished in Paris. But the approval in this case was quite unusually emphatic.[2] The verdict may have been mistaken ; but it was certainly unmistakeable. When all deductions have been made on the score of official pressure it still remains clear, that no dynastic change in the nineteenth century received such emphatic assent from contemporary France as that which ratified the substitution of the Second Empire for the Second Republic.

It is not the lack of extenuating features, but the presence of aggravating circumstances attending the *coup d'état*, that must prevent the historian from accepting any contemporary condonation of it as conclusive. For though the Constitution of 1848 was more worthy of death than many others whose violent suppression history has hitherto condoned, yet the fact remains that it was suppressed by the one man in the world who had sworn to uphold it.[3] And even if it were proved that the illegality of December saved the whole of France from a veritable social cataclysm in the following May, still this hypothetical service was marred by the massacre of innocent spectators in the streets of Paris.

Both these charges have been exaggerated, but neither

---

[1] It is perhaps not wholly irrelevant to observe, that the author of the most famous study on *The English Constitution* won his literary spurs in a series of articles written from Paris on the morrow of the coup d'état in *defence* of it. *Bagehot : Works*, i. 77–137.

[2] Even in 1871 ' it was the opinion of so impartial an observer as the British ambassador [Lord Lyons] that if a free vote could have been taken under universal suffrage a majority would probably have been obtained for the re-establishment upon the throne of Napoleon III.' *Newton*, ii. 31. What is at any rate certain is that no majority could have been obtained for the Republic.

[3] The oath in question ran as follows :—' En présence de Dieu et devant le peuple français, représenté par l'Assemblée Nationale, je jure de rester fidèle à.la République démocratique une et indivisible, et de remplir tous les devoirs que m'impose la constitution.' *Normanby*, ii. 399.

can be denied.   It is true that in all probability when he
actually took the oath Louis Napoleon had no intention
of breaking it : [1] for at first he certainly failed to realise
the impossibility of that legal revision which he was confident that France desired.   But though this fact justified
him in taking the oath originally, it does not acquit the
President of continuing to hold office after he had determined to break the oath in virtue of which he held it.   Yet
even here the argument which condemns the breach of the
oath condemns also to some extent the imposition of it.
Having made their constitution legally unalterable its
framers had proceeded to exact an oath that no attempt
should be made to alter it illegally.   He who would alter the
constitution must break the law, and he who would break
the law must break his promise also.   The promise itself
was but one rivet the more in the chain by which what was
known to be a reluctant country was bound eternally to a
republican constitution.   Oath-breaking is bad.   But it is
an altogether fortunate thing that oaths of allegiance have
no worse effect than to exclude from political life a few
abnormally honest men.   Else all constitutional change
would long ago have been rendered universally impossible,
by the simple device of confining political life to the oath-
bound.   From this fate men's readiness to break oaths,
and not their reluctance to impose them, has saved the
world.   Even though it knows them frangible few governments [2] can resist the desire for the fictitious sense of

---

[1] For historic truth at any rate, Louis had some regard : *v.* his interview
in Jan. 54 with *Du Casse* (*Souvenirs*, 144–150) in which on the ground that
l'histoire est de l'histoire he forbade his Uncle Joseph's biographer to suppress
a stricture of Napoleon's on his father or an inconvenient early letter of his
own about the Strasburg adventure, or to bowdlerise a hitherto unpublished and not very printable St Helena conversation.   Du Casse suggested
euphemisms. " 'Oh, non, non,' me répondit l'Empereur : 'vous auriez tort,
ne faites pas cela.   Il ne faut pas ôter son cachet à la pensée de l'Empereur.' "
[2] Of these few, the Second Republic had originally the honour to be one.
'Le gouvernement provisoire de la Republique—considérant que, depuis
un semi-siècle chaque nouveau gouvernement qui s'est élevé a exigé et
reçu des serments qui ont été successivement remplacés par d'autres à
chaque changement politique. . . . Decrete :—Les fonctionnaires publics . . .
ne prêteront pas de serment.'   Decree of 1 March 48.   But when it became
apparent that France would make the only protest in her power against a
republican constitution by electing a non-republican President, a solitary
oath of allegiance to the Republic was inserted for his especial benefit,

security attained by the imposition of oaths of allegiance.
But were such oaths really unbreakable no government
could be deterred from what would then be a frantic
eagerness to extort a genuine pledge of immortality. That
there may never be lacking a supply of men willing at a
pinch to break such oaths is the humiliating but manifest
interest of mankind.

In one respect the measure of blame attaching both to
broken oath and to bloodshed in Paris is dependent on an
unknown quantity ; for it varies in inverse ratio to the
magnitude of a hypothetical catastrophe, the crisis of
May 1852 from which the *coup d'état* saved France. The
shadow that the crisis cast ahead of it was at least not
hypothetical at all. ' Five weeks ago,' wrote Bagehot,[1]
the tradespeople talked of May 52 as if it were the end
of the world. It is hardly to be imagined upon what
petty details the dread of political dissolution at a fixed
and not distant date will not intrude itself.' Instances
follow from his personal observation during five months
residence in Paris, from which he concludes that the ever-
increasing trade depression and unemployment,[2] created
by the threat of the crisis, could not fail eventually to
make the crisis justify the threat. ' No danger could
be more formidable than six months beggary among the
revolutionary *ouvriers,* immediately preceding the exact
period fixed by European as well as French opinion for an
apprehended convulsion. It is from this state of things
whether by fair means or foul that Louis Napoleon has
delivered France. . . . Clever people may now prove that
the dreaded peril was a simple chimera, but they can't deny

---

[1] Paris, 8 Jan. 52. *Bagehot : Works,* i. 79. Referring to ' the moral
question and the oath,' he adds, ' It certainly does not seem to me proved
or clear, that a man who has sworn even in the most solemn manner to
see another drown, is therefore quite bound, or even at liberty, to stand
placidly on the bank. . . . And supposing I am right, such certainly was
the exact position of Louis Napoleon.' *Ibid.,* 85.

[2] The Paris correspondent of the *Morning Chronicle,* 5 Dec. 51, p. 5,
c. 6, reported on Dec. 3 that ' a week ago more than one-half of the workmen were out of employ.' Contrast Circourt, 4 Nov. 52 : ' The tradesmen
and even the workmen, who have more work on hand than they can do, are
become entirely favourable to the new power.' B.M. Add. MSS. 37,423,
f. 181. Cf. *Flaneur,* 79.

that the fear of it was very real and painful, nor can they dispute that in a week after the *coup d'état* it had at once, and apparently for ever, passed away. I fear it must be said that no legal or constitutional act could have given an equal confidence.' Here we are in the region of pure hypothesis ; but the very success of the *coup d'état* proved on this score a disadvantage to its defenders. It was difficult even for Frenchmen long to realise that a shadow so completely lifted had really lain so heavily on their country ; like men awakened from a nightmare they were conscious for a moment of fugitive and retreating hosts, of some unclutched-at train of vanishing disaster ; surely it had been a dream. It was good to be awake and at work again, but need one have been woken quite so roughly ? For the moment the sweet and overmastering emotion was relief ; only later did the question obtrude itself at all insistently. And the answer later was affected by man's instinctive tendency to believe that what has in fact not happened has never been in any real danger of happening.

There remains the last and gravest charge of all : the massacre of inoffensive citizens on December 4 on the Boulevard Montmartre. Morality is not a matter of counting heads, or even corpses ; but it may be convenient at this place to attempt some guess at the death-roll of the *coup d'état*.

More than guess-work is in fact impossible. For the secret archives retrieved from the Tuileries after the fall of the Empire, which enable us to compute with some certainty the number of proscriptions which followed the *coup d'état*, shed no light on the actual loss of life occasioned by it. We can only therefore compare conflicting and uncertain accounts. Officially the entire number of killed and wounded, soldiers and civilians, was stated to be approximately six hundred.[1] But these figures have seldom been accepted as accurate. The latest and highest estimate of the *Times* exactly doubled them :[2] this estimate

---

[1] *Maupas*, i. 510 : detailed statistics on previous page. See also for favourable and minimising figures *Fleury*, i. 183 ; *Mayer*, 170, 298–304.

[2] *Times*, 28 Aug. 52. Contradicted by the *Moniteur* two days later.

has generally been taken as the maximum, as the official estimate is the minimum, for historical computation of the casualties. But despatches of the British ambassador hitherto unpublished suggest an even higher figure. ' I grieve to say,' he wrote on December 9, 'that I have this day learnt from two different persons, who received the information from the Ministry of the Interior, that the loss of life in connexion with Thursday last, not including the military, but confined to the insurgents and various casualties, amounts to more than 2000 persons.'[1] And a few days later he hints at a higher total still. ' M. Reculot,' he wrote on December 14, ' the French Secretary of Legation at Constantinople, dined yesterday with General St Arnaud and asked the General how many persons had perished in the days of the 4th and 5th of December. The General's reply was, " I am really afraid to tell you how many. Above three thousand who never defended a barricade." '[2]

These two brief despatches, both of which are here quoted entire, would revolutionise our conceptions of the casualties of the *coup d'état* if they could be accepted without reserve. But in the first Normanby names neither of his informants, and in the second he does not claim to have his information even at second hand. Further, since the Pacifico affair he had been on bad terms with Louis Napoleon,[3] and he was now in the thick of a personal quarrel with Palmerston, which turned entirely upon the blameworthiness of the *coup d'état*. It was as much therefore to his interest to exaggerate the casualties, as it was to the interest of the French government to minimise them. None the less, the former despatch at any rate cannot wholly be set aside ; and in the light of it the *Times* figures may now be reasonably held to represent not an exaggerated maximum, but a sober estimate of the casualties of the *coup d'état*.

[1] F.O. France, Normanby to Palmerston, 9 Dec. 51.
[2] *Ibid.*, 14 Dec. 51. ' Secret.'
[3] ' He showed his personal antipathy to the Prince President in a very undiplomatic way, foretelling his impending fall.' So Malmesbury wrote of Normanby's behaviour as his guest at a small dinner-party in Paris on 21 Apr. 50. *Malmesbury*, i. 260.

Even such an estimate as this would credit the *coup d'état* with casualties scarcely more than a tithe of those occasioned in Paris by the June days of '48. But the very magnitude of the fighting then gave to its consequences the dignity of open war : what France never forgave Louis Philippe, and Paris never forgave Louis Napoleon, was the indiscriminate fusillade of an exasperated soldiery upon civilian non-combatants. Had this thing happened as the result of orders or in spite of them ? Had there or had there not, in the one street in which the occurrence was admitted, been firing from roofs or windows ? Could there have been—how could there not have been—the excuse or aggravation of drunkenness ? [1] Such were the horror-stricken questions with which the English press especially resounded. It is difficult perhaps in dealing with an isolated incident to attain a due sense of proportion in such matters ; which demand for their philosophic treatment the multiplication of them into a method of government. But when all allowance has been made for the sensitiveness of an age long immune from European war, the casualties occasioned by the *coup d'état* remain its most decisive condemnation. This fact was fully realised by the ablest of its opponents, who were careful in their denunciations of it to represent the massacre of December 4th not as an accidental accessory but as the deliberate and essential climax of the *coup d'état*. Such a thesis had for the Republicans a double advantage. Not only did it turn the limelight on to the worst act of the villain, but it served to obscure the strange inaction [2] of the heroes. The chief task of literary opponents of the *coup d'état* was to explain why it had only to face literary opposition. There would have been a real opposition

---

[1] The only substantial basis for the charge is the well-attested fact that on the morning of Dec. 2 Fleury offered sums of 2500 francs to a number of brigade commanders from the Prince : some accepted ; *Canrobert,* i. 532, refused. The totally inadequate excuse for the offer was that it might be necessary to buy food for the troops without returning to barracks ; the amount of it where it was accepted worked out at a total of 50 centimes a man for the entire period of the coup. It was Canrobert's brigade which was responsible for the fusillade.

[2] On which see Prévost-Paradol to Taine, 10 Dec. 51. *Gréard,* 180.

came the answer, but for the massacre. There must have been a real opposition, echoed others, witness the massacre. For either answer it was necessary that the massacre should have been deliberate. Otherwise the theory has little to recommend it. Few rulers were personally more humane than Louis Napoleon. Yet granted even that in his eyes Paris was worth a massacre, a massacre would still have seemed the last thing likely to win Paris. Even an accidental massacre had lost Louis Philippe his crown in 1848 : to repeat such an incident deliberately was hardly a plausible method of picking one up for Louis Napoleon in 1851.

But even if he be held innocent of premeditated massacre, Louis Napoleon remains guilty of the bloodshed his *coup d'état* entailed. Like his momentary model [1] William III, in the murder of the de Witts and the massacre of Glencoe, he cannot escape the guilt of deaths which had his own advancement if not for deliberate motive, for result ; which though he did not desire he occasioned, which though he may have deplored [2] he did not avenge, whose authors he screened from justice and even rewarded for their wrongdoing.

In all this Louis did not lack precedent. But in the event he proved less fortunate than his more cold-blooded predecessor. Thanks to the eloquence of his advocates and his ultimate success William III is generally remembered as the single-minded artificer of a great international deliverance. Thanks to the eloquence of his opponents and his own final failure, a fate less fortunate has befallen Napoleon III ; a ruler by instinct generous to a fault, humane to the verge of weakness, himself also in some sort the deliverer of a nation not his own.

---

[1] v. *Simpson*, 204.

[2] ' No man ever more deeply deplored them ; and where the opportunity offered, he gave what indemnity he could to the families of those who had suffered. There are young persons who lost their parents on that day who have been educated at his expense, the cost being defrayed out of his private purse ; and I know myself one instance in which the children have had a regular quarterly stipend paid to them from their infancy, and which is continued without interruption or diminution to this day.' *Gronow*, ii. 179. This was written in 1864.

For him the stain of innocent blood remained [1] a damned spot which no later lustrations could wipe out ; so that a monarch sincerely concerned for the oppressed, for the afflicted, for—in his own phrase—' the disinherited,' survives in the popular memory as the Man, and by the deed, of December.[2]

[1] ' Un boulet que toute sa vie on traîne au pied ' was the Empress's description of the coup d'état at Chislehurst to *Duruy,* i. 66.

[2] Since this book was first published, fresh evidence has come to light which proves that the actual casualties of the *coup d'état* were considerably smaller than those estimated above on p. 173 : see pp. 389, 391, below.

CHAPTER VI

THE EMPIRE AND THE EMPRESS

What's in the *Times* ?—a scold
At the Emperor deep and cold ;
　　He has taken a bride
　　To his gruesome side,
That's as fair as himself is bold :
　　There they sit ermine-stoled,
And she powders her hair with gold.

ROBERT BROWNING.

IT was not until the 31st of December 1851 that Louis Napoleon was formally acquainted by his official advisers that France had accepted his deed of December 2nd. In the interval he affected to regard his position as purely temporary ; though he informed France cheerfully by a proclamation issued a few days after the *coup d'état* that in any case he had accomplished the first part of his task : society was now saved whatever the popular vote should be. For ' Why should the people rise against me ? If I no longer possess your confidence it is not necessary to have recourse to insurrection. An adverse vote in the electoral urn will suffice.'

In a similar strain he now accepted the announcement of the plebiscite. He had transgressed the bounds of legality, he admitted, but only that he might regain right. And for this, ' more than seven million votes have absolved me.' ' I realise,' he added, ' all the grandeur of my new mission, but I am not blind to the grave difficulties of it. None the less—by a right heart within me, by the co-operation of all men of goodwill, who like you will enlighten me with their

177

understanding and sustain me with their patriotism, by the proved devotion of our valiant army, and not least by that divine protection which to-morrow I shall solemnly ask heaven still to accord me—I hope to render myself worthy of the continued confidence of the people.' His private letters at this time breathe a still more complacent sense of virtue. ' What I have done,' he wrote to his old friend Arese, ' has been with the object of saving France years of trouble and strife. Do your duty, come what may.' [1] Perhaps we can only repeat of such professions on the morrow of the *coup d'état*, what its most bitter opponent Normanby had written on the eve of it. ' I impute less to him of selfish feeling than I should to anyone else who acted under the same impulses, because among the strange ingredients which make up his peculiar character there is a sort of mystic fatalism which convinces him that he is predestined to save France ; and it would be I am sure with the best intentions that he would set about the execution of that which he believes to be ordained by fate.' But we cannot do less than record also the ambassador's conclusion : ' It is not under the influence of such hallucinations that the serious affairs of great countries in troubled times can be satisfactorily directed.' [2]

The plebiscite of December 20, in accepting the presidency of Louis Napoleon for ten years, had accepted also the sketch of a constitution which he had propounded to the people ; now on January 14 the finished article was exhibited for their admiration.[3] In this constitution the President was in effect all-powerful : ministers were responsible to him, legislators swore fealty to him, and he retained the sole initiative in the proposal of law. Of the two chambers, the upper was composed of his nominees, and sat in secret ; while the lower could not ask questions, could not contain ministers, could reject but practically could not amend legislative proposals, and could only be reported in an officially edited summary of its proceedings.

[1] *Grabinski*, 116.
[2] F.O. France, Normanby to Palmerston, 1 Dec. 51.
[3] For its text in full, v. *Moniteur*, 15 Jan. 52 ; *Jerrold*, iii. 465–471.

Further, both houses had their chairmen chosen for them by the President. Even so the scheme retained some faint adumbrations of democratic origin and control ; adumbrations to which Louis adroitly drew attention in his first speech to his first legislature under the new constitution.[1]

'What do I see before me ? ' he exclaimed, regarding with a kind of surprised benignity his meek Senators and docile Representatives, ' what do I see before me ? Two chambers, one elected under the most liberal electoral law in the world ; and the other, appointed by me it is true, but independent, because its members are irremovable.' Louis Napoleon had in fact insisted that the Legislature should be elected by universal suffrage ;[2] and it was true that the Senators once nominated could not be removed.[3] Nor did he retain in regard to his upper house the usual power of swamping opposition by an indefinite creation of new peers : for by the constitution their numbers could never exceed one hundred and fifty ; and of the constitution they were themselves interpreters and custodians, armed with a right of veto on all laws contrary to its provisions, as also on any infringing on freedom of worship, the liberty of the individual, the equality of all citizens before the law, and the principle of the immovability of the judiciary. The lower house moreover, sadly shorn as it was of all opportunity for eloquence, did yet retain the fundamental right of voting or refusing to vote both laws and budget. Further, it was elected by a franchise out and away more liberal than that enjoyed by contemporary England. Every Frenchman received the vote at the age of twenty-one ; four Englishmen out of five had at this time no vote at all. True, in

---

[1] 29 Mar. 52.

[2] ' I know that when the constitution was under discussion in 1852 it was strongly urged upon the Emperor that it was dangerous to submit the choice of deputies to the Legislative Body to the same ordeal as that by which H.M. held his own authority.' F.O. France, Cowley to Clarendon. 'Most confidential.' 9 July 57. He even harped on this identity : cf. his reply to an address of the Chamber on 2 March 54. ' Nous représentons tous les mêmes intérêts, car vous et moi, nous sommes les élus de la France.'

[3] They were not as sometimes stated—e.g. by Professor Alison Phillips, Modern Europe, 337 —' dismissible at will.'

France as in England constituencies had their frontiers
arranged to suit the conservative interest : but in France
the electoral districts were at least equal in population ;
whereas in England they differed so fantastically that in
1866 Bright could point scornfully to 'a Parliament, more
than half of whose members are returned by *3 per cent* of
the grown men of the kingdom.'[1] Most important of all,
the French voter was protected by the ballot ; an elementary security for which the fraction of Englishmen who were
enfranchised at all had still another twenty years to wait.

All these advantages however were heavily offset by
a system of official candidature from which England at
that time was entirely free : a system involving an injury
to the spirit of representative government for which no
mere improvements in its mechanism could atone. Still,
even under the burden of this indignity, no assembly whose
members were inviolable and elected by single, secret,
direct, and universal suffrage from equal electoral districts
could long possess these advantages and lack the germs
of real constitutional development. And that development the President hinted not obscurely, it might be his
own wish to foster and encourage. Liberty indeed, he
remarked in a phrase destined to a melancholy notoriety,
could not found, but only crown, the political edifice.
Meanwhile he had at least set things right way up.
'Society had too long resembled a pyramid resting on its
apex : I replaced it upon its base.' But he was careful to
explain that this achievement did not constitute finality : on
the contrary he congratulated his hearers that the present
constitution was in essence flexible ; it had 'only fixed what
could not be left uncertain ; it had not immured the
destinies of a great people in an insurmountable ring wall.'[2]
In fact, the Second Empire differed from the Bourbon and
Orleanist experiments of the nineteenth century, in that
they both started with a mildly liberal charter or constitution, which in practice they proceeded gradually to

---

[1] *Trevelyan : Bright*, 364. Bright calculated that 84 per cent. even of
the adult male population were at that date still totally unenfranchised.
[2] 'Je veux les mener à une liberté sage' was a remark of his about this
time to Prince Czartoriski, who repeated it to *Jerrold*, iv. 37.

render reactionary ; while it, from a foundation almost frankly despotic, proceeded gradually in the direction of parliamentary liberalism. Meanwhile the very machinery devised to diminish the effective control of amendments by the lower house—the free use of small committees of its members, and of an external drafting body, the Council of State—did in effect conduce to the facility of legislation : the President, the original initiator of bills, tended to be moderate and humane in his conceptions, while the committees, though incapable of fundamental opposition, were by no means ill-fitted for the task of converting in detail large ideas into practicable proposals. Hence the actual legislative output of the whole, even in the early most popular and least liberal years of its existence, compared far from unfavourably either in bulk, benevolence, or general utility and good draftsmanship with that of the republican chambers which came before and after.[1]

Although his new legislature was elected at the end of February and at work by the end of March, Louis could not restrain his desire for action even for those few weeks. In the interval, he governed the country frankly as dictator. by a series of decrees. For two months he revelled in the activities of a beneficent despot, translating into sudden action the whims of long months of brooding reverie. It delighted him at a stroke of his pen to accomplish what wrangling deputies in interminable debates had discussed for months and nothing forwarded : it pleased him still more to give sudden substance to fond imaginings of his own long-prisoned imagination. His activities in this respect during the opening months of 1852 were such as to appease the most insatiate appetite for infallible direction from above ; during those months the French *père de famille* could never open his morning's newspaper without lighting on some new decree of indefatigable authority. One day's decree converted the national debt from a 5 per cent. to a 4½ per cent. loan : the usual option of repayment at par was proffered ; but thanks to the rise in public

[1] On this, v. *Jerrold*, iii. 385 *n.* Cf. *Dickinson*, 232, 233.

securities following on the success of the *coup d'état* the holders all but unanimously preferred conversion to redemption. Other decrees established a great network of railways throughout France. The Orleanist regime had generally discouraged and invariably delayed enterprise of this kind : Louis now gave it a sudden and on the whole a well-directed impulse, with the result that the total length of French railways was quadrupled in the next seven years.[1] Private enterprise alone was employed, with no State subvention or guarantee : but the President stipulated that at the close of ninety-nine years all such property should revert to the State. Succeeding decrees multiplied in a similar manner roads, canals, telegraph lines, and harbours. Others followed to check the adulteration of food, discountenance Sunday labour, and to improve the sanitation of slums.

In every case the word was no sooner spoken than the work was begun ; like Aladdin newly endowed with his wishing ring, Louis not only took childish delight in multiplying the activities of his genius, but he would have his behests executed with all imaginable celerity. Paris could not indeed be made to sprout palaces in a night ; yet the wonder-working effects of the Napoleonic talisman must be swift as well as startling.

Unfortunately Louis Napoleon, as fairy prince in the pantomime of these winter months, was not content to seek his effects solely amid the oriental splendours of the Arabian Nights ; from the rôle of Aladdin he could not resist a temporary excursion to the part of Robin Hood. It was the immense possessions of the Orleanist princes which now tempted him to the part—at all times somewhat congenial to him—of benevolent highwayman. In compelling the exiled king to sell within twelve months all real property he possessed in France, Louis was only following the precedent set by Bourbons in their treatment of the Bonapartes, and by Orleanists in their treatment of the Bourbons. But no similar justification could be pleaded

[1] *C.M.H., Thomas*, 299.

for another decree published on the same day.[1] It was an ancient and established principle that upon his accession all the private property of any French prince, by whatever title acquired, became merged instantly in the Crown domain. But Louis Philippe by a legal fiction had evaded this rule ; making over to his sons, on the very day of his election to the throne, the greater portion of his enormous landed estates ; excluding from the gift his eldest son, and reserving to himself a life interest in all property thus transferred. The expedient itself had been of doubtful legality : by a step at least equally dubious in law and far more high-handed in its incidence, Louis now denounced the previous transference ; and declared the estates in question restored to the State domain, from which he pronounced them to have been illegally alienated. A few Legitimists, in their detestation of Louis Philippe, rejoiced at the proceeding ;[2] but the Orleanists, as was natural, bitterly resented it. Louis however brutally declared that the hundred million francs remaining to their princes more than sufficed to maintain their dignity abroad ; and that for the rest they ought to be grateful that his government would continue the annual payment of the 300,000 francs dowry voted by the last regime to the Duchess of Orleans.

Content with this exposition of his moderation, the President proceeded gaily to apply his booty to a score of benevolent purposes ; among them the endowment of mutual benefit societies, the provision of decent Christian burial free of charge for the poor,[3] the establishment of orphanages and asylums, the improvement of workmen's dwellings in large manufacturing towns, and the foundation in the *crédit foncier* societies of a really useful system of agricultural loan and mortgage banks, by means of which the impoverished land-owner was enabled to make long-needed improvements in his small estate. Upon these followed decrees for the provision of public baths and wash-houses, the improve-

---

[1] 22 Jan. 52. For text in full, v. *Register* : 1852, 209 *sq*. For Orleanist criticism, v. *Bazin*, 379–384.

[2] *Papiers Sauvés*, 6.

[3] A concession particularly grateful to the priests, by the odium from which it relieved them. *Arch. Nat.*, F 1ᶜ ¹¹¹., Seine, 30.

ment of hospitals, the reorganisation of pawn-shops in the interests of their *clientèle*, and the reform of the *Bureaux de placements* in such a sense as to make of them a sort of primitive labour exchange. Doubtless Louis imagined that by his act he was creating a multitude of vested interests in France hostile to the Orleanist dynasty, or at any rate financially interested in its continued exclusion from the throne. But naturally the proceeding was regarded as a strange inconsistency in one who had just appealed to France as the defender of private property against the onslaughts of socialism.

The fact was that though Louis had offered himself to France in all good faith as a physician against a threatened severe attack of this disease, yet as a result of his own semi-socialist inclinations the remedies which he so drastically administered were from the first decidedly homeopathic in their character. Unfortunately the patient desired more orthodox treatment ; a hair of the dog that might have bitten him was by no means to his taste ; and the physician found himself denounced in consequence for a charlatan and worse. ' He has the perverse ingenuity of a madman,' wrote the Marquis de Circourt, in a passage eloquent of contemporary conservative opinion in Paris, ' the ingenuity of a madman and the self-confidence of a fatalist. He says he wants eighty million to fill up the deficit, and that the richer classes are alone to pay them ! He speaks about income tax, progressive taxation . . . and the like.' His advisers ' vainly endeavoured to make him understand the wicked folly of such things.' [1] Of these a number now withdrew from his counsels ; some, like Fould, Rouher, and Morny, were but momentarily estranged : others, of whom Montalembert was the chief, were permanently alienated.

But this isolated severity directed against the house of Orleans shrank into insignificance when compared with the measures adopted against the Socialists and Republicans. Many already of the decrees which the President had been

[1] Circourt to Reeve, 1 Feb. 52.   B.M. Add. MSS. 37,423, f. 43.

showering upon the country were animated by motives
primarily repressive. It was no fear of fostering the spirit
of militarism which induced him to reform the National
Guard almost out of existence ; nor any mere zeal for
temperance which led to the licensing and restriction of
cafés and *cabarets*. Frankly repressive in particular had
been the decree dealing with the press ; a decree as drastic
as any previous effort of despotism in this direction, and
only distinguished from its predecessors by one notable
trace of originality. Under the system now inaugurated
newspapers were allowed to commit two indiscretions with
impunity ; only after having been twice ' warned ' did they
ordinarily become liable to suspension. From this system
of one free bite emerged ultimately a new and subtle form
of journalistic sarcasm ; for under it a clever editor could
discover to a nicety the precise degree of daring or veracity
upon which he might venture ; and under exactly how
thin a guise of apparent innocence or admiration he might
convey to the government his disapproval, ridicule, or contempt. Though the general effect of the system was devastating, a few of the most skilfully conducted of Parisian
newspapers throve upon it ; [1] in some cases at any rate
their contributors seem to have entered into the game of
cheating the censor with real zest and enjoyment. It was
a game played eventually with known rules as well as
with established penalties : the least clumsiness in attack
drew upon the offender a sharp rap over the knuckles in
the shape of an official *avertissement* ; an *avertissement* however which a period of good behaviour on the part of the
particular journal, or some public occasion of rejoicing on
the part of the government, might suffice to render *nul et
non avenu*. It was a game which in the playing conduced
to an artful elusive fugitive attack ; and in the player
to that strongest joy in gambling and strangest joy in
games ; the joy of the mouse in playing with the cat.

But drastic as they were, these other measures in the
interests of ' public security ' seemed gentle and humane

---

[1] *La Gorce*: *Empire*, i. 47. See on this subject generally *Pessard*, i.
passim ; *Rochefort*, i. 303 *sq.* ; *Villemessant*, iii. 69.

by the side of the sentences doled out to the republican
or socialist opponents of the *coup d'état*. In this task all
pretence of moderation was flung aside : repression here
was naked, brutal, and unashamed. First the President
put thirty-two departments under martial law. Then he
presented himself by a decree [1] with the right of transport-
ing to Algeria or even Cayenne any member of any secret
society. A month later eighty-eight members of the old
Assembly were either banished or ' momentarily removed '
from France. At the beginning of February tribunals
were created to deal summarily with the hoards of provincial prisoners. These tribunals, the so-called ' mixed
commissions,' consisted of triumvirates, composed in each
case of a general, a lawyer, and a prefect. Their powers
ranged from immediate liberation to transportation to
French Guiana : their proceedings were to be secret, final,
and above all swift. In fact the sole compensation for
the absence of law was the absence of delay ; by the
middle of March the work such as it was was done. Over
twenty-six thousand persons had been arrested,[2] of whom
six thousand five hundred [3] were acquitted and rather more
than five thousand [4] sentenced only to police surveillance ;
of the fifteen thousand [5] actually punished nearly two-
thirds [6] were sentenced to deportation to Algeria ; while
the rest were either handed over to other tribunals for
offences against common law,[7] or expelled from France,[8] or
bidden to reside in some particular fortress or city of it,[9] or
even condemned to the dreaded shores of French Guiana.[10]

It seems necessary to verge on the statistical in the
recitation of these sentences, since to this day a good deal
of loose writing is common on the subject.[11] During the
actual continuance of the Second Empire exaggeration
was inevitable : the government had only itself to blame
if its contemporary published statistics in regard to the

---

[1] 8 Dec. 51.   [2] 26,642.   [3] To be precise, 6501.   [4] 5108.
[5] 15,033.   [6] 9530.   [7] 915.   [8] 1545.
[9] 2804.   [10] 239.
[11] E.g. *Dickinson*, 216. ' Now, transportation meant Cayenne, and it
is said that the number of persons thus dealt with was over 25,000.' In
fact, it was under 250. On their treatment, v. *Delescluze*. On contemporary exaggerations of the figures, v. *Seignobos : France*, 220.

coup d'état were dismissed as valueless. But immediately after the fall of the Empire a secret police court report on these punishments was rescued from the Tuileries, and published among a selection of the Emperor's private papers made and edited under the auspices of the republican government with the object of discrediting the imperial regime as much as possible.[1] The document in question was one which had been furnished confidentially to the Emperor by his chief of police on the eve of his marriage, in response to an express request for an exact account of all persons against whom ' any penal measure whatsoever ' had been taken after December 1851 ; and unless we are to imagine that Maupas took an entirely gratuitous risk in wantonly deceiving the Emperor, his figures must be taken to be correct.[2]

One other fact in regard to these figures ought perhaps to be set forth here, since in general it has been as studiously ignored as these sentences themselves have been eloquently advertised. Deserving of all condemnation though these condemnations undoubtedly are, it is unfortunately the case that neither the Republic which preceded the Second Empire, nor the Republic which followed it, is here in a position to cast the first stone. By the aid of special commissions the Second Republic in 1848, after the June days, arrested over fourteen thousand men ;[3] and voted itself powers to deport whom it would of them without trial ; not, like the majority of the present victims, to Algeria, but to some less comfortable colony of France.[4] The Third Republic in 1871, after the Commune, first shot nearly twenty thousand men without trial [5] and then made prisoners of more than twice that number.[6] Of these prisoners, nearly twelve hundred died from ill-treatment,[7] over a thousand were women, six hundred and fifty were children,[7] and seven thousand five hundred were deported

---

[1] *Papiers et Correspondance*, i. 216, 217, whence come all the figures quoted above.
[2] As such they are in effect accepted even by *Bourgeois*, *C.M.H.*, 140.
[3] *Moniteur*, 7 Oct. 48.   [4] *La Gorce*: *République*, i. 395.
[5] *Bourgeois*, ii. 214.   [6] 43,501. *Hanotaux*, 211.
[7] *C.M.H.*, 505.

to New Caledonia [1]—the most remote of all the colonial acquisitions of the Second Empire. To deal with these prisoners twenty-two courts-martial sat permanently down to 1876.[2] It is true that both republics had greater excuse for their savage attacks on the prostrate Socialists than had Louis Napoleon : nevertheless it was the same fear of the same *Spectre Rouge* which led France to acquiesce in all three of these barbarities. Nor is it wholly due to the greater number of extenuating circumstances that the first and last of these pogroms have in fact escaped the condemnation most justly lavished on the second. Their relative immunity from criticism these others owe in reality to the fact that they were committed by republics. It is doubtless a testimonial to the republican ideal that men who love liberty love the republic also. But this very fact carries with it in practice one real danger to both. Tyranny in a despotism will at least get itself denounced : tyranny in a republic can count on no such practised castigation.

These considerations do not in any way extenuate the President's action. Political crime is nothing the better for having precedents, and something the worse for having imitators. But it is precisely as unprecedented and unparalleled that this particular crime has been denounced, by writers ignorant alike of what went before and after. And it is therefore a fact which deserves to be set on record, that the Third Republic auspicated its regime by dispatching to New Caledonia more than thirty times as many prisoners as the Second Empire had sent to Cayenne ; and that in general its early exiles were not only more numerous but were banished to far greater distances for far longer periods of time.

What chiefly distinguished the present sentences from those of the Second or the Third Republics was the fact that almost from the first, save in exceptional cases, any of Louis Napoleon's exiles could re-enter France upon the signed petition of himself or of a friend, accompanied by an undertaking to abstain from politics and to recognise

---

[1] *Seignobos* : *Histoire*, 7.
[2] *Bourgeois*, ii. 214.   *Hanotaux*, 213

accomplished facts.[1] Recollections of his own exile, and appeals from those who had befriended him when himself a prisoner,[2] quickly led Louis to mitigate to this extent at least the severities which followed the *coup d'état*. One of the charges levelled against the Second Empire by its contemporary republican historians was precisely the fact that it did everything in its power to accelerate this process of return, and that 'gendarmes, convict-keepers, jailers made the strongest efforts to induce those transported or imprisoned to sign their petitions for pardon.'[3]

Hence in January 1853, even before the first collective amnesty, the total number of persons still undergoing punishment of some sort in connexion with the *coup d'état* had sunk to 6153, of whom less than five thousand[4] were in exile : and this number was itself at that time in daily process of diminution by individual submissions.[5] Three thousand more of them were at that time 'pardoned,' on the occasion of the Emperor's marriage. In March 1856, after the birth of the Prince Imperial, a general permission to return was issued to all who would accept the established government :[6] and finally in August 1859 an unconditional amnesty allowed everyone to return without any engagement of any kind.[7] At this last date eighteen hundred political offenders of all sorts were admitted to be still undergoing some form of punishment ;[8] but the total included refugees from the earlier disturbances of June 1848 and 1849, as well as a number of men subject only to police surveillance in France.[9] This final plenary amnesty applied with one single exception[10] to all the exiles of the Second Republic as well as of the *coup d'état*. Almost all

---

[1] *Delord*, ii. 576.
[2] Notably from George *Sand*, iii. 262–270, 282–285, 287–292, 306–311.
[3] *Delord*, ii. 576.
[4] 4042 were in Algeria, 173 in Cayenne, 614 banished from France ; the remaining 1324 were 'interned' in France. *Papiers et Correspondance*, i. 217
[5] *Ibid.*   [6] *Moniteur*, 20 Mar. 56.
[7] *Moniteur*, 15 Aug. 59.   [8] *Constitutionnel*, 25 Aug. 59.
[9] *La Gorce : Empire*, iii. 121.
[10] Ledru-Rollin, exiled in 1849 ; excluded now on the pretext that he had been guilty of common crime ; v. *Delord*, ii. 589. *Ledru-Rollin*, ii. 460–465.

of them availed themselves of the measure ; rightly judging, now that no conditions debarred them from return, that they could serve liberty better in France than out of it. But a few preferred as *émigrés* to deny their presence to ' an enslaved country ' : [1] and among those few was the most illustrious of them all, Victor Hugo. Perhaps he was artist enough to realise that he was well served by the picturesque environment of his exile, and by the halo of a voluntary and not too arduous martyrdom. But even he cannot have guessed the true extent of that service. For its real benefit was that it availed to deflect him in his prime from politics, in which he was just not ridiculous, to literature, in which he was just not sublime.

Meanwhile the event to which all these activities were directed was rapidly looming into view. With the opening of the year 1852 began the last stage of Louis Napoleon's long march towards Empire. The revised constitution, which the recent plebiscite had ratified, was still nominally republican ; and Louis himself in March, at the opening of the new session, had affected an inclination ' to preserve the Republic ' unless popular unrest should force him to give authority a still more stable form. But every month that passed brought with it some sign of an approaching change. The Civil Code became once more the Code Napoléon : the Imperial Eagles remounted the military standards : portraits of Napoleon at Versailles were observed—a small but significant detail—to be labelled now Napoleon I.[2] Everywhere official formulæ halted between a republic already to all real purpose dead, and an empire not yet ready to be born. For once the mortal wound had been dealt, the President was an unconscionable time in killing. Perhaps he hoped that by the delay the republic might have some appearance of dying a natural death : probably he saw that it was desirable to dissever by a decent interval the ending of the old order from the

[1] E.g. *Boichot*, 265 ; *Quinet*, i. 413–425 ; and *cf.* letter of Charras in *Scheurer-Kestner*, 42–46.
[2] F.O. France, Cowley to Granville, 5 Sept. 52.

inauguration of the new. In any case it was characteristic of him, that having decided to change the character of the portrait cast on the French political screen, he effected the alteration not abruptly by the withdrawal of one picture and the substitution of another, but almost imperceptibly by a process of dissolving views. On his election to the presidency he had exchanged civilian costume for the uniform of General of the National Guard ; after the *coup d'état* this in turn gave place to full military uniform.[1] In 1852 he still made his dwelling in the Elysée ; but already he entertained at the Tuileries. On his state box at the Théâtre Français the Republican cypher R.F. gave place to his personal monogram L.N.[2] In church men did not yet pray for him as Emperor ; but they no longer prayed for him as President : *Domine salvum fac Ludovicum Napoleonem*, the petition now employed,[3] needed but the shedding of the Christian name to make it merely regal. On the coinage of this year the name and emblems of the Republic subsisted on the one side, but the head of the new Napoleon appeared upon the other : the superscription remained the Republic's, but the image was already Cæsar's.

Spring turned to summer, and summer verged on autumn, yet still the last step was untaken. His opponents imagined that Louis was awaiting some spectacular opportunity for his proclamation as Emperor by the army ; but the restoration of the eagles to the legions assembled in the Champ de Mars in May, and the official inauguration of the Fête Napoléon in August, were alike allowed to pass with the empire still unmade. One such opportunity Louis Napoleon does indeed seem to have sought, and sought in vain. ' I am credibly informed,' wrote Jerningham, the *chargé d'affaires* at the head of the British embassy during the interval between Normanby's retirement and Cowley's appointment, ' that the French Government recently applied to that of Austria for the remains of the son of the Emperor Napoleon, the Duke of Reichstadt,

---

[1] *Viel-Castel*, i. 249. [2] *Fraser*, 125.
[3] *Delord*, i. 397.

and that the Austrian Government replied that they could not be better placed than where they were, namely by the side of those of the Duke's mother. I am further informed that this reply caused much irritation at the Elysée, and some of the President's household have consoled themselves with the reply that the French army will some day go and take those remains.'[1] Louis had made the return of Napoleon's own remains the occasion of one of his youthful attempts to seize the empire ; nothing is more probable than that he would have liked to inaugurate its actual restoration now by a similar translation of the body of Napoleon II.

This was not the only way in which Austria would seem to have baulked him during this year of a pomp and precedent on which he had set his heart. For some months he nursed the hope of getting himself crowned by the Pope in Paris, so that the Second Empire like the First might reflect the glories of a Carolingian coronation. Difficulties perhaps in any case insuperable lay in the path of this scheme ; for Pio Nono pressed for modifications of the code, or at least of its interpretation, such as Louis Napoleon could hardly have conceded. But it was Austria whose intervention appears to have given the project its *coup de grâce*, by intimating to the Vatican that in the event of its compliance with Louis' request the Emperor of Austria would require the Pope to crown him also at Vienna and in addition to place on his head at Milan the iron crown of Lombardy.[2] It is perhaps no more than a coincidence, though none the less a significant one, that if credence may be attached to either of these unpublished sources both the European monarchs, Austrian as well as Russian, who already possessed an imperial title are now shown to have rebuffed at the outset the imperial pretensions of France ; and that each in turn paid the penalty by suffering defeat and territorial diminution at the hands of this unwelcome colleague.

It was only in September that Louis at last embarked

---

[1] F.O. France, Jerningham to Granville. 'Confidential.' 22 Jan. 52.
[2] Circourt to Reeve, 8 Nov. 52. B.M. Add. MSS. 37,423, f. 187.

on his final passage to the Empire. He adopted once more
the old device of a tour of the provinces. This time his
voyage in his own phrase was a question, 'a mark of interrogation.' It was a mark of interrogation however
which expected the answer 'yes,' and it was addressed
once more not to Paris but to the provinces. But of the
provinces Louis insisted, against the advice of his ministers,
in visiting just the districts which had most distinguished
themselves by their opposition to the *coup d'état*. Down
the Rhone valley he travelled to Lyons and Marseilles ; and
thence through the departments of the South and West where
socialism had been most rife, to Toulouse and Bordeaux.

Once more he was justified by the result. The present
tour had it is true certain advantages over its predecessors, due to the fact that the Prince had now complete
control over the executive machinery of the provinces.
Cheap trains were run by local railways to enable trippers
to visit towns through which the Prince was passing :
and in these towns themselves municipal authorities
would have verged on the munificent in their preparations
for his reception, had not Louis, struck by the magnitude
of the sums so voted, inserted a notice in the *Moniteur* [1]
requesting them to curtail their expenditure, and to
devote to the poor the major portion of the sums already
voted for his reception. The popular enthusiasm was in
any case undoubted ; nor were the cries of *Vive l'Empereur*
of merely official manufacture.[2] But for a moment Louis
seemed still to hang back. 'This greeting,' he said at
Lyons, 'awakens a memory which goes straight to my
heart, rather than a hope which flatters my pride.' At this
same town he received in audience General La Marmora,
who came charged with a friendly letter from the King
of Piedmont. For the moment, Louis told the General,
it must still be his first task to consolidate the power and

[1] 28 Aug. 52.
[2] ' Je vous dis que je viens de voir de mes yeux et entendre de mes
oreilles ce que je n'avais jamais vu et n'avais jamais entendu dans nos
villes du Midi, à aucune de nos époques politiques ; il est impossible, si
l'on n'en a été témoin, de se faire une idée de l'enthousiasme frénétique des
populations sur le passage du Prince Président.' Castelbajac to Reiset,
8 Oct. 52. *Reiset*, ii. 54.

prestige of France : but that done he was determined
'*faire quelque chose pour l'Italie qu'il aimait comme sa
seconde patrie.*' [1]

Only at the end of his tour was the word for which France
waited spoken at last : the Emperor's own acceptance of
the Empire. This was at Bordeaux. The usual banquet
had been held ; the usual after dinner speech ensued. But
this time the speech was explicit. Mere frankness, which
was as far removed from pride as from false modesty, compelled him, said the Prince, to recognise that the overwhelming majority of the French people appeared to desire
the restoration of the Empire : a desire not unnatural
since it might free them from anxiety for the future. ' But,'
he added, ' there is one fear to which I ought to reply.
There are some who doubt, and say " the Empire, that
means war." *I* tell you, the Empire means peace. It
means peace, for France desires it : and when France is
satisfied, the world has rest.' The quiet and colossal
arrogance of this sentence gave mortal offence to the Czar :
as an epitome of European history it contained just enough
truth to render it deftly flattering to France and irritating to the rest of Europe. The neatness of the dictum is
only increased if it be remembered that it was itself the
obverse of a recent saying of the great Austrian Schwarzenberg ; a statesman whose premature death in April 1852
was the most important event of its kind in the history
of the nineteenth century. ' When France catches cold,'
he had remarked, ' Europe sneezes.' [2]

The remainder of the President's speech contained no
sentence to which the most fastidious critic could take
exception. ' I too, like the Emperor,' said Louis, ' have
many conquests to make. I would fain, like him, conquer
unto conciliation the dissident parties, and lead back into
the great main river of the people the separate straggling
streams that are like to lose themselves without benefit to

---

[1] This La Marmora himself told *Ollivier*, iii. 141.

[2] *Reiset*, ii. 41. Next morning, Louis parodied his own parody. In
taking leave of Bordeaux, he complimented its prefect, Haussmann, on the
excellent condition in which he found it : ' adding with a smile, " Quand le
Prince est satisfait, le Préfet peut être tranquille." ' *Haussmann*, i. 474.

any. I would fain conquer to religion, to morality, to the
easing of their burdens that portion of our populace—still
so large—which in the midst of a Christian land knows
hardly at all the teachings of Christ ; which in the heart
of the most fertile country in the world, can scarcely command the bare necessities of life.

' We have immense waste territories to cultivate : roads
to open, harbours to deepen, canals to complete, rivers
to render navigable, railways to link in one. Facing
us over against Marseilles we have a vast dominion to
assimilate to France. We have all our great ports of the
West to bring near to America by speed of communications
which as yet they lack. Everywhere we have ruins to
raise again, false gods to tread under foot, truths to make
triumphant. That is how I would interpret the Empire, if
the Empire is indeed to be restored. Such are the conquests
I contemplate. And you, all of you who surround me, you
who wish like me our country's good, you are my soldiers.'

The speech deserves to be read in French. In its original
form no utterance of the new Emperor's comes so
near to justifying Cobden's praise of the ' absolute perfection of the style of his occasional addresses ' : [1] in
the light of it even Tocqueville's wild remark that ' Louis
Napoleon was the only man living who could write
" monumental French " ' ceases for a moment to sound
extravagant. Among its actual audience, though uttered
in a ' firm and loud voice,' the speech did not create
universal enthusiasm : [2] possibly some more militant
pronouncement would have been more clamorously applauded. But in Paris, in France at large, the report of it
gave rise to sincere and spontaneous emotion ; indeed no
dynasty at its inauguration had ever proposed to itself a
larger or more gracious design. The famous dictum,
L'Empire c'est la paix sounds sadly enough, it is true, to
those who know the sequel. But that is not to say, as
some have said, that it was therefore conscious hypocrisy.

[1] *Morley* : *Cobden*, ii. 352.
[2] F.O. France. Report of British Consul at Bordeaux, enclosed in
Cowley to Malmesbury, 10 Oct. 52.

Not every purpose that is unfulfilled is for that reason
insincere : nor need a man's word be out of harmony with
his thoughts, because it is at variance with his acts. The
failure to seem consistent has less commonly been proof of
hypocrisy than the desire to seem consistent has been cause
of it.

A week later Louis Napoleon re-entered Paris ; and at
once the last preparations for the change of government
were taken in hand. The senate was consulted, and with
the exception of Louis' old friend and tutor M. Vieillard,[1]
voted unanimously for the change. The Senatus Con-
sultum was only to take effect when ratified by the popular
vote, but this ratification was at once forthcoming. On
November 21 and 22, wild and stormy days,[2] the new
plebiscite was taken ; the majority in Louis' favour was
even larger than in the preceding year, seven million eight
hundred thousand voting for the Empire, a quarter of a
million only opposing it, though two millions in that
drenching rain abstained from voting at all. On the eve
of the vote socialist and republican exiles issued last
impassioned appeals to France, holding up Louis Napoleon
to execration, hinting even at the virtue of assassination.
The Comte de Chambord launched a mournful and dignified
rebuke to those who sought the virtues of monarchy from
any but its legitimate source. The *Moniteur*, in successive
columns, reprinted the one and the other ; adding also
minute and detailed accounts of the precautions taken
to ensure the authenticity of the vote : describing the
polling clerks and committees selected by the electors themselves ; the guard set at night over sealed urns deposited
in sealed rooms ; the open counting of the votes in the
presence of the electors, at tables so arranged that they
could freely circulate between them. These last particulars

[1] Whence this letter :

St Cloud, 9 Nov. [52].

My dear M. Vieillard,—How can you imagine that your vote could affect
my friendship in the least ? Come and lunch on Thursday as usual. The
new title I am to receive from the nation will no more change our customs
than it will change my regard for you. Let this be proof of it.—Your
friend, Louis Napoleon. *Jerrold*,.iii. 404.

[2] *Haussmann*, i. 576.

were intended as an answer to Victor Hugo's charge that
the vote was merely falsified. The charge was groundless ;
falsification was unnecessary ; and though now as in the
preceding year official pressure had its part in exaggerating
the result, yet even less than in the preceding year did it
solely or mainly account for it. Now as then the fact
remained unquestionable, that France had greeted the
change with approbation as general, with acquiescence as
nearly universal, as ever she bestowed on any dynasty or
constitution in her history.

To Europe as a whole however the revival of the Empire
in 1852 was a far more serious challenge than the mere
prolongation of the presidency in 1851. For the present
change involved the restoration to the throne of France of
a member of Napoleon's dynasty, and any such restoration
the Powers were pledged by treaty to resist.

Yet no effectual resistance was forthcoming. Now as
often the drama enacted on the high stage of French
politics held the eyes of Europe : but now as a year
earlier the spectators were divided in their sympathies.
Yet though the division and the line of division remained unaltered, a strange reversal had taken place in the
attitude of the audience. At the deed of December 1851
the stalls applauded and the gallery groaned : now at its
apparently logical outcome in 1852 the gods were happy
and the kings dismayed. The *coup d'état* had been
reprobated by England and welcomed by the East : the
new Empire arising from it was condemned by the East
and readily accepted by England. Superficially surprising,
this seeming *volte-face* was in fact consistent and intelligible.
The very liberalism which made England loathe the *coup
d'état* forbade any forcible opposition to the clearly-
expressed will of the French nation, that it would have the
author of it for Emperor. The very spirit of despotism
that made the Czar rejoice in the *coup d'état* as an act of
repression, made him resent the re-erection by a nation
of a dynasty of its own. It was no source of pleasure to the
ancient dynasties of the East to see an Emperor the more

in Europe intruding upon their company with a title as
high-sounding as their own.   And to Nicholas in particular
the numeral with which the new Napoleon qualified his
style seemed an insufferable arrogance : for to recognise
Napoleon III was by implication to recognise not merely
Napoleon I but Napoleon II : the boy whose hour of
Empire it had been no affectation in Europe to ignore,
since France herself had scarcely taken cognisance of it.

From the opening months of 1852 Russia had not
ceased to urge on Louis a pledge that he would abstain
from the imperial title.[1] Finding that the Prince could by
no means be persuaded to take it, the Czar fell back upon
a policy of no emperors between empires ; he even wrote
Louis an autograph letter, delivered to him on November
30, urging him at least to resist the insidious attraction of
the numeral III.[2] This letter, so far from mending matters,
proved an absolute obstacle to any understanding.
Louis affected to be too busy to answer it during his last
two days as President, and unable to answer it after
December 2 ; for how could he salute Nicholas in imperial
style until the Russian government had recognised his
new title ? [3] The Czar meanwhile postponed his recognition of the new Empire in any form, because he had
received no answer to his letter.[4] While direct intercourse
between the two emperors was thus temporarily suspended,
their diplomatic relations were verging on the acrimonious.
In mid-December Nesselrode, the Russian foreign minister,
sent to his ambassador at Paris a despatch in which he
formally protested against the title Napoleon III.   Kisseleff
handed it on to Drouyn de Lhuys, intending that he should
show it to his master.   Drouyn however returned it without
showing it to the Emperor, saying that he must decline to
discuss *un fait accompli*, and had consequently no other

---

[1] F.O. France, Cowley to Granville, 21 Feb. 52. *Cf.* F.O. Russia,
Seymour to Clarendon. ‘ Confidential.’   24 Dec. 51. ‘ Tous mes voeux
sont pour lui,’ said Nicholas, ‘ qu’il se fasse nommer Président, consul
même pour dix ans—pour la vie—rien de mieux : mais pour Dieu qu’il ne
songe pas à se faire proclamer Empereur.’   *Ibid.*
[2] F.O. France, Cowley to Granville, 1 Dec. 52.
[3] *Ibid.*, Cowley to Malmesbury, 19 Dec. 52.
[4] *Ibid.*, Cowley to Lord John Russell, 29 Dec. 52.

observation to make on Count Nesselrode's despatch than
to admire the elegance of its style.[1] The new Empire was
enabled to take up this comparatively independent attitude
towards Russia, thanks to the fact that England had
already officially recognised its existence ; indeed Louis
was profoundly impressed by the fact that the sole Power
which had never recognised the First Empire had been the
first great Power to recognise the Second.

In January therefore, the Czar presented his tardy
credentials ; but relying on the promised co-operation of
Austria and Prussia, he omitted the customary salutation,
Sire, mon Frère.[2] On January 4 Drouyn informed
Kisseleff that for this reason he could not advise Napoleon
to accept them. On the evening of that day matters
appeared to have reached a complete deadlock, since
though the Austrian and Prussian credentials were couched
in customary style, their representatives were pledged
only to present them in conjunction with Russia. Had
Drouyn been allowed his way, France would have resolutely
refused to accept the Russian impertinence ; and the
language held by the Austrian ambassador in Paris to
Cowley shows that in this case Austria would have broken
away from her agreement with Russia, and presented her
own credentials as they stood.[3] But this fact was unknown to the new Emperor ; and when faced with the
dilemma of disobeying his foreign minister or belying his
own speech at Bordeaux, he wisely preferred to submit to
what was after all not a national injury but merely a
personal incivility. On the following day he informed
Cowley through Fould of this decision.[4] ' To give your
Lordship an idea of the way in which business is carried on
here,' Cowley continues, ' he asked me not to tell Drouyn,
" as the Emperor had not yet announced his intention to

---

[1] F.O. France, Jerningham to Malmesbury. ' Confidential.' 18 Dec. 52.

[2] ' Mon Frère,' he told the English ambassador at Petersburg, ' could
only be addressed to one whose authority was from Heaven ' : ' by Mon
Frère, if addressed to a Frenchman, he should designate another person '
[Henri V]. F.O. Russia, Seymour to Russell. ' Secret and confidential.'
22 Jan. 53.

[3] F.O. France, Cowley to Russell. ' Most confidential.' 4 Jan. 53.

[4] *Ibid.*, Cowley to Russell, 5 Jan. 53.

that minister." ' Later in the morning Cowley found the Russian envoy still in ignorance of this sudden solution of a difficulty which twenty-four hours earlier had threatened to bring about an immediate rupture in the diplomatic relations of the two countries.[1] On the same day Kisseleff was received in audience by the Emperor, whom the Czar addressed as ' *notre très cher ami Napoléon, Empereur des Français.*' A familiar and perhaps correct tradition [2] ascribes to Louis Napoleon on this occasion his most celebrated repartee, making him express himself to Kisseleff as very sensible of his master's kindness evinced in his peculiar form of address, ' for we put up with our brothers : we choose our friends.' But Cowley reports only a more commonplace remark. '*Vous voyez,*' said Louis to the Russian envoy, '*je regarde plutôt le fond que la forme*' : adding ' your Emperor has shewn me kindness until now : I will look to the past more than to the present.' [3]

To his own people Louis Napoleon had already explained the reasons for his choice of a title, when he was officially apprised that a new title was his to choose. On December 1 he received a deputation from the Senate ; by whose spokesman he was addressed now for the first time as Sire. In reply, addressing an audience so used to see one régime reared on the ruins of its predecessors, as to expect the present to obliterate by all means in its power the very memory of the past, Louis formally professed himself the beneficiary of all past governments. ' Not only do I recognise the governments which have preceded me,' he said, ' but I inherit in some sort whatever they have done of good or evil.' But just because he accepted the facts of history, he could not ignore the glorious reign of Napoleon nor yet ' the regular though ephemeral title of his son, whom the Chamber proclaimed in a last access of vanquished patriotism.' Although therefore he dated his reign not from 1815, but from the day of his popular

---

[1] F.O. France. Cowley to Russell, 6 Jan. 53.
[2] The story was told to Rothan by Meyendorf, an attaché actually present at Kisseleff's audience. *Rothan*, 403.
[3] F.O. France, Cowley to Russell, 3 Jan. 53.

election, yet he assumed with the crown thus given him the title of Napoleon III. 'Help me, Sirs,' he ended, 'to establish in a land troubled by so many revolutions, a stable government, that shall have for foundation religion, righteousness, justice, and a love for those that suffer. And receive here my oath that I will spare no pains to assure the prosperity of the country, and that I will yield in nothing which touches the honour and dignity of France.'

Next day, the anniversary now of the *coup d'état*, as well as of Austerlitz and of Napoleon's coronation, Louis was proclaimed Emperor, and inducted to the Tuileries. Lavish grants were at the same time made to the numerous members of the imperial family ; over a score of whom received public provision. Throughout his reign this host of cousins was a mere encumbrance to Napoleon III, adding much to the expense [1] and nothing at all to the prestige [2] of his court, receiving from him without gratitude what he had earned for them without help. Two only, it is true, of this miscellaneous collection of Highnesses were capable of inheriting the Empire : the old King of Westphalia, and his son Prince Napoleon. All other surviving members of the family, save Napoleon III himself, were disinherited by the terms of Napoleon's will ; and Louis by his own act, in virtue of the power given to him by the recent plebiscite, had selected Jerome and Prince Napoleon as his heirs. His nomination of them had been apparently as unwilling as it was unpopular. For on 'strangely good authority' it was reported to Lord Clarendon, that the new Emperor's first desire had been to entail his succession by adoption, and to adopt the Comte de Chambord.[3] The idea was palpably impracticable, but not for that reason the less characteristic of its author ; the nephew of

---

[1] For details, see *Papiers et Correspondance*, i. 75–76.

[2] *Cf.* the Countess Bernstorff to her mother, 29 Nov. 52 : 'Louis Napoleon's family is too impossible for anything. . . . The Prince is decidedly the flower of the flock. He isn't exactly imposing, but one cannot deny that he has something distinguished about him.' *Bernstorff*, i. 184–185. Cp. *Greville*, 16 May 50 : 'He is himself by far the best of his family, being well-meaning and a gentleman ; but all the rest are only a worthless set of *canaille*.'

[3] *Maxwell*, i. 346.

Napoleon legitimising the descendant of St Louis would have been just the spectacle with which he would have delighted to astonish France and Europe. But the legitimist Henri V could never consent to become heir by adoption and grace of a Bonaparte ; and the republican Prince Napoleon was the last man living to forgo his dynastic right to any crown. France however was perturbed by the mere prospect of such a ruler. Of distinguished appearance, considerable talent, and real though fitful eloquence, Prince Napoleon had yet contrived to arouse in almost all with whom he had come into contact feelings of political distrust or of personal dislike.[1] The Emperor had felt it wise to mitigate the unpalatable pronouncement which recognised Prince Napoleon as his heir presumptive, by expressing the hope that he might himself be permitted to contract an alliance which should assure direct heirs to the crown.

A happy marriage seemed the one thing now needed to give stability to the dynasty. In France there was no semblance of effective opposition to the restored Empire ; here and there, greatly daring, some Republican journalist would express his opinion of the new Emperor by sticking his stamps on upside down ; [2] but even the most sanguine renounced all present hope of overturning the Empire itself. The general tranquillity of the country was profound ; and Louis was fully aware of the strength of his own position. ' He talked with confidence,' reported Stratford Canning a year later, ' of his hold on public opinion, especially in the provinces, saying that he required no guards, and could go alone into the most retired streets of Paris with safety.' [3] Such was indeed his habitual practice. ' *Tous les jours*,' wrote the anarchist Proudhon of the new Emperor in the first week of his reign, ' *il se promene*

---

[1] *E.g.* ' Le prince est toujours, quoiqu'il fasse, le même homme, sans vigueur, grossier et mal élevé, détesté par tous ceux qui l'approchent.' *Viel-Castel*, iii. 180.

[2] *Pessard*, i. 29.

[3] *Lane-Poole*, ii. 237. Cf. *Ernest*, ii. 74. ' We drove without any kind of escort. Even in the worst faubourgs the people saluted us in a quiet and friendly manner.' This was in March 54.

*seul, à pied, sans escorte, à travers Paris stupéfait de son
audace.'* [1] His marriage, even if it were to be the occasion
of one audacity the more, would at least save the new
Empire from hanging upon the thread of a single and
unguarded life.

During the years of his presidency Louis had felt his
position too uncertain to seek a bride : he had even
pleaded the impossibility of marriage for one in his position
to excuse the continuance of his scarcely veiled liaison.
with Miss Howard.[2] When, however, the *coup d'état*
had brought him within sight of a crown, he at once
renewed his suit to his cousin the Princess Mathilde,[3] to
whom he had actually been engaged until the failure of his
descent on Strasburg in 1836 caused her father to break off
the match.[4] This time the lady herself refused. Her
marriage to a peculiarly unpleasant Russian grandee had
been dissolved on grounds which would allow of its annul-
ment by the Pope ; and she still retained an affectionate
interest in Louis and his fortunes. But by this time she
had formed a literary and artistic circle of her own which
she did not wish to exchange for the confines of any court.
Thereupon Louis allowed his advisers to seek on his behalf
the hand of a foreign princess. They sought in vain.
In June 1852 the Princess Caroline of Wasa, grand-
daughter of Stéphanie Beauharnais, cousin of the Empress
Josephine, was approached on the subject : [5] but her
father under Austrian influence declined the alliance, and
married the Princess instead to the Prince Royal of Saxony.
In December Walewski, French ambassador in London,
asked that Princess Adelaide of Hohenlohe, a niece of
Queen Victoria, might become Empress of the French.
This request also was refused.

---

[1] Letter dated Paris, 11 Dec. 52, to the republican Madier-Montjau.
' Il n'y a pas un homme, même dans le parti républicain,' continues the
writer in disgust, ' qui soit à la hauteur morale de s'y opposer.' *Proudhon*,
v. 114. And *cf.* p. 150 *n.* above.
[2] *Barrot*, iii. 361–364. *Falloux*, i. 504. She was now retired on a handsome pension *Papiers et Correspondance*, i. 172–173. *Cf.* Add. MSS.
37,422, f. 182.
[3] *Canrobert*, ii. 33.   [4] v. *Simpson*, 129.
[5] *Fleury*, i. 214. *Register* : 1852, 254. ' *Malakoff*,' i. 20.

Despite these initial rebuffs, a little patience and persistence would doubtless have sufficed to procure a princess
elsewhere : [1] even a new Empire has its measure of attraction, and a Parisian palace was no poor exchange, under
any title, for the ancient but tedious proprieties of some
provincial court. But Louis Napoleon was now in his
forty-fifth year. At that age he could not afford to await
indefinitely the day when royalty should vouchsafe to
hand him a princess in marriage : ' he had no time to
lose,' he told Malmesbury, ' if he was to leave an heir grown
up.' [2] The same haste was in fact upon him that drove
Henry VIII to his rupture with the papacy—the haste of
a monarch no longer young to furnish a dynasty not yet
old with an heir male, born in lawful wedlock. Emperor
and King alike no doubt had other reasons for their hurry ;
but each could plead reasons of state to justify a marriage
in haste. In this case even before the final repulse of his
ministers' second matrimonial proposal in England, Louis
Napoleon proceeded to engage himself to a bride of his own
seeking, eighteen years his junior, in the person of Eugénie
de Montijo ; a Spaniard of great beauty, though no longer
in the first bloom of youth.

Though Spanish by birth, Eugénie was not without
French predilections. Under the first Empire her father
had formed one of the *afrancesados*, that small body of
Spanish nobility whom Joseph succeeded in rallying to his
cause. In this capacity he had fought and had been
wounded at Salamanca, had retired with the retiring armies
of France to Paris itself, and thence directed in 1814 the
last cannonade against the victorious Allies.[3] There in
exile he wooed a Spaniard of Scottish lineage, María de
Kirkpatrick ; and though he returned to Spain before his
marriage, it was at a convent school in Paris that his
daughter Eugénie was educated. Since 1849 Eugénie with
her mother, now two years a widow, had been frequently

[1] Just too late Louis received the offer of a Swedish princess. v.
Diplomatic Study, i. 251 n.
[2] *Malmesbury*, i. 393. On this ground Morny, almost alone of Louis'
advisers, welcomed the marriage. B.M. Add. MSS. 37,423, f. 237.
[3] *Delord*, i. 486.

in Paris ; and like other foreigners of distinction, had attended the Prince's receptions at the Elysée. But it was only in the autumn of 1852 that Louis seems to have paid any marked attention to Mlle. de Montijo. Mother and daughter were invited, with a number of other guests, to stay at Fontainebleau in November, and at Compiègne for a longer visit in the following month. But Louis' ministers were wholly unprepared for an announcement which he made to them early in January that he had chosen this Spanish beauty for his bride.

To the majority of them the news was not merely unexpected, but in the highest degree unwelcome. The dynasty, to their mind, had need of just such added prestige as a royal alliance might bring it ; and to be foreign without being royal seemed the worst qualification possible for an Empress of the French. Just because the Emperor was in some sort an adventurer, it seemed imperative to his councillors that the Empress should not be an adventuress. Cæsar himself was suspect : then Cæsar's wife must be above suspicion. It was true that among the collateral ancestors of Mlle. de Montijo arduous heraldic researches discovered a Doge of Genoa, a Queen of Portugal, a King of Galicia and the Asturias ; [1] but it was rumoured that researches less arduous would have brought to light nearer ancestors entirely plebeian.[2] Yet after all to say this is but to say that among the progenitors of the house of Montijo, as of most other houses, king and chimney-sweeper were alike discoverable. True, the former alone were discovered ; but the survival of the fittest is a principle more commonly illustrated in a man's ancestry than in his descendants.

With more reason might the Emperor's advisers have dreaded the personal influence of such a bride upon such

---

[1] *Jerrold*, iii. 420

[2] Those interested in these obscurer and nearer relatives of the Empress will find a detailed account in Add. MSS. 37,423, f. 253 and 254. One of them, daughter of a Belgian tradesman, wife of a French consul at Malaga, sister of Eugénie's maternal grandmother, unfortunately died on the very eve of the wedding : ' and her death was concealed until after the marriage of her imperial niece.' Then ' the Montijos and the Empress, after some hesitation, went into mourning.' *Ibid.*

a husband. For though endowed by nature with high
spirit, ready utterance, and singular beauty, the new
Empress yet lacked any real preparation for the rôle she
was so suddenly called upon to fill. There were, it was
rumoured, volcanic elements in her past. Her birth had
been precipitated by an earthquake and had accomplished
itself in the open air.[1] When the Duke of Alva proposed
to her sister instead of to herself she had taken poison and
all but died.[2] Her own engagement now was promptly
greeted by the suicide of one of her admirers in Paris.[3]
Her conduct had not been free from indiscretions ; and her
judgments, often unbalanced in themselves, were almost
always unrestrained in their expression. To the difficult
task of mounting gracefully a precarious eminence—a task
necessarily harder than the mere maintenance of an assured
position—she brought not the natural possession of the
grand manner, that is neither haughty nor familiar, but
the desire to possess it, which in turn is both. Hence her
real grace and charm were marred for many by an apparently
capricious alternation between undignified abandon and
some sudden access of hauteur. Whether for this reason,
or owing to some half-articulate disappointment at the
exaltation of a foreigner over them, the fact remains that
neither her great beauty, her sincere piety, nor her large
charities ever succeeded in making the Empress popular
among the Parisians ; while in her husband's immense
hold upon the affections of the provinces she had at no
time any real share.

More important even than her personal attributes were
her political and religious convictions. These may be
briefly summarised as the precise antithesis of those of
Prince Napoleon, the present heir presumptive to the
Empire. He was a free thinker and an anticlerical ; she
not merely a Catholic but a dévote. The Prince combined a persistent sympathy with Italian nationalism, and
even an occasionally sincere liberalism,[4] with a somewhat ludicrous affectation of republicanism : an affectation

---

[1] *Tschudi*, 16.   [2] *Ibid.*, 26.
[3] *Ibid.*, 51 *n.*   [4] E.g. vide *Commissaire*, ii. 170. *Proudhon*, v. 153.

which in no way debarred him from a luxurious enjoyment
of all the perquisites of the Empire, or even from a very
vigilant insistence on the use of his own princely title.[1]
The new Empress on the other hand disliked Italians,
distrusted nationalism, and was an ardent champion of
the political rights of the Pope. Essentially she was
an authoritarian imperialist : what was not the Pope's
was Cæsar's, and what was Cæsar's was his wife's. But
she too sought her political consolations elsewhere. A
curious cult of Marie Antoinette, whose career she regarded
as destined somehow to be typical of her own, led ' the
Spaniard ' to devote her very honeymoon to a pilgrimage
among the relics of ' the Austrian.'[2] The melancholy
fascination of her prototype soon affected Eugénie's
imagination. Almost she persuaded herself that she was
a Bourbon, and quite that she was a Legitimist. Queen
Victoria after all was a Stuart and a Jacobite ; perhaps
when those heralds had been at work a little longer they
might present Eugénie with as good a title to the ancestry
of her dreams.[3]

All this struck Prince Napoleon as inexpressibly absurd.
It was hard enough to forgive his cousin for marrying
at all, for any marriage stood in the path of his own
succession to the Empire. But play-acting of this kind
revolted his republican instincts ; to which and to the
injury done them he proceeded to testify by appearing
at court functions dressed as something between Hamlet
and a sort of ambassador *de luxe* of the United States of
America. Throughout the reign this personal antipathy
between Prince Napoleon and the Empress was destined
to be a mere nuisance to the Empire : for not even

---

[1] On this, see *Du Casse : Coup d'état*, 81.
[2] *Canrobert*, ii. 52. *Viel-Castel*, ii. 165.
[3] They did in fact discover that the Kirkpatricks were illegitimate
descendants of James II : thereby pleasantly accounting for the Empress's
resemblance to portraits of another sovereign whose career she might
have likened to her own—Mary Queen of Scots. *Tschudi*, 72 *n*. For an
equally ridiculous attempt to establish consanguinity between the Empress
and Marie Antoinette, v. *Nauroy*, 54. The Prince Consort's brother,
more absurdly still, accounted for Palmerston's approval of the marriage
by attributing to him ' a pleasure something akin to that of a father-in-
law ' in the news. *Ernest*, ii. 25.

their hatred of one another could endear either of them
to France. To some trifling extent, it is true, the variety
of political opinions affected by his cousin and his wife
may have enabled Napoleon III to cast his dynastic
net a little more widely; tame Legitimists and still
tamer Republicans might be taught to eat out of the
hands of the Empress or of Prince Napoleon.[1] But the
divergence was not robust enough to broaden really
effectively the hold of the dynasty on the country, or to
achieve the compensations which the Hanoverians had
reaped in England from their quarrels with their heirs.
Nor did the conflicting political views of his *entourage*
find compensation in a resulting equilibrium on the part
of the Emperor. For the rival opinions had no common
characteristic at all, save the militant and unreasoning
method of their proclamation; and the Emperor, essentially
moderate in his individual instincts, was yet more prone to
oscillate between two extremes than to maintain a mean
between them. Hence the political antagonism of his two
chief domestic mentors tended to introduce into his policy
elements not of compromise, but of contradiction.[2]

The full force of these distracting influences was only
seen in the later years of Louis' reign, when a malady
hitherto only occasional in its effects began to impose
the penalty of premature age and permanently weakened
will. It was then too that another unfortunate fact became apparent. In marrying Eugénie Napoleon III had
married for love; and it is at least probable that there
was more love on his part than on hers. But on her part
there was loyalty to the marriage tie; on his there was not.[3]
And the result was soon seen. It was in no way abnormal
that a woman disappointed of domestic happiness should
seek consolation in politics; what was exceptional was that
in this instance the compensation achieved was not merely
political activity, but political power. For just because he

---

[1] On Prince Napoleon's utility in this way, v. *Houssaye*, ii. 230.
[2] On this, v. *Persigny*, 387–408.
[3] ' Je lui ai été fidèle,' he told Viel-Castel in 1857, ' pendant les six
premiers mois de notre union ; mais j'ai besoin de petites distractions, et
je reviens toujours à elle avec plaisir.' *Viel-Castel*, iv. 337.

had given her less than her due as wife, Louis was unable to refuse Eugénie more than her due as Empress.[1] And the political power of which she thus became possessed was destined in the long run to prove disastrous to her husband and to herself. It was this indirect consequence of the Emperor's indiscretions which formed their true political penalty. None of all his numerous mistresses seems to have exercised upon him any real political influence.[2] In this respect there was a sort of safety in numbers : the very vagrancy of the Emperor's affections and the rapidity with which their objects succeeded one another prevented him from mixing passions and politics. But the same fact increased the actual and potential scandal occasioned by his conduct ; and with it the hold which the Empress eventually secured over her husband during the ten years of ill-health which preceded his death. Even here it is characteristic of him that it was only when he ceased to be passionately in love with his wife he began to be politically influenced by her. It was in every respect unfortunate that his first affection for her did not prove lifelong.

For the moment the one concern of the Emperor's advisers was that he should have fallen in love with Eugénie at all. Knowing their universal hostility to the marriage, he merely informed them of his intention without any pretence of asking their advice. On Saturday, January 22, he proceeded to announce his engagement officially to deputations of the Senate, the Legislative Assembly, and the Council of State. The speech in which he did so was a vindication in somewhat militant terms of a step for which Europe had expected some sort of veiled apology. ' Gentlemen,' he said, speaking still with a perceptible German accent,[3] ' I accede to the wish so often

---

[1] ' Longtemps déjà avant la guerre, un familier du Château me disait : " L'Empereur, voyez-vous, a tellement peur des scènes d'intérieur, qu'il serait capable de mettre le feu aux quatre coins de l'Europe, pour se soustraire à une de ces scènes de ménage auxquelles il prête trop souvent le flanc par ses infidélités." ' *Du Barail*, iii. 145.

[2] Of only one of them—Mme. Castiglione—has such influence been even plausibly alleged : and the allegation is entirely unconvincing. v. *Fleischmann*, 150, 172.

[3] *Du Casse: Souvenirs*, 247.

manifested by the nation, in that I am come to announce
to you my marriage.' Thus he began his address to an
audience whom he knew not to desire this particular
marriage at all. ' The union I am about to contract,' he
continued, ' is not in accord with the traditions of ancient
policy : therein lies its *advantage*.' For royal alliances
after all created a false sense of security, and often sub-
stituted dynastic for national interests. ' Furthermore,
the examples of the past have put fears and superstitions in
the heart of the people. They have not forgotten that for
seventy years no foreign princess has ascended the throne
but has seen her race scattered or proscribed by war or
revolution. One woman only seems to have brought good
luck in her train ; and that woman, the kind and gentle
wife of General Bonaparte, was not of royal blood.'

From this universal dispraise of royal marriages, such as
he had failed to obtain for himself, the Emperor excepted
as in duty bound the royal marriage of Napoleon ; so
wording [1] his exception as to retort on Austria its dis-
courtesy to himself. ' True,' he continued, ' the marriage
of Napoleon I with Marie Louise was a great event. It
pleased the nation's pride to see the ancient and illustrious
House of Austria, so long at war with us, sue the alliance of
the elected head of the new Empire. During the last
reign, however, was not the self-respect of the nation
wounded when the heir to the throne vainly solicited for
many years an alliance with a reigning family ; and
obtained in the end a princess accomplished indeed, but
only of secondary rank, and of another religion ? ' This
last allusion to a living and widowed princess was an
unpardonable—and to do him justice an unparalleled—
lapse from Louis' ordinary gentlemanliness in public
utterance ; in a perhaps legitimate desire to humble the
haughty he had permitted himself for a moment to flout
the fallen.

But he soon returned to a foeman more worthy of his
steel : proceeding with a kind of glory to boast himself
of the things that Nicholas had accounted his shame.

---

[1] F.O. France, Cowley to Lord John Russell, 24 Jan. 53.

' When in the face of ancient Europe a man is carried by
the force of a new principle to the exalted level of the old
dynasties, it is not by making old his blazon, by seeking at
any cost to introduce himself into the family of kings, that
he compels recognition. Rather it is by steadfastly
remembering his origin, by maintaining his proper character, by assuming frankly before the face of Europe the
position of *parvenu* : a glorious title when one acquires
it [1] by the free suffrages of a great people.' Freed therefore
from ancient precedent, he found his marriage became his
own private affair. ' She who has become the object of my
choice is of lofty birth. French by instinct, by education,
by the memory of the blood her father shed for the Empire,
she has as Spaniard the advantage of having no relatives in
France [2] on whom honours and dignities must be showered.
Catholic and pious, she will address to heaven the same
prayers as myself for the prosperity of France ; gracious
and good, I doubt not that she will revive in the same
position the virtues of the Empress Josephine.' The
' virtues of Josephine ' were not the dowry which every
man would seek for his bride : but Louis may be pardoned
for thinking the best of his grandmother. Besides it was a
feature of the Napoleonic legend to cry up Josephine and
to cry down Marie Louise ; until to have discovered any
particular vice in the latter was sufficient proof of the
existence of its corresponding virtue in the former. In no
other way could Josephine have acquired the reputation of
a faithful wife.

' I come then, Gentlemen,' concluded the Emperor, ' to
say to France : I have preferred a woman I love and
respect to a stranger whose alliance would have brought
gain not without loss. In placing independence, the
qualities of the heart, family happiness before dynastic
prejudice or the calculations of ambition, I shall not be
less strong in that I shall be more free. Very soon on the
way to Notre Dame I shall present the Empress to the

---

[1] *Lorsqu'on parvient.* The passage was aimed at Nicholas. *Ibid.*
[2] This statement was not strictly accurate : *v.* F.O. France, Cowley to
Lord John Russell, 24 Jan. 53 ; B.M. Add. MSS. 37,423, f. 253.

people and the army : their trust in me assures their
sympathy to my chosen : and you, Sirs, when you have
learned to know her, you will be convinced that this time
too I have been inspired by Providence.'

Unpalatable as such an announcement must have been
in any case, this was hardly the method to conciliate
opposition. A few foreigners it is true were startled into
an amused approval : [1] but the Emperor's own subjects
were surprised and shocked. Circourt complained as of an
act which flouted every decorum, that ' the Emperor had
spoken before France and before the world with the easy
frankness of a citizen who, in his dressing-gown and
slippers, expounds at large before confidential friends the
motives of his determination upon a point of private life.' [2]
Already both in Paris and in the frontier provinces the
choice of Eugénie for Empress had been felt to render less
probable the continuance of peace ; [3] since it could not
but increase the isolation of the new dynasty in Europe.
And now the speech with its direct taunt to Austria
and its indirect defiance to Russia, seemed to make
bad worse.

It was here perhaps that the general sense of his people,
more clearly than the mortified pride of his courtiers,
appreciated the true danger of Louis' choice. That choice
was indeed not commonplace : but it was precisely an
infusion of the commonplace of which this extraordinary
Empire stood in need. It is true that with another
Empress the Second Empire would have lacked much of its
most characteristic brilliance ; it would be as hard to
conceive the Second Empire without the Empress as it
would be to visualise the creations of Charles Dickens save
through the medium of his original illustrators. Yet those

---

[1] *Cf.* an English correspondent of Clarendon's : ' That dear Emperor !
I cannot help admiring the cool manner in which that man does exactly
what he likes ; and what Montaigne would call the *soudaineté de ses idées*
keeps up a continual interest in the play. If he marries next Saturday, I
suppose he will hardly invade England before the Saturday following,
which gives us time to pack up.' *Maxwell*, i. 362.

[2] Circourt to Reeve, 22 Jan. 53. B.M. Add. MSS. 37,423, f. 243.

[3] *Ibid.*, f. 247, 249. But elsewhere in the provinces the marriage was
not ill-received. Cf. *Arch. Nat.*, F 1ᶜ *3 4-6.

illustrators, for all their verve and brilliance, served to
exaggerate into mere caricature types already surcharged
with humour, heightening into broad farce figures which
it had been their truer service to subdue into credible
human individuals. Even so Louis' high-spirited Empress
served but to emphasise the novelty of an empire already
sufficiently unconventional, rather than to make good
what it lacked of stability, sobriety, and political common
sense. Louis may have been right to disdain and his
advisers wrong to desire a royal alliance on the ground that
such a marriage would have given a ' leg up ' to the new
dynasty. But such an alliance would have been beneficial
to his dynasty for a precisely opposite reason ; not that it
would have lifted it up to altitudes otherwise unattainable
to it, but that it might have held it down to the more
customary course of kings ; serving the ship of state in
some sort as an anchor to the commonplace, for lack of
which it was to drift into

> . . . ' the foam
> Of perilous seas in fairy lands—forlorn.'

A homely princess of royal birth and intelligence—even
perhaps for choice of Teutonic stock and Protestant
religion—this might well have been for Louis Napoleon
the truly prudent and profitable alliance. But failing
some placid Hausfrau from Saxe-Coburg-Gotha—and we
find it difficult after all quite to regret the failure—
his actual choice might easily have been worse. In one
respect the cause of its present unpopularity was to be the
measure of its future triumph. France felt that when she
had made a man her ruler he became fit match for the
daughter of any king. The failure of Louis Napoleon to
obtain a royal bride was therefore for the moment a
national humiliation. But eventually the love match
redounded into a subtler tribute to the national pride.
That Napoleon III should have climbed tactfully by dint
of a royal marriage into the company of kings would after
all have been no great achievement. But that he, proceeding from the people and flaunting the fact, should

himself first choose a bride from among the people and then force the proudest dynasties of Europe to welcome her as hostess and guest and equal of their queens—that was a far more indubitable triumph. For it meant that whom France chose might himself choose whom he would and thereby gentle her condition. Even at second hand the virtue worked ; it sufficed to be the choice of the chosen of France to be the peer of any queen.

In some ways the new Empress reigned peerless. She had beauty and charm and courage, and a sense which enabled her to be arbitress of the fashions of Europe. And though she enhanced in some degree the closing catastrophe of the Second Empire, yet she enhanced also and personified its opening splendours. As May Queen, the queen of a day, the radiant centre of a passing but magnificent pageant, she was exactly in her place. No fairer form could have been discovered to grace the fleeting but brilliant triumphs of the new Empire ; no figure more stately or statuesque could courtiers have crowned —before they were withered—with every flower of the spring. Upon no shoulders could have fallen in fact more fittingly the mantle of Mary Queen of Scots or Marie Antoinette.

With a view perhaps to the decrease of its unpopularity the Emperor made his marriage the occasion of large charities and amnesties. There was little difficulty in charity, with a civil list of a million a year ; and ample opportunity for amnesty within twelve months of the *coup d'état*. As we have seen, some three thousand victims of that deed were now very graciously pardoned. But if such indeed were the objects of the *largesse* it failed of its purpose.[1] For though the wedding was celebrated with all procurable pomp, it was marked by an utter absence of enthusiasm.[2] To the finery a trifle too resplen-

---

[1] The préfets were gravely puzzled at what they called 'l'ingratitude des amnistiés.' *Arch. Nat.*, F 1ᶜ *3 15-17.

[2] See e.g. *Times*, 1 Feb. 53, p. 5, c. 4. *Laughton*, i. 279. *Henry Greville*, ii. 33. *Hübner*, i. 106. Cowley attributes the extreme unpopularity of the marriage in part to 'the almost indecent hurry' with which it was concluded. F.O. France, Cowley to Russell. 'Confidential.' 7 Feb. 53.

dent of new officials brave in their new uniforms was added such savour of antiquity as could be furnished by surviving relics of the pageantry of the First Empire. At Persigny's instance [1] every reproducible detail of the former splendours was exactly repeated. It was in the carriage which bore the King of Rome to his christening that King Jerome and Prince Napoleon took their part in the imperial procession ; the Emperor and Eugénie themselves drove in the same coach of glass and gold that had carried Napoleon both to his coronation with his first bride and to his marriage with his second. The new Empress wore the diamond coronet which Marie Louise had worn on her wedding-day, and Louis Napoleon his uncle's own insignia of the Legion of Honour,[2] with the collar of the Golden Fleece worn by the Emperor Charles the Fifth.[3]

Amid so much careful reproduction of past splendours occurred one coincidence undesigned and undesired. Then, as now, the marriage coach had been surmounted by a gilt imperial crown. Now, as then, at the very instant that the procession was starting out through the great archway of the Tuileries, the crown—the same crown regilded—detached itself from its pediment and fell headlong to the ground.[4] Hastily the damage was repaired and the imperial procession restarted. But however slight the

The private account sent to Reeve by Circourt is even more explicit. ' I never witnessed anything more cold and unpopular than the fête of yesterday. The multitude gazed on the pageant with mere curiosity. No enthusiasm, no expression of respect nor of goodwill. Coarse jests passed from mouth to mouth.' B.M. Add. MSS. 37,423, f. 248. The evening before, on her passage from the Elysée to the Tuileries, the bride had been hooted by the crowd. *Ibid.*

[1] *Beaumont-Vassy,* 49. [2] *Delord,* i. 488.
[3] *Times,* 2 Feb. 53, p. 4, c. 6.
[4] *Fleury,* i. 236. Contemporary accounts are silent on the incident, which was naturally regarded as apocryphal, so long as it rested only on late and inaccurate memoirs published after the omen was fulfilled. But the authenticity of the story can now be established : I find it related within a week of its occurrence in an unpublished letter of A. de Circourt dated 4 Feb. 53. Attempts to replace the crown failed. ' A footman picked it up and tried to refasten it : but another shock sent it again to the dust. I have this fact from a field officer who rode close by.' *Ibid.,* B.M. Add. MSS. 37,423, f. 253.

delay, the double omen might well have impressed even
the least superstitious.   Indeed the incident[1] and its
circumstances symbolised not inaptly the true nature
of the parallel between the newly established Empire
and its prototype.   By dint of careful effort the Second
Empire could not wholly reproduce the glories of the
first; only in undesigned disaster could it really rival
its model.   The present splendours were but a pale
reflection of the old : the crowning catastrophe at least
was Napoleonic.

[1] Two other coincidences are so extraordinary as to be worthy of mention
in this connexion : (1) By a chance unparalleled and unperceived, the new
Napoleon on donning the imperial purple was precisely, and to the day, as
old as the first Napoleon when he doffed it : 44 years, 227 days.   (2) And
the date of his donning of it was not only, and intentionally, the anniversary
of Austerlitz, *La Bataille des trois Empereurs*, and of the first Napoleon's
coronation ; it was also, by a double accident, the anniversary of the accession
of both the other reigning European Emperors.   For it was on December 2
that Nicholas in 1825, and Francis Joseph in 1848, had ascended the thrones
of Russia and of Austria.   Of this latter coincidence the ambassadors of
Romanoff and Hapsburg legitimacy availed themselves to establish an
ostentatious *alibi* from the proclamation of their upstart rival.   For they
chose that selfsame hour to assist at Orthodox or Catholic Mass on behalf
each of his own authentic Emperor.   See Wellesley, *The Paris Embassy*, 14.

CHAPTER VII

THE SOWERS

Spectators and not combatants ! No guess
Anticipative of a wrong unfelt,
No speculation or contingency,
However dim and vague, too vague and dim
To yield a justifying cause ; and forth
(Stuffed out with big preamble, holy names
And adjurations of the God in Heaven)
We send our mandates for the certain death
Of thousands and ten thousands !

SAMUEL TAYLOR COLERIDGE.

NOTWITHSTANDING the somewhat provocative manner in which the Emperor had announced his marriage, all the omens of the year 1853 seemed at its outset to augur peace.   To a pacific policy the new empire was publicly pledged by the famous dictum of Bordeaux ; of his pacific intentions the new emperor had in fact given more than verbal proof, by his submission, against the wishes of his own foreign minister, to a personal incivility which could only be refused at the risk of war. 'Peace and cheap corn' was the Prince Consort's reading of Louis Napoleon's ambition · in this year ; 'Peace with dishonour' was the taunt levelled against the new empire by its exiled enemies during its opening months.

And it was not in France only that the continuance of peace seemed assured.   In England the turn of the century had been marked by a spectacle profoundly impressive to contemporary observers, the Great Exhibition of 1851

217

In that novel conglomeration of cosmopolitan industry, following upon a generation of unbroken peace and unprecedented commercial development, the middle classes of England read the opening of a new chapter in the world's history. With a kind of sober glow they reflected, that while in past ages the dynastic ambitions of monarchs had plunged their hapless subjects into war, they themselves, since their recent attainment of power, had prudently maintained a lasting peace. War after all had been but the folly of princes ; its days therefore were numbered with the advent of the people to power.

Such hopes seemed well-nigh justified by the history of Europe since Waterloo. For nearly forty years no real war had broken the peace of Europe, save for the picturesque but barbarous struggle which issued in the independence of Greece : a struggle culminating in the armed and successful intervention of Russia which furnished the reign of Nicholas with its triumphal inauguration. At that time philhellenic sentiment in England had been strong enough to lead it to acquiesce, although grudgingly and with hesitation, in the territorial diminution of the Ottoman Empire necessitated by the establishment of this new Christian kingdom. In the generation which followed, however, the sympathies of the governing classes in England had returned to the Turkish cause. Greece by its name and past had possessed a means of appeal to English sympathies quite unshared by the other Balkan subjects of the Turk ; yet even Greece, once liberated, had failed to fulfil the dreams of the English Philhellenes. They did not recognise that this failure was in part due to the narrow bounds of the new kingdom : indeed, influenced unconsciously by the large-scale maps of classical Greece to which as schoolboys they had been accustomed, they probably hardly realised how narrow those boundaries were. A series of small diplomatic incivilities had further alienated English sympathies ; reinforcing the revulsion of feeling occasioned by disappointment at the non-fulfilment of wholly impossible hopes. Meanwhile in Turkey, external defeat had produced its usual consequence of internal reform ; the personal initiative of the Sultan, in the reign of Mahmoud, and the activities of a reforming minister of English sympathies, under his successor, gave to the Ottoman Empire not only a period of relative prosperity and peace, but even the apparent prospect of some development towards constitutional government. It is easy in the light of later events to pronounce such promise foredoomed to disappointment ; it does not necessarily follow that contemporary observers ought to have condemned such prospects as hopeless in advance. A reforming Sultan, no less than a reforming Pope, received and perhaps deserved more generous treatment from his own generation than from posterity. After all reform is not least praiseworthy where it is most necessary ; nor are reformers least deserving of support when they are most in need of it.

In the case of the Porte no less than of the Papacy, general promise of internal reform was accompanied by a single dramatic act, which appeared for an instant to confer on either government the championship of national liberties as well. Pio Nono in 1847 had protested against Austria's occupation of Ferrara, and by the success of that protest seemed to have made all Italy his debtor. Two years later, against the yet more domineering intervention of a yet more reactionary Austria—backed this time by the now declared ally of all reaction, Nicholas—the Sultan appeared to play an even finer part ; refusing to deliver up to the joint subjugators of Hungary her fugitive defenders. Kossuth and his followers and his children owed it to the more kindly Turk that they were not handed over to the vengeance of Catholic Emperor and Orthodox Czar. What form that vengeance might have taken, glutted gallows and flogged women could testify, throughout the multiform dominions which once more were Austria : indeed on the eve of this demand for further material for justice the Imperial government, sustained in this action also by the Czar, had sentenced to be strangled, and graciously consented merely to shoot, the late Prime

Minister of Hungary.[1] And Turkey in turn owed it to the appearance of the English and French fleets at the Dardanelles that it was able to make good its refusal under threat of war.

But while England and France had seen with sympathy and sustained by armed support the liberal policy of Turkey, these same signs of Ottoman revival had been regarded with a very different eye by Nicholas. When any state adjoining Russia showed signs of ' breaking up,' it normally became an object of affectionate solicitude on the part of its mighty neighbour. No matter how long the illness, so that the patient spared himself all effort such as might unduly tax his waning strength, he could count in all bedside attentions upon the inexhaustible patience of the East. But suffer him at this stage to show signs of setting his house in order for himself, and the self-summoned physician would at once pronounce death imminent and inevitable. And in such circumstances Poland before and Persia afterwards could testify to the accuracy of the imperial diagnosis. The present case proved no exception. Between 1838 and 1844 Reschid Pasha had introduced in Turkey a series of civil and administrative reforms : in 1844 Nicholas on a visit to England remarked to Aberdeen, ' We have a sick man on our hands.' In the years that followed, the reforms continued on the whole to make headway : tax-farming was prohibited, negro slave-markets abolished, education improved and secularised, and the army in particular radically reorganised. This in a neighbour of Russia could clearly be nothing less than the delirium which heralded approaching dissolution : in January, 1853, the Czar thought a second consultation advisable. Addressing himself to the British ambassador at Petersburg, he pronounced the sick man to be now *in extremis* ; this time he added proposals as to a division of the estate. By these, Russia would establish protectorates not only over the Danubian principalities but over Servia and Bulgaria as well : England, in return for her acquiescence in this, and in the possible temporary occu-

---

[1] *Register*, 1849 [341].

pation by Russia of Constantinople, might annex Egypt and Crete.[1]

But England was now in no mood to assist such schemes either as a spectator or as an accomplice. Aberdeen's friendly reception of his earlier overture had it is true given Nicholas some ground for presuming a similar complaisance in 1853 ; but much water had flowed under the bridges since 1844. Russia, then merely the most gigantic of world-states, had now clearly presented itself as the most tyrannical.

This double characteristic of size and oppression served to render Russia obnoxious to most different elements of English public opinion. To some its mere size was a sufficient offence. Russia at this time was not only the greatest Empire in the world, but the greatest Empire the world had ever seen. Its territories—which contemporary statisticians gravely computed to be of an area equal to the moon [2]—stretched their unbroken bulk over three conterminous continents. In Europe itself, Napoleon's prediction seemed so far fulfilled that the Russian dominions there alone more than doubled the extreme size ever attained by his own brief Empire ; and were nearly ten times as large as the next largest existing continental power, the patchwork Empire of Austria : considerably more than half of Europe was already Russian. And behind these enormous European dominions lay others in uninterrupted expanse three times their size in Asia ; which in their turn were severed only by the narrow Behring Strait from a matter of half a million more square miles of Russia in America. Gigantic in itself, this empire

---

[1] Critics of the Crimean War have generally assumed that the Czar's proposal at the opening of 1853 was merely that he might be allowed to confer as a free gift on Servia, Bulgaria, and the other provinces of European Turkey, independence such as they now enjoy. But both his actual words, as reported by Seymour, in asking England's assent, and still more the very substantial *quid pro quo* which he offered in return for it, would seem fatal to the contention. His real suggestion was that Servia and Bulgaria should form in future—what he claimed that the Principalities formed already—an independent State ' under my protection ' : a very different matter. It is impossible seriously to credit Nicholas with the desire of strengthening the Asiatic and doubling the African and Mediterranean dominions of England, without adding an acre to his own.

[2] *Nolan,* i. 5.

seemed more gigantic still, at a time when Europe in general
had already lost America and not yet acquired Africa.
And this empire, in appearance at once so colossal and
compact, was not merely great but growing : with a growth
only the more formidable that it was gradual ; expanding
unchecked and apparently irresistible at the expense of
every state bordering upon its frontiers. Great as had
been the acquisitions which Alexander had made to the
empire towards the North and West, they were hardly
greater than those which Nicholas had already made
towards the East and South. And this incessant process
of advance was the more disquieting that as yet no Power
or combination of Powers had ever finally succeeded in
compelling Russia to disgorge what once she had made her
own. Last straw of all, the monster was threatening to
become amphibious : recent reports showed that the Czar
had put his fleet into a ' wonderfully efficient state.' [1]

It has been the normal and on the whole the beneficent
result of England's pursuit of the Balance of Power that
this object has led her not to divide empire with the
strongest continental state, but to set limits to its growth
by sustaining its weaker neighbours against it. But though
this was the prime cause of the government's rejection of
Russia's overture, it was the latent hostility of the English
people which rendered that rejection really dangerous.
In Nicholas Englishmen were beginning to perceive the
most formidable opponent of all civic and national liberties :
and Kossuth's eloquence had inspired many of them with a
conviction that sooner or later Russia must be fought if
freedom was to be saved.[2] Fear of the Cossack domination
on this score was neither unnatural, nor altogether un-
justified. The Russian Empire was the last home of
European serfdom ; outside of the army, hardly one-fifth
of its subjects were free men.[3] Its religion was the most
obscurantist of all forms of Christianity. Its ruler was
in his own person mediæval pope and mediæval emperor

[1] *Parker*, ii. 223.
[2] *Vide* Bright's letter of 4 Nov. 51, in *Trevelyan : Bright*, 195.
[3] *Nolan*, i. 8.

in one. Externally its moral influence, and at times its
physical force, was everywhere cast upon the side of
despotism and reaction. And inside its ever-expanding
frontiers—a fact perhaps most ominous of all—it was the
very essence of the Muscovite rule, as seen from Europe,
that it consistently sought to obliterate by subjection to its
orthodox slavonic servitude cultures both higher and more
European than its own. Hence this huge half-barbarous
Power, hanging like a pall upon the confines of civilisation,
seemed then, as a century later, an instrument less fitted to
leaven Asia with Europe, than to submerge Europe once
more with Asia.

In choosing the moment of his unfortunate overture
Nicholas had been animated in part by a general desire to
isolate his upstart imperial rival ; in part also by a hope
of English support in a trivial but troublesome dispute
which was the heritage of an older quarrel between his
country and France. For over a century these two
countries, as champions respectively of Greek and
Roman Catholicism, supported at intervals the rival claims
of Latin and Orthodox monks to the custody of certain
Christian shrines at Jerusalem. In February 1852 the
Porte made a settlement of the outstanding questions in
a sense favourable to France ; but shortly afterwards, in
the temporary absence of the French ambassador, Russia
obtained rights incompatible with those just confirmed to
its rival ; the return of the ambassador was followed by
a third pronouncement, in effect reversing the former
reversal, and once more placing France at an advantage.
In all this there was nothing more than a slight aggravation of characteristic Ottoman diplomacy ; but by this
time a dangerous degree of irritation had been engendered
in the mind of Nicholas : a mind which by this time had
not perhaps survived quite scatheless the strain which
omnipotence puts upon human sanity.[1] Neither the
acquiescence of France in some minor concessions to the
Greek Church, nor even Louis' recall at the beginning of

[1] See below, p. 283.

1853 of his too bellicose representative at Constantinople,[1] sufficed to satisfy the injured dignity of the Czar. He mobilised fifty thousand men on the Pruth, and dispatched to Constantinople in February an emissary in whose hands the dispute at once took on an entirely different complexion. Prince Menschikoff was a man of a naturally overbearing manner ; but the nature of his errand was even more provocative than the studied insolence with which it was discharged. Though England was assured that his mission had no other object than the termination of the dispute as to the Holy Places,[2] Menschikoff in fact presented to the Sultan a scheme which would virtually have transferred from himself to the Czar his political sovereignty over the twelve or fifteen millions of Orthodox Christians in the Ottoman Empire. Even before the true nature of his demands was known, the mere manner of the Russian envoy —his arrival at Constantinople accompanied by a large military retinue, at the end of a journey which had comprised ostentatious reviews of the Russian naval and military forces in the Black Sea ; his refusal to pay the customary visits of courtesy to the Turkish foreign minister ; his virtual demand, promptly complied with, for the latter's resignation ; his arrogant behaviour in the presence of the Sultan himself—all these had produced in the Turkish capital a feeling bordering upon panic.

It chanced that at the moment neither the English nor the French ambassador was present at Constantinople : but so serious did the situation appear to the English *chargé d'affaires*, that he took it upon himself to summon the British fleet from Malta. This order was very properly countermanded by the English Minister of Foreign Affairs, upon renewed and formal assurances from the Czar that Russia had no ulterior designs beyond the settlement of the dispute as to the Holy Places. France, on the other hand, originally less inclined than England for a naval

---

[1] *Debidour*, ii. 93 ; *Thouvenel* : ' *Nicolas*,' 79.

[2] *Argyll*, i. 444.   *Diplomatic Study*, i. 163.   The latter work (*v.* Bibliography) is an official Russian source : a fact which must be borne in mind by those who would appreciate the force of this and later citations of it.

demonstration, now against the advice of the latter dispatched a fleet to Greek waters ; despite Cowley's efforts in Paris to avert ' a step conceived in ignorance and haste, and carried out with petulance and obstinacy.' [1]

The isolated action of France on this occasion had the unfortunate effect of confirming the Czar in a conviction engendered by the reports of his ambassador at London, to the effect that no real co-operation was possible between England and the heir of Napoleon. At this very moment England had in fact taken a step which was to render that belief a delusion. She had sent back to Constantinople as ambassador Lord Stratford de Redcliffe, armed with a somewhat vague authority to order the Admiral of the Fleet at Malta to hold his fleet in readiness to sail for the near East.

Stratford Canning was the last—and with all his faults the greatest—of that generation of English ambassadors to whom greatness was permitted. The general European situation under the Second Empire gave to official diplomacy larger powers than remained to it under the Armed Peace ; and those powers, thanks to the still complete immunity of diplomacy from popular control, were concentrated in fewer hands. Of those larger powers moreover a far larger portion were vested at this time in the person of the ambassador ; since the common use of telegraphy had not yet effected its inevitable work of centralisation, by subordinating every embassy to the immediate direction of the Foreign Office.[2] From this fact it followed also that the importance of an ambassador's initiative varied in direct ratio with his distance from his own capital ; and in all Europe there was no capital so distant from St James' as Constantinople.

All these advantages, together with the still unexpended prestige which English diplomacy had inherited from the Napoleonic wars, Stratford de Redcliffe was both capable and desirous of using to the utmost. He possessed already

---

[1] F.O. France, Cowley to Clarendon, 24 March 53.
[2] ' Happily (sic) there was not a complete perfect communication by telegraph between London and Constantinople.' *Kinglake*, i. 100.

ten years' experience of the embassy to which he was now returning, refreshed with a peerage, at this crisis in Eastern affairs. By birth—for he was a Canning ; by conviction—for he was a convert to the cause of Turkish reform from a completely opposite opinion ; by every personal gift of dauntless energy, commanding presence and perfectly polished strength, he was destined to dominate the entire situation which he found awaiting him on his return to Constantinople in April 1853.

To that situation he addressed himself at once with energy and skill. Affecting to believe the Russian assurances that Menschikoff's mission had no other object than the termination of the trouble as to the Holy Places, he induced that unskilled diplomatist to present to the Porte separately this the avowed portion of his demands : with the result that in less than three weeks this tedious ecclesiastical dispute was settled. In effecting that settlement Stratford had the satisfaction of knowing that he was doing a sensible service to the French Emperor. For on his way out to Constantinople the English ambassador had dined with Louis at the Tuileries ; and after dinner his host ' spoke of the Holy Places, and threw the blame of engaging in that question on the *parti prétre* of the Montalembert school and the Legislative Assembly. He himself desired nothing better than to finish the affair.' [1] But Stratford probably derived a purer joy from the knowledge that he had not merely done France a service, but Russia an injury. For Menschikoff had committed a fatal error in consenting to separate the old and avowed grievance of Russia as to the Holy Places, from her new and mysterious demand for a formal and exclusive protectorate over all Greek Christians. He had achieved the professed object of his mission and accepted a settlement of the Russian claims where they were obviously reasonable. But thereby he was forced—unless he were to retire with the greater half of his errand undischarged—to produce openly and

---

[1] *Lane-Poole*, ii. 236. Even Kinglake admits that the disinterment of the question was the work of France ' under a free Parliamentary government.' *Kinglake*, i. 483.

separately the demand for the Protectorate ; a demand
hitherto disavowed, and in its present form clearly indefensible. This he did in an ultimatum addressed to the
Porte on May 5. Four days later Stratford communicated
to the Sultan in a private audience, with every circumstance of solemnity, the fact that he was authorised to
order the fleet at Malta to be in readiness to sail.[1] Thus
encouraged, the Sultan rejected the Russian ultimatum ;
on May 21 Menschikoff left Constantinople with the whole
diplomatic staff of Russia ; a month later Russian troops
crossed the Pruth and occupied the Principalities, an act
of war which the Czar protested was prompted by motives
entirely pacific.

The news of the invasion, in spite of the explanations
with which it was accompanied, gave rise in England to
an outburst of popular excitement : but Aberdeen, as
premier, was working for peace ; and from the Foreign
Office Clarendon at the end of June bade Stratford advise
the Turks to abstain from armed resistance to the Russian
aggression. In France too even Drouyn, the most warlike
of the imperial advisers, was still inclined to a pacific
solution.[2] Moreover, Nicholas himself was impressed by
the unexpected violence of Austria's opposition to his
occupation of the Principalities ; an opposition increased
by the fact that the occupation took place at a time when
an autograph letter from Francis Joseph was on its way to
the Czar, dissuading him from the step.[3] The fact too that
his threatened invasion of Turkish territories had been
followed by the advance of the English fleet, which now at
last joined forces with the French squadron near the
entrance of the Dardanelles, was calculated to suggest to
the Czar that an alliance between the two Western powers
was not really outside the range of possibility.

Russia accordingly accepted the arbitration of the
Powers ; in August the representatives of England, France,
Austria, and Prussia met in conference at Vienna, and

[1] *Lane-Poole*, ii. 266.
[2] F.O. France, Cowley to Clarendon. 'Confidential.' 13 June 53.
[3] F.O. France, Cowley to Clarendon, 11 July 53.

agreed upon a note to be submitted by Turkey to Russia as the basis of a settlement. This note, a vague re-affirmation of previous treaties, was forwarded to either disputant as the unanimous award of the four powers : as such it was promptly accepted by Nicholas ; and all Europe with a sigh of relief pronounced the question settled, and peace assured.

And if to the uninitiated peace seemed assured by the Czar's acceptance of an international award framed by the self-constituted defenders of Turkey, those who were acquainted with the inner history of the negotiations had even better reason for such a conclusion. They knew that before its publication the note had been imparted to the Turkish ambassador at Vienna, and that both he and his dragoman had expressed their entire approbation of it.[1] In view of this fact, and of the advantage of getting Russia out of the Principalities as soon as possible, it was not thought necessary [1] to incur the long delay of sending the entire document in advance to and from Constantinople : a journey which in mere fairness would have involved the corresponding double journey of a duplicate copy to and from St Petersburg. It was known too in Vienna that the Emperor of Russia had offered to evacuate the Principalities the moment Turkey accepted the Note,[2] and that orders for such evacuation were already made out [3] and in the possession of the Russian generals.

But to the common amazement, this note framed by the friends of Turkey, accepted by the unbending Nicholas himself, was now refused by the usually complacent Turk ; unless certain apparently trivial [4] modifications were intro-

[1] All this Clarendon himself told *Greville*, 20 Sept. 53. Kinglake's plea on behalf of Stratford that 'Austria, forgetting its duty as a faithful mediator, had used means of ascertaining that the Note would be acceptable to Russia, but without taking a like step in favour of the other disputant ' [*Kinglake*, i. 348] is a mere misstatement of fact.

[2] F.O. Austria, Westmoreland to Clarendon, 13 Sept. 53.

[3] *Ibid.*, 14 Sept. 53.

[4] Though verbally slight, the modifications were not really trivial. The most important was the addition of the words ' by the Sublime Porte ' to Turkey's undertaking to observe the terms of previous treaties as to ' the protection of the Christian religion.' This addition excluded the assumption of a Russian protectorate. For the complete original text, and the proposed alterations, see *Kinglake*, i. 501, 502.

duced into three clauses of it. The answer was as irritating
as it was unexpected ; since however the alterations in the
note merely served to render explicit the loosely-worded
intentions of its authors, England now urged the acceptance
of the revised version upon the Czar. But Nicholas at an
earlier stage in the negotiation had not merely accepted
without hesitation the proposed compromise when first
made aware of its contents, but he had already, in the
words of the English premier, ' agreed as promptly to an
alteration proposed by the English government in the
interest of the Porte.' [1] He now very naturally refused,
as derogatory to the dignity of Russia, to amend still
further at the instance of Turkey herself a document to
which he had given his formal assent, after it had been
presented to him as the settlement officially recommended
by the peacemakers of Europe.[2]

So just and so moderate appeared at this juncture the
attitude of the Czar, and so indefensible the conduct to
which Turkey had been instigated, that even the British
ambassador at St Petersburg, himself hitherto inclined to
suspect Russia at every turn, now ventured on a confidential protest against regarding as a *casus belli* the Czar's
mere adherence to the original proposals of the Powers.
' Your Lordship will I trust have the kindness to excuse
me,' he wrote, in a sentence which for him was almost
abrupt, ' if I add that having never been alarmed at the
idea of an appeal to the *ultima ratio* as long as Russia was
running counter to those principles of justice and equity
which England is bound to uphold, I should consider such
an appeal as the most grievous misfortune if made when the
Emperor had so far retraced his steps.' [3]

Since in point of fact that ' most grievous misfortune '
did actually occur, as a result of Turkey's unexpected
rejection of the European solution accepted by Russia,
it becomes necessary at this point to determine to what
disturbing agency that rejection itself was due.

That the prime responsibility for the Crimean War must

---

[1] *Maxwell*, ii. 17. [2] *Journal de St Pétersbourg*, 13 Apr. 54.
[3] F.O. Russia, Seymour to Clarendon. ' Confidential.' 13 Sept. 53.

rest upon Louis Napoleon : upon the proverbial sensitiveness of a *parvenu* [1] personally affronted by the Czar's refusal to call him ' Brother ' ; upon the political necessity of gaining the support of the French clericals and the military necessity of blooding his army on some body other than French, all these are statements which have long since filtered through into the textbooks. But like some other such statements, they have become truisms without ever having been truths. That such a thesis should have passed into common acceptance is due to the very different services of which it is capable. In the Emperor's lifetime, it seemed to offer to his detractors a fine example of low cunning ; Kinglake and the English opponents of the Second Empire in particular knew that they could not better alienate England from Napoleon III than by persuading her that in the Crimean War she had been used and duped by him. A generation later, the ablest of Louis Napoleon's French apologists found in a variation of the same thesis the highest tribute which he could pay to the imperial statecraft ; the Emperor had deliberately led England into the war in order to break up the last relics of the Holy Alliance, and so to render possible his war of liberation in Italy. [2] In reality the figure of Louis Napoleon is big enough to carry neither praise nor blame such as this. Perpetually in their estimate of political leaders historians are betrayed by the temptation to exaggerate the element of design and underestimate the element of accident in the conduct of human affairs. Nor are any body of men more careful to confirm them in this habit than political leaders themselves. The historian is prone to the process, because thereby he seems to magnify his office ; but incidentally he magnifies also the figures to whom he attributes such deep and prophetical designs.

That Louis had a sincere desire for the English alliance

---

[1] In speaking of himself as a parvenu (p. 211 above) Louis Napoleon had in fact presented his historians with an idea ; to which the majority of them have clung with a tenacity very excusable in them. Napoleon I, who really was a parvenu, had the sense not to mention the fact ; and the trait has escaped notice in consequence in the most over-analysed character in history.

[2] *Ollivier*, ii., chapters v. and vi.

in general, and for co-operation with England on the
Eastern question in particular, is no doubt true. And he
was no less certainly determined that France should not
submit under his rule to such humiliation on that question
as she had suffered under Louis Philippe in 1840. But
that he had any consistent desire to lead both countries
into war, is a contention which can now be conclusively
disproved. No one can long work among unprinted
documents without being tempted to exaggerate their importance, and the cult of the unpublished has fewer new
facts of real significance to its credit than its exponents
would willingly admit. But of the unprinted diplomatic
correspondence of this period it can at least be claimed that
it renders an ancient theory untenable : a theory which
however has served so long as commonly to have been
given brevet rank as fact. ' There was no need,' writes
Professor Alison Phillips who states it well, ' of the " bellicose
influence " of Stratford to make the Porte reject terms
which were humiliating to his pride : the attitude of France
at least proved that in the event of war Turkey would not
be without allies.' [1] Yet when the news of that rejection
reached Napoleon III he ' did not conceal his disappointment and displeasure ' from Cowley, and urged that more
stringent instructions should be sent to Vienna with a view
of obtaining the compliance of the Porte.[2] Nor can it be
maintained that the Emperor's manifestation of displeasure
was any mere affectation designed to deceive Cowley.
For four days later the Turkish minister in Paris became so
alarmed at the vexation of the Emperor that he called on
Cowley with the object of discovering whether the English
attitude would be more favourable ; and even informed
him that he had been instructed to tell France that Turkey
would never sign the unmodified note ' with its own consent.' This cryptic instruction he interpreted as meaning,
unless it should appear more dangerous to refuse than to
sign : [3] apparently an indication that should England

[1] *Modern Europe*, 341.
[2] F.O. France, Cowley to Clarendon   'Confidential.'   29 Aug. 53.
[3] *Ibid.*   2 Sept. 53.

back the Emperor in the matter Turkey would be reluctantly prepared to give way.

It thus appears that the refusal of Turkey to accept the unmodified Vienna note and thereby to ensure peace, was so far from being Louis Napoleon's revenge on Nicholas, that this ' resentful parvenu ' was deeply displeased and disappointed at the narrow failure of this pacific solution.[1] But that the Czar did indeed owe his present rebuff to a casual act of arrogance in his past seems probable enough. Only it was an older injury to a stronger man for which he was now to pay the penalty.

Towards the close of the year 1832 Palmerston had promoted Sir Stratford Canning to the embassy of St Petersburg : an unwarrantable act on his part since the Czar had already privately intimated to him that Canning was the only man in England to whose appointment he would object. The fact of this previous protest was however generally unknown.[2] Hence it was a matter of general amazement when after the announcement had actually been gazetted, and when Stratford had already received numerous letters of congratulation upon his appointment, Nicholas took the unprecedented step of refusing to receive him at St Petersburg. Stratford on his part refused to ease the position by

---

[1] On Louis Napoleon's efforts for peace both on this occasion and later, see also *Greville*, 2 Sept. 53 ; and 29 Jan. 54.

[2] Palmerston's biographers are silent on the incident : Canning's (*Lane-Poole*, ii. 18–23) is misleading. Apparently unaware of the Czar's repeated private protests before the appointment, he suggests that it was Nicholas who was diplomatically at fault, and Nicholas who was forced to retreat from an untenable position. The private letters of Palmerston and Bligh of 27 Oct. 32, 17 Nov. 32, 14 Dec. 32, 9 Jan. 33, 3 March 33, and 17 June 33 in F.O. Russia under those dates prove that it was Palmerston who was at fault, and Palmerston who had to climb down. They show that contrary to all precedent the appointment was gazetted publicly and unexpectedly in spite of repeated private protests in advance through every possible diplomatic channel : that Palmerston at first claimed to appoint a *persona non grata* on the ground that ' we are the only judges who is the most proper for the service of England ' ; and that when snowed under with precedents against such a procedure he fell back on ' our peculiar constitution ' : ' even if it were the universal rule on the continent that is nothing to us ' : further, that after originally declaring that Nicholas must accept Canning permanently he subsequently offered to withdraw him at the earliest opportunity if only he might be allowed to save his face by sending him at all. But conscious of his impregnable position the Czar refused all concessions, and Palmerston had eventually to give way completely. See also *Reid : Durham*, 315, 316.

any act of voluntary retirement : so the harassed Premier sent him as a special envoy to Madrid, accredited indeed to the King and Queen of Spain, but still styled in his letters of credence ' Ambassador to the Emperor of All the Russias.'[1] And ambassador *in partibus* to the Czar (who meanwhile had to content himself with a mere *chargé d'affaires* at Petersburg) Stratford insisted on remaining for two years ; refusing, for the greater annoyance of Nicholas, a permanent transference to the Spanish embassy ; since his acceptance of it would have ended his phantom tenure of the more coveted post. It is probable that Palmerston resented the rebuff to which he had gratuitously exposed his friend : it is certain that Stratford felt himself to have been outrageously used by Nicholas. This is not to accuse him of any conscious intention of gratifying a private vendetta at the cost of a European war. But such memories did no doubt contribute to his conviction ' that there could be no real settlement in the Near East until the pretensions of Russia had been publicly repudiated and until the Tsar had sustained an unmistakable defeat either in diplomacy or in war. If without war so much the better, but by war if necessary.'[2]

An important factor in the relative contributions of the two men to the war, though not in their relative culpability for it, was the diverse attitude of Nicholas towards them. Against Louis Napoleon he nursed no lifelong enmity. The *coup d'état* in his eyes had been a European service, and up to the time of the usurped title he had wished its author nothing but good. The usurpation itself he had regarded as an injury, but it was an injury for which he had obtained satisfaction ; his recognition of his ' dear friend ' had been an insolence, and to that insolence Louis Napoleon had been forced to submit. Hence having publicly taught the new emperor his place, Nicholas felt christianly disposed towards him.[3] It is easy to forgive an injury when once one has avenged it.

[1] *Lane-Poole*, ii. 24. [2] *Marriott*, 231.
[3] Witness *e.g.* his amicable overtures recorded below, p. 244.

But in his older quarrel with de Redcliffe the Czar had already been buffeted on one cheek ; a fact which rendered more dangerous the sense of symmetry which inspired Stratford with a desire to repeat the operation on the other. Already by exceeding or at least anticipating [1] his instructions he had compelled the Czar to retreat from one untenable position in the matter of the Hungarian refugees : for that very reason the Czar could not submit at the same hands to a second resounding diplomatic rebuff, administered in precisely similar fashion. For once more de Redcliffe took liberties with his instructions. He did not indeed disobey them in the letter : officially, as in duty bound, he recommended the note of pacification to the Porte ; [2] in his own words to Clarendon ' he did his *official* best in support ' of it.[3] But even Kinglake, generally concerned to acquit Stratford and convict Louis Napoleon of bringing on the war, admits that the real thoughts of the ambassador could not have been concealed, and that the ' sagacious Turks . . . would easily resolve to follow his known desires, and to disobey his mere words.' [4] Stratford's dislike of the note was intensified by the fact that its authors had omitted to consult him in advance as to its contents.[5] The one thing, thought Clarendon, that might have made peace tolerable to Stratford was that he should have been himself the peacemaker.[6] Certainly the Great Elchi [7] possessed an exalted conception of the office of ambassador : the rôle as he conceived it, though it might on occasion [8] include the duty of carrying out instructions, yet generally comprised the right of first issuing instructions as to what those instructions should be. Provided that this trifling

---

[1] *Lane-Poole*, ii. 191, 193.　　　　[2] *Ibid.*, ii. 291.

[3] *Ibid.*, 295, Stratford's italics : and v. *Maxwell*, ii. 295.

[4] *Kinglake*, i. 352.　　　　[5] *Ibid.*, i. 347.

[6] ' I have all along felt that Stratford would allow no plan of settlement that did not originate with himself.' 25 Aug. 53 ; *Maxwell*, ii. 18.

[7] The real title conferred on Stratford by the Christian subjects of the Porte was still more eloquent of his reputed power : ' Padishah of the Shah '—Sultan of the Sultan—expressed current and correct opinion as to his influence over Abdul-Medjid. On the absolutely dictatorial nature of that influence, v. *Skene*, 4 *sq.*

[8] Only on occasion. v. *Maxwell*, ii. 66.

preliminary were complied with, the Foreign Office
had no more obedient servant than its ambassador at
Constantinople.

How much or how little Stratford's ' official best ' meant
when it ran counter to his private inclinations, no one knew
better than his chief. A month earlier, when on the news
of Russia's acceptance of the Vienna note all England
with a certain weary relief was speaking of the entire
question as ' settled '—and settled by a veritable dis-
pensation of providence on the very eve of the Twelfth [1]—
we find the following entry in Greville's diary : ' I saw
Clarendon yesterday. Nothing new, but he said he fully
expected Stratford Canning would play some trick at
Constantinople, and throw obstacles in the way of settlement.' [2] ' The titular sultan is for peace,' wrote Clarendon
now,[3] ' but the real sultan thinks that now or never is the
time for putting an end to Russia.' In fact Clarendon
throughout displayed an accuracy as a prophet which is
the measure of his condemnation as Minister of Foreign
Affairs. The only real excuse for retaining Stratford at
Constantinople would have been either ignorance of his
probable course of action or approval of it. Of these,
Clarendon could plead neither. He was wise, not after
the event, but during it and before it. Open-eyed he
suffered himself to be led into the ditch.[4]

Nor was Clarendon the sole accomplice before the act
to a deed which at the time he recognised as criminal.
Aberdeen, the premier, wrote that autumn to Graham, ' I
thought we should have been able to conquer Stratford,

[1] It was in fact on the Twelfth itself that Clarendon told the House of
Lords that the crisis was virtually at an end. *Hansard*, cxxix. 1635. But
Stratford was out for bigger game. A month later, when the question was
well going again, he wrote gleefully, ' The Turks are not sportsmen as you
know, and consequently enter little into such considerations.' *Lane-Poole*,
ii. 300.

[2] *Greville*, 11 Aug. 53.

[3] To Herbert : 11 Sept. *Stanmore*: *Herbert*, i. 197 *n*. And again, later,
ibid. : ' It is to Stratford's amour propre froissé that the obstacles to peace
must be attributed.'

[4] He described Stratford as ' bent on war ' (*Maxwell*, ii. 29), and as
' animated with such a personal hatred of the [Russian] Emperor,' as to
' take a part directly contrary to the wishes and instructions of his government.' *Greville*, 3 Sept. 53.

but I begin to fear that the reverse will be the case.' In the same letter he did not hesitate to speak of ' the dishonesty of Stratford.' [1] That in spite of this opinion he left Stratford at Constantinople was due to his conviction that directly challenged Stratford must prove victorious. His recall would have involved the resignation of Russell who wanted popularity, and of Palmerston who wanted war : and a new cabinet would at once have emerged with Palmerston as its Premier and war as its object.[2] By remaining in office himself, even at the cost of some minor concessions to Stratford and to the warlike desires of the people, Aberdeen could still hope to baulk them both at the last of the actual achievement of their end.

Unfortunately for the cause of peace, the Czar proceeded at this point to throw away all the advantage which he had gained by his prompt acceptance of the Vienna Note, by explaining his reasons for accepting it. Russia's position in opposing a bare refusal to the suggestion that she should modify to her own disadvantage at the instance of Turkey an international award, recommended to her by the great Powers as a fair settlement of the dispute, was technically one of extraordinary strength. But by a fatal error the Russian Chancellor sent to Vienna a reasoned analysis of Turkey's proposed modifications, and Russia's grounds for rejecting them. This analysis revealed the fact that Russia had interpreted ambiguities in the original Note in a sense not intended by its framers, though only explicitly excluded by the proposed Turkish alterations.[3] England and France thereupon refused to follow Austria and Prussia in urging Turkey to accept the original Note—a Note which even the Prince Consort now condemned.[4] Attempts were made early in October to frame a new Note altogether, but by this time Turkey was growing really out of hand. At the beginning of October the Porte launched an ultimatum requiring the withdrawal of the Russian troops from the

---

[1] *Stanmore : Aberdeen*, 270, 271.
[2] On this, v. *Stanmore : Aberdeen*, 254 ; *Morley : Gladstone*, 488.
[3] *Maxwell*, ii. 24. For the document itself see *Diplomatic Study*, i. 214-217.
[4] *Martin*, ii. 517.

invaded Principalities within fifteen days.[1] On October 10 Russia replied with a virtual refusal ; and thereupon a state of war ensued between the two empires. On October 22, at the instance of the French government, the English and French fleets passed the Dardanelles.

Even so, hopes of a pacific issue were not dead. The Czar announced that it was not he who had declared the war, and it would not be Russia who would begin it : his troops would refrain during the winter from taking the offensive, and would merely repel any aggressive movement on the part of the Turks whether in Asia or in the Principalities : these last, however, Russia must continue to occupy ; not necessarily for annexation, but as a guarantee [2] of her antagonist's good faith.

But the Turks possessed no similar ' material guarantee ' for the good behaviour of Russia, whose mere presence in the Principalities they regarded as in itself an unwarrantable aggression. At the beginning of November, they crossed the Danube and defeated the Russians at Oltenitza in the first pitched battle of the war.

Mortifying as was the news of this Turkish victory to the Czar, it at any rate appeared to him a complete release from his engagement to refrain from taking the offensive. And thanks to the activities of Stratford, opportunity for offensive action was quickly forthcoming.

As we have seen, the passage of the combined fleets in October into the Sea of Marmora was less the work of the English than of the French ambassador at Constantinople.[3] But Stratford soon resumed the lead. His despatches at the beginning of November seemed to Queen Victoria to ' exhibit clearly a *desire* for war, and to drag us into it.' ' It becomes a serious question,' she added, ' whether we are justified in allowing Lord Stratford any longer to remain in a situation which gives him the means of frustrating all our efforts for peace.' [4] Her husband shared her views. ' Louis Napoleon,' he wrote in that same month, ' shows

---

[1] *Kinglake*, i. 354.
[2] *Gage matériel*. The phrase was Count Nesselrode's.
[3] *Lane-Poole*, ii. 309.   [4] *Q.V.L.*, 5 Nov. 53.

by far the greatest statesmanship ; . . . he is moderate but firm, gives way to us even when his plan is better than ours. . . . Lord Stratford fulfils his instructions to the letter, but he so contrives that we are constantly getting deeper into a war policy. Six weeks ago, Palmerston and Lord John carried a resolution that we should give notice that an attack on the Turkish fleet by that of Russia would be met by the fleets of England and France. Now the Turkish steam-ships are to cross over from the Asiatic coast to the Crimea, and to pass before Sebastopol. This can only be meant to insult the Russian fleet, and to entice it to come out, in order to bring our fleet into collision with that of Russia according to his former instructions, and so to make a European war certain.' [1]

Three days later the Prince's prediction was fulfilled to the letter : Clarendon in August was not a better prophet than the Prince Consort in November. For the Turkish coat was not merely trailed but trodden on. On November 30 the Turkish squadron on its way from the Bosphorus to Batoum was attacked in the Turkish harbour of Sinope by the Russian fleet, and practically blown out of the water.

It was nearly a fortnight before the news of the catastrophe reached the western capitals ; but when it did, though calmly received in Paris,[2] it produced a violent explosion of indignation throughout England. The disparity of the forces engaged ; the supposed treachery of an attack which was regarded as a breach of the Czar's engagement to refrain from taking the offensive ; most of all, the continuance of the Russian cannonade long after the Turkish crews were completely defenceless, so that four thousand of them were killed—all these caused the action to appear to England not a battle but a massacre. As a result the war-party in the English cabinet, hitherto held in check by the pacific but incompetent premier, now definitely gained the day. Unfortunately too at this

---

[1] 27 Nov. 53. *Martin*, ii. 532, 533. See further on the general contemporary impression that Stratford was working for war, *Greville*, 4 and 8 Sept. 55, and Appendix B, p. 391, below.
[2] *Diplomatic Study*, i. 280.

juncture the French Emperor was inspired with a fresh desire to do something showy with the fleets. He proposed that the Mediterranean squadrons of the allies, which had already occupied the Sea of Marmora, should now enter the Black Sea, and there invite all Russian ships to return to Sevastopol ; this proposal strenuously urged by his ambassador at London was accepted by the English cabinet under pressure of Palmerston's momentary resignation and the popular clamour which it occasioned. Hence at the beginning of January the Black Sea was emptied of Russian shipping, until such time as the Principalities should be evacuated by Russian troops.

It was at once obvious that Sinope and its immediate consequences had immensely increased the probability of a European war. At that prospect Stratford no longer troubled to conceal his glee. A friend [1] who had just seen the allied fleets, in obedience to this latest diplomatic decision, emerging upon the Black Sea, hastened at once to the ambassador with the news : for the actual intrusion of armed vessels into those sacred and forbidden waters was felt by all beholders to be a harbinger of war. As such Stratford hailed it. ' You have brought some good news,' he answered, ' for that means *war*. The Emperor of Russia chose to make it a personal quarrel with me ; and now I am avenged.' ' Thank God, that's WAR ' [2] had already been reported to be his fervent exclamation, on the first news of the Battle of Sinope. A *Nunc dimittis* indeed, but not 'in peace.'

Yet England's eagerness for the war was the work of no one man. Four years earlier in an eloquent oration Cobden had assured his Yorkshire constituents that a widening of the franchise was the security for peace. For ' in proportion as you find the people governing themselves you will find that war is not the disposition of the people, and that if Government desire it the people would put a check upon

---

[1] Lord Bath. Clarendon received the story from Lady Ashburton to whom Lord Bath narrated it in a letter. *Greville*, 24 Feb. 54. The same story is also reported in Malmesbury's diary of the following day. *Malmesbury*, i. 425.

[2] A Dr Sandwith who was with Stratford on the occasion repeated this to Lord *Stanmore* : *Aberdeen*, 254 *n*.

it.' [1] Few prophecies were to receive more swift or signal refutation. In a sense Lord Clarendon's famous phrase was true which described England as ' drifting ' into the Crimean War. But it was the popular breeze throughout that kept her straining at every anchor that would have arrested her course. Against the war was ranged originally almost the whole of the machinery of government : the Foreign Office, the Premier, the *Times*, the Queen, the Prince Consort himself. The four last were all bitterly anti-Bonapartist ; and not only that but by predilection pro-Austrian and even in a sense pro-Russian. [2]

One by one they veered before the wind ; with a conversion which though slow was in the case of the court at least sincere. But the sincerity of the royal conversion did not at once atone for its sloth, and the suspicion that it might succeed in baulking the country of its war seemed for a moment almost to shake the stability of the throne. For by this time the populace was possessed by one wild frenzy for war. When in January 1854 the Czar's rumoured acceptance of a settlement emanating from Vienna seemed for a moment to promise peace there was no longer, as in the previous summer, a general sensation of relief ; only a cry of disappointment that ' the beggar would not fight.' [3] But to be kept from fighting him if he would—that was a state of affairs which flesh and blood could not endure. Two Englishmen only had consistently smoothed the way for war ; Stratford, and his old second in the duel with Nicholas, Palmerston. But against Palmerston unhappily the court had shot its bolt and shot it at the wrong time. Two years earlier, as men now realised, he had been jockeyed

---

[1] 18 Dec. 49.   Yet in that very speech and in the very next sentence he was pouring oil on flames on which the government poured water : in eloquent popular denunciation of Russia ' the black despotism of the North ' and on ' that province of Russia—that miserable and degraded country Austria, next in the stage of despotism and barbarism.' *Cobden* : *Speeches*, i. 432, 433. But for his distinction between the right of denunciation and the right of intervention, with specific reference to his remarks on Russia, *v.* his parliamentary speech of June 1850 on the Pacifico affair. *Hansard*, cxii. 671. And for a most just demolition of alarmist arguments based on the mere *size* of Russia, *v.* a letter of his dated 15 Oct. 49 : B.M. Add. MSS. 37,053, f. 41.
[2] v. *Lorne*, 173.   [3] *Stanmore* : *Aberdeen*, 255.

out of office ; by a process which threatened a dangerous
increase in the power of the crown, and in a cause which
appeared a subservient truckling to the principles of the
Holy Alliance. In consequence the sane and prudent
counsels of the crown lacked for the moment a weight which
they had never more deserved ; else England might have
escaped the Crimean War as she escaped another infinitely
more disastrous. But the Prince Consort who modified the
Note on the Trent affair was not under the recent suspicion
of having rid England of the most English of her ministers
at the behest of Austrian or Russian despots ; and the
Queen was powerless now to recall Stratford for a good
reason because she had lately dismissed Palmerston for a
bad one. Still more helpless was the court now against
Palmerston himself. When in mid-December he had of
his own accord resigned,[1] his colleagues were forced within
a few days to beg him back on his own terms, though those
terms meant war. Neither cabinet nor crown could afford
to seem to have got rid of Palmerston a second time.

The storm thus bowed before quickly abated ; in fact
thanks to the prompt prostration of the cabinet it was only
its aftermath which reached the throne.[2] But for a week
or so the mere suspicion that they had even failed to oust
Palmerston and stifle the war made things distinctly
unpleasant for the court ; for one joyful moment it was
believed half England over that the Prince Consort had

---

[1] Mr *Strachey*, 168, seems half to accept the suggestion of *Kinglake*, ii.
29, 30, that the court was really attempting to repeat in Dec. 53 its *coup
d'état* against Palmerston of Dec. 51. But (1) documents destructive of
the contention were published in the *Quarterly Review* of April 77 :
CXLIII, 373–379. (2) Even before their publication this whole passage
—an afterthought in Kinglake's 1877 edition—was on other grounds a piece
of demonstrably dishonest writing. (3) Evidence apart, it is inherently
more probable that Palmerston *more suo* was having his ' tit-for-tat ' with
the court, than that the court was gratuitously seeking a second round
with him. What really ' remains wrapped in obscurity ' is the source of
the suddenly-started suddenly-stopped press campaign against the Prince.

[2] Those who only consult the files of the *Times* miss the evidences of
this mania ; for the *Times* with all officialdom was working for peace. It
was the Radical papers which really raved for war : the *Morning Herald*,
the *Daily News*, and most of all the *Morning Advertiser* ; *e.g.* leading articles
of 28 Dec. 53, and Jan. 6, 13, 17, 19, and 24 of 54. ' Better,' it wrote,
' that a few drops of guilty blood should be shed on a scaffold on Tower
Hill than that the country should be baulked of its desire for war.'

been committed to the Tower for treasonable correspondence with the Czar ; [1] the only doubt which seems to have
agitated the waiting thousands on Tower Hill was whether
they would be afforded the spectacle of one royal prisoner
or two : the more credulous inclined to the opinion that
' the Queen also had been arrested.' [2] A similar fate was
assigned by rumour to the Premier, Aberdeen.[3] When
Parliament was opened at the end of January Queen
Victoria and her husband were able to drive through the
streets of London without actual insult ; but they found
themselves entirely subordinate features in their own procession ; ' all the *enthusiasm* was bestowed on the Turkish
Minister.' [4] So far as England was concerned the war was
regretted by the government and demanded by the people.
And it was the will of the people that prevailed.

Completely different was the state of affairs in France.
As in England it was the government, so in France it was
the people who wanted peace. This second fact too has
been obscured by another variant of doctrinaire liberalism.
In general it is of the faith to believe that governments
and not peoples are the originators of war. But in this
instance republican propaganda demands an exception in
the case of France. It postulates that Louis Napoleon
had just inflicted on France a government which she
detested, and was forced to lessen its internal unpopularity
by the distraction of a popular war.[5] The truth is that the

---

[1] ' The Postmen some suspicion had
      And opened the two letters,
      'Twas a pity sad the German lad
      Should not have known much better.'—*Lovely Albert*,

a contemporary broadside quoted by *Strachey*, 178. ' My correspondence
with the Emperor Nicholas,' protested the Prince, ' has been confined to
announcements of the births of my children.' *Ernest*, iii. 80.

[2] *Martin*, ii. 562 : *Stockmar*, ii. 499, 500 : cf. *Times*, 18 Jan. 54, p. 8, c. 6 :
Greville, 15 Jan. 54.

[3] *Stanmore* : *Aberdeen*, 256.   [4] *Greville*, 1 Feb. 54.

[5] There is a passage in the *Pharsalia* so exactly expressive of the orthodox
legend that its exponents deserve to be presented with the quotation :

    Non erat is populus quem pax tranquilla iuvaret,
    quem sua libertas inmotis pasceret armis.
    Inde irae faciles, et, quod suasisset egestas,
    vile néfas ; magnumque decus ferroque petendum
    plus patria potuisse sua ; mensuraque iuris
    vis erat : hinc reges et plebis scita coactae.

French people had just obtained the government they desired, and wanted above all things to be left in peace. To baulk them of that desire was on Louis Napoleon's part a gratuitous test of his own popularity ; and great as that popularity then was he needed it all, and final success to boot, to reconcile his subjects to the war.

Not only was peace in general at the moment strongly desired by France, but the prospect of this particular war was doubly and trebly distasteful to her. To devout Bonapartists it seemed a shocking thing that the new Napoleon should at once seek the alliance of the victor of Waterloo. Napoleon's Russian campaign moreover had inspired France with a profound conviction of the invulnerability of Russia : surely it was foolish, as M. Hugo suggested, to begin one's empire with 1812 ? The fact was that Napoleon III regarded England and not Russia as the main cause of his uncle's downfall ; and for that reason among others he preferred the English to the Russian alliance as the corner-stone of his own foreign policy.[1] But France as a whole ascribed Napoleon's ruin to the Russian expedition, and his punishment only to England. For the accident which had thrust on England the thankless task of being Napoleon's gaoler had kept alive anti-English sentiment [2] in France long after all popular feeling against Russia had subsided. Throughout the Crimean War therefore Louis Napoleon, by the unstinted expenditure of his personal popularity, was engaged in forcing France, in alliance with the nation whom at the time she most disliked, into an attack upon the nation whom she held least capable of being attacked successfully. It was a testimony to the immense hold which he had on French public opinion that the Emperor should have succeeded in rallying it to such an adventure in such company at all. The limitation of Russian sea-power did genuinely concern Englishmen ; but it left France entirely cold. And since England had insisted as a condition of the alliance that

---

[1] On Louis Napoleon's deliberate reversals of his uncle's policy, see an article by the present writer on ' Napoleon and the Second Empire,' in the *Times'* Napoleon Supplement of 8 May 1921.

[2] For its persistence, v. e.g. *Arch. Nat.*, BB 30, 367.

neither country should make annexations in any circumstances, the French were inclined to feel that they were fighting in a foreign cause with a stipulation in advance that they should not be paid for it. Nor was there even in France any real religious enthusiasm for the war such as a crusade on behalf of fellow-Christians naturally engendered in Russia. The dispute as to the Holy Places, it is too often forgotten, had been settled satisfactorily nearly a year before the war began ; and the Turk had seldom the attraction for Catholics that he had for Protestants or Jews. Of the clerical and reactionary parties Orleanists generally were bitterly anti-English,[1] and Legitimists were pro-Russian to a man. In point of fact those who in France disapproved of the war least were probably the Socialists and Liberals ; to bring down Russia was to set despotism tottering everywhere, and the same fact which made the war hateful to clear-sighted Royalists made it welcome to clear-sighted Republicans. But Royalists were many and Republicans few ; and clear sight was an even rarer merit among the latter than among the former.

It is not strange therefore that at the beginning of 1854 the Prince Consort should have described the Emperor as being 'in anything but a warlike mood,'[2] though his disinclination to hostilities was but a pale reflection of his people's.[3] So obvious was this fact that Russia now made repeated efforts to detach France from the English alliance.[4] It was a pity, urged Seebach, that the Emperor Napoleon should lose the glory of assuring a pacific solution of the question.[5] Louis himself had written to his representative at St Petersburg, saying that if the Russian Emperor had any proposal to make, he would give it every attention ; but urging that no time should be lost, since ' he could not disguise from himself that matters were in a

[1] But Thiers favoured the alliance. *Cf.* his letter to Ellice of 25 March 53. *B.N. Nouv. Acq. Fr.*, 20,618, f. 292.
[2] *Martin*, ii. 563.
[3] v. Circourt to Reeve, 31 Dec. 53. B.M. Add. MSS. 37,423, f. 405.
[4] F.O. France, Cowley to Clarendon, 29 Dec. 53 ; 19 Jan. 54. 'Confidential.' Admitted by *Diplomatic Study*, i. 282. Cf. *Q.V.L.*, Leopold to Victoria, 13 Jan. 54.
[5] F.O., *ibid.*

declivity which might lead to war.'[1] The only result of his private and indirect appeal was a persistent assertion by the Czar that all the trouble was caused by ' *les bureaux* ' : that if he had to do with the French Emperor alone matters would soon be settled.[2] Louis therefore determined to address Nicholas publicly and directly : and dispatched at the end of January an autograph letter to the Czar. The letter comprised a dispassionate recital of the events of the last year ; it urged that only definite efforts in the direction of peace could now avert definite war ; it then proposed for this purpose a scheme of pacification based upon an immediate armistice, and the simultaneous abandonment of the Principalities by the Russian troops, and of the Black Sea by the allied fleets. Further, should the Czar find it easier to treat directly with the Turk, by all means let him do so ; only when they had settled matters between themselves, let whatever arrangement they should have reached be submitted for final ratification to the Four Powers. These proposals, conciliatory in themselves, were however accompanied by a purposely plain-spoken intimation that their rejection would force France, no less than England, to declare war ; an intimation deliberately made by Louis in unmistakable terms, in order to put an end to the Czar's dangerous illusion that he might be able at the last moment to detach France from England.[3] The severest of the Emperor's English critics admits that this letter was ' in many parts ably worded and moderate in tone,' and that its proposal offered Russia ' a decorous escape from her troubles.'[4] But the Czar rejected the offer, and embittered his rejection with a taunt ; Russia, he did not doubt, would show herself in 1854 what she had been in 1812.

The chief criticisms to which Louis' overture exposed him at the time were that it savoured of self-advertisement ; that in seeking peace in this outrageously public manner he was departing from all the decent usages of diplomacy ;

---

[1] F.O. France, Cowley to Clarendon. 'Confidential.' 30 Dec. 53.
[2] F.O. France, Cowley to Clarendon, 25 Jan. 54.
[3] *Ibid.* [4] *Kinglake,* i. 400, 402.

that his action was theatrical, and displayed moreover a desire for the lion's share of the limelight. These criticisms are probably just. But some higher criticisms and compliments lavished on him in this connexion a generation later, are almost certainly false. Mr Paul, seeking in Louis a satisfying melodramatic villain, describes the letter as being on his part ' a theatrical and obviously insincere attempt to conciliate the man who would not call him brother.' [1] M. Ollivier, seeking in Louis a hero of romance, revolving inwardly for the liberation of Italy a great symmetrical design, postulates also at this point, as a condition and consequence of his argument, the same statement : the Emperor in proposing peace purposed war, foreseeing that his offer would be rejected,[2] and that its rejection would eventually redound to the advantage of Italy. It is the easiest method of writing history well to people it with complete heroes and authentic villains. Not only are such characters artistically invaluable when found, but the discovery of them is actually assisted by the restful process of ignoring evidence. The task of examining evidence is irksome ; and its reward is the risk of losing one's hero and almost the certainty of losing one's villain.

Louis Napoleon at any rate survives the ordeal in neither capacity. The ' open letter ' it is true is less commonly a harbinger of peace than of the sword ; and it has long been a device affected by those who praise the one and seek the other. But with many small crookednesses of method contracted during his long training as conspirator, Louis yet retained in some larger matters an almost childish simplicity of motive ; and in the present instance there is abundance even of published evidence that the Czar's rejection of his overture occasioned its author only an extreme and naïve disappointment.[3] The real charge which Louis incurred by this letter from those acquainted with the facts was of a totally opposite nature. They could acquit him indeed of the offence imputed to him at the

---

[1] *Paul*, i. 329.   [2] *Ollivier*, iii. 184.
[3] Admitted by the Russian *Diplomatic Study*, i. 284. ' It seems positive that he expected great results from it, and that he was much hurt at the failure of this personal effort at conciliation.' And even by *Kinglake*, i. 399.

time that he had acted presumptuously in speaking for
the Queen as well as for himself. For the Emperor had at
first proposed that the Queen should send a similar letter,[1]
but her ministers very sensibly refused to advise her to
write one.[2] Their actual grievance was of a very different
kind. When the draft of the letter was submitted for his
approval, Clarendon disapproved strongly, as altogether
too accommodating, of its two chief concessions, in respect
of the simultaneous withdrawal of the Russian troops
and the allied fleets, and the facilities afforded to the Czar
for separate negotiations with Turkey. Through a lack
of straightforwardness which Clarendon attributed to
Drouyn rather than to his master, England was given to
understand that her objections would be met by radical
omissions, but the letter was none the less dispatched with
merely verbal modifications.[3] Hence England would have
been placed in a most awkward situation if the Czar had
accepted the French Emperor's proposals. A few days
later however his scornful refusal of them rendered
groundless the English fears of being tricked by means of
them into an unsatisfactory peace.[4] But the general impression produced by the letter upon the mind of France
and Europe was not of a kind which entitled it to be regarded as an unmixed success ; and when a month later
Louis offered to repeat the performance on a smaller scale
in another admonitory letter to the King of Greece, Cowley
intervened to dissuade him from the course.[5]

Meanwhile the last faint chance of peace had finally
flickered out. Even the action of the allied fleets in clearing the Black Sea of the Russian flag had not absolutely
rendered war inevitable ; if the fleets were instructed merely
to maintain the neutrality of the Black Sea, protecting
thereby from attack Russian ports, no less than Turkish,
the Czar would accept a naval armistice so maintained,
while reserving his freedom of action on land. Failing

---

[1] F.O. France, Cowley to Clarendon, 25 Jan. 54.
[2] *Ibid.*, 29 Jan. 54.   [3] *Greville*, 15 Feb. 54.
[4] *Ibid.*, 19 Feb 54.
[5] F.O. France, Cowley to Clarendon, 26 Feb. 54.

this, he announced that he must break off diplomatic relations. The allies in reply refused to forbid the Turks free passage between Turkish ports ; the only proper equivalent for a naval armistice in the Black Sea would be, they answered, a military armistice in the Principalities. Upon this, at the beginning of February, the Czar withdrew his ambassadors from London and Paris. He still refused to declare war. But at this juncture Austria, the great Power most immediately concerned by the invasion of the Principalities, volunteered to support the Western Powers in requiring the evacuation of them by a given date. On the strength of this offer, without waiting to secure a definite undertaking of armed assistance from Austria in the event of Russia's refusal, England and France launched an ultimatum. The Czar intimated that the demand was one to which he could return no answer ; even so, however, he reiterated his declaration that Russia would not declare war. But to the allies a negative answer was in effect war ; and war was as a result declared at Paris and London on the 27th and 28th of March. It was characteristic of the English declaration—a document of some length—that in it the use of the word ' war ' was scrupulously avoided.[1] It was the last tribute to peace, the fit finale of a negotiation in which the English cabinet had assented to no warlike measure without first protesting against it, and protested against none without finally assenting to it. But war, however euphemistically declared, was henceforth a fact. For not the most pacific of premiers can at the same time break the peace and keep it. It only remained to this ministry of all the talents to give one crowning proof of its even-handed administration. Even in its incompetence it was impartial : having proved its inability to preserve peace, it owed to itself to prove before it perished its equal inability to wage war.

[1] *Register* : 1854, 531, 532.

CHAPTER VIII

THE REAPERS

La Russie est la pierre angulaire du despotisme dans le monde ; et cette pierre, fût-elle arrachée par la main de despotes, entraînera tôt ou tard dans sa chute tous les gouvernements absolus.

ALEXIS DE TOCQUEVILLE.

IT was characteristic of the Crimean War—and a tribute perhaps to the force of that mere habit of peace which it had so unfortunately broken—that it took longer to get itself declared than almost any other in history. Characteristic also of the war and of its age was the fact that during a considerable part of its actual course negotiations were simultaneously in progress with a view to the discovery of some means for its conclusion. At the outset for some months after the declaration of war, the real centre of interest remained less military than diplomatic. That the combat once joined would prove long and obstinate either side had reason to suspect ; each was therefore anxious to secure the military or at least the moral support of those countries in Europe which remained neutral. Of the great Powers two only—Austria and Prussia—remained outside the range of hostilities ; it was therefore for the favour of these two German states that Russia and her opponents were suitors in the spring of 1854.

Of the two, Russia had recently rendered signal and gratuitous service to the one ; and still more recently had assisted at the grievous humiliation of the other. To Nicholas directly Austria owed Hungary : to Nicholas indirectly Prussia owed Olmütz.[1] Yet of the two it was Prussia whose king intimated to the Western Powers that should they ' let loose revolution as their ally ' they would force him to fight on the side of Nicholas ; while Austria showed at the very outset of the war a disposition to co-operate with the allies, and finally in their company launched the ultimatum which compelled Russia to acknowledge defeat.

The fact was that the very magnitude of her debt to Russia inspired in Austria a perverse desire to deny an obligation which it wounded the national vanity to admit, and would have taxed the national energies to discharge. The diplomatists of Vienna preferred to pass cynically through a sort of moral bankruptcy court ; what could not be repaid could at any rate be repudiated. ' We will astonish the world by our ingratitude,' said Schwarzenberg. And if Austria failed to fulfil his prediction to the letter, it was only because at ingratitude in Austria the world refused to be astonished. One man only paid the country, or rather its ruler, that compliment ; and that one was Nicholas.

It is a bitter thing for a boy who has made a man his hero to discover gradually that his divinity was but of the common clay after all. But it is a worse thing far for a man to be disappointed suddenly in the hopes which he has wreathed about some boy. The one can build new altars to new gods : the other may have lost that faculty for ever. So was it now with Nicholas. He had con-ceived a romantic affection for the fair-haired fatherless boy, whom in a year of universal ruin he had sustained on his tottering throne. It was his habit to have near him a marble statuette of the young Emperor,[2] whom in his own phrase ' he loved as a son.'[3] ' He had been strangely slow to believe that Francis Joseph could harbour the thought of opposing him in arms : and when at last the truth was forced upon him, he desired that the marble should be taken from his sight. But he did not, they say,

---

[1] On this, v. *Diplomatic Study*, i. 41.
[2] *Delord*, i. 545.   [3] *Vitzthum*, i. 36.

speak in anger. When he had spoken he covered his face with his hands and was wrung with grief.'[1] Of all the blows which fell on Nicholas in the last twelve months of his life, none was harder to bear than this.

That in the atmosphere of Vienna youth should grow cold and calculating before its time was perhaps no matter for wonder ; and gratitude once put out of court, calculation seemed to indicate clearly enough to Austria the course her statesmen actually pursued. For Russia at the mouth of the Danube was already threatening Austria herself in the nineteenth century with the fate which Holland at the mouth of the Scheldt had inflicted on the Austrian Netherlands in the eighteenth : the deliberate throttling of her trade by the one great waterway which she possessed. By purposely allowing the mouth of the river to become silted and unnavigable Russia's possession of the mere delta of the Danube had already wrought Austria commercial injury. But her acquisition of the whole Danubian Principalities would have added a far more formidable political threat. It would have given Russia extensive frontiers not only to the east of Austria but to the south ; and poised semi-slavonic subjects of the one between the outstretched finger and thumb of the other. It needed a robuster constitution than Austria's to contemplate with equanimity the friendly but ineluctable hand-grip that would ensue.

Moreover on general grounds the declared object of the allies, the maintenance in its integrity of the Ottoman Empire, was one which harmonised admirably with the Austrian policy of immobility. Nor would this harmony be in the least impaired, even if the Czar were right in his diagnosis. For from the point of view of immobility the preservation of existing institutions was even more desirable when they were dead, than when they were living. That dead men should be buried, and their goods divided, was from the point of view of Austria a dangerous precedent ; the proper thing to do with a corpse was to embalm it, and say that it lived and remained a legal owner of property.

[1] *Kinglake*, i. 427.

The allies might or might not prove successful in their efforts
to arrest or conceal the processes of decay in Turkey : that
such was their object their very critics testified ; and it
was an object eminently deserving of the sympathies of
Austria.

Widely different was the attitude of Prussia. Prussia
like Austria regarded the freedom of the Danube as a
German interest, and was even prepared to admit that the
evacuation of the Principalities might become a European
necessity. Like Austria therefore she refused to give
Russia any formal assurance of neutrality ; and with
Austria she even entered in April into a general defensive
alliance. Neither Power did in fact take any active part
in the struggle : but whereas Austria's attitude towards
Russia was on the whole one of malevolent neutrality, the
King of Prussia throughout sought earnestly to discover
for the Czar, his brother-in-law, some road back to an
honourable peace. In this sense he wrote to Queen
Victoria protesting against the war on the eve of its declaration ; adding that for himself he must prefer the
interests of his own subjects to those of the Turk. It was
war for an idea, war against a shadow, that especially
revolted the Prussian monarch. ' The preponderance of
Russia is to be broken down. Well I her neighbour have
never felt this preponderance, and have never yielded to it.
And in reality England has felt it less than I.' . . . ' I
know,' added the King, ' that the Russian Emperor is
ardently desirous of peace. Let your Majesty build a
bridge for the principle of his life—the Imperial honour.
He will walk over it, extolling God and praising Him.
For this I pledge myself.' Finally the King announced
that Prussia could not join England against Russia : ' the
Emperor is a noble gentleman and has done us no harm.'
Such language, the Queen replied, was unworthy of a great
Power ; from the King of Hanover or Saxony she could
have understood it. As for making a supreme attempt at
peace, so many pacific proposals had been made already
that ' one might almost call the ink wasted on them

another Black Sea.'[1]   Another Red Sea presumably did
not matter.

But it was as much the traditional policy of Prussia
to remain at peace when Europe was at war as to go to war
when Europe was at peace, and Frederick William remained obstinately pacific.   Alleging no better reason than
that he regarded ' Peace as a blessing and War as a curse,'
he met the reproach as to Prussia's abdication of its
position as a great Power with the remark : ' I believe
that the character of a so-called Great Power must justify
itself, not by swimming with the tide, but by standing firm
like a rock in the sea.'[2]   Hence the spring of 1854 saw
England hardly less disappointed in Prussia than the Czar
had been disappointed in Austria ; either combatant was
fain to forgo his hopes of making the struggle European.
Still if great Powers persisted in acting like small ones and
keeping the peace, there was always the possibility that
small states might be induced to act like great ones and
make trial of war.   Early in May the French Emperor
broached this idea to Cowley ; he thought that Sweden,
Sardinia, and perhaps even Spain might join the alliance ;
and that it might be worth while to have them.   For ' if
Russia came out of the struggle with her wings unclipped, she
became mistress of the destinies of Europe.'[3]   This proposal
to rally the smaller nations of Europe against the Russian
colossus was eminently characteristic of its author, save for
the fact—hitherto as unknown as the proposal itself—that in
the case of Spain, Sweden, and Denmark, as well as of Sardinia, it eventually admitted of practical accomplishment.[4]
But the willingness to help grew greater only as the need of
help grew less : for the moment the prospects of the allies
merely sufficed to render it impossible for Nicholas on his side
to obtain assistance from such sources.   Small states even
less than great Powers can afford to fight on a losing side.

---

[1] *Martin*, iii. 42-45.   The letter contains a quotation from Shakespeare,
as well as this pun : conclusive evidence that the Queen was not its author,
and that the Prince Consort was.

[2] *Q.V.L.*, iii. 29.

[3] F.O. France, Cowley to Clarendon.   ' Most Confidential.'   7 May 54.

[4] *v*. p. 349 below.

For the Czar, even to ask the suffrages of the smaller Powers was already a condescension ; to ask and be refused was humiliation unspeakable. That humiliation too he was to taste. One small incident may be related here, as typical in its way of much which the lonely autocrat was destined to suffer in the last year of his life. A Russian of rank who visited the Pope early in 1854 was charged casually at the end of his audience with some polite message for the Czar ; concluding with the well-worn formula, ' I do not forget him in my prayers ' : a formula generally understood in the case of a heretic to imply no more than prayers for his conversion. But Pio Nono's visitor interpreted the remark, or allowed it to be interpreted, as an expression of the Pope's personal good wishes to Nicholas in the war, and the Czar clutched greedily at so unexpected an expression of sympathy. He even took the unusual step of writing an autograph letter to the Pope, thanking him for his kind communication. But all his answer was a letter professing complete mystification, and saying that the Pope could only suppose that His Majesty alluded to expostulations addressed to him some time ago, pleading for the better treatment of Catholics in his dominions.[1] It was not the last time in the diplomacy of the war that Russia was to be reminded of Poland.

Meanwhile diplomatic rebuffs were at once explained and embittered for the Czar by news yet harder to bear : news of the ill-success of Russian armies at the actual seat of war. At the end of March, abandoning upon the intervention of the Western Powers the self-denying ordinance which had committed them to a mere defensive occupation of the Principalities, the Russian troops had crossed the Danube and proceeded successfully to overrun the Dobrudscha. But when in May they laid siege to Silistria, they encountered a resistance of wholly unexpected vigour

---

[1] F.O. France, Cowley to Clarendon, 18 Mar. 54. The story seems worthy of publication, because the Russian official *Diplomatic Study*, published a generation later, asserts boldly and without qualification, that ' the Pope sent to the Emperor Nicholas his best wishes for his prosperity and success.' *Diplomatic Study*, ii. 83.

from a Turkish garrison inspired by two young English
officers, who in this first episode of the war had found their
way to the fighting. The Russian general himself was disabled by a wound ; and on the 20th of June his troops were
forced to raise the siege. By this time moreover Austria
had summoned Russia to evacuate the Principalities ; and
political no less than military considerations demanded
the withdrawal of the invading army. It accordingly
retreated, first to the north of the Danube and finally to
the north of the Pruth. By the beginning of August no
Russian troops were left in Turkish territories : at the close
of it, the Czar caused it to be announced that for the remainder of the war he would limit himself to the defence
of his own dominions. The Principalities themselves were
temporarily occupied by Austria, who informed the allies
that her object was to protect them from Russia, and
Russia that her object was to protect them from the
allies.[1]

But since it was the Russian occupation of the Principalities which had started the war, there was no apparent
reason why her evacuation of them should not have ended
it. Unfortunately the course of these opening operations
inclined neither combatant to peace. All the honours of
the campaign at this stage had gone to the ' sick man ' ;
whose success afforded no direct satisfaction to the military
prestige of his allies, and was yet peculiarly exasperating
to the wounded pride of his opponent. Russia could not
accept defeat, and the allies would not even accept victory,
at the hands of the Turk. Instead, emboldened rather
than satisfied by the Ottoman success, they demanded
from the Czar not indeed any surrender of territory, but
substantial diplomatic concessions : [2] these concessions
Nicholas refused. Doubtless he was convinced that now
as often before in her wars with Turkey Russia would
retrieve in a second campaign all that she had lost in a
first ; while to a second campaign the allies also looked for
some more direct and unmistakable success. At the
moment neither of the Western Powers had great cause

---

[1] *Ernest*, iii. 122.   [2] See below, p. 297.

for jubilation ; England no less than her ally was ill-content ; an imposing fleet had been sent to the Baltic with quite unimposing results. True, the chief fortress on the Äland Islands had surrendered ; but beyond the razing of its fortifications nothing permanent had been achieved. Louis Napoleon had attempted to make use of this small success as a means towards the fulfilment of his earlier proposal for the extension of the alliance. Apparently on his own responsibility, he caused his foreign minister to offer the islands to Sweden.[1] But Sweden was too cautious to throw in her lot definitely with the allies at this stage, though she asked them to continue their occupation of the islands. This however proved im-practicable ; instead it was decided at Paris that the allies should content themselves with razing the fortifica-tions.[2] Before the return of the fleets this work of demoli-tion was very thoroughly carried out ; but in England there was a widespread feeling that the operations of this Baltic Armada bore an unsatisfactory resemblance to those of an historic army that 'went to Spain.'[3] Regarded as a mere appetizer a captured fortress with a couple of thousand prisoners might be all very well : as the *pièce de résistance* in a war for which one had been waiting forty years it was ludicrously inadequate. England 'wanted more.' So far her fleets had done little, and her armies less. ' We are now approaching the sixth month of actual hostilities,' complained the *Times* in July, ' and as yet not a shot has been fired by the land forces of England.'[4]

Moreover as the royal letter to the King of Prussia had observed : ' Shakespeare's words :

"Beware
Of entrance to a quarrel ; but being in
Bear it that the opposer may beware of thee,"

---

[1] F.O. France, Cowley to Clarendon, 27 Aug. 54.

[2] F.O. France, Cowley to Clarendon, 29 Aug. 54. At the end of the war, the King of Sweden endeavoured to obtain for the Aland Islands ' a complicated system of neutrality ' : in this he was however unsuccessful, as well as in his desire for a restriction of the Russian fleet in the Baltic. F.O., Paris Congress Papers. Palmerston to Clarendon, 26 Apr. 56.

[3] On the ' great indignation ' felt in England on this score, v. *Greville*, 22 Sept. 54.

[4] *Times*, 24 July 54.

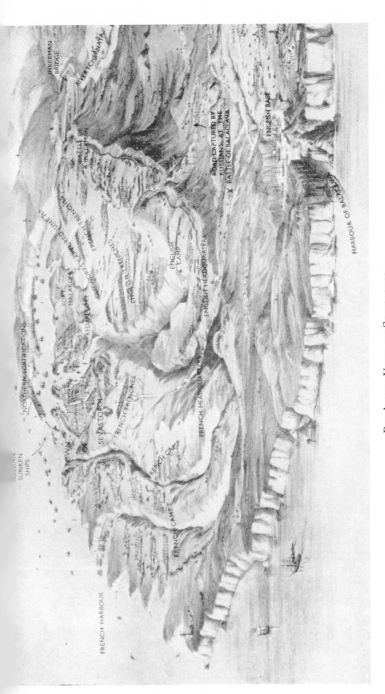

BIRD'S-EYE VIEW OF SEVASTOPOL

From a contemporary English lithograph after a drawing by T. Packer

MARSHAL SAINT-ARNAUD AT THE BATTLE OF THE ALMA

From a lithograph by E. Gambart

are deeply engraved on the hearts of all Englishmen.' [1]
And the Baltic proceedings were obviously not calculated
to make posterity beware ; nor in the months that followed
were similar efforts to carry to remoter shores the terror
of the English navy attended with more marked success.
For the elation with which men learned that the White Sea
Squadron had succeeded in destroying all but one tower of
the capital of Lapland [2] was quickly abated by the news
that the Pacific Squadron, ten days later, had completely
failed to destroy any perceptible portion of the capital of
Kamschatka.[3] Instead it had been forced to retire badly
battered to San Francisco to refit and repair. The ineffective nature of these operations served to create a
demand not merely for more war, but for better war. In
fact it was by this time obvious that if the Russian colossus
was to be brought to the ground at all, the conflict must be
continued by no mere series of pin-pricks at the extremities
of that gigantic frame. Yet the natural alternative—a
mortal blow thrust home at the heart of the Russian Empire
—seemed precluded in advance by memories of the Moscow
Campaign. It was not Nicholas alone who remembered
1812.

It remained therefore for Russia's assailants to discover
some portion of their opponent's anatomy at once vulner-
able and accessible ; and in this quest they finally stumbled
upon Sevastopol. Since it seemed hopeless even to attempt
a blow at the actual heart of Russia, the *Times* conveniently
discovered in this its southernmost fortress a sort of subsidiary heart—' the heart of Russian power in the East.' [4]
Against this might be directed a blow both practicable and
mortal. The decision on the face of it had much to commend it. It was from Sevastopol that the Russian fleet
had sallied forth to destroy the Turkish squadron at
Sinope ; it was to Sevastopol that this same fleet had
retreated with absolute security after the allied warships

---

[1] *Q.V.L.*, 17 March 54. It was not until the next Russo-Turkish war,
in 1877, that this sentiment was translated from Elizabethan to Victorian
verse, and coupled with the name of Jingo.

[2] *Register*, 1854 [403].   [3] *Ibid.*, 1854 [404, 405].

[4] *Times*, 24 July 54, p. 8, c. 3.

had occupied the Black Sea. To encompass its destruction would be to have moved from striking distance of Constantinople the very source and symbol of Russian naval aggression.

Hence in the middle of September the allied armies were transferred from Varna, the pestilent Bulgarian seaport on which they had first been centred, to what was henceforth to be the scene of all their hopes and labours and despairs—the peninsula of the Crimea.

It was in the Bay of Eupatoria, some thirty miles north of the great fortress of Sevastopol, that the allied armies were landed. The Russians, under the command of that same Prince Menschikoff whose disastrous mission to Constantinople had done so much to bring on the war, offered no resistance to the disembarkation ; on September 14 and the three following days thirty thousand French troops with a somewhat smaller English force and a body of seven thousand Turks effected a leisurely landing on the deserted beach. On the 19th they began the southward march, their faces set towards Sevastopol, and by their side, all morning as they marched, the allied fleets sailed slowly. Only in the afternoon, when a third of the thirty miles that divided them from their goal had already been traversed, did they encounter opposition. They had crossed already unopposed a number of small streams running seawards through the salt and sandy plain at right angles to their line of march : now suddenly ahead of them appeared another, somewhat broader than its fellows, having behind it, as they had not, high land towering suddenly from the river bank ; and on the heights, entrenched in strong defensive position, the hitherto invisible Russians. It was the river Alma.

Next day the stream was crossed and the heights stormed ; a French flank attack on the Russian left was followed by a frontal attack delivered by the English in close order on the right ; by four o'clock the Russian general ordered his troops to retire. Ill-led and out-manœuvred, his forces had suffered heavier casualties than they had inflicted on

their slightly more numerous assailants ; and with nightfall
the semblance of an orderly retreat was exchanged for an
undisguised and precipitate flight.

It was at this juncture that the allies were guilty of what
was probably the gravest military blunder of the war. They
failed to attempt an immediate assault upon Sevastopol
from the north. The contention that such an assault
would certainly have been successful is perhaps hardly
warranted, for the statements of the future defender [1] of the
city as to the indefensible position in which it then stood
are less conclusive than some historians have assumed.[2]
By minimising the original defences of the fortress Todleben
enhances the merit of his achievement in defending it ;
and his book, written long after the event, is in fact guilty
of many such attempts to exaggerate a feat which stood
in no need of exaggeration at all.[3] In any case, southern
Sevastopol, which comprised the real arsenal and city and
fortress, was separated from the mere storehouses and
outlying defences on the north by a harbour which was in
fact a considerable inlet, well over a thousand yards wide :
hence it is far from certain that the capture of the northern
works would have sufficed to render the city itself untenable.
Moreover the allied troops were weary and ill-fed ; the
battle, though victorious, had been closely contested ; and
that contest itself had been but the climax of an extremely
arduous week. The French too had as yet no cavalry ; [4]
while the English troops, in the picturesque phrase of their
commander, were ' pursued to the very battle-field ' by
the scourge of cholera.[5] Unlike their allies they had
been shot ashore without tents, without ambulances, and
without baggage animals ; [6] the astonished soldiery on
landing had been bidden to abandon their very knapsacks.[7] But it is probable that, weighty as such considerations were, they would have been overborne by a
capable general at the head of the allied forces ; not

[1] *Todleben*, i. 239.
[2] E.g. *Kinglake*, iii. 23, 27, 43, etc.   *Paul*, i. 356.   *C.M.H.*, 317, 318.
[3] On this, see *Hamley*, 67-72.   [4] *Saint-Arnaud*, ii. 584.
[5] *Martin*, iii. 132.   [6] *Sterling*, 134.   *Nolan*, i. 436.
[7] *Sterling*, 64.   *Steevens*, 77.

because it was easy to go forward, but because it was
fatal to stand still.

But a capable general neither portion of the attacking
armies possessed. Lord Raglan, the commander-in-chief
of the English expeditionary force, had seen service and
borne himself gallantly in the Peninsular War, and had lost
a right arm at Waterloo. Even in the presence of French
staff officers the habit clung to him in the Crimea of alluding
to the enemy as the French : [1] ' What would the Duke do
now ? ' was a question which haunted him much as a
similar question was to haunt his sovereign after the death
of the Prince Consort. The Napoleonic wars were in fact
his last military memory, for since 1815 his duties and
tastes had been political and diplomatic. Even in his
military career he had never had the disposal of a regiment
in a detached encounter ; [2] in the forty years which
followed, his activities had been chiefly displayed as a
Secretary of Embassy, a conservative Member of Parliament, a Privy Councillor, a peer, and a well-known
favourite at court. Cultured, kindly, scholarly, he well
deserved the laudatory epitaph gravely passed upon him
a year later by one of the most sympathetic of his subordinates in the Crimea : none could deny that he was ' a
thoroughly amiable man, of the highest aristocratical
tendencies.' [3] But for years before his appointment, his
life had been not merely civilian but sedentary. Now at
sixty-six, he found himself suddenly thrust into the post
of commander-in-chief of the English army in the Crimea.
Courageous as ever in the field, he knew how to comport
himself with dignity in circumstances habitually beyond
his control ; and though his direction of military operations
was seldom unimpeachable, his description of them was
conveyed in despatches of flawless excellence and lucidity.
Nor, under censure and criticism which he did not always
deserve, did he ever fail to display a magnanimous and
pathetic patience. Whether in the prime of life he could
have proved himself an effective commander of an effective

[1] *Tuckwell*, 40 *n*.   [2] *Nolan*, i. 381.
[3] *Sterling*, 286.

army must remain a matter of conjecture : it is a fact neither uncertain nor to himself discreditable that in his sixty-seventh year he did not prove equal to the Herculean task of evolving such an army from the material placed at his disposal by the British War Office of 1854. Nobody but the British War Office of 1854 could have expected that he would.

Though of appallingly plebeian origin,[1] Saint-Arnaud, the commander-in-chief of the French army, was neither so old [2] nor in actual leadership so inexperienced as his English colleague : long years of actual military service had brought him gradually from entirely subordinate position to responsible and independent command in recent African campaigns ; and though even he was some twenty years older than Todleben, the real defender of Sevastopol, he was at any rate a dozen years younger than his English colleague Raglan. Unfortunately what he lacked in age he made up in illness ; at the time of his appointment he was already in the last stage of a mortal disease, which at times quite incapacitated him from the exercise of his command.

It was this fact probably which led Saint-Arnaud to refuse Raglan's advice in favour of an immediate advance on the evening of the victory on the Alma. Next morning Saint-Arnaud wished to advance, but this time Raglan refused ; the English had borne the brunt of the fighting on the previous day, and their general now found himself fully occupied in extemporising provision for his wounded. Each commander was overruled when he was right and had his way when it was wrong : it took two to act, though one could veto action : a fact which throughout the siege favoured inaction and delay.[3] As a result the

---

[1] *Kinglake*, passim.

[2] The average age of the English generals in the Crimea was just about twice that of the English generals in the Peninsular War. *Graham*, 69.

[3] At the time it was commonly contended either that Raglan alone dissuaded Saint-Arnaud, or that Saint-Arnaud alone dissuaded Raglan. For the first thesis, v. *Nolan*, i. 433, *St Amand*, ii. 195 : for the second (which he admits however lacks the support of any letter or paper of Raglan), *Kinglake*, iii. 300 *sq.* The conflict of evidence is best reconciled by a remark of Napoleon III on 8 Oct. 55 to Marshal *Castellane* (v. 94), ' Je sais positivement que le soir de la bataille de l'Alma, lord Raglan avait

victors now contented themselves with encamping on the field of battle, whence the dying general dictated to his Emperor a despatch announcing the first victory to which French troops had been led by the restored eagles of the Empire. A week later, not unhappy in the opportunity of his departure, Saint-Arnaud was dead.

Even when shorn of its proper consequences, the victory of the Alma was no small achievement ; but to Europe in general, the announcement of it came coupled with a false report,[1] all but universally believed, that Sevastopol itself was fallen. Owing to the prevalence of this belief the military importance of the victory was first unduly exaggerated and then as unduly disparaged ; but upon its true political significance contemporary popular opinion seized at once with extraordinary swiftness and acumen. In all the minor capitals of Europe outside the Balkan peninsula itself, the people were visibly elated, the courts as visibly dismayed. Munich, the Hague, Dresden, Florence, Naples, all witnessed this same ebullition of popular rejoicing and royal perturbation. The Duke of Tuscany especially was loud in his lamentations ; while at Naples Bomba shut himself up, and refused to be comforted by his courtiers.[2]

But nowhere was the news of the victory more welcome than in Paris. For in France the war was still so unpopular as to render it doubtful whether the requisite loan would be subscribed. In fact Drouyn de Lhuys had actually thought it necessary to sound the English ambassador, '*most confidentially*,' as to the possibility of a joint loan, with bonds payable either in London or Paris ; an expedient which Cowley felt bound to advocate to his

écrit au maréchal de Saint-Arnaud de pousser sur Sébastopol, qu'il allait se porter en avant. Le maréchal de Saint-Arnaud ne le voulut pas ce soir-là ; il fut de cet avis le lendemain, et lord Raglan répondit qu'il ne le pouvait plus, à présent qu'il était embarrassé de ses blessés.' Throughout Saint-Arnaud displayed alternately the moods of a sick man too ill to move, and of a dying man in a hurry.

[1] For its origin, v. *Skene*, 316.

[2] *Nolan*, i. 439. He was reported to have sent large sums of money to Russia. F.O. Naples, Lowther to Clarendon, 28 Oct. 54.

home government, on account of the great unpopularity of the war, and the presumable difficulty in raising money for it in France.[1] These particular fears proved groundless : war against Russia on behalf of Turks could always get itself financed : [2] and without English assistance a French loan was so much over-subscribed that half the applications had to be refused.[3] None the less, the speech with which the French Emperor opened his parliament in this year bears witness to the general feeling of his subjects that France had been led into the war by England, in defence of interests not truly French at all. ' To reign in Con-stantinople is to rule the Mediterranean,' protested the Emperor : ' and none among you, gentlemen, I believe, will maintain that England alone has important interests, in a sea which bathes three hundred leagues of French coast.' But the distance of the battle-ground, the exiguity of the national interests at stake, and the absence of any genuine detestation of the foe, combined to give a sense of remoteness to the conflict. France was at war, but without the normal emotional anæsthetics ; and she seemed in consequence to pass judgment on her own contemporary war with something already of the sad clear-eyed aloofness of posterity.

Powerless perhaps to alter this attitude the Imperial government affected almost to encourage it ; carrying forward unperturbed in the intervals of military activities its social legislation for the provinces, increasing rather than diminishing its embellishment of Paris, and inaugurat-ing its preparations for an international exhibition there which should rival next year in time of war that recently

---

[1] F.O. France, Cowley to Clarendon, 22 Feb. 54.

[2] ' On March 4 Rothschild declared during a visit which he paid me that for a war with Russia any sum was at command ; he would furnish at once " as many millions as were desired." ' *Ernest*, iii. 70.

[3] *Jerrold*, iv. 41. ' Je demandai au prince [Jérôme] pourquoi l'on n'avait pas gardé pour les nécessités futures de la guerre le surplus de la souscription. " C'est précisément," me répondit le prince, " l'observation que j'ai faite aujourd'hui à l'Empereur.—Non, me dit-il, on a trop souvent trompé le peuple, je ne veux plus qu'il en soit ainsi. J'ai demandé deux cent cinquante millions, je rendrai le reste, sauf à faire un nouvel emprunt si le premier est insuffisant. Avant tout, il faut tenir la parole donnée." ' *Reiset*, ii. 249, 250.

concluded in London amid dreams of a perpetual peace. In spite of the war it was indeed as a ' Universal Exhibition of the Arts of Peace ' that it was convoked : and the Emperor was so far careful to justify its title that he caused Russia herself at the height of the war to be invited to send her exhibits to it.[1] So civilised was Europe in those days that such an invitation seems to have caused no particular astonishment. A minor precursor to the great exhibition, in the shape of an International Statistical Congress at Paris, served incidentally to illustrate the Emperor's lack of vindictiveness towards personal as well as national opponents. Among a cosmopolitan deputation of three hundred delegates which waited on the Emperor in connexion with the Congress was Albany Fonblanque, the able editor of the Radical *Examiner*. He had known Louis in his English exile and after observing hopefully his first advent to power, had castigated him unmercifully for his use of it since. To his surprise ' the Emperor, instead of passing on, stopped, and said : " M. Fonblanque is an old acquaintance," offered his hand as of old, and entered into familiar conversation about me and mine. It was all very kind. Considering all that has passed, I was and am pleased.' ' You will say,' he added, ' I am about to turn courtier : I can't help it.' [2]

During the early summer of 1854 Louis remained generally in the capital, where his presence was imperatively required by the constant series of personal decisions imposed upon him by a vicious system of government which demanded his immediate direction of all considerable affairs : a heavy burden at best and all but intolerable in time of war. At the beginning of August however he was carried off by the Empress to Biarritz, a watering-place which was to owe much to the homesickness of Eugénie and its proximity to Spain. From Biarritz, upon Napoleon's birthday, the Emperor made an excursion to Bayonne.[3]

---

[1] *Jerrold*, iv. 78.

[2] Fonblanque to Forster, 17 Sept. 54. *Fonblanque*, 46, 47.

[3] At this same city a year later Eugénie succeeded in inducing her husband to attend a state performance of her country's gladiatorial show, the Spanish bull-fight. ' I observed,' wrote *Fraser* (27, 28), ' from the

That his work did not lie altogether lightly upon him is
shown by his answer to the customary adulations of the
local bishop. ' I thank you, Monseigneur,' he replied,
' for the petitions you address to heaven on my behalf :
but I would have you invoke also its protection upon our
armies.' ' Pray,' he added with a touch of melancholy
double meaning, ' for those who fight and those who suffer :
for to pray for them is still to pray for me.' [1]- Earlier in
the same speech he had congratulated himself and France
on a fact which he held to be sufficiently proved by his
mere presence at that extremity of his dominions : ' It
shows,' he said, ' that France, calm and contented, is no
longer troubled with those fears which compel the chief
of the state to remain armed and alert in the capital.
It proves that she can sustain a distant war, without
disturbing the free and regular course of her domestic
affairs.'

This statement was a public reply to a series of re-
monstrances which the Emperor had received from Paris
enlarging on the dangers entailed by his long absence from
the capital in the most inaccessible corner of France. His
disregard of these warnings, at a time when an unpopular
and hitherto unsuccessful war coincided with the worst
famine since 1817,[2] was generally condemned as foolhardy.
' It furnishes another proof of his imperturbable tenacity
in adhering even to the minor details of his plans,' wrote
Prince Chimay to King Leopold at this time. ' Really it
is tempting Providence. His opponents must be extraordinarily disorganised and enfeebled to make no attempt
to profit by such a chance. Here we have the Emperor
absent, not a man, not a minister on the spot strong enough
or daring enough to show the slightest initiative in case of
danger : the marshals divided and jealous of each other,
the old army of Paris broken up, only new regiments to

moment that the first horse was killed the Emperor never raised his eyes
for a moment from the bill of the performance, which was lying in front of
him : indeed the man who had finally to dispatch the bulls was obliged
to come quite underneath the Imperial box to ask permission ; and even
then the Emperor appeared at first not to see him.'

[1] *Jerrold*, iv. 54.   [2] *Senior: Thiers*, i. 206.

take their place, who know nothing of the tactics of street fighting in the capital . . . that is the state of affairs which the Emperor leaves to the lucky chances of his Star.' [1]

Such risks were not the only disadvantages attending the Emperor's absence from Paris ; for the inconveniences occasionally entailed on the English cabinet by Queen Victoria's affection for Balmoral were not to be compared with those inflicted on the French Ministry by Eugénie's affection for Biarritz. ' He will not allow his ministers to consult each other,' reported Cowley, two days after Louis' speech at Bayonne, ' and one of them told me a few days ago that the ministers of War, Marine, and Foreign Affairs had all written to the Emperor upon the same matter in a different sense, and that His Majesty either through inadvertence or inattention had approved the propositions of all three, thus causing the greatest confusion.' [2]

As though unconscious of his shortcomings, Louis proceeded to spend a large part of the next month also away from Paris ; this time in superintending the operations of some 100,000 troops, concentrated for manœuvres between St Omer and Boulogne. This mobilisation had been effected partly as a means of preliminary training for regiments intended ultimately for service in the Crimea : partly too, in the Emperor's words, to show Europe that France, without deplenishing her garrisons, could easily put into the field another hundred thousand men, besides those she had already sent to the East. Incidentally, these manœuvres served another purpose ; for they helped to break the social boycott of the new court which the monarchical party in Paris had hoped to render European. The Kings of Belgium and of Portugal visited Louis at Boulogne.[3] True, their visits were short and their kingdoms small and they left their Queens behind them : still they were indubitably kings of a kind. More important was a four days' sojourn made by the Prince Consort at the camp : an action extremely grateful to the new

---

[1] *Ernest*, ii. 146.
[2] F.O. France, Cowley to Clarendon, 17 Aug. 54.
[3] *Martin*, iii. 102. The Belgian ministry resigned in consequence. *Ibid.*, 118.

Emperor, who received the Prince with tears in his eyes
as he expressed his pleasure at this fresh proof of the
cordial relations between the two Western Powers.[1]

The visit did in fact on the Prince's part involve the
sacrifice of personal prejudice to reasons of state. Six
months earlier he had furiously resented a proposal of his
brother the Duke Ernest of Saxe-Coburg-Gotha, to break
the boycott of the Tuileries by visiting the Emperor.
The visit was paid none the less, and the Duke's memoirs
contain a most interesting account of his conversations
with his host, recorded immediately after their occurrence.[2]
'His manner of receiving me was in every way natural and
easy. . . . He launched forth into a history of the first
and second Empire and of the distinctions to be drawn
between them . . . almost in the form of an academic
lecture. Now that the consciousness of their national
rights had so grown in the people it would, he said, be
crediting him with folly to think that he could once more
tread the mistaken paths of his uncle. . . . Sometimes
during a quiet chat, when he would sit in his arm-chair
smoking cigarette after cigarette and speaking almost like
a man in a dream, he gave me the impression of a German
savant rather than of a sovereign of France. On such
occasions he would recite whole poems of Schiller, and would
pass suddenly from French to German in his talk. . . .
What he admired in the Germans, he said, was that they
had not yet lost the hope of a united Empire. The national
sense of the Germans was really a power far stronger than
all armies. He would be an ardent enthusiast for the union
himself, if he were a German.' 'It seemed to me after my
stay in Paris simply unintelligible,' commented the Duke,
'that he should be considered devoid of abilities. A short
conversation with him suffices to dispel this notion. Not
that he ever tries to express himself on a subject at once
in pregnant words, but every interesting side of it that is
touched on produces a change in his otherwise immovable
countenance which shows the lively interest it awakens in
him. He then expresses himself naturally and sensibly,

[1] *Martin*, iii. 101.   [2] *Ernest*, iii. 61 *n.*

sometimes wittily, but always without empty phrases and declamatory effect.'

Once the subject of Prussian expansion arose. ' Suddenly he fell silent, paced up and down for a while, and then said dreamily, with that inimitable smile of his, " *Ma foi, pour ma France ce m'est bien égal, si on me dédommage sur le Rhin ou en Italie.*" ' [1] It was the utterance, the very action even of the prisoner of Ham ; when pacing, pacing, *pacing* up and down, as a man will long cabined in small room, he had given himself the luxury of letting his thoughts range free and far, where neither stone walls could confine them nor hard facts. Exact phrases, though their hearer and perhaps their utterer knew it not, repeated themselves now in the palace from those far-flung rhapsodies of the prison-house.[2]

Curiously enough when Duke Ernest's brother the Prince Consort met the Emperor six months later at Boulogne he was immediately struck by another consequence, this time physical, of that long imprisonment ; though he no more than his brother recognised its source. The weather as it happened was oppressively hot. But the Prince noticed that his host was ' very chilly, complains of rheumatism, and goes early to bed.' [3] For the rest however he found him ' not so old or pale as his portraits made him, and much gayer than he is generally represented ' ; amazed that his visitor did not join him in his after-dinner cigarette, extremely frank in discussion of all topics of home and domestic policy, though prone at times to vague and impracticable schemes, such as one for the union of Spain and Portugal under his late guest King Pedro.[4] The Emperor dilated on vague advantages : the Prince

---

[1] *Ernest*, iii. 62–76. The Emperor's speech to his Legislative Assembly in Dec. 54 referred publicly, after a separate mention of Austria, to ' Germany, whose union and prosperity we desire.' *Jerrold*, iv. 57.

[2] Cf. *Simpson*, 219–234. Later he realised that he had only changed prisons after all. On 10 May 60 he wrote to thank Mme. Cornu, who had ransacked libraries for him when he was in prison, for some new good office in connexion with his *Life of Cæsar* : it reminded him he said of her kindness to the prisoner of Ham. ' Les extrêmes se touchent,' ended the letter, ' et les Tuileries sont aussi une prison.' *B.N. Nouv. Acq. Fr.*, 1067, f. 290.

[3] *Martin*, iii. 109.   [4] *Ibid.*, 101–105.

bristled with practical objections. For example, was
Portugal to become a province of Spain, or Spain of
Portugal ? ' Oh,' replied Louis, ' one could easily tell the
Portuguese "I am making you a present of Spain," and the
Spaniards "I am making you a present of Portugal." '
Naturally Albert was unconvinced.[1]

But it was only on the last evening of the visit, after
three dusty days among the soldiers, that the Emperor
unburdened himself of his two darling projects : ' the one
to see Lombardy free from the maladministration of Austria,
the other to see Poland restored.' Once more the Prince
protested : Austria needed her military frontier, she could
not give up the line of the Mincio. ' The Emperor objected
that this still left a large portion of Italy in the hands of
Austria. I defied him to trace another tenable boundary
on the map. He replied, that if military frontiers were an
essential point for the existence of States, France also had
claim to one. My answer was, that France had the best
military frontier, her flanks covered by neutral Switzerland
and neutral Belgium. He denied that neutrality was a real
protection, as it was rarely maintained in time of war.' As
to Italy, he would be glad if even the Milanese only could
be freed ; and for Poland ' he would be content with ever
so small a nucleus, and perfectly so with the Grand Duchy
of Warsaw.' He thought Galicia well governed, and would
be willing to concede the retention of both Austrian and
Prussian Poland. Germany therefore could not object.
Besides, ' he had been in Germany during the passing
through of the Poles who fled their country after the
revolution, and nothing could have exceeded the enthusiasm
and national feeling for them.' To this second scheme
Louis reverted a month later in conversation with the English ambassador in Paris ; asking Cowley whether England
would object to the re-establishment of the kingdom of
Poland. In reporting the proposal Cowley was the less
enthusiastic since he had reason to fear that for the hypothetical kingdom there was already waiting a hypothetical
king, in the person of Prince Napoleon.[2] How far the

---

[1] *Martin*, iii. 118.   [2] F.O. France, Cowley to Clarendon, 8 Oct. 54.

ambassador's suspicions were well-grounded it is impossible
to determine ; but it is not improbable that Louis would
have been happy to bed out his preposterous cousin at
any inconvenient distance from Paris.

For the moment Prince Napoleon was out of the country.
Tired of seeing him about in black velvet, Louis early in
1853 had created him a general. This step had attained
its object in forcing the Prince to wear uniform on occasions
of ceremony ; but it had incidentally given rise to keen
resentment in the army.[1] For though he was endowed
with a fitful eloquence and occasional but undeniable
political insight, the Prince's virtues were hardly even at
that time considered military. On the outbreak of hostilities
it had been thought necessary to follow up this high
military promotion by some sort of apprenticehood in war.
Prince Napoleon was accordingly sent to the front as a
representative of the French dynasty, as the English was
already represented by the Duke of Cambridge. Both
generals were present at the opening of the Crimean
campaign, and praised in despatches ; both retired on the
approach of winter ; the one sick to Malta,[2] the other
sick to Constantinople. Each was announced to return ;
neither did. Instead they proceeded to Paris, where their
presence had a generally depressing effect ; [3] since it was
interpreted less as a sign of their own ill-health than of
the unfavourable prospects of the siege.[4] In the case of
the Duke no permanent harm was done ; but Prince
Napoleon sustained a lifelong injury. In his case a
dynasty with urgent need of military prestige had
incurred in the person of its one representative at the
front the suspicion of personal cowardice. Of this fact

---

[1] *Castellane*, iv. 426.   [2] *Verner*, i. 85.

[3] ' Le Duc de Cambridge est arrivé a Paris exaspéré contre son gouvernement, découragé et décourageant à l'excès. Il a presque reproché à Lady
Cowley d'avoir laissé partir son fils pour l'exposer inutilement à des périls
sans gloire.' Chimay to *Ernest*, iii. 161, 162.

[4] ' The two princes, who have just arrived in Paris, are both, it is said
by those who have seen them, in a perfect state of health. . . . For the
honour of the Duke of Cambridge it should be said that personally he does
not claim to be ill.' ' *Malakoff*,' i. 89.

the French Emperor was very sensible : [1] and in the
hope that his cousin might rally his physical and moral
forces, he at first forbade his return to France ; allowing
him only to retreat to Constantinople. But the hope
proved vain ; within a few months the Prince was back in
Paris ; in the eyes of France branded unjustly perhaps
but indelibly a Napoleon and a coward.[2]

Louis' own contributions to the war so far had chiefly
taken the form of a series of not very helpful military inventions. At all times he had a good deal of the White
Knight in his composition, and just now he was particularly
prolific in new devices. He invented and introduced a
new carbine into his army, and further devised a rocket
of enormous calibre and unparalleled soaring-power, from
which he expected great results.[3] To the British Admiralty
he communicated an invention based on experiments he
had carried out on the resisting power of wrought iron :
he had discovered some wonderful angle at which even a
two-inch plate of iron would resist any shot—' the shot
splitting. He thought an application of this to floating
batteries to be the way for taking Cronstadt without any
loss.' [4] Apparently however the angle proved elusive, for
Cronstadt remained untaken and even unassailed by any
such unfair advantage. But with unabated enthusiasm
the Emperor continued his inventions : on a December
morning three months later he conducted the British
ambassador mysteriously to the garden of the Tuileries,
and there showed him a model of yet another device ; a
life-sized tent for cavalry which he had invented for use
in the Crimea.[5] This invention also remained untested.
For even at the outset of the war, horses were far from
plentiful ; and such cavalry as existed were by this time,
through lack of forage,[6] in rapid process of conversion into
infantry.

[1] F.O. France, Cowley to Clarendon, 21 Nov. 54.
[2] His old nickname Plonplon was emended to Craint-plomb.   *Viel-
Castel*, iii. 118.   *Cf.* cartoon above, facing p. 208.
[3] *Martin*, iii. 116.   [4] *Ibid.*, 116.
[5] F.O. France, Cowley to Clarendon, 8 Dec. 54.
[6] This was so great that in this month, Dec. 54, a mare and foal could be
bought in the English lines for two shillings.   *Campbell*, 212.

But not all of Cowley's interviews with the Emperor were of such a trivial nature. A month later Louis both wrote and spoke to the English ambassador, urging certain drastic reforms in order to impart new vigour into the languishing operations in the East. The Emperor advanced two main propositions, both of which give proof of a genuine desire on his part not merely to hasten the conclusion of the war, but also to maintain the alliance intact after the war was over. He urged first that during the actual hostilities France should take the lead on land and England on sea. The present attempt of each Power to equal strength in both services was at best, he urged, a wasteful arrangement. ' Besides,' added Louis, ' what will be the result at the end of the war ? Why, that I shall have a navy of which you will be the first to be jealous ; and that you will have expended millions to raise an army which will then be useless to you.' This eminently sensible proposal was followed by another of more doubtful wisdom, but no less clearly indicative of a sincere intention to remain permanently on good terms with his ally. He urged that England should adopt conscription. ' Something of the kind,' he said, ' you must do, or you will lose all your former reputation. It is already sad to hear how opinions have changed on the Continent as to your being a formidable Power.' [1]

Neither of the Emperor's suggestions was adopted by his ally : but the interesting fact is that they should have been made at all. For throughout his reign there was in England a party never wholly discredited and sometimes numerous and influential, which attributed to Louis a deep design for the ultimate invasion of this country. There is no lack of evidence now to discredit this hypothesis ; but perhaps no single fact is more difficult to reconcile with it than this long-unnoticed interview. For in it this would-be invader of England gratuitously endeavoured at once to avert the growth of a French fleet

---

[1] F.O. France, Cowley to Clarendon. 'Confidential.' 24 Jan. 55. Three weeks later de Tocqueville wrote to an English friend urging the same course for the same reason. *Tocqueville : Correspondence*, ii. 93.

GRAVES AT THE HEAD OF THE HARBOUR OF BALACLAVA

From a lithograph after a drawing by William Simpson

"GENERAL FÉVRIER" TURNED TRAITOR.

"RUSSIA HAS TWO GENERALS IN WHOM SHE CAN CONFIDE—GENERALS JANVIER AND FÉVRIER."—*Speech of the late Emperor of Russia.*

'Death lays his icy hand on kings'

From John Leech's cartoon in "Punch," 10 March 1855

such as alone could render possible the landing of a French
expeditionary force on English soil, and at the same time
to promote the growth of an English army which would
render such an invading force completely impotent even
if it were landed. It seems at first sight a matter for regret
that the knowledge of such an endeavour, as of Louis'
earlier attempt already recorded in this volume [1] to avert
a naval competition between the two countries, was withheld from contemporary England. Such regrets, though
natural, are possibly wasted. To posterity alone were the
facts to be revealed ; but to posterity alone perhaps would
the facts have been evidence. To the contemporary
alarmists they might have been but an added proof of
foreign duplicity. No honest invader, it would have been
argued, would have been at such pains to conceal his
nefarious designs.

The Emperor's statement as to the rapid decline in
England's military prestige was even at this early stage
of the war only too well founded. For a generation or
more, on the strength of her military performance in the
Napoleonic wars and her militant diplomacy since, England
had been vaguely credited with immense resources in the
field. Now she was suddenly seen to be reduced in a few
weeks by the demands of a comparatively trifling expedition
to the most desperate expedients for the raising of troops.
Two months earlier the Prince Consort had been driven
to anticipate Louis Napoleon's advice, urging that the
Government should avail itself of powers still nominally
remaining to it under an obsolete act, to 'complete' by
ballot the deplenished ranks of the Militia.[2] In December
Parliament had actually passed a highly unpopular Foreign
Enlistment Act, for the raising of fifteen thousand foreigners
who were to be first drilled in England, and then sent out
to fight for it.[3] The recruits so obtained were chiefly
German ; but on this matter even Palmerston proved cosmopolitan. 'Let us get as many Germans and Swiss as

---

[1] P. 40, above.   [2] *Martin*, iii. 146.
[3] v. *Greville*, 18, 22, and 24 Dec. 54.

we can,' he wrote six months later to his Secretary for War
—for by this time England in her desperate need of men
and of a man had made him her prime minister—' let us get
men from Halifax ; let us enlist Italians ; let us increase
our bounty at home without raising the standard. The
only answer to give to objectors is, the thing *must* be done,
we *must* have troops.' [1]

That these shifts should have been necessary was due to
the utterly unexpected course which the Crimean expedition
had taken after the opening victory on the Alma. For a
week afterwards, as we have seen, Europe had been filled
with rumours—explicit, detailed, and to all appearance
authentic—to the effect that Sevastopol itself had fallen :
rumours which were at least so far intelligent, that the fall
of the fortress might possibly have been the real result of
a prompt attack delivered on the morrow of the battle.
But after a week of enthusiasm and illuminations came news
of a very different kind. Instead of pursuing their triumphant progress directly to the city, and attacking it from
the north, the allied armies had proceeded to make a
circuitous inland march behind Sevastopol, in order to
assault it more easily from the south. This deviation was
due to the prompt decision of Menschikoff, after his first
defeat, to sink a portion of the Russian fleet at the mouth
of the harbour ; an act which, by rendering impossible
any effective naval co-operation in an attack on Sevastopol,
deterred the allied commanders from attempting to deliver
a frontal attack from the north. The flank march however
was carried out so far successfully that by September 27
the allied armies had safely emerged again upon the sea
coast at Balaclava, this time to the south of Sevastopol.

At this point Raglan was guilty of a decision which was
to cost his army dear. It had originally been intended that
the harbour of Balaclava should serve as base of supplies
for both armies, but inspection at once revealed the fact
that it was not large enough for such double use. In these
circumstances the French would seem to have had the
prior claim to the place ; [2] since they had hitherto held the

[1] 10 June 55. *Ashley* ii. 98.   [2] *Hamley,* 79. *Kinglake,* iii. 102.

right of the allied line, and whichever army took that
position now was bound for geographical reasons to have
its base at Balaclava. But as in the order of march the
English chanced to have entered the place first, Canrobert,
Saint-Arnaud's successor in the command of the French
army, consented to waive his strict right, and 'generously
and wisely' gave Raglan the choice of position and of
duties.[1] To be on the right or outer side of the line was
to assume, in addition to the inevitable hardships of the
siege, the brunt of any attack from the Russian field army ;
but in the opinion of Raglan, and of his naval adviser
Lyons, the harbour of Balaclava was so infinitely preferable
to any other in the neighbourhood that the possession of
it would more than outweigh any disadvantage on this
score.[2] Accordingly they chose to remain where they were,
and the French marched on to the westward ; where in
Kinglake's phrase ' the forbearance they had shown was
rewarded '[3] by the discovery of two bays which were at
least as serviceable for the landing of supplies as the harbour
which they had resigned to the English.[4]

Meanwhile a week had elapsed since the victory of the
Alma ; and even from that week's grace the Russian
position had derived material benefit. The garrison, which
some days earlier had numbered only a few thousand men,
was now reinforced by the crews of the disabled fleet :
earthworks were springing up on the hitherto ill-defended
land side of the town : while guns from the sunken ships
were fast being mounted on the extemporised bastions and
redoubts. Menschikoff himself with the bulk of his army
had retired to the inland of the Crimea, to await reinforcements : but he had left in the city the one soldier of genius
whom the war discovered : a Russian colonel of engineers,
Todleben.

---

[1] *Kinglake,* iii. 103.   [2] *Hamley,* 80.   *Kinglake,* iii. 104.
[3] *Kinglake,* iii. 104.
[4] It seems necessary to insist on these details, since *Paul,* i. 357, makes a
grievance of the fact that the English were allotted at once the worse
harbour and the more arduous position : omitting to observe that although
not strictly entitled to it, the English commanders were given their choice
in the matter ; and that they availed themselves of it to choose the worse
combination, under the impression that it was the better.

Even so however what the allies had lost in time they
had well-nigh gained in place : at the end of September
they were in a position to deliver a surprise assault upon
the weakest part of the fortifications of Sevastopol ; an
assault which Todleben himself afterwards asserted could
not have failed of success.[1] The attack in point of fact
would probably have been a more difficult matter than the
Russian writer maintains : but even so if only as the lesser
of two evils it was plainly incumbent upon the allies to
attempt it. Again, however, their generals [2] shrank from
so hardy a decision. Moreover it was contrary to all
precedent to assault a fortress without preliminary bombardment. And the siege guns were still at sea. From
the point of view of an attack in ceremony this might
have seemed the less important that at the moment there
was nothing very particular for them to bombard. But
General Burgoyne, the head of the English artillery,
assured Lord Raglan that if only he would wait for the
guns the place could be reduced in three days.[3] Unfortunately the guns themselves took three weeks in coming :
and in those three weeks Todleben had been so busy that
when at last the cannonade was opened it continued for
eight days without result. The effect of waiting for the
siege guns had been to necessitate a siege.[4]

And now indeed the position of invaders and invaded
was signally reversed. A month earlier sixty thousand
allies had confronted some forty thousand Russians : now
themselves a shrunken force they were faced by Russian

[1] But see p. 259 above.
[2] Again Kinglake asserts, upon the authority of one unnamed officer,
that Raglan was dissuaded from advance by his French colleague. (Kinglake, iii. 237 : followed as usual by Paul, ii. 357.) But in this case he was
not writing of a dead man : Canrobert issued a formal denial that any
such suggestion had ever been made to him by Raglan, and his denial
was confirmed by English officers in high command : e.g. Major-General
Taylor and Marshal Burgoyne. v. Wrottesley, ii. 327–330 : Times, 4 Aug.
68. Though abounding in unintentional inaccuracies, it is only under the
exigencies of a certain private vendetta (on which see Bibliography, p. 382
below) that Kinglake deliberately distorts facts ; save where the facts are
themselves guilty of running counter to his main thesis, that Lord Raglan
was a great general. Unfortunately the preponderance of facts which do
conflict with this thesis, over those which do not, is considerable.
[3] So Aberdeen told Argyll, i. 502.
[4] On this, v. Windham, 71 ; Bostock, 245.

troops hardly short of a hundred thousand men. Then victorious and in superior numbers they were marching forward to a surprise assault upon an almost open town : now with an initial repulse behind them they were sitting down to besiege an enemy of twice their own strength, established in what was fast becoming an all but impregnable fortress. But besides all this a most notable reversal had been effected in the moral of the two combatants. In the Russian ranks the unreasoning panic caused by a first defeat had been followed by elation and confidence perhaps equally unreasoning, when it was discovered that their original fears were groundless. On the part of the allies the first effervescence of the attack had been followed by a no less natural depression ; when it was seen to be the preliminary not of a vigorous assault but of an arduous and interminable siege.

It was a siege in which it was soon hard to discern who were the besiegers and who the besieged. By mid-October even in form the assailants had become the assailed. On the 25th of that month Menschikoff delivered a surprise attack upon the rear of the English position at Balaclava. The battle contained many incidents glorious to the allied cavalry : a brilliant and successful charge by an English heavy brigade arresting the Russian advance ; an English light brigade hurled to death in a madly magnificent attempt to execute a palpably impossible order, and just saved from annihilation by the admirable initiative of a French cavalry officer who launched his regiment on the Russian batteries to cover their retreat—such events as these entitle the name of Balaclava to appear as a most honourable memento in the battle-roll both of the French and English armies.

None the less the battle was a victory for the Russians. They had captured a Turkish standard and seven English guns : and what was far more serious, they had seized and retained the outer line of the allied position at Balaclava and with it a portion of a most important roadway ; thereby not only straitening most uncomfortably the disease-smitten quarters of the English, but infringing for months to come upon their best line of communication with their base.

Eleven days later Menschikoff renewed the attack. Very early upon a drizzling Sunday morning heavy with November fog, he directed a massive assault upon the English right ; which he succeeded in taking entirely by surprise. All day long on the dull and dirty plain a confused battle went forward ; the cannon smoke clinging heavily to the damp earth, men tramping mournfully to their deaths knee-deep in mire ; their very drums [1] so sodden with rain as to emit only strange soul-depressing noises at once unmilitary and unmelodious. In the end Menschikoff's attack was repelled : for in spite of his superior numbers and the co-operation of a sortie from Sevastopol itself, the English succeeded in holding. their own until the arrival of French help enabled them to repel the entire Russian assault. This time the victory was plainly with the allies ; but never was victory less ex-hilarating in its results.[2] For by this time the war was no longer waged on even terms. A Russian victory at Inkerman would have left the allies no alternative but to abandon the Crimea, and hardly even the ability to do that : but even the Russian defeat did not now, as at Alma, render possible a successful assault upon Sevastopol. It only allowed the allies to maintain throughout a Russian winter the parody of a siege : where the besiegers were not only outnumbered by those whom they essayed to besiege, but lacked the barest equipment for their own proper maintenance even as an effective army of observation.

Upon this, winter fell suddenly in mid-November ; led in by a storm that swept away by the thousand the frail tents from the wind-swept plateau, wrecked a score of ships with their freight of clothes and stores, and converted into a mere morass the six-mile up-hill cart-track which now alone connected the cholera-stricken English camp with its source of supplies at Balaclava.

[1] *Saint-Amand*, ii. 217.
[2] Thus Clarendon to his wife, 15 Nov. 54. ' No further news to-day, but everyone is miserable about the so-called victory.' *Maxwell*, ii. 50.

And it was now that England received, in regard to the expedition launched so light-heartedly against Sevastopol, the worst reverse of all.   The first letters of soldiers and war-correspondents from the Crimea in September had been cheerful enough : everyone was glad to have exchanged the inglorious inaction of Varna for a definite and audacious military adventure.   Moreover with its ideal autumnal climate, its pleasant villages and smiling vineyards—the latter in the full perfection of their harvest of black grapes,—the Crimea appeared at first sight to the British officer ' a paradise for campaigning purposes.' [1] But within a few weeks he had found another name for it. The grapes were eaten now, and the fruit-trees felled for firewood ; long before Christmas the very roots of the vines had been hacked out to meet the imperious necessity for fuel.[2]   Then it was that news came trickling home of very different import ; news which moved England at first to incredulity, and finally by the road of indignation to reform.   Reports were received, denied, repeated, and at last overwhelmingly confirmed, of horses without hay, waggons without roads, doctors without the most necessary drugs for the treatment of disease which the lack of elementary sanitary precautions rendered rampant among men half-fed, half-clad, half-sheltered, and wholly overworked.   The Crimea was notoriously destitute of timber ; the military authorities in supplying the troops with food made no distribution of fuel, and no provision for any kind of cooking.   Yet the Commissary General at Balaclava [3] expressly stipulated that all coffee should be sent out from England not merely unground but unroasted : quashing the protests which the request evoked even from the Comptroller of Victualling at home, by the remark that ' the soldiers will no doubt find some means of overcoming any difficulty that may arise from the want of mills and coffee-roasters.' [4]

Forty years earlier, though cattle could only be brought

---

[1] *Home*, 22.   Cp. *Bernard*, 108.   [2] *Ibid.*, 24.
[3] On whom see *Sterling*, 143.
[4] *Sebastopol Committee*, vol. iv. p. 10, Q. 17,752.

to him by sailing-vessels from the north of Spain, Wellington had made it clear at Torres Vedras that circumstances must be regarded as exceptional which forced him to put his troops on salt provisions for two days in the week.[1] But salt pork on seven was the fare of the British army in the Crimea during the opening months of the siege, although cattle in plenty were collected at Constantinople.[2] Generally however it was only the six miles cart-track which separated the army from the necessities for lack of which it died. The fact that it had often to be eaten raw, did not prevent salt pork as sole food from being a common source of scurvy : lime juice in plenty lay at Balaclava from the middle of December, and Raglan was informed of the fact ; yet only at the beginning of February was it issued to the troops.[3] As they were fed, so were they clad. Greatcoats were stacked by tens of thousands in piles at Balaclava ; while in camp men perished of mere cold.[4] Thanks to their landing without knapsacks [5] the mass of the troops had practically no clothes at all save those they wore : [6] night or day, knee-deep in mud in their trenches, or ankle-deep in mud in their tents, the ordinary soldier must sleep or be shot at in the same single and verminous suit.

But it is needless here to repeat in detail the whole miserable tale : of vegetables rotting in harbour for lack of the mere order to distribute them, of boots in ample quantities, but for the left foot only, and even when at last they were distributed in pairs so much too small that men walked frost-bitten and barefoot through the snow ; worst of all—until Florence Nightingale and her following lightened even these—of hospitals [7] so ghastly

---

[1] *Wellington Despatches*, vi. 561.
[2] Admitted even by the whitewashing *Chelsea Board*. Appendix, 572. *Tulloch*, 112.
[3] *Sevastopol Commissioners' Report*, 8. *Chelsea Board*, 24.
[4] *Register*, 1855 [190]. *Tulloch*, 43.   [5] *Supra*, p. 259.
[6] *Sevastopol Commissioners' Report*, 23.
[7] On the French superiority in all these matters, and especially the last, see *Sterling*, 132, 164, 165, 151. *Wrottesley*, ii. 186. On the mismanagement as a whole see William Russell, *Letters on the War* (reprinted from the *Times*) ; Roebuck's Sebastopol Committee, May 1855 ; *Crimean Commissioners' Report and Appendix*, Jan. 56 ; *Chelsea Board's Report*, July

as to render preferable for their inmates not merely the
death that was their one way out, but even the life that
was their broad way in. Rather in passing be it recorded that the same evidence [1] which demonstrates the
almost incredible sufferings of the troops demonstrates also
their display under those sufferings, of a general level of
courage, patience, and heroical endurance,. only equalled
by that of the garrison of Sevastopol itself in the last weeks
of the siege. But hardly even that deadly final bombard-

56 (a whitewashing counter-move to the former); and *Tulloch* (a conclusive
rejoinder to that counter-move by one of the original commissioners). On
the appalling condition of the hospitals in particular, see *Cook*, i. 177, and
authorities there cited. *Kinglake*, vol. vi. cap. viii., that Raglan may
appear a general, throughout minimises the mismanagement.

[1]   CAMP BEFORE SEBASTOPOL.
                                        8th April 1855.

Dear Wife I now take the opportunity of writin to you these few lines
hoping to find you and the children all in good helth as this leaves me at
present thank God for it. Dear wife I would have sent you more before
this but the reason of it is we are quite tired of eating this hard bisket so
that we are forced to buy Bread, and that we pay dear for the price is two
shillings for a pound and a half of bread and to shillings for a pound of
chese so that runs away with what little money that we have got and if
it was not for it the half of us would have been dead . . . in drawing shot
and shell to our guns. We have to do the work instead of the horses
there is no one knows the hardships that we have only ourselves. They
talk in England about sending us out potatoes and preserved vegetables and
all such things but there is none of it reaches the hard fighting soldiers:
the staff of the army clames all. . . . It makes the blood broyle in my
veans when I see the way that we are treated but I hope the Lord will
witness all these dowings and punish them accordingly for the way that
they have treated us. . . . The Russians all ways attack us at night they
will never give us fair daylight for it since the battle of Inkermann they
will always remember the beating they got on that day. Dear wife I have
got to inform you that we are going to take the field tomorrow morning
for the grand attack of Sebastopol and I hope the Lord will strengthen
us for the battle and it will be the greatest battle that ever was known
and I hope there will nothing come to prevent us pulling it to the ground.
For we have had hardships enough lying on these frozen hills looking at
that confounded place. I never should die happy to think that I should
have to leave this place without seeing the downfall of Sebastopol and
so many of my poor comrades laid low in this awful place. Dear wife
I hope if it is the Lord's will I am laid low that he will provide for you
and the poor children. I shall rite if the Lord spairs me to return from the
field as soon as it is taken for I am sartin that it will be taken. Dear wife
give my kind love to your mother and to your sister and to your brother
and his wife and to all enquiring frends. Dear wife do not let my mother
know nothing about the matter now to conclude with my kind love to you
and the children till death A. SMITH.

     Fare well good night and God bless you all.
     B.M. Add. MSS. 38,983, f. 141. They do not alter much, these letters
or these men.

ment was more destructive of human life : in the seven months of the winter, apart altogether from men killed in action, or dying of their wounds, the British regiments mainly concerned in the conduct of the siege suffered an average mortality in disease alone ranging from forty-five to over seventy per cent.[1]

At a time when soldiers' letters and war-correspondents' despatches were still uncensored, mismanagement such as this could not long be concealed or continued. Hence the end of January 1855 brought ignominious defeat to the government of Aberdeen ; a minister whose career deserved a better end. A week later, after three other politicians had failed to form a cabinet, the Queen was forced to take for her prime minister the man whom three years earlier she had dismissed from the Foreign Office.[2] Palmerston it was who now threw his unbounded and unabated energies into the task of saving from extinction the remnant of the British army in the Crimea.

But at this moment the eyes of Europe were turned suddenly from the death of thousands to the death of one. Far from the scene of conflict, whose every distant rumour he yet followed with intense and feverish solicitude, Nicholas still ruled in St Petersburg, in the loneliness of absolute power. To all appearance the strong man had only become stronger when at last the sacred soil of Russia was assailed ; when to the customary devotion of his subjects was added a new impersonal exaltation, the tribute of a people stirred profoundly alike by religion and patriotism to the waging of a Holy War. Now as ever the indomitable Czar seemed but to collect new energy from his

---

[1] *Tulloch*, xxv.

[2] But she still kept a tight hand on him : witness this rather important unpublished letter dated Windsor Castle, 12 Jan. 56.

'The Queen wd. wish to remind Lord Palmerston that she has not of late recd. those accts. from him of the *Cabinets* which he used to give her and to which she attached so much value as they enabled her to follow exactly the *business* proceedings and discussions of the govt. about the different important affairs that were brought before them and to refer to them thereafter if necessary. The Queen therefore asks Lord Palmerston to be so good as to continue these reports as heretofore.' B.M. Add. MSS. 39,168, f. 47.

difficulties ; defending his policy, denouncing his opponents, preparing for war ; and when the war was once begun pledging his last rouble to its support, arming an Empire for its continuance, above all personally and perpetually inspecting and dispatching to the Crimea regiment upon regiment of patient peasants, of whom only the fittest would survive the horrors of the road to die beneath the walls of Sevastopol. Nor was there anything in this distant aspect of him to reveal to the Russian soldiers, privileged to see once their Emperor before their death, that the Emperor they saluted was himself a dying man. True he was now in his sixtieth year : but his herculean frame was still unbent ; and the known austerity of his habits seemed to promise him years of life. But he came of a comparatively short-lived stock, and had moreover been himself in ill-health during the greater part of the negotiations which preceded the war ; indeed it is probable that this lack of his customary physical serenity contributed not a little to the failure of those negotiations.[1] Historians are wont to hymn as the triumphs of national movements or the outcome of inevitable tendencies results which would not in fact have been achieved at all but for the defective metabolism of one ruler or the deranged digestive processes of another. The map of Europe has seldom lacked some frontier due to the pathological condition of one man.

But Nicholas was now diseased not only in body but in mind. Even before the outbreak of war he had been bitterly aggrieved by England's rejection of his proffered confidence, still more by Austria's crowning duplicity and ingratitude ; and the war itself in its earlier stages had but added to his mortification. Isolated in Europe, foreshadowed by a premonition of his own approaching death,[2] he saw his reign, that had at one time bidden fair to be a continued triumph, closing over him in shadow and confusion. With ever more frantic energy he dispatched fresh

---

[1] On this, see letter to the *Times* by Dr A. B. Granville. *Times,* 5 Mar. 55. *Nolan,* ii. 149. *Reiset,* ii. 233.
[2] *La Gorce : Empire,* i. 352, 353.

regiments to the Crimea ; with emotions of elation or dejection ever more disproportionate to their causes he received in return from the Crimea alternate rumours of success and failure. Chilled and feverish, one bitter morning in mid-February, he sallied forth in spite of his doctor's warnings [1] to review one regiment the more ; and returned to his palace with death at his heart. Three days later a messenger announced the decisive defeat by the despised Turks of an attack in force which he had himself specially ordered to be delivered upon their position at Eupatoria. Whether other news would really have meant new life for the Czar may perhaps be doubted : it was soon seen that this news meant death. On the first day of March it became clear that he had only a few hours left to live.

The last bulletin of king and commoner is the stark announcement of one fact. But a penultimate privilege remains to royalty : the king though mortal is never moribund. He may be confessed to be dead ; he must never be accused of dying. Of this conventional immunity Nicholas refused to avail himself. To the three chief cities of his Empire he sent a curt telegram, ' The Emperor is at the point of death.' [2] Then he sent for his counsellors, and committed his son to their care. He had hoped, he said, to leave things very differently ; the hard work done, and the Empire prosperous and at peace. He asked that his thanks might be conveyed to all the defenders of Sevastopol. Then he bade his wife say the ' Our Father ' with him. At the petition ' Thy will be done,' he broke off. ' Always ! Always ! ' he repeated. A few hours later, about noon on Friday the second of March,[3] he died.

---

[1] *Delord*, i. 591. [2] *Rambaud*, 670.

[3] Here as always Gregorian dates are given. But Russian Style in the nineteenth century was twelve days late, so that the Czar did really fall to his General Février.

CHAPTER IX

THE AFTERMATH

The glories of our blood and state
Are shadows, not substantial things ;
There is nc armour against Fate ;
Death lays his icy hand on kings :
Sceptre and Crown
Must tumble down,
And in the dust be equal made
With the poor crooked scythe and spade.

J<small>AMES</small> S<small>HIRLEY</small>.

IT is not easy now to realise the emotion with which
Europe learned that Nicholas was dead. For a generation that gigantic form had towered above its fellows, the
very symbol of unshaken strength : storms that laid low
all lesser growths had, for this one, but served to enhance
its eminence and affirm more surely its tried and triumphant
stability. And now suddenly the mighty tree was fallen,
with a crash that for an instant afterwards made the
myriad voices of the forest seem silence. For a moment
men did not hear the guns about Sevastopol, and listened
hardly at all to the nearer thunders of the *Times*. Nicholas, who had so long dominated Europe in his life, dominated
it for a few hours yet more absolutely in his death.

But not long in silence. It was only on March 1 that
the first faint intimation had reached the western capitals
that the Czar was even ill : hard on its heels next day
followed the tidings of his death. In England the news
was proclaimed that night in provincial theatres after the
first act of the play, and greeted in many of them with
frantic outbursts of applause.[1] And on Sunday from

---

[1] *Charles-Roux*, 9.

every pulpit hurriedly rewritten sermons pointed a moral with Nicholas. Here indeed was ὕβρις abashed, overweening insolence assuaged, the inordinate pretensions of an autocrat most suddenly abated and abolished.[1] Here in fact, had one but had time to think of it, was the fittest opportunity since it first was penned of quoting the finest apostrophe in English prose : ' O eloquent just and mighty Death ! whom none could advise, thou hast persuaded ; what none hath dared, thou hast done ; and whom all the world hath flattered, thou only hast cast out of the world and despised : thou hast drawn together all the farre-stretched greatness, all the pride, cruelty and ambition of man, and covered it all over with those two narrow words, *Hic iacet !'*

But for France the death of Nicholas spelt no mere judgment on the dead, but hope for the living. It was a death at which in the words of the Austrian ambassador ' all Europe breathed more freely ' : [2] but in France especially the news of it was at once translated into hopes of peace. For it was against Nicholas far more than against Russia that France had been at war ; and now that the shadow of the iron Czar had been lifted off Eastern Europe, the real object of the war was accomplished : his mild and pacific son could never exercise within or without his frontiers the personal domination of Nicholas. On Monday morning a rise of nearly five per cent. in French stock on the Paris *bourse* testified to the confidence with which the news of Nicholas' death was accepted in Paris as an omen of peace.

These hopes were destined to disappointment. It was true that Alexander lacked his father's strength ; for that very reason he could not begin his reign by an abrupt disavowal of his father's policy.[3] Nor could the allies in default of real diplomatic concessions afford to abandon a struggle which had yielded no striking military success. In quest of the former, negotiations were set on foot not very

---

[1] So, the *Times*, 3 Mar. 55, p. 8, c. 3. *Illustrated London News*, 10 Mar. 55, p. 217. *Record*, 5 Mar. 55, p. 2.
[2] *Charles-Roux*, 8.   [3] v. *Rousset*, ii. 86.

hopefully at Vienna : in pursuit of the latter the French
Emperor now took up with renewed ardour a scheme
with which he had already been toying for some weeks.

For some time past he had been dissatisfied with the
small part which he was playing personally in the war.
His uneasiness on this score was increased by the slow
progress of the siege, and by the apparent reluctance of
the allied generals to bring matters to a decisive issue.
In these circumstances the Emperor imagined that his
mere presence in the Crimea would give an impetus to the
languishing war ; lessening the evils of a divided command,
and setting a limit upon its interminable delays. Moreover he had now devised a detailed plan of campaign
which would, he believed, compel Sevastopol to capitulate
by the end of April ; this plan he desired to supervise in
person.

Such were the reasons for his decision given by the
Emperor to Palmerston in his formal communication
of it at the end of February : [1] a communication which
to the English premier was more unwelcome than unexpected. For a fortnight earlier Cowley had informed the
government of the Emperor's reported intention, and set
forth in detail the disadvantages of the proposal. These
were obvious and overwhelming. Even a successful excursion, a brief and brilliant campaign, would remove the
Emperor from Paris for a dangerous distance for a dangerous
time : failure, or the mere absence of success, might render
his return impossible altogether. ' I have not met with a
person,' Cowley reported, ' who does not deprecate the idea.
The funds have fallen considerably since these reports
have been prevalent, and the Emperor must at all events
have the consolation of feeling how necessary his life is
felt to be for the continued tranquillity of France. . . .'
What made matters worse was that ' those who know
the Emperor are convinced that he would be found
wherever the danger is greatest.' [2] How accurately this

---

[1] *Martin*, iii. 228 *sq.*

[2] F.O. France, Cowley to Clarendon. 'Confidential.' 16 Feb. 55.
And on the disquiet which the report created in the provinces, cf. *Arch.
Nat.*, BB[30] 368.

report reflected French opinion on the Emperor's project is shown by the contemporary correspondence even of convinced opponents of his regime. 'We feel that, for the present, his life is necessary to us,' wrote Tocqueville, 'and it would be exposed to many risks. He ought to incur some military risks if he is present at a battle or an assault, and his courage and his fatalism will lead him to many he ought to avoid.'[1] One main object of the Emperor's journey was in fact the desire to retrieve in his own person the injury done by Prince Napoleon to his name. The Prince himself the Emperor intended to take back willy-nilly to the front; Plonplon knew this, and roundly declared that he would not go.[2] All Plonplon's hopes at this time were bound up in the failure of the siege, which he incessantly predicted. If only the whole expedition would fail, his own early retreat from it would become an evidence of military perspicacity. And if he could stay behind while the Emperor failed in person, there were even political possibilities. Why should not the house of Bonaparte also have its July days, and renew its youth in a younger and more liberal line? And who so fit as Plonplon to be the Napoleon of Peace? One chief cause of the Emperor's final abandonment of his excursion was probably his tardy realisation of the fact that he could not really frog-march his cousin to the front, or yet wisely leave him behind to plot mischief in Paris.

But other deterrents were forthcoming in abundance. The English government at once took every step in its power to wean the Emperor from his project. First Cowley wrote a confidential letter of protest to Drouyn, destined really for the Emperor's own eye.[3] Then Clarendon came over and interviewed Louis in person at Boulogne, urging that this French assumption of the supreme command by throwing the English part in the campaign still further into the background might put an undue

---

[1] *Tocqueville: Correspondence*, ii. 96.
[2] F.O. France, Cowley to Clarendon. 18 Feb. 55.
[3] *Ibid.* 25 Feb. 55.

QUEEN VICTORIA CONFERRING THE GARTER ON NAPOLEON III
From the painting by E. M. Ward, R.A.

Copyright of H.M. The King

INTERIOR OF THE MALAKOFF FORT AFTER ITS CAPTURE

From photographs in the possession of the author

strain on the alliance.[1]   In the Crimea itself some English
officers actually welcomed the idea : ' I live in hopes,'
wrote one of them as early as April 1854, ' of seeing Louis
Napoleon take the supreme command of the Allied Armies.
. . . He is brave and clever and more likely to be a good
general than anyone I hear of.' [2]   But on the whole
Clarendon's argument was justified, and he was so far
successful in his use of it as to secure the Emperor's assurance that he would not go off on the instant, but would
wait till all was ready for the ' *dernier coup de main.*'
' *C'est le mot,*' repeated the Emperor, catching at Clarendon's phrase, ' *le dernier coup de main.*' [3]   French history,
indeed, afforded illustrious precedent for the apparition
of royalty at this precise conjuncture before the walls of
a besieged city : at no other moment had the *Grand
Monarch* himself been wont to cast his conquering eye upon
fortresses about to be French.   But such prompt prostration could only be counted upon if besieged no less than
besiegers observed the rules of the game : and however
entirely the allied forces might be relied on for their part,
a like regularity could not safely be assumed in Sevastopol.
For Sevastopol contained Todleben.

The Emperor however was still in confident mood.
Early in April Lord Granville was sent over to Paris to
reinforce the effect of Clarendon's dissuasions.   ' This is
my bill of fare for this year,' remarked his host after
dinner, ' a visit to London, a victory over the Russians
in the Crimea, and a reception of the Queen of England
in Paris before the end of summer.' [4]   The visit to
London at any rate could be put in hand at once :
perhaps it might serve to distract him from this Crimean
excursion.   Arrangements in fact were already in train
for it, and on Monday April 17 the Emperor landed with
his Empress at Dover, setting foot on English soil for the
first time since his exile.   The Prince Consort was there
to meet them, and escorted them to London.   The pro-

---

[1] *Martin*, iii. 233.
[2] Lt.-Col. *Sterling*, 230, 242.   So also Admiral *Heath*, 200.
[3] *Martin*, iii. 233.   [4] *Maxwell*, ii. 79.

cession through the capital, between the yet suburban terminus of their arrival and the station from which they were to depart for Windsor, occupied nearly two hours ; for at Louis' request the passage was made not as originally intended at a trot, but at walking pace.[1] It was noticed that civilly as the Emperor was greeted in the West End, his most cordial welcome was from the artisans of Lambeth and the Borough ;[2] in England as in France it was the common people who received him gladly. Carlyle, jogging down Piccadilly in an omnibus shortly before the Emperor's arrival, cast a baleful eye upon the preparations ; and rejoiced like the aristocrat he was to discover the street lined only with ' two thin and thinnest rows of the most abject-looking human wretches I had ever seen or dreamt of—lame, crook-backed, dwarfish, dirty-shirted, with the air of pickpockets and City jackals, not a *gent* hardly among them, much less any vestige of a gentleman.'[3] Carlyle's lifelong detestation of Louis Napoleon is interesting, since superficially there were some striking analogies[4] between the circumstances of the *coup d'état* and the dismissal of the Rump by his own hero Cromwell. But fundamentally the two men were the poles asunder.[5] The cult of Cromwell led Carlyle not illogically to the cult of Frederick and the new military Prussianism ; of which Louis Napoleon's humaner nationalism was the eventually defeated antithesis.

One slight success was achieved by the new Emperor even in the more aristocratic portion of his journey. In driving through St James' Street Louis pointed with his hand to King Street to call his wife's attention to the small house in which he had lived during the most penurious period of his exile. This simple gesture was noticed and

---

[1] *Illustrated London News. Cf.* Malmesbury to Derby, 14 Apr. 55. ' The Emperor is very anxious that he may be seen as much as possible in public. He is very angry at Walewski's fright about attempts on his person.' *Malmesbury*, ii. 17.

[2] *Times*, 17 Apr. 55.   [3] *Froude*, ii. 174.

[4] v. *Trevelyan: Nineteenth Century*, 300.

[5] Ten years before the *coup d'état*, Louis Napoleon had included both Long Parliament and Cromwell under a common condemnation, ' parce que ni le Long-Parlement ni Cromwell ne firent légitimer leur pouvoir par une élection libre.' *Fragmens Historiques*, 13 n.

approved. An Emperor who remembered that he had
been an exile need not fear to be reminded of the fact.

For Louis the crowning moment of the day was doubtless
that of his actual reception by the Queen at the great
gateway of Windsor Castle. Twice only had he seen her
before, even at a distance : once as an eighteen-year-old
girl going to prorogue her first parliament,[1] at a time when
he had himself just returned from his enforced visit to
America after his attack on Strasburg, and was delayed
in London for a few days in quest of passports real or
forged which should take him to his mother's deathbed in
Switzerland ; and once again a few months before his
ill-fated attack on Boulogne, when in the last profusion
of his pretender's court at Carlton Gardens he had paid
forty pounds for a box at the gala performance at Covent
Garden, on the occasion of the Queen's state visit after
her marriage in 1840.[2] And now, on a beautiful spring
evening, to the strains of his mother's song—*Partant
pour la Syrie*—he was welcomed by this same Queen as an
equal and an ally ; and thereby formally received into
the comity of European princes.

For the Queen too it was a moment to be remembered.
' I cannot say what indescribable emotion filled me,' she
wrote in her *Journal,* ' how much all seemed like a wonderful dream. I advanced and embraced the Emperor, who
received two salutes on either cheek from me, having first
kissed my hand. I next embraced the very gentle, graceful,
and evidently very nervous Empress.' Dinner followed
in St George's Hall ; and conversation at once turned to
the war. Louis feared a disaster, ' and that is why I want
to go out,' he added ; ' our generals,' he was afraid, ' would
always shirk responsibility.' The Queen urged the distance, and the danger. He admitted the distance was a
disadvantage ; but as for danger ' there were dangers
everywhere.'

Next day, spent comparatively quietly at Windsor,
confirmed the Queen in her liking for her guests ; ' they
behaved,' she wrote to her Uncle Leopold, ' really with

---

[1] *Martin,* iii. 104, 248.   [2] *Ibid.,* 251.

the greatest tact.' [1] In the afternoon there was a review of the household troops of Windsor amid an enthusiastic crowd that pressed upon the Emperor ' in such a way,' wrote the Queen in her diary, ' that I grew very nervous, as he rode on a very fiery beautiful chestnut, called Phillips, and was so exposed. He rides extremely well, and looks well on horse-back, as he sits high.' The day ended with a banquet and a ball in the Waterloo Room, which was rechristened for the occasion ' the Picture Gallery ' ; another instance of ' great tact.' [2] The Queen danced a quadrille with the Emperor, ' who dances,' she wrote, ' with great dignity and spirit.' Indeed her other visitors observed that the Queen was ' evidently pleased with her guests.' [3] At eleven on Wednesday morning a council of war met, from which the Queen vainly endeavoured to extract her husband and the Emperor some time after two. The gentlemen were slow in the council chamber, because the Emperor had if possible to be dissuaded from his projected expedition to the Crimea ; and he was not to be dissuaded easily. The ladies without were in a hurry, because at four Louis was to be invested with the Garter, ' and important preparations for the royal toilettes, with a view to this august ceremonial, were indispensable.' So Queen and Empress with their ladies, lunched alone. After the Investiture in the throne room was over, and the usual oaths taken of fidelity and knightly service to the Queen, the Emperor in walking back with the Queen to his rooms, made her a little speech of his own : ' *Je remercie bien votre Majesté. C'est un lien de plus* ; *j'ai prêté serment de fidélité a votre Majeste, et je le garderai soigneusement.*' Then after a pause : ' It is a great event for me, and I hope to be able to prove my gratitude.' To this declaration volunteered by a man ' not profuse in phrases ' the Queen attached a considerable importance.[4] Dinner and a concert filled this last evening at Windsor ; but left a little time too for further talk. The Emperor spoke of the Revolution of

[1] *Q.V.L.*, iii. 117. [2] *Henry Greville*, ii. 208.
[3] *Ibid.* [4] v. *Q.V.L.*, iii. 125 : *Martin*, iii. 247.

'48 ; of the horror of the June days ; of how in the thick
of them he had met the Duke of Cambridge out driving
and had turned aside his half-joking question whether it
was for him they were fighting in Paris : ' *et cependant
déjà on se battait pour moi alors !* '

Next morning the whole party left for London, where
Emperor and Empress were to lunch in state at the Guild-
hall.   The Queen and the Prince Consort accompanied
their guests as far as Buckingham Palace, but precedent
forbade that they should themselves go with them to the
luncheon.   Even without such escort, their reception was
unparalleled.[1] ' One great cheer attended their progress,'
wrote a spectator. ' It was indeed a curious thing to see
the London populace literally drunk with enthusiasm.
The ceremony itself was very well managed, and the
Emperor made an excellent speech ; adroit and in good
taste.'[2]

Adroit and tactful the Emperor's speech undoubtedly
was, alike in its ready reference to his exile, and in its
acceptance of the corporation's praises only as an impersonal tribute to the popularity of the alliance.   But for
the rest he strayed a little from the *banalité* of a Guild-
hall speech.   The two great Western Powers, he said,
were not mere accidental allies in war, but essential comrades in peace.   ' England and France are naturally
agreed on the great political and humanitarian questions
which are stirring the world.   From the shores of the
Atlantic to those of the Mediterranean, from the desire to
abolish slavery[3] to our hopes for the amelioration of all
the countries of Europe, I see for our two nations, in the
moral as well as the political world, only one road to
follow, one goal to seek.'   These were the things to
bind them, and there were ' only unworthy considerations, or petty rivalries that could separate them.'   As

[1] *Times*, 20 Apr. 55, p. 6, c. 3.
[2] *Henry Greville*, ii. 208.   Cf. *Argyll*, i. 546.
[3] A subject on which the Emperor felt strongly, despite his sympathy
with the South in the Civil War.   *Cf.* his letter of 30 Dec. 58 to his Minister
of Algeria and the Colonies prohibiting a form of indentured labour which
later governments discovered to be unexceptionable as ' slave trade in
disguise, I will have it on no terms.'

for the present war, in spite of all difficulties they would in the end succeed. 'For not only are our soldiers and sailors men of tried valour ; not only do our two countries command incomparable resources, but above all—and here is their immense superiority—they are in the van of all generous and enlightened ideas. The eyes of all who suffer turn instinctively towards the West.' [1] To such sentiments the ears of aldermen were unaccustomed from the lips of kings. More proper fare was presently provided in the shape of ' sherry 109 years old, and valued at the rate of £600 the butt.' [2]

Friday, the Emperor's birthday, was devoted to the still unstaled delights of the Crystal Palace. Brilliant weather, immense crowds, unbroken enthusiasm, marked this as every other function of the visit. True, at the requisite moment the fountains refused to play, but this was the only hitch in the entire week. In the evening followed a last and more detailed council of war,[3] and next morning came the almost tearful farewells.

On the whole the Emperor had every reason to congratulate himself on the results of his visit. Queen Victoria was strongly Orleanist in her predilections : [4] her most trusted continental adviser, King Leopold, was by his marriage closely attached to the old French dynasty, and as bitterly opposed to the new : she had herself been visited, only a week before Louis arrived at Windsor, by the exiled Queen of the French. That the Queen had consented to receive him at all he owed primarily to the political situation ; though even so the visit would have been impossible, had the Prince Consort reported unfavourably from Boulogne. But that a state visit had been made the basis of a personal friendship with the Queen, Louis owed entirely to his own efforts. ' He has done his best to please her,' wrote Greville : ' talked to her a great deal, amused her, and has completely succeeded.' [5]

[1] *Times*, 20 Apr. 55, p. 7, c. 5.   *Jerrold*, iv. 72.   *St Amand*, ii. 271.
[2] *Register*, 1855, 69.   [3] *Panmure*, i. 165.
[4] On her original disinclination for relations with the Bonapartes, v. *Maxwell*, ii. 43.
[5] *Greville*, 20 Apr. 55 : see also *Vitzthum*, i. 164.

Of the measure of his success the Queen's diary bears witness. On Monday the Emperor receives negative praise : he is ' so very quiet ; his voice is low and soft, and " *il ne fait pas de phrases.*" ' [1]   On Tuesday he has become ' very quiet and amiable, and easy to get on with. Nothing can be more civil or amiable or more well-bred than the Emperor's manner—so full of tact.' [2]   By Wednesday ' his manners are particularly good, easy, quiet, and dignified, as if he had been born a king's son and brought up for the place.' [3]   And so the steady crescendo of praise goes on, culminating on his departure in a passage more than usually prodigal of italics.   ' That he *is* a very *extraordinary* man with great qualities, there can be *no* doubt—I might almost say a mysterious man.   He is evidently possessed of *indomitable courage, unflinching firmness of purpose, self-reliance, perseverance, and great secrecy* ; to this should be added a great reliance in what he calls his *star*, and a belief in omens and incidents as connected with his future destiny, which is almost romantic : and at the same time he is endowed with a wonderful *self-control*, great *calmness*, even *gentleness*, and with a *power of fascination*, the effect of which upon those who become more intimately acquainted with him is most sensibly felt.' [4]   This testimony is the more striking that in the next paragraph the Queen conscientiously endeavoured to redress the balance of the man's present charm by recalling his past conduct ; ' his attempts at Strasburg and Boulogne, and this last, after having given a solemn promise never to return or make a similar attempt.'   This promise—as the English Foreign Office papers were to show conclusively half a century later—was never really given : [5] Louis did not break because he did not make any such engagement ; but the story was one of which no intimate of the Orleanists could remain in ignorance. The Queen's conversion from the Orleanist presentation of Louis Napoleon's character is only the more remarkable when it is remembered that she continued to accept in its entirety the Orleanist misstatement of his conduct.

[1] *Martin*, iii. 240.   [2] *Ibid.*, 241.   [3] *Ibid.*, 249.
[4] *Q.V.L.*, iii. 122.   [5] *Simpson*, 125.

The Emperor's letter on his return to Paris conveyed to the Queen and to England the one thing lacking to complete their satisfaction in the visit ; in the shape of an assurance that he had practically decided to abandon his expedition to the Crimea.[1] Three days afterwards an event occurred which conceivably had its part in confirming the decision. In the cool of the evening the Emperor was riding up the Champs Elysées towards his new park the Bois de Boulogne, when a well-dressed and good-looking Italian advanced towards him, with his hand to his breast pocket as though about to present a petition. Instead he produced a pistol ; but though he fired twice at the Emperor from a distance of only a few yards, he entirely failed to wound him. Pausing only to assure the bystanders that he was unhurt, Louis ' who behaved with the utmost calmness ' [2] rode forward on his way, neither hastening nor slackening his pace.[3]

Both on his way home, and in the evening at his public appearance at the Opéra Comique, Louis was received with spontaneous and genuine enthusiasm ; [4] more than ever Paris had been made to feel that for the moment the life thus threatened was necessary to France. In answering next day the loyal congratulations of his Senate the Emperor affected to believe that this very necessity absolved him from all danger. ' I fear nothing,' he said, ' from the attempts of assassins. There are existences which are instruments of the decrees of providence : so long as I have not accomplished my mission, I incur

---

[1] *Q.V.L.*, iii. 118.

[2] F.O. France, Cowley, 29 Apr. 55. Besides the double-barrelled pistol with which he made the attempt, the would-be assassin was also armed with ' a pair of loaded pistols, a large dagger clasp knife and a razor —all of English manufacture.' *Ibid.* He was guillotined a fortnight later. ' It was with the greatest difficulty ' and ' only after repeated and unanimous representations on the part of his ministers . . . that His Majesty's assent to this execution was obtained.' F.O. France, Cowley, 14 May 55.

[3] *La Gorce*: *Empire*, i. 368 ; *Register*, 1855, 74.

[4] ' J'ai vu le soir à neuf heures l'arrivée des voitu.es impériales au théâtre de l'Opéra Comique et je dois dire que si je lisais ce que j'ai vu, je n'y croirais pas, j'accuserais les journaux d'adulation. Les cris de Vive l'Empereur tonnaient comme des décharges d'artillerie se prolongeant au loin. J'ai vu des gens pleurer.' *Viel-Castel*, iii. 140.

no danger.' For the rest ' confident,' he said, ' in the affection of the people,' he forbade any other addresses of congratulation to be presented to him from France at all.[1]

For the moment the incident had no untoward result. It cast no cloud over the alliance, and unsuccessful assassination merely gave its unfailing fillip to the popularity of its intended victim. But the price was to be paid with interest later. The attempt was only one of a long series made upon the Emperor's life by assassins fresh from England. Two years earlier Louis had protested on the subject to his old friend Malmesbury. ' You know,' he said, ' I am neither fanciful nor timid, but I give you my word of honour that three men have been successively arrested within fifty yards of me armed with daggers and' pistols. The last fired at the gendarme and wounded him. I have taken great pains to have these attempts hushed up. These men all came straight from England, and had not been twelve hours in France. Your police should have known it and given me notice.' [2] The sense of grievance time and again repeated and repressed was destined to blaze out at last on the occasion of the Orsini attack three years later ; with results permanently damaging to the good understanding between the Western Powers.

Meanwhile during the whole winter of the Crimean War intermittent and apparently interminable negotiations were proceeding at Vienna. As early as August 1854, when the Czar's enforced evacuation of the Principalities seemed to have removed the *casus belli* altogether, Austria had concocted with the Western Powers proposals known as the Four Points ; which were presented to the Czar as the increased demands to which the allies were entitled by their opening victories in the war. Of these Four Points, two were calculated to deprive the Czar of his political protectorate over portions of the Turkish subjects or dominions ; while two were directed against

---

[1] *St Amand*, ii. 278.

[2] 20 Mar. 53. ' I put the above conversation on paper as soon as I returned to my hotel, so I can answer for its being almost textually correct.' *Malmesbury*, i. 392, 393.

his commercial and strategic monopoly of the Black Sea. It is probable that had these Four Points been presented by the Four Powers, Nicholas would have accepted them at once. But since Prussia had not associated herself with the demand, he refused at first to consider it. At the beginning of December, however, under the influence of the new successes of the allies in the Crimea, Austria proceeded to translate her invitation into a sort of ultimatum : if peace were not assured on the basis of the Four Points by the end of the year, Austria would lose no time in deliberating with the French and English sovereigns upon effective means to obtain the object of their alliance. Upon this, even Nicholas gave way ; nursing at his sick heart such feelings towards Austria as Austria herself forbore to contemplate, the Czar at the beginning of the new year had accepted the Four Points in principle as a starting-point for negotiation.

But Russia had stationed as her ambassador at Vienna her ablest diplomatist, Prince Gortschakoff : and Gortschakoff, while winter and disease were wasting away the allied armies before Sevastopol, employed his every art to dissuade Austria from opening any actual conference upon the Four Points. In this task of importing sloth to Vienna he was assisted by an action to which England was driven at this time, owing to this same process of attrition in the Crimea. Through lack of the most elementary necessities, the English troops were suffering far more severely than the French ; moreover England, unlike France, had no immediate means of raising fresh levies to take the place of those which the gross incompetence of her administration was threatening with extinction. In this necessity, that some troops other than French might be left to oppose Russia in the Crimea,[1] the English government fell back upon an eighteenth-century device ; proceeding now from the individual enlistment of aliens to seek the corporate service of a hired army.

[1] In Jan. 55 the French Army in the Crimea had grown to 78,000 men ; while the effective force of the English had sunk to 11,000. *Hamley*, 176. *Sterling*, 171.

The state which came to hand for this purpose was Piedmont. It is true that as a result of negotiations thus initiated, it was finally arranged that Piedmont should not be formally subsidised ; and that her troops should be carefully exempted from the status of mercenaries. For by a step flattering to the *amour propre* of both parties alike, Sardinian troops were spared the indignity of serving as mercenaries, and England escaped the public confession that mercenaries were necessary to her. Instead she merely gave free transport to the Sardinian troops, and undertook to advance to the Sardinian government as a loan at 3 per cent half a million pounds every six months the war lasted.[1] In return Piedmont undertook to raise its contingent from the 10,000 which England had originally asked, to 15,000 men.[2] Disraeli in the House of Commons attacked the proposal as a mere subsidy in disguise ;[3] and it is true that the necessary funds were advanced to the Sardinian government at a rate of interest considerabiy lower than the English exchequer itself was at this time forced to pay for consols.[4] Throughout the campaign the English War Office, to an extent occasionally most wounding to the susceptibilities of the Sardinians,[5] insisted on treating them as subordinates in virtue of this loan.[6]

The action of Cavour in making England's necessity Piedmont's opportunity has rightly been praised as the supreme example of his statesmanship. In the teeth of popular opinion, which naturally resented the plunging of his country into so remote a quarrel in so subordinate a rôle, Cavour's insistence carried the day ; and funda-

[1] *Register*, 1855, 395.
[2] *v.* F.O. Sardinia, Hudson to Clarendon. 'Confidential.' 15 Dec. 54.
[3] *Register*, 1855, 182.
[4] *v.* Gladstone's annotations of F.O. draft to Hudson ; F.O. Sardinia, Hudson drafts, 20 Jan. 55.
[5] Cf. *Bianchi*, 65.
[6] 'The Queen and the Prince urged objections to letting the Sardinian 15,000 go with the French, as they consider that force as being part of our contingent, being paid out of money advanced by us.' Palmerston to Panmure, 28 Feb. 55. *Panmure*, i. 87. Cf. *ibid.*, 105, 125, 135, 154, 281, 312, 347, 460. Nesselrode's circular on Piedmont's action declared that England was understood to have taken the Sardinian troops ' under its command—we will not say in its pay.' *Register*, 1855, 107.

mentally his act displayed one of the rare examples of real foresight in history. None the less, its actual consequences have not escaped exaggeration.

The generation which followed the attainment of Italian unity was one which contained for the new kingdom much hardship and disillusion. To carry her through those dull days Italy had urgent need of all the moral support on which by any means she could lay hands. Naturally she found it most easily in contemplating the recent shining hours of her deliverance. But deliverance was not enough. If the nation were now to stand upright it was essential that she should feel that by her own strength or at least her own cunning she had risen to her feet. The *sine qua non* of her actual independence was Austria conquered for her : but the condition of her moral independence seemed to be an Austria conquered by her. An achievement destined in fact to be most heavily indebted to foreign help had been heralded in advance with the proud phrase *Italia farà da sè*. After the event the conviction that that boast was true was so much needed that if grounds enough for it did not exist it was necessary that they should be invented. Where her history had not made good the boast, her historians were tempted to make good the history. It was scarcely indeed deniable that Italy could not have been made with Austria undefeated, and there were dates enough before and after to show that Austria could not have been defeated by the Italians themselves. Without the intervention of France in 1859 nothing in fact could have been done at all, though once the Austrian prop had been removed the native despotisms came toppling down easily enough. But if the French intervention could itself be attributed to Piedmont's intervention in 1855, Italy could claim at least the initiative in her own deliverance. Along such lines it might even be possible to justify the essence of the original boast. *Qui facit per alium facit per se* : and in so far as her deliverer could be shown to have been a mere tool in her hands Italy after all had done it for herself. All was yet well if it could be shown that into the little that Louis Napoleon had done for her he had been tricked or terrified, bribed, bullied or cajoled by Italians, and especially by Cavour.[1]

It is in the highest degree unlikely that Austria really kept out of the war merely because Piedmont came into it. Certainly the allies themselves, with the facts before them, never imagined that they were either forced or free to choose between the armed support of Austria and Sardinia : had they envisaged such a choice they would obviously not have chosen the latter. Further, even if Austria had joined the allies in the fighting, instead of only in the ultimatum which secured for them the fruits of their victories, it would from that hypothesis remain a wholly hypothetical deduction that Napoleon III would even so have been permanently deterred from the accomplishment of his lifelong design of extruding her from Italy. His own conception of the Austrian alliance would actually have accelerated it.[2]

But even if a contingency is remote it is wisdom to provide against it if it is also ruinous ; and unlikely as the double eventualities of Austrian action and French inaction were, it was the true function and justification of Cavour's policy to have made them less likely still. The fact remains however that precisely in proportion as Cavour's action was a service to his own country was it almost a disservice to the Western Powers. For if he really averted a real Austrian co-operation in the war, then he had deprived

[1] This thesis survives in its integrity in the latest, and despite its vehement partisanship the best, biography of that statesman : W. R. Thayer's *Life and Times of Cavour.* Flattering to Italian nationalists, the contention was also most useful to French clericals, who knew that they could not more effectively rouse their countrymen against the Emperor's Italian policy than by representing him as the dupe of Cavour. To this incongruous alliance the thesis owes not only its birth but its survival. For when opponents who give each other the lie on all other points pay tribute to each other's veracity on one, the simple are apt to suppose that their single common assertion must be singularly true.

[2] As early as 6 March 54, long before the Sardinian intervention, he proposed to Duke Ernest to hand over the Danubian Principalities to Austria in return for her retirement from Lombardy. This offer, coupled with that of a free hand in Serbia, was conveyed in person by the Duke to the Austrian Emperor ; by whom it was declined. ' I then realised,' wrote the Duke, ' that all Napoleon's expectations of gaining the desired end by conventions, treaties and compensations were purely chimerical, nor could I conceal this fact from the Emperor of the French,' with the result that when at last he was convinced of it ' his interest in the Eastern war cooled with increasing rapidity.' *Ernest,* iii. 66, 105, 106.

the allies of a vastly greater reinforcement than he brought
them in the Sardinian contingent. The dispatch of that
contingent was in any case a service rendered not to France
but to England.[1] It was in fact to prevent France from
monopolising the war that England had asked Piedmont
for troops.[2] Yet it was the opposition of England which all
but prevented the all-important campaign of 1859 ; and it
was the benevolence of Russia which alone made the fighting
of it possible.[3] In revenge merely for Austrian neutrality
Russia became the well-wisher of Piedmont even though
Piedmont had attacked her unprovoked. It is not really
certain that these good wishes would have been weakened
if Piedmont had not fought against her and Austria had.

More pro-Italian than he was already Louis Napoleon
at any rate could hardly be made : his Italian sympathies
had already been abundantly testified,[4] and were in no

[1] On this see Reiset to Napoleon III, 4 Sept. 55. *Reiset*, ii. 305.

[2] *Thayer*, i. 325. In this respect they proved something of a disappointment. ' The English Army is as compared with the French a mere
handful of men, and in consequence its commander has not the influence
due to the nation. The remedy may be found in the increase of the force.
I was in hopes that the Sardinian Army would have been able for this,
but as they are not fit for trench work, and set up rather as a separate
army than as a portion of the English force, my expectations in that
direction are not fulfilled.' Panmure to Simpson, 31 July 55. *Panmure*,
i. 322. ' It has not done a day's work in the trenches,' complained Prince
Albert to Clarendon on 17 Sept. 55, 'and but for the 16th [on the Tchernaya]
would not have heard a shot fired.' *Martin*, iii. 366.

[3] As early as May 56 Count Stackelberg, the envoy sent by the Czar
to inform Victor Emmanuel of his accession, was ' doing all in his power
not only to excite the Sardinian government but to influence the passions
of the Sardinian people against Austria. . . . He hints that in case of necessity the assistance of Russia would not be withheld.' F.O. France, Cowley to Clarendon. ' Most Confidential.' 30 May 56.

[4] *V. supra*, pp. 61, 62, 139, 193, 269. Shortly before his election to the
presidency, the Prince's chances were discussed by some English officers
in the presence of Gronow. Thereupon ' Alvanley informed us that he
had not very long before passed some days with the Prince at Colonel
Dawson Damer's country seat, and he observed that he had never met
with a more agreeable person ; that the Prince was very communicative,
and would sit up smoking cigarettes till two or three o'clock in the
morning ; and that upon one occasion, in a long political discussion, he
had said, among other things—" It is fated that ere long I shall become
Emperor of France, avenge the defeat of Waterloo, and drive the Austrians
out of Italy ; and the time for this is not far distant." Next morning
Louis' remarks were repeated by Lord Alvanley to his host, whose comment was, " Prince Louis is a charming person : he has a thousand good
and agreeable qualities ; but on the subject of politics, my dear Alvanley,
he is as mad as a hatter." ' *Gronow*, i. 283.

sense at all a creation of the Crimean War. But exaggerations apart, the war did give Cavour a most valuable opportunity of advertising the existence and ambitions of Piedmont ; and that advertisement gained greatly in effectiveness by the skill with which he contrived to give to the Sardinian intervention eventually the appearance of an equal partnership in the general alliance, in lieu of a paid particular service to England.

It was largely the success of Gortschakoff's dilatory manœuvres at Vienna which had induced England in the first instance to prefer Piedmont in the hand to Austria evasive in a singularly impenetrable bush. The same statesman now lost no time in pointing to this very preference as a further reason why Austria should do nothing in haste. Nor did Napoleon III mend matters at this juncture by inserting in the *Moniteur* [1] an official assurance that if Austria joined the Western Powers she would have her Italian possessions guaranteed to her ' for the entire duration of the war.' It hardly needed a Gortschakoff to convince Austria that such an undertaking given with the air of a man who makes a very handsome offer betrayed a radically unsound conception of the map of Italy after the peace.

Hence it was only in the middle of March that the long-expected conference of Vienna opened at all. From that time for something over two months, albeit with many a creak and groan of lumbering machinery, the reluctant artificers of diplomacy were yet seriously at work in the effort to forge peace. Of the Four Points already conceded by Russia in principle, Gortschakoff granted with only graceful reluctance the practical consequences of the two first : thereby securing to Austria the two points about which alone she was primarily concerned ; to wit, the political freedom of the Principalities, and the commercial freedom of the Danube. Austria appeased, Gortschakoff could afford to be less accommodating in his interpretation of the third point, the ending of Russian preponderance in the Black Sea ; to the contention of the Western Powers

[1] 22 Feb. 55.

that this could not mean less than the exclusion of all Russian warships from those waters, he replied that he was unable to see why it should mean more than the free admission to the Black Sea of warships of all nations. If this interpretation were not acceptable, he had others in store ; only it was always a fortnight's journey to Petersburg for fresh instructions ; and if Easter fell late this year, was it on that account not to be observed ? Hence in spite of the arrival of special envoys from the allied capitals —Drouyn de Lhuys from Paris, and Lord John Russell from London—the conference which had made real progress in March, advanced hardly at all in April.

At this juncture Austria contributed a complicated suggestion of her own, based partly on the limitation of the Russian navy, partly on the admission of foreign warships on a sort of sliding scale, in such a way as to maintain an automatic but precarious equilibrium in the Black Sea.[1] In their anxiety to attain either peace with Russia, or the aid of Austria in the war, the envoys of the Western Powers decided to go home and urge this new compromise, or some variant of it, upon their respective governments. In France Drouyn would probably have been successful, in spite of the desire of the French army for a more clearly victorious peace. But the English cabinet not only rejected the proposal for itself as utterly inadequate, but succeeded, by the extremely energetic and determined action of its ambassador in Paris, in procuring Drouyn de Lhuys' resignation.[2]

---

[1] For details, v. *D'Harcourt*, 113–147.

[2] Of this successful intervention by Cowley, who ' had a strong personal opinion against the Austrian proposals,' *Argyll*, a member of the English cabinet, wrote very sensibly (i. 554), ' This was all very well for once, and it was a great escape, but I could not help feeling that it indicated a very dangerous situation. If Cowley had really gained such an ascendancy over the Emperor, and if he allowed it to appear to his own ministers, the French people would soon come to know of it, and a proud nation would ill bear the idea that their policy, at a very difficult conjuncture, was determined by the will of a Foreign Ambassador. Granville . . . [from Paris] wrote me a very curious letter about the strength of the language which Cowley allowed himself to use against the Austrian proposals—a letter which seemed to indicate that he wished me to give some note of warning. I accordingly wrote to Clarendon, pointing out the danger, and urging that Cowley should be reminded of it.'

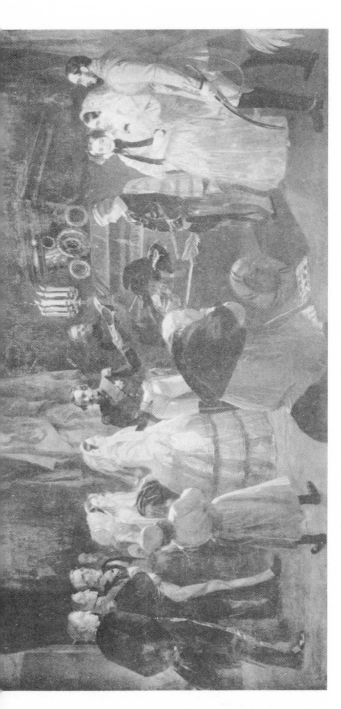

QUEEN VICTORIA'S VISIT WITH NAPOLEON III TO NAPOLEON'S TOMB
From the painting by E. M. Ward, R.A.

REMOVING THE KILLED AND WOUNDED FROM THE GREAT REDAN

The English envoy, Lord John Russell, adopted a more circuitous course.　He too tendered privately his resignation to the Government,[1] but at the request of his colleagues he consented to remain in office, and even to repudiate in public with extreme vehemence proposals which he had himself privately supported.　In the parliamentary debate raised upon the issue by a now no longer negligible peace party, he distinguished himself by the vigour of his denunciation of any such 'simulated peace.' Any momentary popularity which this sudden access of warlike enthusiasm gained for him was however promptly extinguished by a manifesto to which the Austrian government was naturally provoked, revealing the fact that at Vienna Russell, no less than Drouyn, had promised his whole-hearted support to the Austrian proposal.[2]　Upon this, there was nothing for it but that the Foreign Minister should really resign : his conduct seemed not merely indefensible but unintelligible.　It would appear in fact to have been due to an illusion momentarily current among English politicians, and later perpetuated by the skill of an English historian.[3]　In common with the majority of his countrymen, Lord John imagined that the Austrian proposal had been rejected at the instance, and in the interests, of the French Emperor.　It was in fact the case that in his strenuous campaign for its rejection, Cowley in Paris had called in the aid of the military : at his own request [4] he was allowed by the Emperor to be present at the decisive audience with Drouyn, which resulted in the resignation of the French statesman and the rejection of his pacific proposal.　At that interview Cowley appealed [5] to Marshal Vaillant, who was also present : the latter 'confined himself to stating that the army would not be satisfied with a peace on those terms.' [6]　At the time, in his private despatches for the month of May 1855, the English ambassador rightly made no secret of the truth,

---

[1] *Walpole* : *Russell*, ii. 263.　　[2] *Martin*, iii. 294, 305.
[3] *Kinglake*, vii. 328 *sq*.
[4] 'And most heartily do I rejoice that the Emperor granted it' he commented, with reason. F.O. France, Cowley.　'Confidential.'　7 May 55.
[5] *Senior* : *Empire*, i. 240.　　　　[6] *Ibid*.

that it was the French Emperor who desired peace, and he himself who by arduous exertions and with no little difficulty was endeavouring to avert any acceptance of the Austrian proposal, or rather of an improvement on it of Louis' own devising, whereby the Russian Black Sea fleet would be limited in future to the number of ships actually remaining at the end of the war. But in the course of a conversation six years later [1] he wisely minimised his own share in the transaction by exaggerating Vaillant's : [2] though even then he revealed the fact that it was he who had asked the Emperor to take Vaillant's opinion.[3]

The impression which Kinglake [4] later launched upon historians,[5] by dint of a judicious exploitation of this interview, was also at the time itself mysteriously propagated in the English cabinet.[6] Russell seems to have been persuaded to repudiate his own peace policy by the false assurance that peace now would be unwelcome and injurious to the French Emperor, whom he considered ' the most faithful ally who had ever wielded the sceptre or ruled the destinies of France.' His biographers and apologists are probably right in accepting this, his own justification of his action, as sincere. But with one accord they have concluded that because sincere therefore it must have been well founded.[7] Cowley's contemporary secret despatches now prove that it was false. Lord John himself, unlike

---

[1] With *Senior*: *Empire*, i. 238 *sq.*

[2] Doubtless he had received the warning referred to above, p. 304 *n.*

[3] *Senior, ibid.*, p. 240.   [4] *Kinglake*, viii. 344–350.

[5] E.g. *Paul*, i. 396, 397. ' Lord Clarendon, who was sincerely desirous of peace, could not move a step without France, and the Emperor was still bent on war. . . . It is impossible to blame him. But England had been brought to a pretty pass when she must needs shape her policy to keep him on the throne.' This is an exact reversal of the truth. In general, Kinglake writes in bad faith knowing the facts ; and his disciples in good faith, ignorant of them.

[6] On ' the incredible ignorance of facts even among leading politicians as to the Vienna proposals, which ' Lord Grey and Gladstone alone seem to have actually read,' see *Vitzthum*, i. 169. Cf. *Morley*: *Gladstone*, i. 547. Gladstone himself was one of the few men not even momentarily deceived as to the cause of their rejection. ' All that I can see and hear,' he wrote on May 14, ' tends to the conclusion that the English Government, and the English Government alone, is the cause which has prevented peace from being, in substance, made within the last three weeks.' *Argyll*, ii. 32.

[7] *Walpole*: *Russell*, ii. 263, 266. *Reid*: *Russell*, 264, 265. So too *Maxwell*, ii. 86.

his biographers, discovered this fact for himself : only a few weeks later he complained bitterly that he had been deceived ; that he had been ' allowed to suppose, like the public, that the Emperor's rejection had been spontaneous, instead of having been suggested and urged upon him by us.' [1]

Behind the whole matter lurks the darker question ' Who tricked Lord John ? ' : a question which historians and biographers have failed not merely to answer but to ask.   Palmerston and his Foreign Minister Clarendon were dead-set at the time on a continuation of the war, [2] or at least on the frustration of this particular attempt to end it.   The latter at any rate must have read the most important despatches of his most important ambassador. Yet the substance of Cowley's despatches is such that only an extraordinary economy of truth on the part of Clarendon or Palmerston or both could have left any of their colleagues under the impression that Louis Napoleon desired the failure of the negotiations.

Their failure had in any case for consequence the relapse of Austria into a condition of complete neutrality : for that country not unnaturally made the allies' evasion of the peace an excuse for its own evasion of the war.   Already, at the beginning of June, the repudiation by the allies of the Austrian proposal had led to the abandonment of the negotiations at Vienna : now Austria proceeded to declare that as a further result of this repudiation she regarded her own obligations under the December treaty as acquitted : she accordingly reassumed her original freedom of inaction.   Thereby without repairing the well-nigh irreparable breach in her relations with Russia, she succeeded in forfeiting all effective claim upon the gratitude of the

---

[1] *Greville*, 7 Sept. 55.   His informant was Russell's brother, the Duke of Bedford.

[2] For reasons far from frivolous.   Later events fully justified Herbert's conviction that ' to have left unfinished a great military enterprise like the siege of Sebastopol . . . would have had a very disastrous effect in Asia, and that the prestige of success was necessary for our Indian Empire.' *Stanmore* : *Herbert*, ii. 10.   The question of military prestige had a practical urgency for England as well as for Louis Napoleon : a fact which writers on these negotiations have ignored.

allies. These last now declared themselves betrayed by
Austria's evasion of the treaty in June, just as Russia
had declared herself betrayed by Austria's conclusion of it
in December.

Austria's refusal to translate moral support into military assistance was the more disappointing to the allies
that even yet things were going none too well with them in
the field. It is true that with the coming of spring the
worst sufferings of their armies were over : sickness abated,
reinforcements arrived, and the English contingent became
once more a fighting force. The simultaneous arrival of
warm weather and warm clothes put fresh heart into the
troops ; and a delighted sergeant was able to report ' The
men are beginning to swear again.' [1] The war too, which
had tended to languish during the period of negotiations,[2]
was naturally renewed with added energy after the Vienna
conference had broken down. But April which brought
new vigour to the troops brought also new embarrassments
for their generals. A newly-installed submarine cable
enabled Louis Napoleon now for the first time to direct
operations immediately from Paris. In multiplying his
telegraphic instructions to his generals, Louis found some
consolation for his abandonment of any personal expedition
to the Crimea.

Such an expedition, though attended with dangers far
outweighing its advantages, yet had at least some advantages to be outweighed : this new method of intervention was merely mischievous. It was true that Canrobert
needed stimulus of some sort. Though a brave soldier
he had proved a timid general, refusing for his troops
risks which he would have faced cheerfully in his own
person.[3] Possessed of every quality that would endear him
to his soldiers,[4] save the ability to lead them to victory,

[1] *Kinglake*, vii. 342.
[2] ' I told the Emperor that while we were negotiating at Vienna our
Admirals ought to bo shelling Odessa ; but he said the war must bo
carried on according to the " civilised ideas of 1855." ' *Malmesbury* to
Derby, 14 Apr. 55. *Malmesbury*, ii. 17.
[3] *Sterling*, 155. *Denormandie*, 228.
[4] On their devotion to him, v. *Castellane*, v. 97.

he had by the extreme severity and simplicity of his own life,[1] by his personal encouragement and supervision, and by his perpetual presence in their midst, done much in the dark winter just over to preserve his troops from the utter disorganisation and discomfort which reigned in the English camp ; to which Raglan, from his house at Balaclava, paid only the most rare and fleeting visits.[2] But in that crowning and impersonal courage that will dare failure to achieve success, resolutely shouldering responsibility and accepting all the consequences of action, Canrobert had proved himself utterly deficient. For this supreme fault of irresolution no combination of virtues could in any general have atoned ; but in this case the many virtues of Canrobert came to the assistance of his one vice. Naturally too prone to take advice if it were given him, his affable manner and accessible habit of life secured that it was given him in plenty. Lacking now for the first time the crisp command of authority behind him, he sought support instead in the conflicting suggestions of subordinates. And so well apprised had been the French general by these means of the disadvantages of any particular course of action, that throughout the winter, though his troops were clamouring for action,[3] he had done little more than advance laboriously his trenches towards Sevastopol. Nor had a combined bombardment of the town in the beginning of April proved more successful than its predecessor which had closed the autumn campaign in the previous year.[4]

It was at this conjuncture that Louis Napoleon sent an imperious summons to his commander-in-chief, urging him to take the offensive without further delay.

To understand the gravamen of the Emperor's charges upon his generals during this and the following months, it is necessary to bear in mind one elementary fact which is not always remembered. From beginning to end the siege of Sevastopol was strictly no siege at all. At no

---

[1] *Bocher*, 70.   [2] *Kelly*, 125. *Graham*, 68, 72.
[3] *Sterling*, 174.
[4] Owing to its failure the assault which was to have followed it—*cf.* p. 281 *n.* above—was never delivered. *Shadwell*, i. 371.

time was the fortress cut off from communication with the interior. At the beginning of the ' siege ' the garrison had been suffered quietly to send away all non-combatants : [1] in the course of it they received immense accessions of men, ammunition, and supplies : [2] at the end of it they merely retreated from the southern to the northern side of the harbour. For by reason of their still unbroken line of communications the surrender of the fortress did not involve the surrender of the garrison.

It was against a siege so abnormally shorn alike of its ordinary inconveniences for the besieged and of its ordinary prize for the assailants that the French Emperor was now protesting. Versed in the theory of war, though remote from the actual conditions of the campaign, he had convinced himself that common sense and the very elements of strategy rendered futile any further assault upon Sevastopol until the investment of it had been first completed. If it were replied that the peculiar geographical conditions rendered any such hermetical investment all but impossible [3] given the actual resources of the besiegers, Louis was ready with an alternative plan of campaign. At the time when he meditated a personal appearance in the Crimea, he had intended to leave an army of observation to guard the siege-works before Sevastopol, and himself with the bulk of the troops to advance into the interior of the Crimea, towards Simferopol ; thereby threatening the Russian lines of communication, automatically completing the investment of Sevastopol, and in all probability forcing the enemy to give battle. Convinced that the strength of French troops was in the open field, while that of the Russians lay behind walls, he did not doubt that in the pitched battle thus provoked the allies must prove victorious. This was the plan which Louis now required his still hesitating general to put into immediate execution.

Forced now either by opposing his Emperor to assume the responsibility of taking no risks, or by obeying him to take risks for which he was not responsible, Canrobert had

---

[1] *Hamley*, 91.   [2] *Ibid.*, 194.   v. *Argyll*, i. 478, 494–495.
[3] On this, v. *Siege of Sebastopol*, i. 12, 13.

less hesitation than usual in preferring the second course :
but it was soon evident that his allies would have none of
it. Instinctively they preferred to go through with the
task on which they had laboured so long already, rather
than to let go even an imperfect grip upon Sevastopol for
the sake of some new and showy programme sprung on
them from Paris. Lord Raglan, at all times more capable
of vetoing foolish proposals than of initiating wise ones,
had little difficulty in showing that this particular proposal
was one to be vetoed.

Upon this Canrobert came at last to a decision of his
own. On the morning of May 16 he telegraphed in
cypher to the Emperor begging that he might be allowed
to resume a subordinate position ; the one he occupied,
as he very simply and justly observed, was beyond his
strength. The Emperor as wisely assented ; three days
later the astonished army learnt that General Canrobert
had returned to his post at the head of the division which
he had commanded before Saint-Arnaud's death ; while in
his place as general-in-chief appeared an older soldier of a
sterner school—General Pélissier.

Pélissier was a short stout Norman, in every way the
antithesis of his predecessor. In many of the finer qualities
of heart and character, the latter was his superior. But
whereas the very virtues of Canrobert were his weakness,
Pélissier drew strength even from his faults. In manner
brusque to the verge of brutality, he knew how to render
criticism not indeed superfluous but impossible.[1] The
merest orderly officer who found himself in the simple
tent which served Canrobert for head-quarters was encouraged by his kindly familiarity to easy and expansive
conversation ; in the presence of Pélissier even the direct
emissary of the Emperor, charged with dictatorial instructions fresh from Paris, found his injunctions faltering,
his explanations trailing off into silence. Not the least
of the new general's merits as a commander consisted in
the fact that he had learnt how not to obey. By his
troops—whom, unlike Canrobert, he was perfectly prepared

---

[1] *Rousset*, ii. 191 *sq.*

to send by thousands to their deaths,—he was respected, trusted, and above all feared.

The appointment of Pélissier produced a no less notable change in the relation of the French and English head-quarters. Hitherto, although by the spring of 1855 the British army formed less than one-sixth of the total effective forces of the allies in the Crimea,[1] yet its general had retained a considerable and at times almost controlling voice in the common military counsels of the allies. For though far from a competent commander, he was at any rate a *grand seigneur* : and possessed, by the side of his previous French colleagues, of qualities verging upon personal eminence. With the coming of Pélissier this position was reversed. Bitterly criticised in the English press, and rated severely by a dour Scotch Secretary for War,[2] Lord Raglan was now perceptibly more worn and aged than in the opening months of the campaign.[3] The relatively increased influence of the French commander carried with it however no bitterness in the English camp. For Pélissier's plan of campaign was none other than the original English design ; that of a steadfast maintenance of the siege, and a refusal to be turned aside by any dis-tractions whatsoever.

At the outset the new commander was fortunate enough to be able to report to Paris some tangible successes. A naval expedition was despatched to Kertch, at the mouth of the Sea of Azov ; and without opposition immense sup-plies of corn, rations for 100,000 men for four months, were taken and destroyed. Against Sevastopol itself operations were vigorously pushed forward ; on June 7 a combined attack, following upon a third bombardment, delivered the outer line of the Russian fortifications into the hands of the allies. It was a great gain, the first

---

[1] *D.N.B.*, liii. 241. That total in June 1855 was 188,000 men. *Ibid.*

[2] After assisting on May 18 of this year at a presentation of medals by Queen Victoria to wounded soldiers, the Secretary for War was asked : " " Was the Queen touched ? " " Bless my soul, no," was the reply. " She had a brass railing before her, and no one could touch her." Mrs Norton then said, " I mean, was she moved ? " " Moved ! " answered Lord Panmure, " she had no occasion to move ! " ' *Malmesbury*, ii. 24.

[3] *Sterling*, 201.

decisive victory of the year ; bought at the cost of some six hundred English casualties and six thousand French.

On the whole the policy of adventure had been justified by its results. Pélissier resolved to attempt one audacity the more. The expedition to Kertch had been achieved on the Queen's birthday ; now he would celebrate a greater anniversary with a greater feat of arms. On June 18, their common capture of Sevastopol should wipe out for French and English the last ill memories of Waterloo. True this observance of the anniversary demanded the neglect of some customary precautions : the English trenches were still 250 metres distant from the Redan ; and nearly twice that distance separated the French siege-works from the Malakoff. But while the besiegers were advancing their approaches the besieged would be strengthening their defences ; and hitherto the allies had lost far less by rashness than by delay in following up an initial success. Against his better judgment, the English general assented to the assault ; on the appointed date it was badly bungled and decisively repelled. A week later Raglan sickened suddenly ; and at the end of the month he died.

The defeat which had thus given his death-blow to the English commander narrowly failed to procure his dismissal for Pélissier. His last unsuccessful assault upon the Malakoff, no less than his previous successful attack upon the outworks, had been executed in absolute disregard of the imperial instructions from Paris. And he had conveyed the news of its failure to Paris with even more than his usual bluntness ; as though unaware that in a soldier disobedience that fails is unpardonable. After vainly endeavouring to obtain from Pélissier details of his recent losses or present plans, the Emperor wrote to him at the beginning of July pointing out that his operations, undertaken contrary to the ordinary law of sieges and against express instructions from Paris, had already cost the army 20,000 men ; that since his last repulse he had refused, in spite of repeated requests, to furnish necessary information either in regard to the losses he had incurred or the plans which he proposed. In consequence he must consider himself under definite orders either to submit to the French War Office an immediate and detailed report of his intentions, or to refrain from any serious steps for which he had not obtained previous telegraphic confirmation from Paris ; failing this he was to hand over the command to General Niel.[1] The letter ended with an assurance that no one had been told of its contents, and that the general was therefore perfectly free to adopt any of the three courses prescribed. But there can be no doubt that had it reached its destination, Pélissier would have resigned. Fortunately he remained ignorant of the fact that it had ever been written. For thanks to the urgent expostulation of General MacMahon, who was passing through Paris on his way to the Crimea, Louis caused the letter to be taken from the post at Marseilles.[2] Thus arrested in mid-career, it served as a harmless vent for the feelings of its author, and secured to its intended recipient a practical immunity from further reproaches.

In justice to the Emperor it must be remembered that his position during the last four weeks had been one of peculiar strain and difficulty. The failure of the Vienna conference had been an unmixed disappointment to the great bulk of the French nation. From the outset of the war many in France had held that an army predominantly French was being employed to defend interests primarily English. This party had latterly been greatly augmented by the perfectly correct suspicion that it was due almost entirely to England's insistence and the Emperor's personal loyalty to his ally, that the recent Austrian proposals had not issued in peace. Whether the Four Points together were worth the fighting for seemed to many Frenchmen doubtful : the continuance of the struggle for a disputed reading of a single one of them— and that one a point purely maritime—was almost universally regarded as an undue deference to the naval interests of England. And the Emperor knew, what

[1] *Ollivier*, iii. 309–310.
[2] *Du Barail*, i. 444–446. *Rousset*, ii. 293.

France merely suspected, that the casualties were enor-
mously in excess of those which the War Office had been
allowed to publish.[1]   Added to this was a growing conviction that England was availing herself of the French alliance
to extort naval concessions from Russia at a time when she
had proved both on land and sea her incapacity to extort
anything unaided from anybody.   This conviction England
owed to naval failure in the Baltic followed by military maladministration in the Crimea, and the loud proclamation of
both by the one English journal read outside of England.

For his rejection of the Austrian proposals in deference
to the wishes of his ally, Louis was soon to be richly rewarded.   To his fidelity to England he owed both the
French capture of Sevastopol, and the conclusion of a victorious instead of an indecisive peace.   But at the moment
things looked cheerless enough.   The resignation of his
able Foreign Minister, Drouyn, weakened the Emperor
just where he could least afford to be weakened; for
admirably served as was the Second Empire in its internal
administration, its diplomatic service was almost uniformly
contemptible.   An incompetent natural son of the great
Napoleon, Walewski, was now promoted from the London
embassy to take Drouyn's place; his post in turn was
filled by Louis' early friend and fellow-conspirator Persigny,
who was and remained ignorant of the very elements of
his business.[2]

[1] By July 1855, 201,500 French soldiers had been sent out : of whom
37,000 had been killed outright, and 74,000 sent home sick or wounded;
of these 34,000 had died.   *Ernest*, iii. 182.
[2] The following letter of Aug. 55 shows the Emperor trying to teach
him the alphabet of his profession.   ' Mon cher Persigny, Walewski m'a
remis votre dépêche.   Je dois, à ce sujet, vous faire, dans votre propre
intérêt, une recommandation bien importante.   Quand on occupe une
position officielle comme la vôtre, il faut se pénétrer de cette vérité qu'on
n'est pas maître de développer ses idées personnelles, quelque bonnes et
utiles qu'elles soient.   Car un ministre ou un ambassadeur ne peuvent
donner d'autorité à leurs paroles que si l'on est bien convaincu qu'ils sont
les échos fidèles de leur gouvernement ; et si, par malheur, cette conviction
venait à s'affaiblir, ils perdraient toute influence et toute importance
politiques.   Il faut donc, lorsque vous communiquerez une idée au gouvernement anglais, qu'il soit bien persuadé que vous êtes l'organe officiel et
fidèle de mes vues et de mes intentions.   Or, dans votre dernière communication au gouvernement anglais, qui contient, je l'avoue, de bonnes
choses, vous vous êtes avancé sans savoir réellement si telle était la détermi-
nation actuelle de mon gouvernement.'   *Persigny*, 185.

This weakening of his diplomatic service, entailing fresh labours on his part to repair the shortcomings of his agents, overtook the Emperor at a moment when he had placed his policy in unprecedented isolation from the general body of public opinion in France. So swiftly and completely did military and diplomatic triumphs follow upon the failures of 1855, that historians have commonly failed to realise how seriously French public opinion was at the time perturbed by them. At the time prophets of disaster were numerous, and the course of the campaign gave ample opportunity to the pessimists. In the spring of 1855 especially the royalist salons in Paris were all agog with hints and rumours of disaster; if only things would go a little worse the same causes which had already upset a cabinet in England might serve in France to bring down a dynasty. Never therefore was military success more necessary to the Emperor than at the moment when he was confronted with the news of the worst defeat in the war; a defeat incurred as the result of operations undertaken in express disobedience to his own commands. Further, he was faced with alarming reports as to the health of the allied armies; for the return of summer, though it had meant the lightening of many of their burdens, had meant also the return of one most formidable foe, the Asiatic cholera. The Sardinian recruits in particular had been decimated by the disease. And all the while summer itself was passing, and in the distance loomed an evil by the side of which even cholera seemed endurable enough: the prospect of a second Crimean winter in the face of the unconquerable ruins of Sevastopol.[1]

Upon all these things in public the Emperor put a brave face. The check of June 18 was announced in the *Moniteur* without explanation or excuse, in the same bald terms in which Pélissier had announced it to the Emperor. A special session of the Legislative Assembly was convoked: another levy of 140,000 troops was raised; another war

---

[1] 'The dark prospect of another winter looms before us. It must be looked in the face, but it is a precious ugly thing to look at.' General Codrington to Sir George Brown, 27 July 55. *Martin,* iii. 319 *n.*

loan issued and five times over-subscribed.[1]   All this was done gravely, soberly, and at once ; not without sorrow, but without vain lamentations.   Doubtless the absence of clamour in press and parliament was due in chief to the absolute power of the existing government. But the silence in this instance was not all servility, and the spectacle of a nation setting itself sternly yet without reproaches to retrieve a severe reverse was one which did not lack a dignity of its own.

The disappointment and depression caused by the failure of June 18 proved in any case more acute than lasting.   The allies soon realised that though that check might for the moment have counteracted the moral ad-vantage of the success which it immediately followed, yet it had by no means cancelled the permanent gain ensuing from the capture of the outworks.   Moreover the Russians did not long allow their foes to indulge in vain regrets ; for after no great delay they decided to make one final effort to crush the forces of the besiegers.

Since the decisive repulse at Inkerman in the previous autumn the Russian relieving army had remained inactive. Now at last, strongly reinforced, it made another tardy attempt to fulfil its mission.   To such action it was indeed driven by the two successes obtained by the allies in the spring.   The capture of the outworks of Sevastopol, sorely straitening the resources of its defenders, prompted the relieving forces to action from in front : the previous demolition of their own food supplies drove them to action from behind.   Unless the relieving army now attempted to justify its name, it would itself cease to be an army, and there would be nothing left for it to relieve.   And if Pélissier's early successes rendered action necessary, his subsequent repulse seemed to render action hopeful ; one supreme effort more, and these disheartened and diseased besiegers might yet be swept back into the sea.

It was the same River Tchernaya from which they had been driven back in November that the outer army of the

Russians now attempted once more to cross on August 16. In the autumn their assault had been delivered upon the English camp from the bridge of Inkerman, near the mouth of the river ; now, strongly reinforced, they crossed it near its source by the Traktir bridge, and fell upon the position of the French. As before, the attack was launched in the early morning : as before a convenient mist from the river valley screened the first advance. But this time rumour had preceded action : the French in consequence were prepared for the attack. By nine in the morning the sixty thousand Russians who delivered it were already in retreat ; long before midday the battle was over. Eight thousand Russians had fallen killed or wounded in the course of it : while the French had bought their decisive victory comparatively cheaply with only 1500 casualties. In this battle the Sardinian contingent, hitherto and thereafter attacked by no other foe than disease, had one of its divisions in action : a hundred and sixty Italians were wounded, and twenty-eight of them were killed.[1] Until the very end of the battle their share in it was practically confined to artillery support,[2] but the little they had to do they did well. It was a great thing for Cavour that his expedition should now at last have taken part in a real battle ; and he proceeded to exaggerate judiciously not indeed the valour of his countrymen but the opportunity which they had had for displaying it. Never was achievement so well advertised, and never was advertisement more successful.[3] By the end of the war the Piedmontese had almost persuaded themselves if not Europe that at the crisis of the Crimean War they had advanced to the support of a tottering cause, and by their impulse turned the wavering scale in favour of the allies.

For the moment, however, it had not occurred to anyone to ascribe the victory of the Tchernaya to anyone but the French : and to the French the news arrived most

---

[1] *La Gorce: Empire*, i. 424. *Paul*, ii. 14.   [2] *Russell*, 60.
[3] E.g. *C.M.H.*, 991, ascribes this French victory exclusively to the Piedmontese.

opportunely, on the eve of the return visit of the English
Queen to the Emperor.   Moreover, minute as was the
Sardinian share in it, the battle itself was far from un-
important.   For it represented the last real attempt of
the Russians to prevent a bombardment, which the allies
were now for the first time able to render really effective.
How effective that bombardment would be, or how desperate
had been the Russian need of averting it, the besiegers
themselves hardly at first realised.   But within the city
the boldest began to contemplate a prospect which the
weakest still forbore to put into words.   The moment of
feverish elation which had followed upon the success of
June 18 was quite over now.   When the news of the
French victory on the Tchernaya penetrated the fortress
its defenders realised at once the frustration of their hopes
of any successful diversion from without.   And on the
very next morning the enemy opened his new and devastating cannonade, which continued all but unbrokenly for
twenty days.   Thanks to the loss of the outworks, this
new bombardment proved far more deadly than any of its
predecessors.

Indeed southern Sevastopol as a whole was now clearly
becoming untenable : but still the commanders of the
garrison persisted in their defence.   Preparation, it was
true, was made for a final retreat, by the construction
of a pontoon bridge across the harbour ; whereby at the
last instant the remnant of the garrison might retire to
the safety of the northern heights.   Meanwhile, though
the continued holding of the southern side should cost
a thousand men a day, it was resolved that it should be
defended to the last.[1]   The decision was inspired by no
hope and dictated by no necessity : further resistance could
only at a fearful cost delay for a few days the abandonment of the fortress, nor would such abandonment itself
involve the surrender of the garrison.   To delay that
abandonment was now merely to diminish the size of the
garrison that would retreat, and to incur the grave risk

[1] Gortschakoff to the Russian Minister of War, 1 Sept. 55, v. *Hamley*,
275.

that in the confusion of a final assault, it might fail to make good its retreat at all.

But there are occasions in war—and in no department of it more than in the defence of a besieged city—when resistance which subserves no military aim is yet not accounted waste : or more properly in war as in peace waste may take forms so splendid that few dare pronounce it purposeless. So now for no material cause, the defenders of Sevastopol resolved that having held Sevastopol for Russia thus far, they would hold it to the end.

What they decided to do they did, though at terrible cost. Throughout the last fortnight of August and the first week in September, the pitiless bombardment continued ; a bombardment that merited Gortschakoff's description of it as ' *un feu d'enfer.*' Daily upon the doomed and devoted fortress the murderous fire continued : every twenty-four hours during these dreadful last three weeks cost the garrison the better part of a thousand men.[1] The incessant labours of the night—which now more frantically than ever alternated with the murder by day—could no longer make good the damage done to the fast crumbling earthworks ; all that the uttermost efforts of the defenders could achieve was to maintain the real covering of their powder magazines, and to hide a little while from the enemy the true nature of the havoc which their fire had wrought elsewhere.[2] Even for this small end an ever larger number of the ever-shrinking garrison had to be employed by day as well as by night : and to dig by day was death in ever shorter time under the fire of the ever-approaching batteries of the besiegers. At intervals indeed the thunder of the enemies' cannon would die down suddenly ; and the now normal din of the bombardment be succeeded by a heard and ominous hush. At this sinister silence the garrison would hurry their wearied reserves from the subterranean penetralia of the fortress to man its uttermost remaining defences : for such a silence must needs precede the final agony of the assault. But the defenders, massed thus upon the circumference of

---

[1] *Wood*, 382.   [2] *Register*, 1855, 257.

their works, and nerved to repel an impending attack, would find that they had advanced only to be exposed once more to a renewed and redoubled cannonade ; a cannonade the more murderous that its victims were crowded to receive it in the least sheltered portions of their defences.[1] Time and again during the last hours of the siege the grim jest was repeated, nor did repetition ever wholly rob it of its effect.   For it was on each occasion impossible for the defenders to be certain that this time at least the assault was not about to be delivered in earnest.

Nevertheless the final attack when it did come, took the defenders by surprise.   Unlike its predecessors of the 7th and 18th of June, it was delivered neither at daybreak nor at night-fall, but at noon.   September 7, the anniversary of Borodino, was purposely allowed to pass without attack : [2] the morning of September 8 was occupied only with a deliberately desultory cannonade.[3]   But at noon, while many of the Russian troops were taking their midday meal [4]—retiring for the purpose to the dismal subterranean dens which afforded them now their sole shelter and repose—French and Zouave regiments attacked the Malakoff ; in the space of half an hour, despite the desperate efforts of the defenders, they had gained precarious possession of the key of Sevastopol.   After this it availed the Russians nothing that four other French attacks upon other bastions of the fort ended in failure ; or that the English assault upon the Redan was decisively repelled.   For the loss of the Malakoff alone sufficed to render the whole town indefensible.   Six times the Russians endeavoured to recapture this all-important position ; [5] from twelve till after seven the intermittent struggle continued ; [6] but in the end the French, after desperate encounters, were left in possession of the fort.   Only at

---

[1] *La Gorce : Empire*, i. 429.   [2] *Ibid.*, 430.
[3] *Nolan*, ii. 466.
[4] When the troops were relieved for this purpose, in order to avoid the vastly greater mortality caused by introducing new troops into the works before retiring the old ones, the contrary course was pursued : hence during the actual changing of the guard, the Malakoff was for a moment stripped of most of its defenders. *Hamley*, 276.   *Steevens*, 274 *n.*
[5] *Nolan*, ii. 467.   [6] *Times*, 27 Sept. 55, p. 7, c. 2.

dusk did the Russian general begin his perilous retreat : during the night of the 8th he succeeded by one of the most brilliant feats of the entire war, in effecting unmolested the withdrawal of the garrison by bridge and boats to the northern side of the harbour. Then the last ships were sunk, the remaining magazines exploded, the city behind them fired, and the bridge itself destroyed.

And so, committing his vessels to the deep and his city to the flames, Todleben concluded worthily his great defence. For a whole day after his going the fire still kept the foe at bay ; as though unwilling that even now the foreigner should set foot within the place. It was only on the morning of the 10th, walking warily among the still smouldering embers, that the victors entered into possession of their prize : smoking ruins where had once stood Sevastopol—and would yet stand Sevastopol again.

CHAPTER X

THE PRINCE AND THE PEACE

Say not the struggle naught availeth,
  The labour and the wounds are vain,
The enemy faints not, nor faileth,
  And as things have been, they remain.

For . . . not by eastern windows only
  When daylight comes comes in the light.
In front the sun climbs slow, how slowly !
  But westward, look, the land is bright !

ARTHUR HUGH CLOUGH.

DURING that same summer of 1855, while the armies about Sevastopol were painfully approaching the prize of their long labours, and the garrison within awaiting the last agony of the inevitable assault, very different scenes were transacting themselves in a very different city. Far away from the bleak shores of Crim Tartary, as though careless altogether of that inhospitable sea for whose ' neutralisation ' half Europe was in arms, Paris seemed given up to a round of more than Parisian gaieties. The new court sought occasion for festivities ; the great exhibition gave excuse for them ; and an unwonted influx of foreigners furnished spectators in abundance to both. These last indeed might well have imagined that Paris regarded the conduct of a European war as an inconsiderable distraction, a mere πάρεργον beside the serious business of amusing oneself.

The most notable event in that summer's pageantry had it is true its obvious connexion with the war. At the close of the English parliamentary session, two days after the battle of the Tchernaya, Queen Victoria herself, with her husband and the Prince of Wales, had come to Paris to return the Emperor's visit. It was an occasion which few could fail to find moving. For though Victoria had spent a few quiet days in Paris in the year before her accession,[1] yet no reigning sovereign of England had set foot within its walls since that December day, four centuries and more ago, when a ten-year-old boy, the ill-fated Henry VI, had been crowned there king of a distracted country. And in those four centuries there was scarcely a continent or ocean where English and French had not fought in well-matched rivalry for Empire. Could this indeed be the end of all that strife ? At any rate the event was worth the watching.

Upon Louis, who had gone to Boulogne to meet his guests, other and nearer memories from the past must have pressed with questions no less challenging. Although the morning was perfect, and a broiling sun beat down upon the placid Channel, the English squadron was late ; the Emperor rode up to the heights above the town, that he might thence be able to catch the first glimpse of its coming. No sail was visible on the horizon, but in the castle behind him and the harbour before, Louis could hardly fail to find the wherewithal to occupy his thoughts. For in the one he had been imprisoned, in the other wounded and all but drowned, on another August morning fifteen years ago.[2] That was after another landing at Boulogne, when as an exiled pretender he had failed ignominiously to win over its tiny garrison to be his first regiment in a new return from Elba. But suddenly he was jerked back into the present, and almost once again to death in those same waters of Boulogne. Halting his horse but a short distance from the overhanging cliff, he had let fall the reins upon its neck in order to manipulate with both hands a pair of field-glasses which he had raised to his eyes. Suddenly the horse started forward, the Emperor's hat flew off, and it was only by dropping the glasses to the ground and reining in his steed with whatever of skill and muscle

---

[1] *Martin*, iii. 357.   [2] *Simpson*, 167 *sq.*

he still possessed, that he succeeded in pulling it back upon
its haunches within a few feet of the cliff's edge. A less
expert equestrian would scarcely have escaped disaster :
as it was, the Emperor later maintained that no bombs or
bullets of would-be assassins had ever shown him death so
nearly as he had seen it for one moment on the cliffs of
Boulogne.[1]

For the rest, the day passed without mischance. In the
evening the Emperor found himself driving down his new
Boulevard de Strasbourg with the Queen of England by his
side ; through crowds whose enthusiasm was somewhat
damped by the fact that the visitors arrived several hours
late, and that the Queen drove through Paris in the straw-
bonnet in which she had crossed the Channel.[2] The remainder of the visit however was a brilliant success. In
the deepening twilight the cavalcade passed through the
Emperor's new park—the Bois de Boulogne—to his palace
at St Cloud, where the Queen found ' everything magnificent, and all very quiet and royal.' [3] The eight days of
her ' most eventful, interesting and delightful visit ' were
fully occupied alike for host and guests. There were of
course the inevitable balls, state dinners, visits to the opera
and to the Exhibition itself. But there were also quiet
breakfasts with the Emperor upon bright summer morn-
ings, ' the coffee quite excellent, the cooking very plain
and very good, the servants very quiet and attentive ; ' [4]
intimate confabulations protracted by long exchanges
between Albert and the Emperor of old German songs and
memories ; [5] drives incognito through the city ; confidential
discussions about the war, the commanders, the alliance,
and the general understanding of the two nations. The
Emperor told the Queen something of his difficulties with
his ministers ; how one had even warned him that the
English alliance had reconciled France to the fall of Louis
Philippe. ' I answered him,' continued the Emperor,
' " Louis Philippe n'est pas tombé à cause de son alliance

[1] *Vizetelly*, 84.   [2] *Guardian*, 29 Aug. 55
[3] *Martin*, iii. 322.   [4] *Ibid.*, 325.
[5] *Ibid.*, 324.

avec l'Angleterre, mais parce qu'il n'était pas sincère avec l'Angleterre." ' But no difficulties of detail should deter him from breaking through the anti-English tradition : for himself he cared only ' *pour les grandes choses.*' [1] Later the Queen broached the somewhat delicate question of her relations with the exiled Orleanists in England ; Walewski had given her to understand that her mere refusal to drop these friends and relatives in their adversity would be displeasing to the Emperor. 'That,' replied the Emperor, ' was just like Walewski : ' adding that of course he quite understood that she could not abandon friends in misfortune.[2] The Queen was impressed by her host's ' tact and good feeling ' in what might have been an awkward discussion, and particularly gratified to find all Louis Philippe's restorations at Versailles intact ; neither there nor at St Cloud had any of his handiwork been destroyed.[3] Later in the reign, indeed, the Pont Louis Philippe, an insignificant iron structure, was rebuilt more spaciously in stone. But although rebuilt it was not renamed, for Louis Napoleon had none of his successors' desire to obliterate the emblems of preceding reigns.[4] The Third Republic could not rest until it had removed every symbol or name or date that could remind Paris that ever a Second Empire had existed. Ten, twenty, thirty years after its downfall, if any stray cipher of the Empire was found to have survived unnoticed upon some distant cornice, gangs of republican masons were dispatched post-haste to deface it, prompt as fire-brigades to extinguish whatever might kindle memories of the departed regime.

But it was through streets still proclaiming themselves the handiwork of the new Empire that Louis with his guests drove daily in this brilliant summer's week. ' Paris

---

[1] *Martin,* iii. 332. *Cf.* pp. 28, 29 above.

[2] *Martin,* iii. 344. ' Perhaps the Emperor knew that he had not a great deal of tact,' was the Prince Consort's reply to a previous question of his host about Walewski. ' " None at all," said the Emperor.' *Ibid.,* 118. Yet Walewski was his chosen representative at his most important embassy.

[3] *Q.V.L.,* iii. 136, 138. His monogram survived in 1854 on the plate and even the napkins of the Tuileries. *Ernest,* ii. 60.

[4] v. *Fraser,* 56. And on his equal respect for the insignia of the Bourbons, v. *Castellane,* v. 102.

is signally transfigured,' wrote the Prince Consort some
days later to his Uncle of the Belgians, ' by the Rue de
Rivoli, the Boulevard de Strasbourg, the completion of
the Louvre, the great open square in front of the Hôtel de
Ville, the completion of the Palais de Justice, and restoration of the Sainte Chapelle, and specially by the laying
out of the ornamental grounds in the Bois de Boulogne. . . .
How all this could have been done in so short a time, no
one comprehends.' [1] Yet at every turn there was enough
of the old to recall memories and contrasts of other days.
Once while they were out driving together the Emperor
suddenly drew the Queen's attention to the Conciergerie :
repeating thus the little gesture that had been so successful
in London.   ' That,' he said, ' is where I was in prison : ' [2]
and indeed fifteen years earlier he had been a hand-cuffed
prisoner within its walls.   On another day host and guests
visited the Hôtel des Invalides ; and by torch-light, in a
heavy thunderstorm, to the strains of ' God save the Queen '
played in slow time from the organ, the grand-daughter
of George III upon the arm of another Emperor of the
French, surveyed the coffin of Napoleon.[3]

This scene was the climax though not the conclusion of
the visit, which was favoured with the same unbroken
sunshine and enthusiasm which had marked the Emperor's
stay in England.   On their way home the Emperor once
more accompanied his guests to Boulogne.   There they
reviewed an army of forty thousand men, on the very sands
where Napoleon had mustered his army for the invasion
of England.[4]   It was only after dinner, at about eleven,
that they drove through the illuminated town to the actual
embarkation on the Queen's yacht.   Even then the final
farewells were postponed.   It was a magnificent moon-
light night, and the Emperor put out with his guests a
little way to sea.   After they had left the harbour, he was
shown over the yacht and admired its size : he would have
one like it, but smaller, for himself.   ' I said he must build

[1] *Martin*, iii. 153.   [2] *Martin*, iii. 325, v. *Simpson*, 185.
[3] *Martin*, iii. 338.   *Q.V.L.*, iii. 139.
[4] *Martin*, iii. 344.

one of the same size; to which he replied, "*Cela va pour la Reine des Mers, mais pas pour un terrestrien comme moi.*" [1] It was the last of a series of compliments and courtesies which certainly did not lack their effect. 'Wonderful it is,' wrote the Queen a week later, 'that this *man*—whom certainly we were *not* overwell disposed to—should become *personally* our friend, and this entirely by his *own personal* qualities, in spite of so much that *was and could* be said against him. . . . Without attempting to do anything particular to *make* one like him, or ANY personal attraction in outward appearance, he *has* the power of *attaching* those to him who come near him and know him, which is *quite incredible.*' [2]

'I know *no* one,' she continued in the same letter, ' who puts me more at my ease, or to whom I feel more inclined to talk unreservedly, or in whom involuntarily I should be more inclined to confide, than the Emperor. He was entirely at his ease with us . . . never making *des phrases* or paying compliments—so full of tact, good taste, high breeding. . . . He is quite *The Emperor*, yet in no way playing it; the court and whole house infinitely more *royal* and better managed than in poor Louis Philippe's time, when all was in great noise and confusion.' [3] ' I felt,' she added—' I do not know how to express it—safe with him. His society is particularly agreeable and pleasant; there is something fascinating, melancholy, and engaging, which draws you to him, in spite of any *prévention* you may have against him.' [4]

But the Emperor's conquests after all concerned France less than did his army's; and even the festivities which this royal visit crowned could not really distract Paris altogether from the fate of the combatants before Sevastopol. Little as the country was interested in the ostensible cause of the struggle, it had not ceased to concern France that her armies, upon whatever quarrel engaged, should fight with honour and success. The emotion with which men had learnt of the failure of the assault in June had been

---

[1] *Martin*, iii. 349.
[2] *Q.V.L.*, iii. 140.
[3] *Ibid.*, 139.
[4] *Martin*, iii. 157.

none the less profound that it was not clamorous in its
manifestation ; and in the brilliant summer months which
followed it had been something of an affectation in Paris
as in her ruler to admit no abatement of the former festivities.   Just because the fortunes of war had been dubious,
all action must be avoided which might seem to admit
that its ultimate issue had been placed in doubt.   Nero
has fiddled desperately before now, lest men should even
suspect that Rome was burning.

How far these uninterrupted festivities were from arguing
a real indifference as to the war was soon seen when at
last from the Crimea there came news of decisive success.
For a moment when the first despatch was posted respecting
the capture of the Malakoff, Paris still hung back ; fearful
that a rumour so often falsified might prove false once
again.   But when next day a fuller telegram announced
that Sevastopol had really been abandoned by the Russians,
and the cannon of the Invalides boomed out their confirmation of the news—still more when the detailed reports
which followed proved that the victory had been not
merely decisive, but French—then at last Paris abandoned
herself to rejoicings so whole-hearted and enthusiastic as
to betray by contrast how forced had been the former
gaieties.   Nor was the present ebullition of gladness any
mere martial ardour ; the news was welcome as an achieved
triumph in war ; but it was more welcome still as conveying
a renewed hope of peace.

But in England the news gave rise to very different
emotions.   Already, a fortnight before the capture of the
Malakoff, Palmerston had protested in advance against the
assumption that the end of the siege should automatically
be regarded as the end of the war.   On the contrary ' our
danger will then begin : a danger of peace, not a danger
of war. . . . We shall not yet have obtained those decisive
successes which would entitle us to insist on such terms as
will effectually curb the ambition of Russia for the future.' [1]
In this attitude the Premier had the general support of

[1] *Ashley*, ii. 100.

military opinion. The War Office by dint of large expenditure had at last placed itself in a condition to conduct war ; and it was anxious now for an opportunity of effacing the memory of its earlier ineptitudes. After having to fight when one was not prepared, it would be the crowning unfairness to be prevented from fighting when one was. And throughout England there prevailed well-grounded confidence, not confined to the War Office itself, that that body could not fail to improve in 1856 upon its performance of 1855.[1]

But if a precipitate peace were to be deprecated while Sevastopol still stood, a thousand times more was the prospect of it rendered unpalatable by the circumstances of that city's fall. For that fall had spelt not only a French victory but an English defeat. Of this fact Raglan's successor had made no secret. ' The assault on the Malakoff,' he wrote in a curt telegram, ' has been successful, and the work is in possession of the French : the attack of the English against the Redan did not succeed.'[2] Both to this despatch, and to its longer successor, its readers took grave exception on grounds of style :[3] indeed it may be admitted that Simpson, while no more fitted than his predecessor for the command of men, was much that predecessor's inferior in the command of words.

But defeat for its announcement involves a heavier tax than victory upon a general's prose ; and the tale of it is in any case exposed to sterner criticism. Else the very bluntness of Simpson's first announcement might have impressed England, as it impressed France,[4] by its proud disdain of excuse, extenuation or euphemism of any kind. But his second and fuller despatch was a confused confession of an enterprise plainly mismanaged : and details later forthcoming from other sources made the tale worse hearing still. For on the heels of the news that the attack had been made with an inadequate force, and without proper provision for its support, appeared a detailed account

---

[1] *Martin*, iii. 389.   [2] *Times*, 10 Sept. 55, p. 6, c. 6.
[3] E.g. *Nolan*, ii. 482. Cp. *Panmure*, ii. 407.
[4] And not a few of the British troops actually serving in the Crimea ; v. *Campbell*, 334.

in the *Times*[1] suggesting that the attacking troops had
refused to deliver the attack, and the supporting force
refused to support it. ' Someone had blundered ' again :
but in this instance the unreasoning command of a general
had not been redeemed by unreasoning obedience in the
men.

Briefly, Europe was informed that in the actual attack
on the Redan the front rank had entered it with ease ;[2]
but that though it was at first but feebly defended, the
utmost gallantry and exertions of their officers had failed
to induce the men to any further advance. It had been
in vain that boys fresh from school stood erect upon the
wall, exposed to every shot as they beckoned their troops
to follow them :[3] in vain that with orders, oaths, and
finally even with fists[4] they strove to get them forward ;
the men would only shoot from behind the shelter of the
parapet, until the Russians reinforced drove them back
into their trenches. The incident was due to the operation
of entirely exceptional causes : but of the result there were
no two opinions in the English camp; in the words of
' Redan ' Windham—the one man in authority who emerged
from that day's proceedings with military reputation not
merely intact but enhanced—it was felt to be ' the greatest
disgrace that had ever fallen on the British soldier.'[5]

In part the disaster had been due to General Simpson's
decision that certain divisions ' should have the honour of
the assault from the circumstance of their having defended
the batteries and approaches against the Redan for so many
months, and from the intimate knowledge they possessed

---

[1] *Times*, 26 Sept. 55, pp. 6 and 7. The publication gave rise to natural
indignation : ' I trust the army will lynch the *Times* correspondent,'
wrote the gentle Herbert next day. *Stanmore*: *Herbert*, ii. 1. But the
Times report was endorsed by the later accounts of officers concerned :
Campbell, 317 *sq*. *Ranken*, 52. *Sterling*, 311, 327 *sq*. *Windham*, 205 *sq*.
Wood, 373.

[2] *Hamley*, 282.   [3] *Campbell*, 317.

[4] *Windham*, 206.

[5] ' He put his hand on my shoulder and said, " I could have forgiven
them if they had been beaten out, but they would not go in. These may
be the last words I shall ever say to you, but I declare they are true." . . .
I shall be anxious to see how his report is worded. If he praises the
gallantry of the men, I shall lose the last shred of faith in public documents.'
Campbell, 319.

of the ground.' [1]   The choice proved doubly unfortunate.
The divisions in question had suffered heavy casualties in
the last few months : and the gaps thus created in their
ranks had recently been made good by large drafts of raw
recruits.[2]   Moreover the actual war experience even of the
rest had been largely a training in taking cover ; and when
suddenly bidden to storm their old familiar obstacle no
heroism of their officers could rally them effectively from
defence to attack.   The men were oppressed by memories
of previous failure in June ; and still more by reports that
this Redan which they were now again bidden to assault
had in the interval been elaborately mined : so that as
soon as they had succeeded in ousting the last Russian from
the fort they must expect themselves to be blown sky-
high with their conquest by their retreating foes.[3]   Such
a belief naturally did not enhance their appetite for
victory.[4]

The immediate importance of the incident was due to
the partial and mischievous publication of the facts.   Such
publication was calculated and perhaps intended to make
the event thus advertised seem intolerable [5] as the last
act of the war : [6] it was not to such a scene as this that
England had looked, when eighteen months ago she had
let loose the war which was to revive in alliance with the
new Napoleon the glories won in conflict with the old.
Hence it was in vain that the allied victory was announced
in England as an occasion of national rejoicing ; in vain

[1] Simpson's despatch, 9 Sept. 55.   *Times*, 22 Sept. 55.
[2] *Times*, 27 Sept. 55, p. 6, c. 2.   Cp. *Siege of Sebastopol*, ii, 539.
[3] *Times*, *ibid*.   *Calthorpe*, ii. 412.   *Windham*, 188.
[4] The report was true as well of the Malakoff as of the Redan : but
the Russians were prevented by the French from blowing up the former ;
(*Calthorpe*, ii. 408, 417 : *Skene*, 309), and after the failure of the English
attack on the Redan they purposely refrained, on their evacuation of it,
from exploding their magazine there, lest they should kill the English
wounded.   *Sterling*, 334.   *Shadwell*, i. 385
[5] 'The Queen cannot conceal from Lord Clarendon what *her own* feelings
and wishes at this moment are.   They *cannot* be for peace *now*, for she is
convinced that this country would *not* stand in the eyes of Europe as she
ought, and as the Queen is convinced she *would* after *this* year's campaign
. . . it would cost her more than words can express to conclude a peace
with *this* as the end.'   *Q.V.L.*, iii. 163.
[6] Kinglake avoided it by closing his history with the death of Raglan.

that Pélissier in the despatch announcing his own success
praised the valour of the English troops, deliberately
exaggerating by one-third the distance that their charge
had to cover.[1] In London there was no general illumination [2] and England as a whole cried the more vehemently
for war. The government affected to be pleased by the
cry : but in reality it was an encore of doubtful import ;
less an intimation that the performance was good, than a
demand that it should be bettered.

To this clamour in any case, with no too curious enquiry
as to its motives, press and premier lent willing ear.
Palmerston composed a 'long and able memorandum ' to
the effect that Russia was not yet ' half beaten enough ' ; [3]
while the *Times* explained to its docile readers that the
capture of Sevastopol must only be regarded as ' a preliminary operation.' [4]

But there were limits to the persuasive powers even of
the most potent of newspapers and most dictatorial of
prime ministers. Europe as a whole refused to regard as
a mere prelude to the real business of war, an operation
which had cost the lives of more than half a million men.
From the Tuileries the French Emperor did for a moment
urge upon his victorious general a further and vigorous
advance ; [5] by the admission of the Russians themselves
such an advance immediately after the fall of Sevastopol
must almost certainly have compelled the evacuation of
the entire Crimea.[6] But Pélissier had no wish to risk the
laurels he had already won ; [7] and neither success to follow
nor failure to retrieve could stir Simpson to any adventure
whatever. After prodding him vainly for the better part

---

[1] *Nolan*, ii. 480. It was out of deference to the susceptibilities of the
British Army that the title Duc de Malakoff was given him, instead of
Duc de Sebastopol, as had been at first intended. F.O. France, Cowley
to Clarendon, 14 Aug. 56. ' The French army are trying to soothe us
with compliments so overdone that we cannot help seeing through the
grimaces which accompany them.' Cobden to Bright, 30 Sept. 55. *Morley* : *Cobden*, ii. 172,
[2] *Register*, 1855, 148.   [3] *Argyll*, i. 589.
[4] *La Gorce* : *Empire*, i. 252.
[5] *La Gorce* : *Empire*, i. 446.   *Paul*, i. 420.
[6] v. *Martin*, iii. 369 n.
[7] *La Gorce* : *Empire*, i. 447.

of two months Palmerston had him replaced [1] by Sir
William Codrington, an officer who proved unable to
attain success even by its easiest avenue. He failed
although he succeeded a failure.

But by this time it mattered little who held the English
command, for by this time the French Emperor had
come to acquiesce in the passive rôle adopted by his own
commander-in-chief. On merely military grounds, further
action in the Crimea soon became unpromising enough.
The Russians, once they had recovered from their first
disarray after the fall of Sevastopol, lost no time in
strengthening their position to the north of the harbour,
and in placing the remaining Crimean towns in a posture
of defence. To advance inland now towards Simferopol
was but to invite a second winter's siege of some second
Sevastopol ; and such a siege once started must have
rendered peace all but impossible for the allies until it
too should have been carried to a triumphant conclusion.
Even so the process was capable of indefinite repetition
and gave promise of no definite result. France moreover
had reasons of her own for wishing the war ended. An
entire reversal had by this time been effected in the condition and achievements of the allied armies in the Crimea.
In the first winter the French troops, with something less
than their share of the honours of battle behind them, were
in health and efficiency immensely superior to the English
contingent. Now, satisfied with the almost undivided
glory alike of the last victory in the field and the last
triumphant assault upon the fortress, they were yet in
all matters of equipment, organisation and consequent
physical well-being as much behind the English as they
had hitherto been in advance of them.[2]

But it was not the military situation only which inclined

[1] Simpson resigned, and gave as the cause of his resignation ' a rough
telegraphic message, or as we now call it a telegram, from Panmure.'
Palmerston to Argyll, 13 Oct. 55. *Argyll*, i. 585.

[2] Deaths from disease in the last four months of 1855 showed, as compared with the corresponding period in the previous year, a decrease of 80
per cent. in the English mortality, coupled with an increase of over 60
per cent. in the French. *Longmore*, 17 *sq*. *Graham*, 120. *Home*, 64.

France to peace. As yet the apparent prosperity of the Empire had been unaffected by the financial burdens of the war ; but those who best knew the real resources of the country knew best that they could not without grave injury sustain a long continuance of such expenditure.[1] Indirectly too, by the far larger armies which she was employing in the war, France as compared with England was incurring a far heavier tax on the vitality of the nation as a whole. No single French interest was served by the continuance of the war ; nor after the capture of the Malakoff could even the honour of the army demand further vindication. As a result, the English people had not more longed for war in the autumn of 1853, than did the French for peace in the autumn of 1855.

The desire, it was true, though as deeply felt was less loudly proclaimed. Peace in its advocates is ever less clamorous than war ; and political advocacy of any kind at this period was necessarily more restrained in France than in England. But though no regime more than the Second Empire had muffled the ordinary organs of public opinion, no ruler more than Louis Napoleon was quick to catch the faintest nuance of popular censure or approbation. He did not allow men to shout, but he was very far from deaf.[2]

It was however no easy task which confronted the French Emperor if he were to combine a due deference to the ardent desires of his own subjects for peace with a loyal observance of his obligations towards an ally still bent on war. In England Palmerston, hitherto the Emperor's staunchest ally, was now become his most formidable opponent. Not merely had the English premier the wildest ideas of the conditions which could be imposed

---

[1] A fact later admitted even by the militant Cowley. 'Time tends to prove that there was far greater necessity for France to make peace than I had any idea of at this period last year.' F.O. France, Cowley to Clarendon, 13 Feb. 57.

[2] At the Archives Nationales, Series F 1c III. and BB 30/367, *sq.*— reports of prefects and procureurs généraux from the departments— both give the impression of a government with its ear to the ground, extraordinarily anxious to inform itself of every movement of popular opinion.

on Russia,[1] but he had not the faintest conception how overwhelming was the desire of France for peace. Like the rest of his countrymen he attributed the Emperor's anxiety for it merely to ' the Cabal of stock-jobbing politicians by whom he is surrounded ' who ' *must* give way to him if he is firm.' [2] Like them too he was honestly unaware that the objects of the war were mainly English and the sacrifices of it mainly French. And thanks to the circumstances attending the failure on the Redan, and the advertisement given to them by the *Times*, Palmerston still seemed to have behind him the public opinion of England in his demands for another campaign.

It was in this emergency, while matters seemed drifting hopelessly to an indefinite prolongation of the war, that the French Emperor rendered to his country and to Europe what was perhaps the greatest service in the region of mere diplomacy that ever he rendered to either. But one emotion remained strong enough at this moment to reconcile the apparently irreconcilable antagonisms of England and Russia : Satan only could cast out Satan : mutual jealousies could be dwarfed by common fear. It was to Louis' discernment in recognising, and skill in utilising, a potential factor of such fear, that Europe owed it that the capture of Sevastopol proved a preliminary not—as the *Times* had wished—to a lasting war, but to a speedy peace. Before the startled vision of friend and foe he let loom for an instant the lamentable figure of Poland.

Already, within a few days of the news that Sevastopol was fallen, he had sent an urgent message to England,

[1] ' He seems to have laid down no principles on the subject, but merely thinks the more you can get the better. The more you ask the more you are likely to get, and whatever is worst for Russia must be best for England.' Herbert to Gladstone, 16 Nov. 55.   *Stanmore: Herbert*, ii. 12.

[2] Palmerston to Victoria, 17 Jan. 56. The few Englishmen on the spot knew better. From Paris three days later the Duke of Cambridge wrote to the Queen : ' France wishes for peace more than anything else on earth, and this feeling does not confine itself to Walewski or the Ministers—it extends itself to all classes. The Emperor alone is reasonable and sensible in this respect, but his position is a most painful one, and he feels it very much. The fact is that public opinion is much more felt and more loudly expressed in this country than anybody in England at all imagines.' *Q.V.L.*, iii. 166, 167.

asking ' us to engage not to make peace until the conditions respecting Poland agreed to in 1815 were recognised and fulfilled by Russia.'[1] Clarendon at once wrote objecting to a proposal which he regarded as 'ill-advised and inopportune.'[1] From that moment the Emperor sought peace. Despite his injunctions to his own general the moment for reaping the full military advantages of the Crimean success had been allowed to pass unused ; despite his suggestions to his ally the result of military success even if it were gained was to be politically useless. To free Poland he was willing to spend France further ; but not for barren advantages upon the Black Sea.

The manner in which England met his suggestion was such as to convince the Emperor that his ally would be no partner in a war of liberation. But if he could not make war for Poland, by Poland he might make peace. The evident repugnance with which the British government regarded the mere prospect of such a crusade was proof that here he had the means of making a continuance of the campaign unpalatable not only to his enemy, but to his ally.

It was therefore to the gaze of Russia next that Louis proceeded to conjure up his most uncomfortable apparition. In that country the new Czar, upon the fall of Sevastopol, seemed to have abated nothing of his hopes or claims : the proclamation [2] which he issued to the defenders of the city breathed still the old confidence in a divine protection of Holy Russia ; an affectation peculiarly exasperating to the English people, accustomed themselves also in their wars to claim a monopoly of that favour. To accuse the Deity of pro-Russian proclivities seemed the unpardonable blasphemy of all. The new Czar's utterances it is true were in this respect a trifle less full-blooded than his

[1] Clarendon to Granville, 16 Sept. 55. *Maxwell,* ii. 93. F.O. France, Cowley to Clarendon, 16 Sept. 55. *Argyll,* i. 583. *Fitzmaurice,* i. 121. And more generally, on the attitude of Palmerston on the same matter, and his frustration of Louis Napoleon's repeated efforts to extract some advantage for Poland from the war, v. *Diplomatic Study,* i. 287 ; ii. 340.

[2] A proclamation ' in which there was the same assumption of being on the side of God and the only true religion which so much disgraced the state papers of Nicholas.' *Nolan,* ii. 488.

father's ; there was an element of modesty for example in his proclamation to Moscow, on the eve of a tour of his southern provinces with which he sought to counteract the impression produced by the fall of Sevastopol. Providence, he admitted, had sent a year of sad trials to Russia. ' But. . . the Lord has always given her His tacit support.' [1] Nicholas would never have been content with that. In the general course of his voyage however Alexander abstained from any overture for peace ; busying himself instead about the rebuilding of his Black Sea fleet, and issuing decrees for the still further increase of his army.

It was while the Czar was thus engaged that Louis Napoleon revealed to him with sudden sobering effect the price of further war. Though refraining from open negotiations for peace, Russia was not unwilling by means of informal intermediaries [2] in Paris to ascertain the true disposition of the French Emperor towards her. One of the first men thus employed was Pfordten, the prime minister of Bavaria, ostensibly a visitor to the closing exhibition of Paris ; it was through him that Louis conveyed to the Czar his deliberately disquieting intimation. He desired peace, he said, and for the present was willing to make it on most moderate terms. ' But if by the spring no understanding shall have been attained, I will appeal to the nationalities, and in particular to the nation of Poland.' [3]

It only remained that these secret overtures should be converted by means of a formal mediation into direct negotiations for peace. The formal mediator was found once more in that old arbitrator Austria. Conscious that she had gravely offended the Western Powers by her final refusal in the spring of 1855 to fulfil the spirit of her promise, and to translate her former mediation into armed intervention in their favour, Austria in the months that followed

[1] *Register*, 1855, 266.   [2] E.g. *Beust*, i. 142.
[3] *La Gorce : Empire*, i. 455. ' It was impossible in our time,' he told Duke Ernest in September, ' to carry on great wars, and make great political arrangements, which were opposed to the interests of the nations. The voice of the nations would always break through again.' *Ernest*, ii. 195.

had endeavoured by an extremely benevolent neutrality to ingratiate herself once more with her former benefactor Russia. But a benefactor estranged is not easily restored to a condition of benevolence : and the fall of Sevastopol had now convinced Austria that in this case the effort was no longer worth the making.

Already Louis Napoleon had hinted to Russia that she would be wise to come to terms quickly. Now he proceeded to intimate to Austria and the German neutrals in general that it might be worth their while to accelerate Russia in her processes of thought. This intimation also was circuitous in form ; but unlike the other it was public in its occasion. The first great exhibition of Paris was closing ; and in closing it the Emperor made a speech. The *Palais de l'Industrie* was an immense building ; previous speakers in it had been completely inaudible ; for this reason only a few perfunctory remarks completely non-political in character were expected. But the Emperor's first words startled the great crowd into astonished attention by being uttered in a voice which carried loud and clear to the remotest corner of the building. For the rest his opening sentences were in no way remarkable in themselves. The mere fact that Paris had held this most successful exhibition, and entertained so distinguished and cosmopolitan a gathering of visitors, in the midst of a severe war, was proof, said the Emperor, both of France's confidence in itself, and of Europe's confidence in France. ' All of you,' he continued, ' who think that the progress of the agriculture, the industry, and the commerce of one nation contribute to the welfare of all others, and that the more reciprocal relations are multiplied, the more national prejudices are effaced, I would have tell your fellow-citizens, in returning to your homes, that France entertains no hatred against any nation, and that her sympathies extend to all who wish, like her, the triumph of right and justice.'

But from this soothing exordium Louis passed abruptly to a disquieting conclusion. ' Tell them,' he continued, ' that if they desire peace they must openly express wishes

either for us or against us ; for in the midst of a serious
European conflict indifference is a bad calculation, and
silence a mistake.' [1]   The beginning of the speech had been
applauded as a mere tribute to its declamation : the close
was marked by an outburst of astonishing enthusiasm, in
which the three thousand English who were present were
particularly vehement.   Members of the diplomatic corps,
without waiting for the rest of the proceedings, made off
as soon as they could do so unobserved : the Prussian
minister, Count Hatzfeld, actually ' climbing over seats and
disarranging the carefully laid folds of diplomatic ladies'
dresses ' [2] in his haste, followed with slightly more decorum
and delay by his Austrian colleague Baron Hübner.   The
English ambassador was observed to watch the exodus
with a very obvious relish.   Exactly what missives the
retreating ministers sent home after their race to the
telegraph office can only be guessed ; but certainly they
sufficed to throw both the Germanies into a state of extraordinary perturbation.   So great was the commotion,
especially in Austria, that the French foreign minister
thought it wise to issue a diplomatic circular explaining
that the Emperor had meant no more than he said.   But
Austria retained an uncomfortable conviction that though
meaning no more he probably meant no less.   Moreover in
the private ear of Austria also Louis had caused to be
murmured that unblessed word Nationality ;   a word
which spelt to Austria not Poland only, but Hungary and
Italy as well.   It was a hint to which there was already
Piedmont to give point.

Accordingly Austria proceeded to produce yet another
scheme of pacification ; including besides the old statement
of the three points already accepted by Russia, a new and
more stringent version of the fourth, which ensured the
neutralisation of the Black Sea.   In addition a still more
unpalatable demand was now included for the cession of
half of Bessarabia.   Moreover Austria was now prepared
to present these terms with a plain intimation that their
rejection would involve the recall of her ambassador from

[1] *Nolan*, ii. 629.   [2] ' *Malakoff*,' i. 94, 95.

Petersburg. In his anxiety to obtain the certain support
of Austria, Walewski submitted these proposals to the
British government with a peremptory and unwarrantable
request that they should be accepted as they stood.   The
English cabinet naturally resented such cavalier treatment ;
but so urgent was the Emperor's language that it agreed to
the presentation of the terms with the addition only of a
few minor inconveniences for Russia ; [1] one of which
however, the neutralisation of the Sea of Azof, was of a
nature which Austria would certainly refuse to urge, and
Russia almost certainly refuse to yield.

At this point Louis resolved upon a new and even more
direct personal intervention. Already once he had allowed
England to dissuade him from a peace to which both he
and France had been inclined ; he could not afford to be
baulked of it again by a concession still more distasteful
to his people. [2] Accordingly by the ordinary channels of
diplomacy [3] he first conveyed to the British government
his grave objections to this new demand, which he regarded
as at once useless and provocative. Then, availing himself
of the intimate relations which in the last six months he
had established between himself and the English sovereign,
he wrote a letter direct to Queen Victoria. [4] Once more
he made play with Poland. He had spoken of Poland
before that Russia might be persuaded to accept moderate
terms : he returned to Poland now, that England might
be persuaded to grant them. [5] The letter began with an
apology for its form, on the plea that it was written in haste ;
and for its matter, on the ground that ' we have reached

[1] v. *Argyll*, i. 597.
[2] As also to the small English peace party. Thus *Greville*, 5 Dec. 55 :
' My own opinion and hope is that he will refuse to give way to us now
as he did last May.'
[3] F.O. France, Cowley to Clarendon, 22 Nov. 55.
[4] 22 Nov. 55. *Martin*, iii. 524.
[5] ' How does it illustrate the madness of our combative countrymen
when one can only turn with hope for peace to the coercion of a Bonaparte
upon the deliberations of our Cabinet.' Cobden to Bright, 18 Sept. 55.
Morley : *Cobden*, ii. 176. *Cp.* Gladstone to Panizzi, 14 Dec. 55. ' My wife
has been . . . what Louis Napoleon is to England. She covers all my
shortcomings.' B.M. Add. MSS. 36,717, f. 239.

one of those critical moments when we ought to speak very frankly to one another.'

Frank the letter certainly was. ' I begin,' wrote the Emperor, ' by repelling any idea which might lead to the belief that the French government would be constrained to make peace, although the conditions were not good, just as I should myself refuse to entertain the idea that the English government would be forced to continue the war if the conditions of peace *were* good. We are, I take it, both of us free in our actions, we have the same interests, we desire the same result ; an honourable peace.' Then came a review of the military situation, which entailed an implied though not an explicit reminder that even now the French troops engaged were three or four times as numerous as the English. During the greater part of the war the disparity had been in fact far greater ; but England as a whole at no time realised that there existed any disparity at all. Here then was the Queen, wrote her ally, with 50,000 foot and 10,000 horse in the East ; and here was he with 34,000 cavalry and 200,000 infantry : but both of them together, though capable of injuring Russia, unable by mere continuance of the present operations to *subdue* her. Three courses remained ; either to make the war smaller, reducing it to little more than a mere defensive blockade, by which the allies at a minimum of expense to themselves might impose large expenditure and inconvenience on Russia ; or to make the war greater, by launching a universal appeal to nationalities, with a bold proclamation of the independence as well of Poland and Finland as of Hungary, Italy and Circassia ; or to make the war end, by securing an understanding with Austria, enabling the allies to mobilise against Russia so overwhelming a body of troops and of public opinion, as would compel her to accept an equitable peace. The third course seemed the more attractive that it was not the allies who had been invited to make concessions to secure the support of Austria, but Austria which had voluntarily adopted and even strengthened the old terms of the allies. ' To such an offer, how can we reason-

ably reply by a refusal, or by equivocations tantamount to
a refusal ? '

The Emperor concluded his undiplomatic epistle on
another note. ' If,' he concluded, ' your majesty's government were to say that the conditions of peace ought to be
of quite another kind ; that our honour and interests
demand a remodelling of the map of Europe ; that Europe
would never be free until Poland was re-established, the
Crimea restored to Turkey, and Finland to Sweden, then
I could comprehend a policy which would contain an element of grandeur, and would place the results to be gained
on a level with the sacrifices to be made. But to deprive
ourselves gratuitously of the support of Austria, for micro-
scopical advantages, advantages which we could always
claim later, that is a step which I cannot bring myself to
regard as reasonable.' [1]

The Emperor's letter, though unwelcome, did not come
to England as a surprise. A week earlier, his remark that
France had no hatreds ' had generally been interpreted as
a rebuke of Palmerston's bellicose attitude.[2] And a month
before he had informed his ally that he was meditating
the recall of 100,000 men from the Crimea ; on the ground
that public opinion in France would not tolerate the maintenance of so large a force in complete inactivity for six
months' useless exposure to the hardships of a Crimean
winter.[3] This recall if it were executed would mean an
immediate adoption of Louis' first alternative, ' a sort of
war ' at the minimum of expense and effort ; it suggested
also a step towards his second and more formidable proposal of war on a grander scale for grander objects. For
once out of the Crimea it was improbable that the army
would ever return to it ; if the winter's refreshment in
France were intended as a prelude to a spring campaign
at all, that campaign would presumably be fought on a
new and nearer field. To be in France from the Crimea
was already to be half-way to Poland.

The general effectiveness of Poland as an argument

---

[1] *Martin*, iii. 524–526.   [2] *Argyll*, i. 598.
[3] *Martin*, iii. 383.

depended upon the fact of its partition, and the consequent injury threatened not only to Russia but to the two German Powers by any project for its reunion. It was in turn this latter threat which carried weight with the English court. The nation as a whole was influenced by a more general anxiety. Eager as England still was to weaken her foe, she was by this time yet more anxious not to strengthen her ally. For by this time the course of the war had already set France in the place of Russia as the strongest continental power : and to be the strongest power on the Continent was automatically to be invader-in-ordinary to the Island. It was the perpetual disability of British foreign policy, for this reason, that it never succeeded in destroying one source of anxiety without creating another in the process. At the moment it was just embarking upon one of those difficult and delicate periods during which it was left halting between two opponents.

As the result of the Emperor's letter, and of the explanations which ensued, the English cabinet reluctantly assented to forgo its demand for the neutralisation of the Sea of Azof.[1] Hence it was with only minor additions that the Austrian proposals were ultimately dispatched from Vienna in the middle of December. Two days after their dispatch the news reached England of Russia's capture of the Turkish fortress of Kars ; a final military success which Russian diplomacy endeavoured, but endeavoured vainly, to use as a means of further mitigating the already moderate peace terms of the allies.

But however moderate was his missive, it was a glacial reception which awaited the Austrian ambassador, when at the end of December he reached St Petersburg with the ultimate ultimatum of his country. Even the tentative affability of Austria in the summer had failed to secure Russia's forgiveness of her previous shortcomings : this last lapse rendered her offence unpardonable. And if the messenger were distasteful,[2] his message was more un-

---

[1] *Argyll*, i. 599.
[2] The Czar would have preferred the mediation of Prussia. F.O. France, Cowley to Clarendon, 16 Sept. 55.

welcome still. Mild as were its terms, they yet implied
on the part of Russia a definite acknowledgment of defeat.
Not merely was she to yield in December what she had
refused in June, but she was to pay for that refusal by a
cession of territory ; a cession small in extent but considerable in its consequences. Never before in her history
had Russia ceded by treaty territory which by treaty she
had obtained.[1] And small as it was the surrender now
demanded would sever her entirely from the waters of the
Danube.

Hence at the beginning of January the Czar replied by advancing counter-propositions : conceding the Four Points,
but no more. Contrary to the spirit of her understanding,
Austria communicated these counter-propositions to the
allies, by whom they were at once rejected. Forced
therefore to present her ultimatum as an ultimatum,
Austria in a last attempt to conciliate Russia added ten
days to the time limit originally imposed : but if an
answer absolute and affirmative were not forthcoming by
January 18, Russia was given to understand that Austria
would be driven to keep her word.

Whether the threat of even so portentous an occurrence
would prove effective seemed for the moment doubtful.
Throughout Europe the news that the ultimatum had been
met by counter-propositions was regarded as a sign that
negotiations had failed. And in Russia there was known
to remain a strong war party : less numerous indeed than
that which desired peace, but more articulate, and far more
accessible to the court.

But many causes combined to render the Czar desirous
of peace. Apart altogether from that disturbing threat
of a future campaign in Poland, the internal situation of
Russia was already grave enough. Far better than his
opponents, the Czar after his recent tour could realise to
what utter exhaustion his subjects had been reduced by
the drain of this continued campaign at an inaccessible
extremity of his empire. Even before the death of Nicholas
their own officials estimated that 170,000 Russians had

---

[1] *Martin*, iii. 422.

died ; and at the time of Alexander's accession a supplementary return raised the figure by nearly fifty per cent.[1]
And even the latter total had been doubled in the nine
succeeding months ; by the end of the war the Russians
calculated that they had lost half a million men.[2]

The fact was that the famous utterance of Nicholas as to
the efficacy of General Février was not the only boast of his
for which history had reserved a tragical fulfilment. Fulfilled also and to the letter was his proud prediction that
Russia would show herself in 1854 what she had been in
1812. But in this instance the Russian Expedition was to be
made and rued by Russians. It was not Generals January
and February only, but Russia herself that was turned
traitor ; so that the things which should have been her
strength became to her now an occasion of falling. And
not merely the Czar, but uncounted multitudes of his
subjects perished in consequence. The Russian winter it
is true took its toll, and no light one, of the allied armies in
the Crimea. But while it decimated Russia's invaders it
all but annihilated her defenders. It was against Russia's
own armies that her whole natural armoury was mobilised ;
her swamps, her snows, her distances, her lack of railways
and of roads. The very shells fired from Sevastopol had
to be carried two on a bullock three hundred and fifty
versts ;[3] while the men who fired them had first to face
three solid months of marching for the privilege.[4] It
took four weeks to cover even the last hundred and twenty
miles in the Crimea itself, between the isthmus of Perekop
and Sevastopol.[5] And on that march the casualties were
no mere one in ten ; it would be nearer the truth to say
that ten men must start for every one who could be counted
on to reach his journey's end. The Russia of 1854 was in
very truth the Russia of 1812. But the causes which made
her then invulnerable at the heart made her wound now

[1] *Martin*, iii. 275.   [2] *Ibid.*, 482.
[3] *Ibid.*, 482 n.   [4] *Canrobert*, ii. 568.
[5] *Skrine*, 160.   'The Russian dead who lay in piles among the Inkerman ravines were scrupulously clean, but they were half starved ; their
uniforms were thin and ragged.   Not a single article of value was found
on their persons—only long tresses of hair and portraits of their women
folk.'

most mortal at the heel. In either case the fact was discovered through an accident. The allied armies in 1854 had been forced by the failure of their intended *coup de main* to lay siege in form to Sevastopol ; just as the Russian generals of 1812 had been forced by the failure of their intended defence to fall back before Napoleon. Neither foresaw that by their very failure they had imposed upon their foe a necessity infinitely more injurious than any they could have inflicted on him by success. Yet in fact the midwinter march of relieving armies to Sevastopol had been as devastating to the strength of Russia as had been the advance on Moscow to the grand army of France.

Ten years later, when, in that way wars have, the Crimean War was beginning to look a little foolish as it became a little remote, it chanced that the Cesarevitch lay dying on the Riviera ; and Alexander in passing through France on his way to his son's deathbed found time to give an audience to his old adversary Canrobert. In melancholy and luminous retrospect the Czar lamented the Russian decision to defend Sevastopol at all. Undefended its capture would have been a barren triumph to the allies ; Russia's resources would have remained intact. As it was, ' we found ourselves,' he said, ' in the position of 1812 with the tables turned.' ' It was your luck,' he added, ' to commit the fault of not attacking Sevastopol after the Alma, when you would certainly have taken it : it was our misfortune to defend it as energetically and obstinately as we did. If you had shown more wisdom or we less energy, we should have won the war.' [1] And after dilating on the fearful wastage of men and material inflicted on his peasant armies, the Czar concluded with a sad reflection on the irony of history.

It is indeed against that sombre back-ground of Russian peasantry that all who would rightly understand the tragedy of the Crimea must conceive of it throughout. In front, the little prancing figures whose sayings and doings form the substance of this book : of this, and of others in abundance written and to be written still. But

[1] *Canrobert*, ii. 568 569.

behind—unnumbered thousands of suffering men, whose fate we do perhaps well to leave alone. It is not they who hold the stage, but the few be-medalled mighty ones : kings, courtiers, counsellors, Eminences and Excellencies of all kinds. Of these we read the correspondence and ransack the despatches, weighing their contentions, appraising their motives, making of their very follies a peg for our poor cleverness. But those Russian peasants escape our computation. They wrote no memoirs, they left no monument, their names are perished as utterly as themselves : within a hundred thousand the very number of them that died is unknown. Without count, without cause of theirs, they were led to the slaughter ; fighting at a command they could not question in a quarrel not their own. In so far as the issue of it affected them at all, they fought that their sons might be the serfs their fathers were. Victorious they had died in their chains : beaten they were to receive the little liberty they ever knew. History had its ironies for the Achæans as well as for their kings.

Helpless, hopeless, inarticulate, the almost animal suffering of untold multitudes of men remains the cost and condemnation of the war. From the mere surmise of it the historian may be forgiven if he turn hastily away ; and come scurrying back to the personages and protocols that are his proper quest and prey. At least one such personage was now actually affected by what lay behind ; for the new Czar was a humane man, and something already of the sufferings of his subjects was known by this time even to their Emperor.

Gloomy as was the prospect within his frontiers Alexander could find no comfort at all beyond them. Any momentary hope which his advisers had built upon rumours of dissension between the allies had now completely disappeared. For as soon as he had won his ally's assent to the launching of the Austrian ultimatum, the French Emperor had dispatched Seebach post-haste to Petersburg with the announcement that ' no power on earth should induce him to separate himself from England, or to take

any other line than that to which he had bound himself
in conjunction with her.' This private pronouncement
' which the Emperor made with great energy,' [1] was borne
out by his public utterances. He told the Imperial Guard,
recently recalled from the Crimea, that he had recalled
them not because the war was over, ' but because it is
only just to relieve in their turn the regiments which have
suffered most ' ; continuing in his best oracular manner,
' there is now in France a numerous and veteran army ready
to show itself wherever circumstances may demand.' To
Russia and to the German Powers as well there was a world
of vague menace in that phrase ' wherever circumstances
may demand ' : it was naturally construed as one hint
the more of a potential campaign in Poland.[2]

This was on December 29. Twelve days earlier a treaty
had been publicly ratified which proved that the western
alliance was not merely intact, but in imminent danger
of growing ; a treaty which added fresh force to the
French Emperor's threat that if the war were continued
it should be delocalised. England and France had signed
with the king of Norway and Sweden a treaty, by which
that monarch bound himself never to cede, lease or alienate
any of his territories to Russia ; and the Western Powers
in return pledged themselves never to allow Russia to take
them.[3] The treaty, it is true, was defensive : but its terms
so far as they went were stringent, and they were without
time limit ; moreover Russia rightly suspected that worse
lay behind.

The diplomatic history of the Crimean War contains no
stranger chapter than one which has hitherto remained
unopened ; revealing an entire series of secret overtures
made towards the allies during the summer and autumn
of 1855 by the smaller states of Europe. As we have seen [4]
the conception of some such coalition of the minor European
Powers against Russia had floated vaguely before the mind
of Louis Napoleon at the very outset of the war : save in

---

[1] *Greville*, 26 Dec. 55. Cf. *Martin*, iii. 407. *Maxwell*, ii. 109.
[2] *Paul*, i. 8. v. *Martin*, iii. 423.
[3] *Nolan*, ii. 631. 　　　　　[4] *Vide*, p. 253 above

the case of Piedmont, however, it was only when the Russian Goliath was tottering to his fall that the slings of these small giant-killers were offered to the allies. In general the same fact which led to the offer of their services led also to the rejection of them ; but it is none the less of interest that the offers should have been made, and in some cases seriously considered.

Of these offers the Swedish was in fact the most important. Some two months before the ratification of the published defensive treaty the King of Sweden had secretly intimated to the French Emperor his willingness to ' take an active part in the war against Russia, if the allies were disposed to attack that power seriously, in the North : ' [1] not unreasonably however he added that he must remain neutral if the hostilities were confined to their former distant field. If the allies should decide to accept his offer of help, he required only that they should give him notice before the end of January.[2]

Significant in itself, this offer was rendered additionally important by another which had preceded it. As early as July 1855 the King of Denmark had secretly intimated to Walewski that he was ready to follow Sweden in any measures which that country should decide to take against Russia. The overture was made with extraordinary precautions against discovery. It was conveyed by an agent whose visit to Paris had ostensibly no other object than to present Napoleon III with a portrait of the King of Denmark. His own ministers were kept in entire ignorance of the King's project : but this he explained was immaterial, as he was prepared to dismiss them on the spot if they proved refractory.[3]

That the Scandinavian Powers should have the will, could they but summon the courage, to strike a blow at Russia was in no way wonderful : more remarkable was the momentary prospect of help to the allies from the monarchies of the Peninsula. In the case of Portugal rumours of such assistance actually found their way into

---

[1] F.O. France, Cowley to Clarendon. ' Confidential.'   30 Oct. 55.
[2] *Ibid.*   [3] *Ibid.*, 31 July 55.

the public press : but they seem to have been based merely on the known needs of England, the historic attachment of Portugal to her cause, and the recent example of Piedmont. For when the Russian minister questioned the Portuguese government on the report, he was told that nothing had hitherto occurred to warrant it : and the English representative contented himself with urging Portugal not to allow Russia to extract any formal promise of continued neutrality.[1]

But at Madrid a more enterprising ambassador was engaged in an active intrigue for the winning of Spanish support. The rumours of Portuguese intervention seemed to Lord Howden to afford a stimulus by means of which Spain might be brought to fight : in the middle of February 1855 he telegraphed to Clarendon his belief that ' if Portugal could be brought to follow Sardinia ' Spain could be brought to follow Portugal.[2] Pride, and the desire to rescue Spain from its present diplomatic isolation, would, he thought, prove sufficient incentives.[3] The idea at any rate of such action Howden proceeded to instil into the Spanish premier's mind, ' with the chance of a favourable fermentation there ' : nor had he any reason to be disappointed with the result. For on the same evening that it was propounded, the suggestion was conveyed to the Council of Ministers, and by them favourably received.[4]

The desire of the Spanish government to emulate the exploits of Piedmont was natural enough. In this the worst-governed of all the three peninsulas there was at the moment a ' Progressive ' coalition in power ; the government of General Espartero was in fact midway in its career from the successful revolution of 1854 which had given it birth to the unsuccessful revolt of 1856 which was to mark its death. With the attempts of this moderate reformer to curb Carlist conspiracy and clerical domination Louis Napoleon was in natural sympathy ; and Espartero for his part was not blind to the advantages which any

[1] F.O. Portugal, Pakenham to Clarendon. 'Confidential.' 18 Feb. 55.
[2] F.O. Spain, Howden to Clarendon, 18 Feb. 55.
[3] *Ibid.* 'Confidential.' 1 Mar. 55. [4] *Ibid.*

opponent of reaction might secure by alliance with the
Western Powers against Russia. His ministers were even
more enthusiastic. In June General Tavala sought a confidential interview with the British ambassador, in order to
assure him that his ' one wish in the world ' was ' to signalise
his passage through power, however short it might be, by
sending a contingent to the allies.' [1] ' For God's sake,' he
continued, ' give me the means of this, put me in the way of
making the proposition : do ask us officially to send troops,
as a peg on which I may hang the question.' Howden was
encouraging but evasive. ' I told him I was willing to
enter into any conspiracy he chose by which 25,000 Spanish
troops might be sent to join the allies in the East ' : but
Spain must make the first proposal.[1] A week earlier
Clarendon had in fact intimated to Howden that though
England would welcome the alliance she could not in any
way attempt to cajole Spain into fighting.[2] But even
without this, Espartero's government proceeded in the
following month to make a definite offer that it would
furnish the allies with a contingent of Spanish troops : [3] an
offer ostensibly based on gratitude to France for defending
the Spanish frontier from an otherwise inevitable Carlist
invasion.[4] But the Spanish government did not conceal
its hope that by this means Spain might show herself
worthy of her former glories, might escape from her
present diplomatic isolation, and be admitted once more
to share the councils of Europe. With these objects,
Marshal Espartero offered in August to have ready by
next spring 60,000 men ; adding that he considered ' himself not too old or infirm to command them.' [5] In point
of fact by Crimean precedents he was hardly old or
infirm enough.

From this time to the beginning of October the Spanish
government grew ever more anxious to participate in the

---

[1] F.O. Spain, Howden to Clarendon, ' Confidential.' 22 June 55.
[2] F.O. Spain. Draft. Clarendon to Howden, 13 Jan. 55.
[3] F.O. France, Cowley to Clarendon. ' Most Confidential.' 2 July 55.
[4] F.O. Spain, Howden to Clarendon. ' Confidential.' 8 Aug. 55.
[5] F.O. Spain. *Ibid.*, and Otway to Clarendon. ' Confidential.' 14
Aug. 55.

war : [1] but as its eagerness to offer its services increased the desire of the allies to accept them declined. At first disposed to favour the suggestion, the French government now saw more fully the disadvantages of a Spanish alliance at this stage of the war ; and in this view the English government concurred. By the autumn of 1855 the prospect of another campaign was becoming remote, and England's pressing need of foreign reinforcements had in any case abated. Moreover by this time much of Espartero's personal popularity in Madrid was spent ; it was doubtful whether he could still have committed his country to so important an adventure. By the end of October the extreme reserve of the allies convinced him that his help was no longer wanted ; and November saw the complete extinction of the proposal.

These offers of help to the allies by the smaller European states remained in the actual train of events not merely unutilised but unknown. But even without them the outlook for Russia was black enough. With Austria on the verge of hostilities, the Quadruple Alliance stronger and more united than ever, the chief Scandinavian Power already in defensive alliance with the enemy, the Czar was left with only one Power to whom he could look even for the most passive of diplomatic support. Prussia alone of the great Powers had hitherto declined all co-operation with the allies : but even Prussia was not proof against the menace of a Polish campaign. For the envoy who had first conveyed Napoleon's threat to Alexander [2] had purposely disclosed it on his way to Bismarck.[3] Frederick William in consequence wrote a letter to the Czar, urging him instantly to yield.[4] Nicholas himself might have thought twice before renewing the war under such circumstances : Alexander upon second thoughts decided to accept the peace. On January 16th, two days before the term of Austria's extended ultimatum, Russia announced her unreserved acceptance of the allies' demands.[5]

---

[1] F.O. Spain, Howden to Clarendon. 'Confidential.' 30 Sept. 55. F.O. France, Cowley to Clarendon, 7 Oct. 55.
[2] *Supra*, p. 338.   [3] *Paul*, ii. 2.   [4] *La Gorce : Empire*, i. 459.
[5] Even so, the *Times* did not despair of war, *v.* Leading Articles, 18 and 19 Jan. 56. Cf. *Dunoyer*, i. 345.

It only remained to choose the scene of the congress which should convert the present preliminaries into a treaty of peace. The resulting choice formed not the least of the moral advantages accruing to the new Empire from the war. By common consent Paris was the capital chosen for this the greatest gathering of international diplomacy since the Congress of Vienna. Russia had proposed Paris, relying on the pacific disposition of the French people ; and England had seconded the proposal, in order that throughout the negotiations her envoys might have immediate access to the sole Frenchman to whom they could look for support,[1] the Emperor himself. The Congress was opened on the 25th of February, under the nominal presidency of the French foreign minister, Walewski : an ineffectual and pretentious personage who owed his office to the fact that he was a natural son of Napoleon. Actually the direction of affairs was in the hands of the French Emperor, whose no light task it was to keep the peace between the peacemakers. Who those peacemakers should be was itself a disputable question. It went without saying that Russia, Austria and the two Western Powers should be represented at the Congress : but to Napoleon III Piedmont owed it that she was admitted to all its sessions,[2] and Prussia that she was admitted to any of them.[3]

From the Emperor's point of view that the Congress of Paris might atone for the Congress of Vienna, the more Powers that were represented at it the better. But his divergence from the English attitude on these two points had a more particular significance, forming the prelude to a long series of services which in the next ten years he was spontaneously to render to the champions of new Italy and new Germany. The Crimean War, luckily for the German Powers, had affected the French and English courts in precisely opposite ways. The Prince Consort emerged from it anti-Prussian and pro-Austrian : Napoleon III pro-

---

[1] *Martin*, iii. 432, 447.
[2] *Ollivier*, iii. 339.   Cf. *Cavour*: *Lettere*, 20 Feb. 56.
[3] *Q.V.L.*, iii. 171.

Prussian and anti-Austrian. The Emperor's attitude was itself not new; only it was now confirmed by the fact that the defeat of Russia left Austria now the outstanding anti-nationalist Power in Europe. And against Austria [1] Louis Napoleon was seeking two swords in Piedmont and Prussia.

Although the outlines of the peace were defined by its preliminaries, there was room enough for contention in regard to details. No great trouble was caused by the original Four Points ; even the third, the rock on which the Vienna negotiations had split, was conceded without difficulty in even more absolute form. Now that her own Black Sea fleet had gone to the bottom, it seemed hardly a disadvantage to Russia that the Black Sea should be closed to all battle-fleets afloat. Strenuous opposition was however offered by her envoys to the cession of Bessarabia ; the capture of Kars since the dispatch of the Austrian ultimatum entitled Russia, they contended, to a mitigation of this demand. But England stood to her guns and the Emperor stood by his ally ; Austria moreover on this point displayed a vehement determination to see Russia removed from any contact with the Danube. And so, adding one black mark the more against Austria to a score long and black enough already, Count Orloff consented to cede the territory.[2] By the end of March the treaty stood ready for signature : a treaty whereby the Black Sea was neutralised, Russia shorn of Bessarabia, the navigation of the Danube made free to all nations and placed under international control, and Turkey formally admitted into the concert of the Powers of Europe. This last provision was not the mere visionary optimism, the absurd apotheosis of the blameless Turk, for which it has sometimes been derided since ; it was largely an entirely practical reversal of a situation artificially created for the advantage of Russia. In 1815, by excluding the Eastern Question from

---

[1] 'The Emperor spoke with detestation of Austrian Policy.' Paris Conference Papers. Clarendon. 'Confidential.' 24 March 56. ' It was difficult to make England understand that Napoleon thought of nothing less than of weakening Prussia.' *Ernest*, iii. 202.

[2] *Maxwell*, ii. 120, is strangely in error on this point.

the deliberations of the Vienna Congress, Alexander I had made the relations of Russia with the Porte a purely domestic matter, in which Europe could claim no concern. Hence all other European aggressions were forbidden to all smaller European Powers by the inviolable arrangements of Vienna ; but this the most tempting field of expansion remained conveniently open to the most expansive Power of all. It was this exceptional prerogative of which Russia was deprived by the Congress of Paris : henceforth Turkey, like any other European state, might appeal from individual aggression to the common treaty right of Europe.

The barrier thus set to the onward march of Russia in the Balkans formed the truly permanent portion of the work directly achieved by the Crimean War. Fifteen years sufficed to annul the neutralisation of the Black Sea ; and less than half as many more to restore to Russia all but a fraction of her loss in Bessarabia. Only French aid had enabled England to gain these terms, and without French aid she could not keep them. But even before the fall of the Empire had opened the door to these detailed demolitions of their handiwork, had come a larger disillusion to any members of the Paris Congress who hoped that in becoming by courtesy and for a cause incorporate in the body of Europe, the Turk would cease to be by nature and choice Asiatic. So completely by the time of the next considerable Eastern crisis had all hopes and promises of Ottoman reform been stultified, that in 1877 even Stratford Canning himself set his still powerful face against any new crusade on behalf of the Crescent.

From this however it does not follow that even in its immediate objects the Crimean War was totally without effect. For though the Western Powers failed to make Turkey European, they at least succeeded in preventing it from becoming Russian. True the sick man was the sick man still, but Russia at any rate had ceased to be the heir.

This direct but negative achievement was not however the most important of the results of the war. Its larger heritage consisted in the profound *bouleversement* which it

effected in the established order in Europe. How much
that was to mean few save the French Emperor himself
can have realised at the moment ; [1] but already before the
separation of the Congress one small indication had been
given of the commotions to come.

With the conclusion of the peace with Russia the ostensible objects of the Congress were accomplished. It had
however a further achievement to its credit, in that it had
given the sanction of international law to certain principles designed to mitigate the severity of maritime war.
A stranger postscript to its work was to follow, in the shape
of a supplementary session devoted to a general discussion
of the affairs of Europe. It was this session which gave
Cavour his sole direct compensation for the intervention of his country in the war. As a result of it Victor
Emmanuel had it was true been received in the autumn of
1855 as the guest of Napoleon III and Queen Victoria in
Paris and in London ; and this public reception of him,
overshadowed though it was by the recent exchange of
visits between his hosts, was yet valuable as advertising the existence of a monarch who had never before set
foot outside the borders of his own country.[2] But the
extreme eccentricity of his manners, to which perhaps this
very isolation had contributed, had prevented the advertisement from being altogether successful. The impression
made by Victor Emmanuel in Paris was far from favour-
able : [3] both in word [4] and deed [5] he outraged *les convenances*
of a court which was anything but strait-laced. Cavour
who accompanied his king on both visits was on tenter-
hooks the whole time : [6] a raising of the eyebrows in
Paris seemed to portend far more terrible possibilities at
Windsor. But in England everything went off admirably.
Fresh from his Parisian exploits Victor Emmanuel found
himself welcomed with almost embarrassing enthusiasm
by delegates from the Bible Societies and Exeter Hall.

[1] ' Don't worry,' he said to Cavour when all was over, ' I have a presenti-
ment that the present peace will not last long.' *Cavour : Lettere*, ii. 227.
[2] *Maxwell*, ii. 106.   [3] *Ibid.*
[4] *Malmesbury*, ii. 38. *Bernstorff*, i. 322.
[5] ' *Malakoff*,' i. 101, 102.   [6] *Thayer*, i. 367.

' Totally forgetting,' complained Greville, ' that he is the most debauched and dissolute fellow in the world,' [1] they hailed him effusively as the morning-star of some new reformation. [2] The king's merits were not those which his Puritan admirers might have been expected to appreciate : his faults were precisely of a kind which they commonly regarded as unpardonable. But his government had recently been excommunicated by the Pope ; and excommunication covers a multitude of sins. It is fair to add that during his whole stay in England Victor Emmanuel was guilty of nothing worse than a few harmless gaucheries ; [3] ' he behaved himself,' as his delighted Premier observed, ' like a perfect gentleman.' [4] In one respect however even the English visit proved a disappointment. ' The king did not much like my shrug of the shoulder,' wrote Clarendon, ' when he asked me what he was going to *gagner* by all this, and whether we could not manage for him *une petite extension de territoire.*' [5]

In this respect Cavour at the Congress fared no better. Throughout he conspicuously failed to commend himself to the President of that Congress, Walewski. The Emperor it was true remained eager to do anything in his power for Italy, short of wrecking the peace. He sounded Austria about a complicated scheme of Cavour's which would have entailed the cession of Parma to Piedmont ; but Austria said she would fight first. Then he revived his own old suggestion first formulated a couple of years ago at the very outbreak of the war : let Austria give up Lombardy and Venetia, and keep instead the Danubian Principalities, which she had been occupying for the duration of the war. This scheme with something of the pride of authorship Napoleon III now urged as ' the only sensible solution of the Italian question.' [6] But again Austria would have none of it ; and at the moment, as he explained to Cavour, it was clearly impossible for the

---

[1] *Greville*, 11 Dec. 55.
[2] The *Times* described their addresses as ' pert paragraphs of nonsense.' 4 Dec. 55, p. 6, c. 6.
[3] E.g. *Malmesbury*, ii. 38.   [4] *Cavour: Lettere*, ii. 157.
[5] *Maxwell*, ii. 106.   [6] *Cavour: Lettere*, ii. 227.

Emperor to make her rejection of it a *casus belli*. After
all it had not been the Sardinian intervention but the
Austrian ultimatum which had secured for France the
peace for which she longed ; to repay Austria for such a
service by immediately launching an ultimatum at her
own head would have been politically indecent even if in
the state of French public opinion it had been practically
possible. Cavour himself, unlike some of his admirers,
had the sense to see this ; and fell back without vain
protests upon the policy of moral compensation.

Even here he was at first unsuccessful. Towards the end
of March he addressed a note to the English and French
representatives at the Congress, lamenting the grievances
of Italy ; but both this note and another addressed to the
same Powers on the same subject three weeks later remained
unanswered. Willing and anxious as he was to secure some
ventilation for the grievances of Piedmont Napoleon III
was on this occasion not prepared to sacrifice the interests
of France. He declined to do anything which might
endanger the Peace. Only the success of his personal
interventions had kept the peacemakers pacific as it was : [1]
and until their essential business was done he refused to
allow Cavour to throw any fresh apple of discord among
them. Before embarking on the war Cavour had sought
to stipulate as a condition of his country's intervention
that the Italian question should be considered at the
eventual peace congress. But that condition had been
refused then,[2] and the fulfilment of it could not be exacted
now. Hence the official proceedings of the Congress were
terminated and the peace itself was signed before the name
of Italy had been so much as mentioned.[3]

But ten days later at a subsidiary meeting Italy was
allowed an unofficial advertisement of her wrongs. The
debate was purely informal and academic, and was ostensibly directed to a general survey of any outstanding
questions which might threaten to disturb the newly

---

[1] 'None of us can resist him,' Clarendon told Vitzthum, 'when he gets
us face to face in his own room.' *Vitzthum*, i. 182.
[2] *King : Italy*, ii. 7.	[3] *La Gorce : Empire*, i. 479.

concluded peace. But though the discussion ranged from
the anarchy in Greece and the iniquities of the Belgian
press to the Prussian grievances as to Neufchâtel, it was
only when it touched upon Italy that it became of real
interest. To Italian grievances Walewski devoted a passing reference, Clarendon an eloquent oration, and Cavour
himself a statement which was all the more effective from
its unexpected moderation. The Austrian envoy wisely
refrained from reply, contenting himself with the unanswer-
able observation that the whole topic lay outside the scope
of the Congress. In consequence he had no instructions
on the question and so was unable to discuss it. Nothing
as a result was done, and not all even of what had been said
was published, in the authorised account of the session.[1]
The effect of the whole incident has been exaggerated ;
for it was a symptom rather than a cause of what was to
follow. Cavour was 'greatly disappointed' with 'this
meagre result,' said Clarendon later,[2] adding ' he did not
conceal his irritation from me.' But in public he dis-
guised his disappointment bravely ; displaying throughout
the Congress a reasonable and patient optimism which
were the more admirable from the way in which both the
war and the peace had cheated him of his hopes. In the
final assault upon Sevastopol England had at least had a
share though an unsuccessful one : the Sardinian army had
taken no part in it at all. It was left with a very minor
share in one minor engagement as its sole military achievement in the war : an achievement which might do something to supersede the memories of Novara, but could not
obliterate them as handsomely as Cavour had hoped.
Like England, Cavour had been apprised of the Emperor's
alternative of extending the war if he could not end it ;[3]
but unlike England he had every reason to welcome such
an extension of it. The end coming as it did had been to
him a bitter disappointment ;[4] it left him with only
moral compensations, and even of those with something
less than he might reasonably have expected.

[1] *Thayer*, i. 385.   [2] *Times*, 18 Feb. 62, p. 5, c. 6.
[3] *Cavour: Lettere*, ii. 155.   [4] *Ibid.*, 175.

Curiously enough it was the representative of England who gave him his only momentary hope of more : a phrase of Clarendon's in a private and friendly interview left him with the impression that Piedmont might count on England's armed support in an almost immediate war against Austria.[1] For a moment Cavour dreamed of a campaign that very summer ; as soon as La Marmora was back from the Crimea an ultimatum should be launched at Austria cast in terms which she could not but reject.[2] First however he must interview the Emperor. But Napoleon III, though benevolent as ever, proved far more pacific in tone than Clarendon, and to this extent less encouraging to his interviewer. ' Go over to London,' he said at last, ' have a good talk about things with Palmerston, and then come and see me on your way back.'[3]

Cavour took the advice not knowing all its wisdom : in London he found himself received very civilly, invited to witness a naval review, and greeted with many expressions of platonic sympathy. But with Palmerston he could hardly get a word of any sort; and he was quite perspicacious enough to realise how completely his high hopes had been misplaced. The bellicose language of her plenipotentiary at Paris had led him to believe that England was as anxious as Piedmont to avenge in a new war her lack of success in the Crimea. Disappointed and disillusioned England certainly was. But the real effect of her disappointment was a disposition to fight shy of any continental warfare in the future. And a very few days in London effectively opened Cavour's eyes to the fact.[4] Cutting short his stay there, and hardly even pausing to thank the Emperor for the cold douche which he had vicariously administered, Cavour hastened back at the end of April to Turin. Empty-handed as it seemed, he brought back no substantial prize : only he could plead

[1] *Cavour : Lettere*, ii. 217. On 17 Feb. 62 in the House of Lords Clarendon denied the use of it in any such sense or context as Cavour had understood. v. *Times*, 18 Feb. 62, p. 5, c. 6.
[2] *Cavour : Lettere*, ii. 218.   [3] *Ibid.*, 225.
[4] Cf. *Mazade*, 140. *Thayer*, i. 393.

that in the face of Europe he had won an honourable mention for Italy.

One country there was whose very name remained unmentioned throughout the entire proceedings of the Congress. From that Congress Piedmont had extorted an advertisement and the Turk a testimonial ; but Poland the peacemakers of Europe passed by on the other side. After all they had effected a settlement of sorts, and were entitled perhaps to a moment of easy optimism as to their creation. And how should such optimism be attained, or a man see at all of his handiwork that it was good, if he reserved not to himself that right of the deliberately averted gaze ? That her fate should have escaped discussion was one of the chief cares—and in the event one of the chief triumphs—of the Russian emissary Count Orloff. This triumph had not been easily won. For though England remained indifferent in the matter, the French Emperor, even when forced to forgo his design of fighting for Poland, still sought to obtain some alleviation of her lot by the peace. With that object he determined to bring the whole question of Poland before the conference.[1] But Count Orloff ' entreated the Emperor not to allow the Polish question to be discussed in Conference,' and ' *promised* in return an amnesty with very few exceptions,—the restoration of landed property to its former owners, reforms both religious and civil, the reintroduction of the Polish language, and a vice-royalty in the person of one of the Emperor's brothers.' [2] So earnest were these assurances that both the Emperor and Walewski thought they might rely upon them : [3] the Emperor moreover allowed himself to be influenced by Orloff's plea, that the new Czar should be allowed the credit of making these reforms at the time of his coronation with the grace of voluntary concessions,[4] instead of grudgingly and of necessity, under the plain compulsion of Europe. Three months however

[1] F.O. France, Cowley to Clarendon, 7 July 56.
[2] F.O. France, Cowley to Clarendon. 'Confidential.' 6 June 56.
[3] *Ibid.*, 7 July 56.
[4] *v.* F.O. Paris Congress Papers, Clarendon to Palmerston, 15 Apr. 56.

sufficed to show that what was not given of necessity would not be given at all ; and that promises made by Russia in secret would remain unfulfilled. Unsupported by his ally and unsuspicious of his foe, Louis Napoleon had in effect let slip an opportunity never afterwards vouchsafed to him of securing some real alleviation in the lot of the least fortunate nation in Europe. Now, as in 1831 [1] and in 1863, he suffered himself to be turned back from the service of Poland.

In this same Congress of Paris Louis Napoleon attempted also a smaller service to a smaller nation : seeking by every means in his power to secure for the Danubian Principalities, now freed from Russian aggression, a similar freedom from Turkish misgovernment. 'The great fault committed by the Congress of Vienna,' he told Cowley, ' was that the interests of the sovereigns were only consulted, while the interests of their subjects were wholly neglected ; the present congress ought not to fall into a similar error. . . . It would be disgraceful to England and France, if they had not the will or power to establish a state of things in the Principalities that would be in accordance with the wishes of the people.' [2] But on this point the Emperor was faced not merely by the indifference, but by the strenuous opposition of England : whose ministers argued logically enough that it would be preposterous to permit a war undertaken in defence of the territorial integrity of Turkey to end in the practical amputation of two Turkish provinces. The fact was that Louis Napoleon though as anxious as England to check the growth of Russia had none of England's desire to maintain the dominions of Turkey. From the first he had been haunted by a sort of shame at having the Turk for ally at all. 'I was surprised,' wrote Malmesbury describing a long after-dinner talk with the Emperor in 1853, ' to hear him repeatedly calling the Turks " *Bêtes— des amis si bêtes que cela* ! " ' [3] This sense of disgust Louis never outgrew. In 1857 under cross-examination by

---

[1] v. *Simpson*, 85.
[2] F.O. Paris Congress Papers, Clarendon to Palmerston. 'Confidential.' 9 Mar. 56. Cf. *Martin*, iii. 465.
[3] 24 Nov. 53. *Malmesbury*, i. 412.

Prince Albert he was driven to a practical confession of it. ' "Do you really care," asked the prince, "for the continuance of the integrity of the Turkish Empire ? " The Emperor said, " If I asked him as a private individual, he did not care for it, and could muster up no sympathy for such a sorry set as the Turks." I interrupted, that I had thought as much.' And the murder was out. [1]

Here in fact lay the secret of all the English and French differences as to the future of the Principalities ; and in the actual congress England supported by Austria succeeded in frustrating the Emperor's design for their future. But in this case his purpose though postponed was not finally defeated. For in the following year England was temporarily disabled by the Indian Mutiny from throwing her full force into continental affairs ; and the French Emperor, though offering his sympathy and support in the actual suppression of the mutiny, yet availed himself of that disability to insist, against the wishes of England, Austria and Turkey, on the reversal of a falsified vote against union extorted by Turkish pressure from the Principalities. ' The maladministration of the Turks was such,' he told Cowley in the spring of 1857, ' that it was impossible that Christian powers should not sympathise with those Christian subjects of the Sultan, who asked for a better government. His Majesty could understand that Turkey, Austria and Russia should oppose the Union of the Principalities, since in union there would be strength, and it must be the desire of these Powers, each for its own specific reasons, to keep those provinces in a state of weakness ; but for his own part he was convinced that the surest barrier against the future encroachments of Russia, was to be found in strengthening the Principalities ; and as this was the principal object which England and France must have in connection with those countries, he conceived that their true policy was to aid in developing those

[1] *Martin*, iv. 101–102. Even before fighting the Pope in 1831 Louis had tried to fight the Turks in 1829: v. *Simpson*, 52. *Cf.* B.N. Nouv. Acq. Fr. 1067, f. 129.

resources which produce strength.' [1] Eventually the Emperor's arguments, or at least his importunity, prevailed : and to his disinterested advocacy this outlying Latin nationality in the East—the legendary offspring of the legions of Diocletian—owed first a federal dualism under a single prince, and finally a complete legislative and administrative union.

But the various and vexatious questions which the Congress left unsolved cast no apparent cloud upon the prosperous conclusion of its labours. Festivities and banquets, decorations and promotions gave to the passing days an air of universal triumph. In dispensing these hospitalities and honours the Emperor took evident delight. To ask a couple of generals to dinner, and at dessert rise and toast them suddenly as Marshals,[2] to be the centre and source of the general festivities, this was at once the sign and satisfaction of his own success. Sometimes however he made these banquets the occasion of more serious pronouncements. At this juncture the project of a Suez Canal was beginning to take substance in the teeth of the bitter hostility of Palmerston, De Redcliffe and Lord John Russell, who fought the scheme stubbornly at every stage, denouncing the canal until it was half-dug as impracticable, and then with even greater vehemence as opposed to the highest interests of Turkey and of Egypt. With these the interests of England chanced to coincide : since the canal obscurely, but all the more dangerously for that, constituted a menace to her Indian Empire. To the overcoming of obstacles raised by this opposition Lesseps was now devoting the same unconquerable optimism which throughout his life was both his strength and snare. In the present instance, more fortunate than in his earlier or later undertakings, he could count on the wholehearted support of Louis Napoleon. To this the Emperor

---

[1] F.O. France, Cowley to Clarendon. 'Confidential.' 12 May 57.
'It is difficult to argue with His Majesty,' added Cowley, ' for on this question at least his philanthropy far exceeds his respect for Treaties.' *Ibid.* And what is to be done with an Emperor, whose philanthropy exceeds his respect for Treaties ?
[2] Canrobert and *Bosquet*, iv. 297, 298.

testified at the close of a farewell dinner-party to the assembled plenipotentiaries by informing the Turkish envoy ' that he took the greatest possible interest in the scheme, which seemed to him a universal benefit ; that he had studied it in all its aspects and acquainted himself with all the documents bearing on it, and earnestly wished its success.   But the enterprise, admirable as it was in every way, had given rise to certain objections and obstructions, especially in England.   For his part he could not consider that these objections were well-founded, and he quite hoped to see them removed.   At the same time he was not disposed to rush matters, for fear of compromising their success.   Instead, relying upon the happy alliance which united the two peoples, he looked to the future—and to a very near future—for an agreement upon this question.' [1] In such an utterance Napoleon III was seen at his best : sustaining, as he did not always sustain, a remote and beneficent design with a statesmanlike appreciation of the proper method for its attainment.   To this policy he adhered with admirable persistence and good temper ;   as when three years later after some particularly discouraging despatch from London he gave Lesseps an interview, told him not to worry, ' you can count on my support and protection,' but added, ' It is a squall : we must shorten sail.' [2]   It would have been well for Louis Napoleon if he could always have pursued his own dreams with the same combination of undiscouraged idealism and practical common sense.   As it was the opening of the Suez Canal by the Empress was destined to furnish his chequered reign with almost the last and certainly not the least-deserved of its triumphs.

For the moment deserved and undeserved good fortunes seemed to pile themselves upon him.   As the fall of Sevastopol had crowned the first great exhibition of Paris, so the Congress of Paris was to receive what to the French Emperor himself must have been yet a more signal benediction.   On March 16 a child was born to him, and that child a son.   Twice before he had been disappointed of

[1] *Lesseps : Souvenirs*, ii. 429, 430.   [2] *Ibid.*, 692, 693.

that hope ; now it seemed that the Prince had postponed
his coming only that he might receive a yet more imperial
welcome. Three years earlier, socially boycotted in his
own capital, and in the eyes of foreign courts a very dubious
adventurer indeed, Louis Napoleon had contracted a
marriage which to the delight of all his enemies seemed to
have set the final seal upon his ostracism. His boldest
friend would not then have dared to predict, that the son
born of that marriage would find awaiting him an inheritance scarcely inferior in its seeming splendour and security
to that which Napoleon himself had won for the first Prince
Imperial of France. In extent the new Empire was in no
way comparable to the old, but under it France had become
once more the first nation of the world. Unaugmented in
territory it had received in the last two years an immense
increase in prestige ; victories infinitely less brilliant than
those of the First Empire had yet sufficed to obtain for it
a European sanction and a semblance of stability such as
that Empire had never been able to possess. Indeed the
one thing that now seemed lacking to it was an heir.

It was at six o'clock on the morning of March 16 that
the cannon of the Invalides once more echoed through
Paris : not the mere one and twenty that should suffice
for a girl ; but a full salute of a hundred and one guns,
proclaiming that the Emperor had indeed a son. The
dramatic effect of this distinction was wasted, since Paris
still slept : [1] but when it did awake to the news its rejoicings were instant, spontaneous, and all but universal.
This ' universality of the manifestation ' was the feature
that most impressed the *Times* correspondent as he walked
round the illuminated city in the evening, even in ' back
streets and lanes where I believe no lights were ever hung
before.' [2] No more striking contrast could have been

---

[1] The many stories which represent the city as hanging upon the tale
of the guns, anxiously awaiting the fateful twenty-second detonation
(accepted even by *La Gorce*: *Empire*, i. 465) are mere inventions: confusedly
reminiscent of the actual occurrence on the occasion of the birth of
Napoleon's own son. v. *Times*, 18 March 56, p. 8, cc. 5 and 6. The present
Prince Imperial was born at 3.14 a.m. *Viel-Castel*, iii. 218.

[2] *Times*, 19 March 56, p. 8, c. 1. Cp. *Thouvenel*: *Empire*, 263. *St
Amand*, ii. 386.

conceived than that between the forced and official celebrations which had greeted the bride, and the genuine enthusiasm evoked by arrival of the heir. That arrival had been none of the easiest. For eighteen hours on end the state bodies had been in permanent session : [1] while the Emperor during the prolonged sufferings of the Empress had been pacing the palace in an agony of apprehension. Nor were his fears ungrounded ; both mother and child were in imminent danger of death.[2]

It chanced that the Prince's birthday was Palm Sunday : and for text that morning the court chaplain took the familiar sentence, ' *Beatus qui venit in nomine Domini* ' : [3] applying it, in words careless of precedent or consequence, to the triumphal entry of this new prince into his capital. Perhaps as he listened the Emperor may have thought of exits as well as entrances ; certainly his own far more subdued response to the congratulations of his senators two days later seemed to display a desire to ' touch wood.' In the baptismal register after his son's names he had written the words *Fils de France*. On this title he now dilated. ' It was,' he said, ' a revival from the usage of the *ancien régime* ; but not for that reason a meaningless piece of antiquarianism. For truly, gentlemen, when an heir is born to perpetuate a national institution, that child is something more than the scion of a family ; he is the whole country's son ; and this name of his points him to his duties.' Then after urging that for a Napoleon, the elect of the people, this title must mean not less but more than for the children of the ancient kings, he put into words a thought which even if unspoken could hardly have been absent from the minds of his hearers. For more than two centuries the crown of France had not passed once in direct succession from father to son. And now who was Louis Napoleon, and what was this his child, that he should hope

[1] *Jerrold*, iv. 111.
[2] ' The Empress has suffered dreadfully and irons had recourse to, which have marked the infant's head. It was *touch and go* with mother and child at one moment.' Holland to Panizzi. Paris, 20 March 56. B.M. Add. MSS. 36,717, f. 418.
[3] *Nolan*, ii. 729.

to escape their common fate ? Another memory, more recent and particular, pressed still more insistently on all. Not fifty years ago another Child of France had been cradled in Paris : born amid every circumstance of imperial splendour ; yet destined to die childless and his father's only child, an exile and an exile's son, the last direct descendant of a deposed and discredited dynasty.

No present splendour could quite have banished from men's minds such memories as those. But in such case the common course would have been silence from ill-omened words. The utterances of the present Emperor however were rarely commonplace. In the days of his own long exile and imprisonment, despite the utter pros-tration of his fortunes, he had proclaimed insistently his unalterable conviction that he would live to rule France. But now that his highest dreams seemed realised ; assured not of Empire only, but of peace, of victory, of a son ; himself all powerful in a country which his own rule had made once more the first Power in Europe ; now he spoke only with a tentative and melancholy modesty, as though he who from the depths had foreseen the height, from the height also foresaw the *débâcle*. Not all the acclamations, he said, which surrounded the cradle of his son, could pre-vent him from pondering on the destiny of those born in the same place under like circumstances. ' If,' continued the Emperor, ' I hope that his will be a happier fate, it is because trusting in God I cannot doubt that protection, when I see Him raise up again, by a marvellous combination of circumstances, all that it had pleased Him to beat down forty years ago : as though He wished to strengthen, by martyrdom and misfortune, the new dynasty which had issued from the ranks of the people. History too,' he con-tinued, with a plain reference to the fate alike of the First Empire and of the Orleanist regime, ' history has lessons that I shall not forget. It teaches me that the favours of fortune must never be abused ; it teaches me too that a dynasty can only hope for stability by remaining faithful to its origin, and by devoting itself entirely to the popular interests, for whose service it was created.' The speech ended with a hope of better things. 'This child whose birth was consecrated by the peace, by the blessing of the Pope telegraphed within an hour of his birth, by the acclamations of the French people whom the Emperor loved so well—this child will I hope prove worthy of the destinies that await him.' The reply 'created considerable emotion' among its immediate hearers :[1] in a similar strain later in the day the Emperor responded to the congratulations of the plenipotentiaries of the Peace Congress. 'I am happy,' he said, 'that Providence has granted me a son at a moment when an era of general reconciliation is dawning upon Europe. I will bring him up imbued with the idea that nations must not be egotistical, and that the peace of Europe depends upon the prosperity of every nation.'

A fortnight after the birth and baptism of the Prince, the delegates of the Congress of Paris met to attach their names to the issue of their labours : signing at midday on March 30 the formal treaty of peace. This too was on a Sunday : and for this occasion as for the last French Catholics discovered, in the twice repeated *Pax vobiscum* of the Gospel, a happy coincidence in the liturgy for the day. In this case the coincidence was more than accidental ; since but for it the protestations of Clarendon and Cowley on behalf of their country against the signing of the peace on Sunday [2] might not improbably have prevailed. As it was, fearing that further opposition might cause real umbrage, they finally consented to this small outrage upon Protestant opinion. That opinion had been in no way especially perturbed by the Sunday slaughter of Inkerman : [3] perhaps after all it might be lawful to make peace also on the Sabbath.

Hence without further ado the treaty was signed and sealed : and forthwith the delegates proceeded in state to the Tuileries ; there to present to the Emperor their

---

[1] *Times*, 21 March 56, p. 8. c. 6.
[2] F.O. Paris Congress Papers. Clarendon. 29 March 56.
[3] But Raglan himself objected to fighting on Sunday. *Walker*, 104.

congratulations on the peace concluded 'under his auspices,' [1] and to the Empress the eagle's quill with which it
had been signed. Louis in his reply went out of his way
to rebut a persistent rumour that the English plenipotentiaries had been less than lukewarm in their desire for
peace, and that they had even opposed unnecessary
obstacles to its attainment. 'Turning to Lord Cowley and
Lord Clarendon he added, that peace had been rendered
possible by the spirit of conciliation they had exhibited.'
As a result 'it was clearly understood by the Congress that
in the opinion of the Emperor the question of peace and
war had rested with England.' [2] For the rest the speech
expressed satisfaction that the present peace was one which
a great nation could accept without degradation ; and
therefore formed a settlement affording reasonable hope of
real permanence and stability. In part this was perhaps
an answering gesture to the many flattering overtures
which the Russian diplomatists throughout the negotiations
had not ceased to make towards the Emperor : in part it
was certainly a hinted reference—the sole complacency
which Napoleon III permitted himself—to the now dis-
carded provisions of Vienna.

The note of triumph in the Emperor's speech was so
modest as scarcely to be perceptible, but matter for it
was obvious to all. Forty-two years ago on that very day,
Paris had capitulated to the armies of the allies ; at whose
head on the morrow Alexander of Russia had ridden in
triumph through the conquered capital. And now not
only had this position been reversed, but the new Alexander
had even deigned to make the memories of that contrast
the basis of an appeal to the new Napoleon. 'The Emperor
Alexander '—so he had suffered his trusted emissary [3]
Seebach to remark—'the Emperor Alexander counts upon
the Emperor Napoleon III taking the same interest in
his fate, as his uncle the Emperor Alexander took in the

---

[1] v. Q.V.L., iii. 186.
[2] Clarendon to Victoria, 1 Apr. 56. 'The Emperor's remark,' continued
Clarendon, 'produced a great effect. It was uncalled for but generous.'
Martin, iii. 472.
[3] F.O. France, Cowley to Clarendon 'Confidential.' 17 Jan. 56.

fate of Napoleon I.' Nor was this all. Less than four
years ago the Czar Nicholas had haughtily refused to accord
to this upstart Emperor the customary salutation of kings :
now his son and successor was pressing upon Louis the
highest royal order of his realm, and pressing it in vain ;
even though he offered to come to Paris himself in order
to perform the investiture in person.[1] It would have been
difficult to imagine a reversal more signal and complete.

And this reversal Louis might well regard as something
more than a personal or dynastic success ; in some measure
at any rate it stood for a truly national triumph. Seven
years earlier France had taken him, outcast and exiled,
and raised him up to be her ruler. But in those seven
years he also might almost claim, that what the French
people had done for him in France, he himself had done for
France in Europe. France too, in his own words,[2] had
formerly been ' disinherited of her rank in the councils of
Europe : ' now she was ' prosperous, peaceful, and respected.' So far as the external situation was concerned,
this was no more than the truth : from being the outcast
he had made her in effect the arbiter of Europe.

Internally the matter was more doubtful. The success
achieved by Louis' speeches from the throne had other
causes than their intrinsic excellence, or even than the
height to which he had raised that rostrum in Europe.
At least in part they owed their acclamation to the echoing
silence which their author had himself secured for them ;
down which, as down deserted corridors, his oracular
utterances rang mournfully and alone. The eminence of
his own political position in France was the result in large
part of the absence from public life of all eminence besides.
That absence he himself recognised and deplored ; only a
few weeks ago he had lamented to Cowley ' that there
were no statesmen in France.' [3] Such an admission at
the time was striking enough. For so high stood the

[1] Paris Congress Papers. Clarendon to Palmerston. 'Confidential.'
25 Feb. 56.
[2] 3 March 56 : speech in opening the Legislative Assembly.
[3] F.O. France, Cowley to Clarendon, 29 Jan. 56.

prestige of the imperial diplomacy at the moment that the
Comte de Chambord himself in a letter to a friend expressed
the intention of availing himself in the event of his restoration of all the ability which surrounded the Emperor.
The letter was intercepted and shown to Louis Napoleon.
' All the ability which surrounds me ! ' was his comment :
' he won't reign long if that is all he can count on.' [1]   In
neither case did the Emperor show any sign of recognising
the cause, even in the act of realising the result.   Eighteen
months earlier a remark of his to the Duke of Newcastle
had displayed a more just appreciation of the position.
' Former governments,' he said, ' tried to reign by the support of perhaps one million of the educated classes.   I have
tried to lay hold of the other twenty-nine.' [2]   The claim
was justified, for the attempt was certainly made and
made with considerable success.   Broadly speaking, it is
true that the more aristocratic governments which preceded and followed the Second Empire had neither its
care nor its attraction for the common people.[3]   But
fatally true also was the admission which Louis' very
claim implied.   He had brought the twenty and nine from
the wilderness and lost the one million that mattered.
For that one outraged and righteous million included
almost all the political and diplomatic experience, above
all, all the eloquence of France.

It was across this gap and emptiness immediately en-
circling his throne that Louis Napoleon had to fling his
utterances to his people.   Over the empty stalls he knew
how to get them across to the pit ; and had his isolation
no graver disadvantages than this it would have involved
nothing worse than some playing to the gallery.   But it
had other and graver consequences.   Single-handed he

---

[1] *Reiset*, ii. 352.   [2] *Martin*, iii. 121.

[3] ' If the chances of the Bonaparte dynasty have appeared at various
periods greater than those of the Orleanists it is not as people will often
imagine owing to the afterglow of the first Napoleon, but to the popularity of his nephew.   The working classes had never been treated as
kindly as they were under the legislation which bore the name of the
Prince Imperial, and the unheard-of commercial expansion of those days
made their lives incomparably happier than at any other period in the
nineteenth century : after more than forty years they have not forgotten
it.'   *Dimnet*, 50.   Cf. *Bodley*, 577 *sq.*, and authorities there cited.

was forced to attempt work which was utterly beyond his strength. Even in 1856 his intimates were aware that the price was increasing physical ill-health.[1] But here it was the essential vice of the imperial system that this price he could not pay alone. Illness which the absence of competent subordinates accelerated in the Emperor, the absence of competent subordinates was to render fatal to the Empire. It was indeed the tragedy of the reign, that the Emperor's illness allowed him just time enough to acquire the strongest hand in Europe ; and then intervened to disable him from playing it even tolerably. ' It was a very sad sight,' wrote Prince Albert's brother, describing a visit which he paid to the Emperor just after the fall of Sevastopol, ' to see this man, who knew himself just arrived at the summit of his position, and secured in the possession of his power, in a state of the plainest physical decay.'[2] Never in fact had ruler of France more brilliant chances than those which Louis Napoleon had won for his country at the end of the first half of his reign. And never were advantages more miserably thrown away.

The turning-point however was not yet. Although his disease was already harder upon him than men knew, the Emperor had left another five years in which he was only exceptionally under its sway, before the longer period when it was exceptional for him to be free from it. And in the interval he was to put his hand to a task which no other hand than his would have attempted, and no lesser help than his could have achieved. That task was the Liberation of Italy.

The history of that work—by far the most considerable achievement of Louis Napoleon's life—we hope to recount elsewhere. Meanwhile we may take our leave of him at

---

[1] ' At present the whole business of the country passes through his hands. The disorganised state of the Emperor's health is not generally known.' F.O. France, Cowley to Clarendon. ' Confidential.' 27 June 56. ' The poor Empress is in very low spirits about him,' he added in a private letter. ' She said that people mistook him—that because he had a calm exterior, they thought he had no feeling—whereas it was impossible to exaggerate the misery which the war had caused him, to which she attributes much of his illness.' Wellesley, *The Paris Embassy*, 101.

[2] ' Frequently he was tormented by such pains that he had to pause in his speech. When he was sitting he was sometimes unable to rise without assistance.' *Ernest*, iii. 193.

the apparent pinnacle of his fortunes : successful abroad, and for the moment, save in the Orleanist salons, popular even in Paris ; while from the provinces he could command a veritable devotion.[1] There was no power on the Continent that would not welcome his alliance : for the moment he seemed almost to have justified Cousin's description of him as the ' Emperor of Europe.' Hitherto ' the Emperor ' *sans phrase* meant Nicholas : henceforth it meant Napoleon. The implied hegemony had not been easily won ; but once attained its retention would seem to have been a relatively easy matter, especially for a ruler both schooled in person by adversity and profoundly convinced by his uncle's fate of the need of moderation in good fortune. Common prudence, and the abstinence from further fantastic adventure, seemed all that was now needed to secure for his reign a monotonously prosperous conclusion, with all the posthumous titles of statesmanship which history awards easily to final political success.

That choice was not made, nor those prizes gained. But the career is perhaps not less worth following for that. The habit of seeking change pursued Louis Napoleon even when change was become to his own disadvantage ; but it was other men's ills as well as his own good that he could not leave alone. And for this reason the expenditure and exhaustion of his power was a process in many ways more fruitful than the acquisition of it, although it led him eventually to astonish by his failures a world which had hardly ceased to be amazed by his success.

---

[1] Witness the scenes of frantic enthusiasm which greeted two months later his sudden excursion to the inundated valleys of the Loire and of the Rhone. 'The Emperor's reception at Lyons, Valence and Avignon seems really to justify the account given of it in the *Moniteur*. A private account says that he was affected even to tears at the manner in which he was received by the Lyons people.' *Times*, 5 June 56, p. 9, c. 2. Cp. *Castellane*, v. 139–143, 'Toujours les cris de " Vive l'homme de cœur ! Vive notre sauveur ! Vive le père du peuple ! "' 'I am assured that his Majesty encountered considerable personal risk in some of the frail boats in which he embarked for the purpose of ascertaining what could be done to alleviate the distress.' F.O France, Cowley to Clarendon, 6 June 56.

APPENDIX A

BIBLIOGRAPHY

THE following bibliography refers only to that portion of Louis Napoleon's life dealt with in this volume. The date given, unless otherwise stated, is that of the first edition. The place of publication is only mentioned when it was not the capital of a country sufficiently indicated by the language. Where the author's name is given in brackets the work was originally anonymous. Pseudonyms are in inverted commas. For the saving of space works cited once only are not repeated below where they have been sufficiently described in the footnote in question. For a similar reason I have omitted from this bibliography all books which I have consulted with purely negative results ; and even ·of the others have practically confined the list to those which I ˉhave actually had occasion to refer to in the notes.

Agresti = O. R. Agresti. *Giovanni Costa : his life, work, and times.* 1904.
Amigues = Jules Amigues. *L'état romain depuis 1815 jusqu'à nos jours.* 1862.
Argyll = The Duke of Argyll. *Autobiography and Memoirs.* 2 vols. 1906.
   Edited by his widow. Argyll was the last survivor of the Aberdeen cabinet, and his memoirs throw some new light on the 'drift to war' in 53.
Ashley = Hon. Evelyn Ashley. *Life of Viscount Palmerston.* 2 vols. 1879.
   A revised edition of the earlier 5-vol. work by the same author and Lord Dalling. Ashley was Palmerston's private secretary ; but neither he nor Dalling quite rose to his opportunities.
Audebrand : Souvenirs = Philibert Audebrand. *Souvenirs de la tribune des Journalistes, 1848–1852.* 1867.
Audebrand : Napoléon III = The same. *Un café de journalistes sous Napoléon III.* 1888.
   Collections of anecdotes of small interest or importance.
Bagehot : Life = *The Life of Walter Bagehot,* by his sister-in-law, Mrs Russell Barrington. 1914.
Bagehot : Works = *The Works of Walter Bagehot.* 9 vols. 1915.
   Like the Brownings, Bagehot chanced to be in Paris for the *coup d'état* and the few months before it. Both the private letters in the Life, and the open letters in the Works, contain valuable contemporary impressions on the event by an acute and impartial observer.
Barante = *Souvenirs du Baron P. de Barante.* 1899–1901. 8 vols.
   Author a remote cousin of Queen Hortense : vols. 7 and 8 cover

this period. Not memoirs at all, but correspondence chiefly with Royalists. Of small value except as an indication of royalist opinions.

Barrot=Odilon Barrot. *Mémoires.* 4 vols. 1875–6.
Valuable for period of his premiership of Louis Napoleon's first cabinet. But largely a compilation of parliamentary speeches : republished as *inédit* matter already printed in contemporary press : and where new not always true. v. *Quentin-Bauchart*, i. 468 *sq.*

Barthez, E.=Docteur Barthez. *La Famille Impériale à Saint Cloud et à Biarritz.*
Barthez (1811–1891) was doctor to the Prince Imperial : charming and intimate description by a shrewd and kindly observer in letters to his wife.

Bastide=J. Bastide. *La République française et l'Italie.* 1858.
Defends the French government's dealings with Italy in 1848.

Bazin=René Bazin. *Le Duc de Nemours.* References are to the 3rd edition. 1907.
Useful on the negotiations for the ' Fusion.'

Beaumont-Vassy=Vicomte E. de Beaumont-Vassy. *Histoire intime du second Empire.* 1874.
Neither 'intime' nor 'histoire' ; just not empty.

Belgiojoso=H. R. Whitehouse. *A Revolutionary Princess.* 1906.
References are to the French edition of 1907.

Belouino=Paul Belouino. *Histoire d'un Coup d'État.* 1852.
The most substantial of the contemporary Bonapartists' apologies for the *coup d'état.*

Bernard=Albert Bernard. *Souvenirs de la promotion de L'Empire.* 1916.
Letters of a young French officer, 1852–4.

Bernstorff=*The Bernstorff Papers.* The life of Count Albrecht Bernstorff, by Dr Karl Ringhoffer. English translation. 2 vols. 1908.
Bernstorff was Prussian minister at Vienna (1848–52) and Naples (1852–7).

Beslay=Charles Beslay. *Mes Souvenirs.* 1873. Neuchâtel.
A republican ex-member of the Constituent Assembly, present at the last meeting of the Legislative Assembly on 2 Dec. 51.

Beust=Friedrich Ferdinand, Count von Beust. *Memoirs.* Translated and edited by Baron Henry de Worms. 2 vols. 1887.
Gossipy reminiscences of no great value.

Bianchi=Nicomede Bianchi. *La politique du Comte de Cavour, 1852–1861.* 1885.
Some 200 letters from Cavour to Azeglio, then Sardinian ambassador at St James'.

Blessington=R. R. Madden. *The Literary Life and Correspondence of the Countess of Blessington.* 3 vols. 1855.
A friend of Louis Napoleon during his English exile.

Blount=*Memoirs of Sir Edward Blount.* 1902.

Bocher=Charles Bocher. *Lettres et Récits Militaires.* 1897.
An Orleanist, brother of the orator, served in the Crimean War.

Bodley=J. E. C. Bodley. *France.* 2 vols. 1898.
References are to the one-volume edition of 1899.

Boichot=J. B. Boichot. *Souvenirs d'un prisonnier d'État.* Leipzig. 1867.

Bosquet=*Lettres du Maréchal Bosquet à sa Mère, 1829–1858.* 4 vols. Pau. 1877–9.

Bostock=Deputy Surgeon-General J. A. Bostock. *Letters from India and the Crimea.* 1896.
A scathing indictment of administrative imbecilities in the Crimea.

Bourgeois, C. M. H.=Emile Bourgeois. Cambridge Modern History, vol. xi., ch. 5.
Republican and anti-clerical. A partisan epitome of the history of the Second Republic.

378 BIBLIOGRAPHY

Bourgeois : *France*=The same. *History of Modern France, 1815–1913*. 2 vols. 1919.
Fairer and better work.
Bourgeois : see also Clermont.
Broglie=Duc de Broglie. *Souvenirs, 1781–1870*. 4 vols. 1886.
Buffoni=Lisabe Buffoni. Chap. 12 in vol. 2 of General Pepe's *Narrative of Scenes and Events in Italy*. 1850.
Calthorpe=[S. J. G. Calthorpe]. *Letters from Headquarters : or the Realities of the War in the Crimea*. 2 vols. 1856.
Vividly written : defends Raglan.
Campbell=Lt.-Col. C. F. Campbell. *Letters from Sebastopol*. 1894.
Letters written from Nov. 54 to May 56. Defends Simpson.
Canrobert=*Le Maréchal Canrobert*, by Germain Bapst. 4 vols. 1903–4.
Practically autobiographical : largely dictated and partly corrected by Canrobert. References are to the second edition.
Cassagnac=M. A. Granier de Cassagnac. *Souvenirs du second Empire*. 3 vols. 1879–82.
Strongly Bonapartist : partisan and untrustworthy.
Castellane=*Journal du Maréchal de Castellane, 1804–1862*. 5 vols. 1895–7.
Cavour : *Lettere*=Luigi Chiala. *Lettere edite ed inedite di Camillo Cavour*. 6 vols. 1882–7.
References are to the second edition.
Chambolle=H. Chambolle. *Retours sur la vie*. 1912.
Edited by his son. Chambolle was a republican deputy, a friend of O. Barrot, present at the last meeting of the Legislative Assembly on 2 Dec. 51.
Charles-Roux=Francois Charles-Roux. *Alexandre II, Gortchakoff et Napoléon III*. 1913.
Vol. I. on 1855–6. Good on Franco-Russian relations, but inadequately documented.
Clermont=Bourgeois (E.) and Clermont (E.). *Rome et Napoléon III*. 1907.
Clermont deals with Louis Napoleon's crime in 1849, Bourgeois with its punishment in 1870 (see above, pp. 87–89). Both portions of the book are valuable, and ably argued : but the work is not quite without polemic purpose, and it deserves a more critical appreciation than it has hitherto received.
Clough=A. H. Clough : *Life, Letters, and Prose Remains*, edited by his Wife. 2 vols. 1869.
C.M.H.=*Cambridge Modern History*. Vol. XI. 1909. The Growth of Nationalities.
Cobden : *Speeches*=*Speeches* by R. Cobden. Edited by J. Bright and T. Rogers. 2 vols. 1870.
Commissaire=S. Commissaire. *Mémoires et souvenirs*. 2 vols. 1888.
A republican deputy who took part in the rising of 13 June 49.
Cook=Sir Edward Cook. *The Life of Florence Nightingale*. 2 vols. 1913.
A good biography.
Dandolo=E. Dandolo. *The Italian Volunteers and Lombard Rifle Brigade*. 1851.
An inside account of the siege of Rome, by one of its defenders. The Italian original was published immediately after the event in 1849.
Daudan=X. Daudan. *Mélanges et Lettres*. 4 vols. 1876.
Davidson=A. F. Davidson. *Victor Hugo, his life and work*. 1912.
A good biography, which deserves to be better known.
D.N.B.=*Dictionary of National Biography*.
Debidour=A. Debidour. *Histoire diplomatique de l'Europe*. 2 vols. 1891.
Delescluze=Charles Delescluze. *De Paris à Cayenne*. Paris. 1869.
Author a victim of the *coup d'état*, who only returned to France in Aug. 1859.

Della Rocca=General Della Rocca. *Autobiography of a Veteran.* English Translation. 1899.

Delord=Taxile Delord. *Histoire du second Empire.* 6 vols. 1868–75.
   Mildly republican, as became the editor of the *Siècle.* A somewhat dreary external chronicle of events : less prejudiced than might be expected from the date of its composition, but deprived by it of many important sources of information at that time unpublished.

Denormandie=M. Denormandie. *Temps passé. Jours présents.* 2nd edition. 1900.

D'Harcourt=B. d'Harcourt. *Les quatre ministères de Drouyn de Lhuys.* 1882.
   Chapter I useful on Drouyn's relations with Lesseps in 49: and Chapter II on the equally abortive negotiations of April 55.

Dickinson=G. Lowes Dickinson. *Revolution and Reaction in Modern France.* 1892.

Dimnet=Ernest Dimnet. *France Herself Again.* 1914.

Diplomatic Study=*Diplomatic Study of the Crimean War from Russian Official Sources.* Tr. 1880.
   Anonymous and poor translation of a Russian official publication inspired by Gortschakoff. Useful for its admissions, which are strangely frank at times : but in general its narrative is thoroughly unreliable.

Du Barail=Général Du Barail. *Mes Souvenirs.* 3 vols. 1894–6.

Du Casse : *Coup d'état*=Baron P. E. Albert Du Casse. *Les dessous du Coup d'état.* 1891.
   Important for attitude of Prince Napoleon and his father during the *coup d'état.*

Du Casse : *Sébastopol*=The same. *La Crimée et Sébastopol de 1853 à 1856.* 1892.
   Contains interesting papers, of no great importance, relative to the Crimean War, which chanced to come into the author's hands.

Du Casse : *Souvenirs*=The same. *Souvenirs d'un aide de camp du roi Jérôme.* 1890.

Dunoyer=Charles Dunoyer. *Le Second Empire et une nouvelle restauration.* 2 vols. London. 1865.
   Author a liberal Royalist, an advocate of the ' Fusion.'

Duprat=Pascal Duprat. *Les tables de proscription de Louis Bonaparte.* 2 vols. 1852. Liège.
   Author a republican representative : declamatory, but useful for detailed lists of names and trades of the victims of the proscription after the *coup d'état.*

Durrieu=Xavier-Durrieu. *Le Coup d'état de Louis Bonaparte.* London. 1852. Also published at Geneva.
   A republican ex-member of the Constituent Assembly present at the barricade fighting in Dec. 51 : but his narrative is inaccurate, and of small value.

Duruy=Victor Duruy. *Notes et Souvenirs.* (1810–94.) 2 vols. 1901.

Ebeling=Ad. Ebeling. *Sketches of Modern Paris.* 1867. English translation, 1870.

Ellesmere=*Military Events in Italy, 1848–49.*
   Author a Swiss mercenary in the Austrian army. Translated by the Earl of Ellesmere.

English Family=G. Mazzini. *Letters to an English Family.* 1844–54. Vol. 1. 1920.

Englishman=[A. D. Vandam]. *An Englishman in Paris.* 3 vols. 1892.
   References to the 1 vol. edition of 1893. Attributed at the time, but wrongly, to Sir R. Wallace.

Ernest=Ernest II., Duke of Saxe-Coburg-Gotha. *Memoirs.* Translated from the German. 4 vols. 1888.
   The duke, a brother of Prince Albert, was the first European prince

to visit the Tuileries : and remained an important intermediary between Napoleon III and the German courts.

Evans=T. W. Evans. *Memoirs.* 2 vols. 1905.
Evans was the Emperor's American dentist.

Falloux=A. F. P. de Falloux. *Mémoires d'un royaliste.* 2 vols. 1888.
Minister of Education in Louis Napoleon's first cabinet : valuable for period of its duration : Jan.-Dec. 49. Clerical.

Farini=L. G. Farini. *The Roman State from 1815 to 1850.* English translation by W. E. Gladstone. 4 vols. 1851-4.
Author a well-informed Liberal politician, deputy at Turin in 48, and Minister of Education in 1850. A transparently honest man, indignant at injustice wherever he saw it, and able to see it on both sides.

Faucher=Léon Faucher. *Biographie et Correspondance.* 2 vols. 1868.
References to the 1875 edition.

Fay=Général C. A. Fay. *Souvenirs de la guerre de Crimée.* 1867.
Author an aide-de-camp of Marshal Bosquet, with whom he served in the Crimea.

Fitzmaurice=Lord E. C. P. Fitzmaurice. *Life of the second Earl Granville.* 2 vols. 1905.

' *Flaneur* '=*Ten Years of Imperialism in France. Impressions of a flaneur.* 1862.
Written in Paris by an intelligent observer.

Fleischmann=Hector Fleischmann. *Napoleon III and the women he loved.* Eng. translation by A. S. Rappoport. n.d.

Fleury=Général Fleury. *Souvenirs, 1837-67.* 2 vols. 1897.

Fonblanque=E. B. de Fonblanque. *The Life and Labours of Albany Fonblanque.* 1874.
Editor of the *Examiner* : one of Louis Napoleon's English acquaintances.

Fragmens Historiques=*Fragmens Historiques : 1688 et 1830.* Par le Prince Napoléon Louis Bonaparte. 1841.

Fraser=Sir W. A. Fraser. *Napoleon III.* 1896.
A collection of anecdotes, several of them about the Emperor.

Froude=J. A. Froude. *Thomas Carlyle.* 2 vols. 1884.

Gaillard=Léopold de Gaillard. *L'Expédition de Rome en 1849.* 1861.
A clerical writer, indignant with the anti-Papal and pro-Italian attitude of the Emperor in 1860 ; whose work contains telling, and, in its author's eyes most damaging, evidence that the President in 1849 was really tarred with the same brush.

Garibaldi=Giuseppe Garibaldi. *Autobiography.* Authorised English translation by A. Werner. 3 vols. 1889.

Giraudeau=Fernand Giraudeau. *Napoléon III intime.* 1895.
Bonapartist propaganda, but its author had access to some unpublished material, and cites adequately and accurately his published authorities.

Gourdon=E. Gourdon. *Histoire du congrès de Paris.* 1857.
A detailed account of the sessions and transactions of the Congress.

Grabinski=Comte Joseph Grabinski. *Le Comte Arese, un ami de Napoléon III.* 1897.
Republishes the valuable letters of Louis Napoleon, Conneau, and Arese, which first appeared in Bonfadini's Italian life of the last-named in 1894. His additions from other sources are sometimes erroneous, *e.g.* p. 62 ; sometimes interesting and important, *e.g.* p. 35 *n.*

Graham=R. H. Vetch. *Life of Lt.-Gen. Sir G. Graham.* 1901.
Includes letters written from the Crimea.

Gréard=Octave Gréard. *Prévost-Paradol.* 1894.

Greville=C. F. G. Greville. *Journal of the Reign of Queen Victoria.* 8 vols. Ed. Henry Reeve. 1888.

Gronow=*The Reminiscences and Recollections of Captain Gronow.* Being anecdotes of the camp, court, clubs, and society, 1810–1860. 1862, 63, 65, and 66.
   References are to the indexed 2-vol. edition of 1892, of matter first published in four separate series.
Guizot=*Lettres de M. Guizot à sa famille et à ses amis.* Paris. 1884.
Hamley=General Sir E. B. Hamley. *The War in the Crimea.* 1891.
Hanotaux=Gabriel Hanotaux. *Histoire de la France contemporaine.* Vol. i, n.d. [1903.]
Hansard=*Hansard's Parliamentary Debates.* 3rd series.
Haussmann=Baron Haussmann. *Mémoires.* 4 vols. 1890–93.
Hautpoul=Général Marquis Alfonse D'Hautpoul. *Mémoires.* 1906.
   Ch. xiii. on his ministry in Louis Napoleon's second cabinet. The memoirs end in 1850, though the author lived till 1865.
Heath=Admiral Sir M. G. Heath. *Letters from the Black Sea, 1854–5.* 1897.
Heine=H. Heine. *Lutèce.* (Correspondance addressée de 1840–1843 à un journal allemand.) Paris. 1853.
Henry Greville=Henry Greville. Leaves from the Diary of Henry Greville. Edited by the Vicountess Enfield. 4 vols. 1883–1905.
Hohenlohe=*Memoirs of Prince Chlodwig of Hohenlohe.* 2 vols. English translation. 1907.
Home=Surgeon-General Sir A. D. Home. *Service Memories.* 1912.
Houssaye=Arsène Houssaye. *Souvenirs de jeunesse, 1830–1870.* 2 vols., n.d. [1896.]
Hübner=*Neuf ans de souvenirs d'un Ambassadeur d'Autriche.* 2 vols. 1904.
   Hübner was Austrian ambassador at Paris, 1851–9. The book is edited by his son.
Hugo : *N. le Petit*=Victor Hugo. *Napoléon-le-Petit.* 1852.
Hugo : ' *Histoire* '=Victor Hugo. *Histoire d'un crime.* 1877.
   The second is an amplification of the first : published, and, despite the author's own statement, in all probability written, twenty-five years after the earlier declamation. Throughout the author is in bad faith : his misstatements are due not to the credulity of honest anger, but to deliberate artistic and calculated literary invention.
Hugo : *Choses Vues*=Victor Hugo. *Choses Vues.* Nouvelle série. 1899.
   Fragmentary but valuable : since this posthumous series contains passages really written at the dates alleged, and not written up later for publication. In all these three works references are to the Nelson edition.
Hugo : *Actes*=Victor Hugo : *Actes et paroles.* 3 vols. 1875.
Jerrold=Blanchard Jerrold. *Life of Napoleon III.* 4 vols. 1874–82.
   The two first volumes on Louis Napoleon's early life contain important material : but the book declines rapidly in value after '48. Throughout it is apologetic and partisan : owing much both of its information and its bias to the Empress.
Johnston=R. N. Johnston. *The Roman Theocracy and the Republic.* 1901.
   Fair but dull.
Joigneaux=Pierre Joigneaux. *Mémoires d'un représentant du peuple.* 2 vols. 1890.
   Author a republican exile after the *coup d'état.* Contains little information.
Kelly=General Sir R. D. Kelly. *An Officer's Letters to his Wife during the Crimean War.* 1902.
   Dull but honest impressions.
Key=Sir A. C. Key. *Memoirs.* 1898.
King : *Italy*=Bolton King. *A History of Italian Unity.* 2 vols. 1898.
King : *Mazzini*=Bolton King. *Mazzini.* 1902.

Kinglake =A. W. Kinglake. *The Invasion of the Crimea.* 8 vols. 1863–80.
This finely written but untrustworthy work is chiefly remembered by what Sir A. W. Ward has recently described as its ' magnificent portico,' ' the opening volumes with their splendid indictment of the author of the *coup d'état.*' [Cambridge Modern History of English Literature, xiv. p. 94, 1916 : where the same book is more marvellously praised for its accuracy.]
In view of such commendation I have thought it worth while to examine somewhat curiously the foundations of this ' portico,' certainly of its kind a monumental structure. The following facts emerge, and deserve publication : (1) Kinglake himself, in his preface, declared this portion of his work—*i.e.* in his own words ' an important part of the first and nearly the whole of the second volume '—to be based ' upon unpublished writings or private information.' ' For the present,' he continued, ' this portion of the book must rest upon what, after all, is the chief basis of our historical knowledge—upon the statement of one who had good means of knowing the truth. In the meanwhile, I shall keep and leave ready the clue by which, in some later time, and without further aid from me, my statements may be traced to their sources.' Although this undertaking has been in print for some sixty years, the promised clue has never been forthcoming. Further, as the result of my own communications with Kinglake's publishers, and of an extensive correspondence with his relatives, most kindly undertaken on my behalf by his late biographer, the Rev. W. Tuckwell, I find that neither the one nor the other have possession or knowledge of any documents by means of which this mysterious promise could be fulfilled. Careful search for such papers has been made for me by the two nearest of Kinglake's surviving relatives, in each case without result. Both of them emphasise the fact that the author before his death ordered the bulk of his papers to be destroyed. In thus consigning them to the fire instead of to the light, the author must be assumed to have been the best judge of their destination. But it is time that historians should know that all his more dramatic charges against Louis Napoleon rest now only on the *ipse dixit* of a writer who broke his promise to substantiate them. (2) Not only does the structure lack foundation, but it possesses bias. The author was Louis Napoleon's unsuccessful rival for the favour of his most famous English mistress, the so-called Miss Howard. Though the fact of this quarrel has been referred to in print several times in the last twenty years, no authoritative confirmation of it has hitherto been forthcoming. As a result of the same correspondence I have the story now on the authority of a very near relative of the historian, who cited it as a fact perfectly well known to the older members of the family.

La Gorce : *République* =Pierre de La Gorce. *Histoire de la seconde République française.* 2 vols. 1887.
Clerical and conservative throughout, but only really unfair in his account of the Roman expedition.

La Gorce : *L'Empire* =Pierre de La Gorce. *Histoire du second Empire.* 7 vols. 1894–1905.
Finely written : the only real historian of the Second Empire. But his dislike of the Emperor's Italian policy leads him to idealise the pre-Italian period of the reign, and to underrate the unpopularity of the Crimean War.

Lagrange =F. Lagrange. *Vie de Mgr. Dupanloup.* 2 vols. 1883.

Lamartine : *Mémoires* =A. de Lamartine. *Mémoires Politiques.*

Lamartine : *Orateur* =Louis Barthon. *Lamartine Orateur.* 1918.

Lane-Poole =Stanley Lane-Poole. *Life of Stratford Canning.* 2 vols. 1888.
Embeds much valuable material : but reflects the influence of Kinglake.

Laughton=J. K. Laughton. *Life and Correspondence of Henry Reeve.* 2 vols. 1898.

Lebey=André Lebey. *Louis-Napoléon Bonaparte et le Ministère Odilon Barrot.* 1912.
  Of greater length and smaller value than the author's previous studies of Louis Napoleon's earlier career.

Lecanuet=R. P. Lecanuet. *Montalembert d'après son journal et sa correspondance.* 3 vols. 1895.

Ledru Rollin=A. P. A. Ledru-Rollin. *Discours politiques et écrits divers.* 2 vols. 1879.

Lefranc=Pierre Lefranc. *Le Deux Décembre.* Paris. 1870.
  A republican deputy who took part in the talking against the *coup d'état.*

Lesseps : *Mission*=M. Ferdinand de Lesseps. *Ma mission à Rome, mai 1849.* 1851.
  Naturally the most important source for the Lesseps negotiations. But allowance must be made for the author's desire to prove that their failure was not his fault.

Lesseps : *Souvenirs*=The same. *Souvenirs de quarante ans.* 2 vols. 1887.

Limet=Charles Limet. *Un vétéran du Barreau Parisien : Quatre-vingts ans de souvenirs, 1827–1907.* 1908.
  An Orleanist friend of Ollivier. Little of interest.

Lireux=A. Lireux. *L'Assemblée nationale comique.* 1849.

Loftus=Lord Augustus Loftus. *Diplomatic Reminiscences, 1837–1862.* [1st series.] 2 vols. 1892.

Longmore=Surgeon-General T. Longmore. *Sanitary Contrasts of the Crimean War.* 1883.
  Corrects some of Kinglake's mistakes in this particular connexion.

Lorne=Marquis of Lorne. *Lord Palmerston.* 1892.
  Contains some new matter not in Ashley.

Lubbock=Percy Lubbock. *Elizabeth Barrett Browning in her Letters.* 1906.
  The Brownings were in Paris from Sept. 51 to June 52 : *i.e.* over the period of the *coup d'état.*

Lushington=H. Lushington. *The Italian War, 1848–9.*
  Articles reprinted in 1859 from the *Edinburgh Review* of 1851, by an English visitor to Rome after the siege.

Lytton=*The Life of Edward Bulwer, 1st Lord Lytton.* By his grandson, the Earl of Lytton. 2 vols. 1913.

Magen=M. H. Magen. *Mystères du 2 décembre.* 1852.
  Anti-Bonapartist account of the *coup d'état.* Like Kinglake withholds proof of his more dramatic charges (*e.g.* p. 120) on plea that others would be compromised by their publication at this date : like Kinglake never produced the evidence at all. Fellow-republicans convict of occasional inaccuracy. *v.* Schoelcher : *Crimes,* 133.

'*Malakoff*'=W. E. Johnston. *Memoirs of 'Malakoff.'* 2 vols. 1906.
  Extracts from reports to the *New York Times* from W. E. Johnston, its Paris correspondent, during the Second Empire : edited by his son R. M. Johnston.

Malmesbury=Earl of Malmesbury. *Memoirs of an ex-Minister.* 2 vols. 1884.
  Author a lifelong friend of Louis Napoleon, on whom his gossipy memoirs—professedly a contemporary diary—throw some interesting sidelights.

Manin=*Documents et pièces authentiques laissés par Daniel Manin.* Traduits et annotés par F. Planat de la Faye. 1860. 2 vols. 1860.

Marriott=J. A. R. Marriott. *The Eastern Question : an historical study in European diplomacy.* 1917.
  A useful outline.

Martin=Sir Theodore Martin. *Life of the Prince Consort.* 5 vols. 1875–1880.
   Valuable on the Crimean negotiations. Vol. iii. based on an examination of some fifty folio volumes of the Prince's papers on the Eastern Question. Anti-Palmerston.

Martinengo Cesaresco=Martinengo Cesaresco, Contessa. *The Liberation of Italy, 1815–1870.* 1895.

Mauduit=Hippolyte de Mauduit. *Révolution militaire du 2 décembre 1851.* 1852.
   An ill-written and inaccurate defence of the *coup d'état*, by a legitimist turned Bonapartist present in Paris at the time.

Maupas=C. E. de Maupas. *Mémoires sur le second Empire.* 2 vols. 1884.
   A son-in-law of Colonel Vaudrey ; one of the chief actors in the *coup d'état*, of which his memoirs contain a detailed and valuable though naturally a partisan account.

Maxwell=Sir Herbert Maxwell. *Life of the Fourth Earl of Clarendon.* 2 vols. 1913.
   In spite of occasional inaccuracies a good and impartial biography : Chapters 13 to 16 useful on the Crimean War.

Mayer=M. P. Mayer. *Histoire du deux décembre.* 1852.
   Bonapartist.

Mazade=Charles de Mazade. *Le Comte de Cavour.* 1877.

Mazzini=G. Mazzini. Life and Writings. 6 vols. 1864–70.

Melun=Vicomte Arnaud de Melun. *Mémoires.* 2 vols. 1891.

Merruau=C. A. Merruau. *Souvenirs de l'Hôtel-de-Ville de Paris.* 1875.

Metternich=*Mémoires, documents et écrits divers laissés par le prince de Metternich.* 8 vols. 1884.

Millelot=M. N. Millelot. *Clamecy en 1851.* 1869.
   Republican : a pamphlet intended eventually as an appendix to Ténot's *Province, q.v.*

Morley : Cobden=Lord Morley. *Life of R. Cobden.* 2 vols. 1881.

Morley : Gladstone=Lord Morley. *Life of W. E. Gladstone.* 3 vols. 1903.
   References are to the 2-vol. edition of 1905.

Nauroy=Charles Nauroy. *Les secrets des Bonaparte.* 1889.

Newton=*Life of Lord Lyons.* 2 vols. 1913.

Nolan=Nolan's *History of the War against Russia.*
   In 40 shilling parts, n.d. References to the 8-vol. collected edition. One of the first and very far from the worst examples of history while you fight.

Normanby=The Marquis of Normanby. *A Year of Revolution in Paris.* 2 vols. 1857.
   As English ambassador Normanby was on intimate terms with Lamartine and other of the republican leaders in 1848. Not invariably accurate, but both this book and his F.O. despatches, which it often reproduces almost textually, illustrate the anti-republican feeling of France in 48, and the republican leaders' appreciation of the fact.

Ollivier=Emile Ollivier. *L'empire libéral.* 17 vols. 1895–1915.
   The second half of vol. ii. and the first half of vol. iii. touch upon this period : but the work is only important on the latter years of the Empire. The author exaggerates Louis Napoleon's desire to bring about the Crimean War.

Ossoli=M. F. Ossoli. *Memoirs.* 3 vols. 1852.
   In Rome during the siege.

Panmure=*The Panmure Papers.* 2 vols. 1908. Edited by Sir G. Douglas and Sir G. D. Ramsay.
   A selection from the correspondence of Fox Maule, Second Baron Panmure, Secretary for War in Palmerston's first cabinet : important on the last year of the war.

Papiers sauvés =*Papiers sauvés des Tuileries.* 1874. Published by Robert Halt
    Less important than the
Papiers et correspondance =*Papiers et correspondance de la famille impériale.* 2 vols. 1870. to which they are a sequel.
    Editing partisan, designed to discredit the fallen dynasty : but the documents themselves are valuable.
Parker =C. S. Parker. *Life and Letters of Sir James Graham.* 2 vols. 1907.
Pasolini =P. D. Pasolini. *Memoir of Count Giuseppe Pasolini, 1815–1876.* English abridged translation by the Dowager Countess of Dalhousie. 1885.
Paul =Herbert Paul. *A History of Modern England.* 5 vols. 1906.
    Well-written, but on the Crimean War wildly partisan.
Persigny =Fialin Duc de Persigny. *Mémoires.* 1896.
    Real memoirs by Persigny would be of great value. These however are brief, random, and isolated recollections, edited by an admirer. They exaggerate the importance of Persigny's interventions throughout.
Pessard =Hector Pessard. *Mes petitits papiers.* 2 vols. 1897–8.
Pierre =Victor Pierre. *Histoire de la République de 1848.* 2 vols. 1873–5.
Proudhon =*Correspondance de P. J. Proudhon.* 14 vols. 1874–5.
Q. V. L. =*The Letters of Queen Victoria.* 1907.
    References are to the 1908 edition.
Quentin-Bauchart =A. Quentin-Bauchart. *Etudes et souvenirs sur la deuxième République et le second Empire.* 2 vols. 1902.
    Author a deputy imprisoned for a few hours after the *coup d'état* who became an ardent and lifelong imperialist a few days later. Written after the fall of the Empire, and published by his son. Little of value.
Quinet =Edgar Quinet. *Lettres d'exil.* 4 vols. 1885–1886.
Rambaud =A. Rambaud. *Histoire de la Russie.* 1878.
Ranc =A. Ranc. *Souvenirs : correspondance, 1831–1908.* 1913.
    A republican exiled after the *coup d'état.*
Randon =Maréchal Randon. *Mémoires.* 2 vols. 1875.
    Minister of War, Jan.-Oct. 51 : Governor-General of Algeria 52 : Marshal 56.
Ranken =Major George Ranken. *Six Months at Sebastopol.* 1857.
    Leader of the ladder party in the last English assault on the Redan.
Reclus : *Favre* =Maurice Reclus. *Jules Favre.* 1912.
Reclus : *Picard* =Maurice Reclus. *Ernest Picard.* 1912.
Register =*The Annual Register.*
Reid : *Russell* =S. J. Reid. *Lord John Russell.* 1895.
Reid : *Durham* =S. J. Reid. *Life of Lord Durham.* 2 vols. 1907.
Reiset =Comte de Reiset. *Mes souvenirs.* 3 vols. 1901–1903.
    Met Louis Napoleon at Arenenberg in 36 ; secretary to the French embassy at Turin 1848–51 ; at St Petersburg 52–53 ; at Turin again 55. Kept a diary : less doctored than most French memoirs.
Ribeyrolles =C. A. Ribeyrolles. *The Prisons of Africa.* Melton Mowbray. 1857. English translation.
    Republican. Formerly editor of *La Réforme.*
Richard =Jules Richard. *Comment on a restauré l'Empire.* 1884
Rochefort =Henri Rochefort. *Les aventures de ma vie.* 5 vols. 1896.
Roon =*Denkwürdigkeiten aus dem Leben des General-Feldmarschalls Kriegsministers Grafen von Roon.* 2 vols. 1892.
    Roon was present as a young officer attendant on the Prussian general whom King Frederick William sent to pay his respects to Louis Napoleon on the occasion of the latter's visit to Strasburg in July 52.

Rothan : *La Prusse* = G. Rothan. *La Prusse et son Roi, pendant la guerre de Crimée.* 1888.

Rothan : *Souvenirs* = G. Rothan. *L'Europe et l'avènement du second Empire.* 1890.

Rousset = C. F. M. Rousset. *Histoire de la guerre de Crimée.* 2 vols. 1877.
  The earliest real history of the war.

Russell = Sir W. H. Russell. *The War.* 1856.
  A reprint of the famous *Times* letters.

St Amand I. = Imbert de Saint-Amand. *Louis Napoléon et Mademoiselle de Montijo.* 1897.

St Amand II. = The same. *Napoléon III et sa cour.* 1900.

Saint-Arnaud = *Lettres du Maréchal Saint-Arnaud.* 2 vols. 1855.

Sand = George Sand. *Correspondance.* 6 vols. 1882–4.

Scheurer-Kestner = Auguste Scheurer-Kestner. *Souvenirs de jeunesse.* 1905.
  A friend of many of the exiles of Dec. 51.

Schoelcher : *Crimes* = V. Schoelcher. *Histoire des crimes du Deux Décembre.* London. 1852.

Schoelcher : *Gouvernement* = The same. *Le gouvernement du Deux Décembre.* 1853.
  The former volume is much the more valuable of the two : it is cited in the one-volume, London, not the two-volume, Belgian, edition. Quite uncritical as to what he heard, the author is a far better witness of what he saw than most of the opponents of the *coup d'état*. But, save for the Baudin episode, he saw little. For Schoelcher's relations with other exiles, *v.* B.N. Nouv. Acq. Fr. 22,135.

Seignobos : *France* = Ch. Seignobos. Vol. vi. of Ernest Lavisse's *Histoire de France Contemporaine.* 1921.

Seignobos : *Histoire* = The same. Chapter 1 of vol. xii. Lavisse et Rambaud, *Histoire générale.* 1901.

Senior : *Italy* = N. W. Senior. *Journals kept in France and Italy, 1848–1852.* 2 vols. 1871.

Senior : *Thiers* = The same. *Conversations with M. Thiers, M. Guizot, and other Distinguished Persons.* 2 vols. 1878.

Senior : *Empire* = The same. *Conversations with Distinguished Persons during the Second Empire from 1860 to 1863.* 2 vols. 1880.

Shadwell = Lt.-General Shadwell. *Life of Colin Campbell, Lord Clyde.* 2 vols. 1881.

Siege of Sebastopol = English official publication of that title. 1859. 3 vols. + 1 vol. of maps and plans.

Siboutie = Docteur Poumiès de la Siboutie. *Recollections of a Parisian, 1789–1863.* Edited by his daughters. English translation, 1911.

Simpson = F. A. Simpson. *The Rise of Louis Napoleon.* 1909.

Skene = J. H. Skene. *With Lord Stratford in the Crimean War.* 1883.
  The work of an admiring subordinate at Constantinople.

Skrine = F. H. Skrine. *The Expansion of Russia.* 1903.

Soissons = Comte de Soissons. *The True Story of the Empress Eugénie.* 1920.

Sonolet = Comte Fleury and Louis Sonolet. *La société du second Empire.* 4 vols. 1911.
  Contains some interesting illustrations.

Stanmore : *Aberdeen* = Lord Stanmore (then Sir A. Gordon). *Life of Lord Aberdeen.* 1893.
  Author a son of Aberdeen : but the book is impartial, and contains original documents : one of the best volumes in the ' Queen's Prime Ministers Series.'

Stanmore : *Herbert* = Lord Stanmore. *Lord Herbert of Lea : a Memoir.* 2 vols. 1906.

Steevens = Lt.-Col. N. Steevens. *The Crimean Campaign with the Connaught Rangers.* 1878.

Sterling = Lt.-Col. Sir A. C. Sterling. *The Highland Brigade in the Crimea.* 1895.

Stockmar = Baron Stockmar. *Memoirs.* English translation. 2 vols. 1872.
Fragmentary memoirs arranged by his son : useful for his dealings with the Prince Consort.

Story = Henry James. *William Wetmore Story and his Friends.* 2 vols. 1903.
Kept a diary in Rome during the siege.

Tchernoff : *République* = J. Tchernoff. *Associations et sociétés secrètes sous la deuxième République.* 1905.

Tchernoff : *Empire* = The same. *Le parti républicain au coup d'état et sous le second Empire.* 1906.

Ténot : *La Province* = E. Ténot. *La Province en décembre 1851.* 1865.

Ténot : *Paris* = The same. *Paris, décembre 1851.* 1868.
Republican, but both works are of real historical value : the first a vindication of the provincial insurrection after the *coup d'état* from exaggerated imperialist charges of Jacquerie : the second a refutation of some of the contemporary Bonapartist apologies for the proceedings in Paris. Draws heavily on Schoelcher, *q.v.*

Thayer : *Cavour* = W. R. Thayer. *The Life and Times of Cavour.* 2 vols. 1911.

Thayer : *Italy* = W. R. Thayer. *The Dawn of Italian Independence.* 2 vols. 1894.

Thirria = H. Thirria. *Napoléon III avant l'Empire.* 2 vols. 1896.
Vol. ii. covers the years 1849–51. Useful for full citations from the contemporary French press.

Thouvenel : *Nicolas* = L. Thouvenel. *Nicolas 1er et Napoléon III, 1852–4.* 1891.

Thouvenel : *Empire* = The same. *Pages de l'histoire du second Empire, 1854–1856.* 1903.

Tocqueville : *Correspondence* = Correspondence and Conversations of A. de Tocqueville with N. W. Senior, 1834–1859. Edited by M. C. M. Simpson. 2 vols. 1872.
Chiefly conversations.

Tocqueville : *Remains* = Memoir and Remains of A. de Tocqueville. 2 vols. 1861.
Chiefly letters—some identical with those in *Correspondence* above.

Tocqueville : *Souvenirs* = Souvenirs de A. de Tocqueville. 1893.
Extremely fragmentary memoirs published posthumously. Of some use for June to Oct. 49 : the period of his tenure of the Ministry of Foreign Affairs.

Tocqueville : *Œuvres* = Œuvres complètes d'Alexis de Tocqueville. Vol. VII. Nouvelle correspondance. 1866.

Todleben = General F. E. I. Todleben. *Défense de Sébastopol.* 2 vols. and maps. 1863–1870.
Written long after the event, with the object of exaggerating an achievement which needed no exaggeration. For detailed criticisms see Wrottesley, ii. 322–326.

Tolstoy = Leo Tolstoy. *Sevastopol.* 1855.
References are to L. and A. Maude's translation. 1905.

Trevelyan : *Bright* = G. M. Trevelyan. *The Life of John Bright.* 1913.
Chapters 10 and 11 contain a sympathetic account of the English peace party during the Crimean War.

Trevelyan : *Garibaldi* = G. M. Trevelyan. *Garibaldi's defence of the Roman Republic.* 1907.
A story which deserved the good fortune of being so finely told.

Trevelyan : *Nineteenth Century* = G. M. Trevelyan. *British History in the Nineteenth Century.* 1922.

Tschudi=Clara Tschudi. *Eugénie, Empress of the French.* 1906. Translated from the Norwegian by E. M. Cope.

Tuckwell=Rev. W. Tuckwell. *A. W. Kinglake.* Biographical and Literary Study. 1902.
A pleasant sketch.

Tulloch=Colonel Sir A. Tulloch. *The Crimean Commission and the Chelsea Board.* 2nd edition. 1880.
A convincing reply, by one of the original commissioners, to the whitewashing report of the Chelsea Board, and to Kinglake's minimising of the mismanagement in the Crimea.

Vandam=A. D. Vandam. *Undercurrents of the Second Empire.* 1897.

Vermorel : 1848=A. Vermorel. *Les Hommes de 1848.* 1869.

Vermorel : 1851=The same. *Les Hommes de 1851.* 1869.
Interesting examples of the kind of criticism of the *coup d'état* and its antecedents which it became possible towards the close of the Empire to publish in Paris.

Verner=Colonel W. Verner. *The Military Life of the Duke of Cambridge.* 2 vols. 1905.

Véron=L. D. Véron. *Nouveaux Mémoires d'un bourgeois de Paris.* 6 vols. 1853–5.
One of the Emperor's journalist friends : editor of the *Constitutionnel* : vol. vi. of his rambling memoirs contains some fabrications on the *coup d'état* : pro-Morny, anti-Maupas.

Viel-Castel=H. de Viel-Castel. *Mémoires sur le règne de Napoléon III.* 6 vols. 1881–84.
An intimate of the Princess Mathilde : scurrilous, and at times amusing : but quite untrustworthy.

Villemessant=H. de Villemessant. *Mémoires d'un journaliste.* 6 vols. 1872-8.
Editor of the *Figaro* under the Second Empire.

Vitzthum=Count C. F. Vitzthum von Eckstädt. *St Petersburg and London, 1852–1864.* 2 vols. English translation. 1887.
Saxon minister at St Petersburg 52–3 : and in London 53–6. Friend of the Prince Consort ; throws interesting sidelights on the diplomacy of the Crimean War, but capable of amazing inventions *v.* Loftus i. 251–3.

Vizetelly=[E. A. Vizetelly]. *The Court of the Tuileries.* 1907.

Walker=General Sir C. P. Beaumont Walker. *Days of a Soldier's Life.* 1894.
Served in the Crimea, Sept.-Dec. 1854.

Walpole : Russell=Sir Spencer Walpole. *Life of Lord John Russell.* 2 vols. 1889.
A competent biography, but with a good deal of special pleading for its hero. Chapter 26 for the Vienna negotiations. Throughout it exaggerates the divisions in the Aberdeen cabinet.

Walpole : Studies=The same. *Studies in Biography.* 1907.

Weill=Georges Weill. *Histoire du parti républicain en France, 1814–1870.* 1900.
The best work on its subject : of which it contains a useful bibliography.

West=Sir A. West. *Recollections, 1832–1886.* 2 vols. 1899.
Visited the Crimea in 1855 and kept a diary.

Wheeler=*Letters of Walter Savage Landor.* Private and public. Ed. by Stephen Wheeler. 1899.

Whitehouse=H. R. Whitehouse. *The Life of Lamartine.* 2 vols. 1918.

Windham=*The Crimean Diary and Letters of Lt.-Gen. Sir C. A. Windham.* Edited by Sir W. H. Russell. 1897.

Wood=General Sir Evelyn Wood. *The Crimea in 1854 and 1894.* 1895.
Expanded from articles in the *Fortnightly Review.*

Wrottesley = Hon. George Wrottesley. *Life and Letters of Sir John Burgoyne.*
2 vols. 1873.
Vol. ii. useful for the Crimea, where Burgoyne was in charge of
the British engineering department until March 55. Pp. 330–342
interesting on Kinglake.

In addition to the abbreviations above, some others have been employed
in the footnotes which refer to manuscript sources consulted. The con-
traction Arch. Nat. is prefixed to citations of MSS. located at the Archives
Nationales, B.M. to MSS. at the British Museum, B.N. to MSS. at the
Biblothèque Nationale, and F.O. to the English Foreign Office Papers at
the Record Office. In every case as exact a reference as possible follows ;
but whereas precision is admirably easy in the citation of documents at
the British Museum and generally also at the Bibliothèque Nationale, it is
necessarily somewhat cumbersome in the case of the Foreign Office Papers.
And for portions of the material at the Archives Nationales lack of paging
renders it impossible to do more than indicate the box or bundle in which
the paper quoted would be found. To do even this it is sometimes necessary
to employ such a jumble of various-sized letters, numbers, and asterisks
as almost to defy the resources of ordinary type.

APPENDIX B

A REPLY TO CRITICISMS

DURING the nearly thirty years since this volume was first published, it
has been challenged specifically on only three points. In one instance,
I am charged with a bias in favour of Louis Napoleon ; in the other two.
with a bias against him. I will deal with the two last first. In 1924 his
great-grandson, the Earl of Kerry, published a collection of the private
papers of the Comte de Flahault, under the title *The Secret of the Coup d'état.*
To this volume Philip Guedalla prefixed a preliminary study, in which he
stated (p. 18) that there was now ' a considerable body of evidence that
Louis Napoleon's action in December was taken in order to anticipate a coup
by the exiled royal family,' a story which ' Mr Simpson dismisses rather
summarily ' (p. 126, above) : in the same preface he claimed (p. 22) that
these newly published documents established a figure for the total casualties
of the *coup d'état* ' less than one half of Mr Simpson's ' estimate. To these
criticisms it may suffice if I quote from the reply which I wrote at the time
in the *Times Literary Supplement.*
' In regard to the casualties and the Maupas report, I do not think that
its discoverers at all exaggerate the importance of their find. The arguments
adduced in its support by Lord Kerry and Mr Guedalla seem to me entirely
convincing ; and if any further point in its favour were needed it would,
I think, be afforded by its concluding paragraph. A plea for ruthless
repression is exactly what Maupas would have added to a *bona fide* report
really intended for the President's private eye ; it would have been the last
thing likely to be included in any dressed-up account originally composed

for purposes of propaganda. For myself, so long as I had only undocumented official figures to set against contemporary estimates four times as numerous from our Embassy, themselves claiming to be derived by more channels than one from the French Ministry of the Interior, I could only —and professedly as " guesswork "—strike a rough balance between them, by doubling the one and halving the other. For the one source had no less interest in minimizing the figures than the other in exaggerating them. But I should now gladly accept the final official version of 600 as approximately correct.

' On the other hand, I find the documents less convincing as an argument for an Orleanist plot to anticipate the *coup d'état*. There are, I think, still three main obstacles to a belief in such a plot. (1) The late date of Palmerston's memorandum, which was only composed in 1858, and not published until after his death. Now Palmerston disliked the Orleanists, liked to hit back smartly, and had been dismissed in 1851 ostensibly for excusing the *coup d'état*. Had he been fully convinced by his own evidence, he would hardly have refrained from making full use of it. (2) Practically the whole of the Orleanist movements recorded in the memorandum—including all for which Palmerston named his informants, and all for which there is real corroboration external to the memorandum—admit of far more simple and innocent interpretation. A running to and fro of the Orleanist princes immediately *after* the *coup d'état*—hurried confabulations and excursions *then*—all these, though capable of a worse construction, *prove* no more than a natural alertness on their part to retrieve anything they could from the confusion ensuing upon the *coup*. Orleanist phrases as to being in Paris by the 20th would be a natural reply enough to Bonapartist deeds in Paris on the 2nd. After all, after the February revolution in 1848, Louis Napoleon not merely talked of being in Paris in three weeks, but *was* there in three days. But that does not make his coming its cause. So it is one thing that the Orleanists should have sought to snatch an advantage, when things had already been thrown into the melting-pot by their opponent. That I never doubted, and that these papers confirm. But it is quite another thing to show that they had already arranged to throw things into the melting-pot themselves. It was this second contention that I pronounced unconvincing, and the present papers leave me less convinced of it than ever. (3) For the decisive argument against it—in default of evidence to the contrary far stronger than any yet forthcoming—is the silence of Louis Napoleon himself. Useful to him even as a defence of the *coup d'état*, evidence of such a plot would have been invaluable after the much more unpopular act with which he followed it—the confiscation of the Orleanist estates. No act in his life was he so hard put to it to defend ; he had alienated by it—as these very papers show—his wisest advisers and best friends. The one argument which would have vindicated him triumphantly, in their eyes and the world's, would have been evidence that the millions of which he seemed arbitrarily to have deprived the Orleanists *could* not safely be left to them, since they had recently plotted mischief from which only his own *coup* had for the time saved France. Such was the President's need, that if he produced no evidence it could only have been because he had none ; and such were his powers, that if he had none it could hardly be but because there was none. As it was, this very correspondence shows us one of his well-wishers branding the act as " unjust," another as " infamous," a third as " an act of spoliation " ; and Palmerston himself, in February 1852, explicitly protesting (p. 214) " it is not justified by any action on the part of those against whom it is directed." And as it was, Flahault in reply could report no more valid motive on the part of the President than a belief (p. 216) that the Orleanists were " corrupting the English Press and embittering the English Court." Men in dire straits do not use pea-shooters when they possess pistols. '

This letter was published on August 14, 1924 ; and from that day to this no fragment of evidence has been forthcoming from any quarter to confirm the existence of an Orleanist plot preceding and justifying the deeds of December 2. I think therefore that I was right in brushing the story aside, and that it may now be taken as definitely established that no such excuse really existed for the perpetration of the *coup d'état*. On the other hand, the fresh evidence of the Maupas report, reproduced photographically in that volume, still seems to me to demonstrate that Mr Guedalla was right in regarding my original estimate of the casualties of the *coup d'état* as twice too high. This admission I confirmed in a note added to the last edition of this book ; and I have no desire to qualify it now.

The remaining charge imputes to me an opposite bias. In October 1933 and April 1934 Professor Temperley contributed two well-documented articles to the *English Historical Review*, on ' Stratford de Redcliffe and the Origins of the Crimean War : articles the general tenor of which, as of the same author's volume on *The Crimea* published in 1936, was to exonerate Stratford. In the first of these articles he speaks of me as ' clearly concerned to shift the responsibility of war from the shoulders of Napoleon III,' adding ' Mr Simpson repeats the old story that Stratford was animated throughout by personal feeling against Tsar Nicholas, who had refused to have him as British ambassador in 1831.' [1] But what I did in fact was not just to ' repeat an old story ' (though I should not assent to the implication that an old story is less likely to be true than a new one) : what I did was to demonstrate (p. 232, above) from unpublished documents the impact and magnitude of the injury done by Nicholas to Stratford. Indeed Professor Temperley made no attempt, either in his articles or in his book, to refute the testimony I adduced to that injury ; for in fact it was irrefutable : what he did do, in effect, was to dispute its relevance. Now it is no doubt possible, as Professor Temperley seems to have held, that Stratford was altogether immune, in his conduct of the negotiations which preceded the Crimean War, from any desire to have his ' tit for tat ' with Nicholas. On the other hand it is also possible that in the course of them the great ambassador was profoundly, even if unconsciously, affected by the unprecedented personal rebuff which the Czar had earlier inflicted on him. After a careful reading of all the evidence amassed by Professor Temperley, in addition to that which I had already examined for myself, I am still of the deliberate opinion that the latter is the more probable interpretation. I neither think, indeed, nor thought (*vide* p. 233, above) that Stratford was guilty of the enormity of seeking to avenge a private injury by a European war. But I both thought, and think, that he was not unwilling to confront Nicholas in 1853, as he had successfully confronted him in 1849, with the alternative between war and a public and humiliating retreat, at a time when to build a bridge for that retreat was the true task of diplomacy.

Here as elsewhere, however, the difference between Professor Temperley's view and mine is a difference less on facts, than on the proper interpretation of facts. He did not, for example, question the authenticity of the doubly attested utterance of Stratford which I cited on p. 239 above : ' You have brought good news, for that means *war*. The Emperor of Russia chose to make it a personal quarrel with me ; and now I am avenged.' What he did do was to explain : ' this last utterance, once the war was certain, seems a legitimate outburst due to war psychology.' [2] Possibly. But *in vino veritas*. For it is also possible that it was precisely in such moments of rare excitement that the real mind of this polished and formidable diplomatist was most truly revealed.

---

[1] *E.H.R.* vol. 48, pp. 601, 602.
[2] *Times Lit. Supp.*, 21 March, 1936.

Similarly it sometimes happened that the same diplomatic documents left a different impression upon Professor Temperley's mind and mine ; nor should I dream, where this was the case, of claiming a greater weight for my personal judgment than for his. What, however, I can with some confidence maintain, is that the impression which Stratford's despatches to Clarendon made on me corresponds with the impression they made on their recipient at the time. This fact, at least in the most crucial instance, Professor Temperley himself would not I think have disputed. For he admits that ' at the time . . . Clarendon blamed Stratford for the failure ' of the Vienna Note. ' But,' he continued, ' it is not usually recognised that Clarendon at least and at last recognised the error of this judgment. In an article, revised by himself ten years later, Clarendon refers to the " Vienna Note " and to the great responsibility undertaken by Stratford in causing its rejection. He adds : " The interpretation, afterwards put upon that note by Count Nesselrode, showed that he [Stratford] was right." This is a very remarkable admission, for Clarendon confesses that Stratford was right in thus disobeying.'[1]

Now the passage which Professor Temperley thus summarises actually runs as follows.[2] ' No man ever took upon himself a larger amount of responsibility than Lord Stratford, when he virtually overruled the decision of the four Powers, including his own Government, and acquiesced in—not to say caused—the rejection of the Vienna Note by the Porte, after it had been accepted by Russia. The interpretation afterwards put upon that note by Count Nesselrode showed that he was right ; but, nevertheless, that was the point on which peace and war turned.' I must confess that the impression left upon my mind by the original passage, which I have here quoted entire and without omissions, differs materially from the impression I should have gathered had I been dependent upon Professor Temperley's summary of it. From the summary I should have supposed that the stress was upon Stratford's rectitude : from the original that it was upon his responsibility. In their true context, as I wrote in the *Literary Supplement* at the time[3] the words seem to amount to little more than ' a rather grudging concession that Nesselrode's subsequent interpretation of the Note presented Stratford with a subsequent justification for his action, on which he could hardly have counted at the time. Certainly the admission, for what it is worth, is sandwiched between what appears to be a double reaffirmation, ten years after the event, both that Stratford, more than anyone else, was responsible for the rejection of the Vienna Note ; and that the rejection of the Vienna Note, more than anything else, was responsible for the war. If this is a recantation, it is anything but a handsome one.' And if we restore, not merely Professor Temperley's half-sentence to the context of its surrounding paragraph, but the paragraph itself to the context of the surrounding article, his use of it seems even more remarkable. For the entire article is a devastating review of Kinglake's famous two first volumes (on which see p. 382, above) ; and contained a smashing demolition of his whole elaborate thesis that England had been led or tricked into the war by Louis Napoleon : on the contrary, ' by far the largest share of that responsibility rests with this country.' And whereas there is no proof that Clarendon inspired the article's meagre and dubious exoneration of Stratford, there *is* conclusive evidence that he did directly inspire its unambiguous exculpation of Louis Napoleon. For to Reeve, the actual author of the article, he wrote, while it was in the press : ' Kinglake would induce people to believe that the Emperor was under an urgent necessity to turn away

[1] *E.H.R.* vol. 49, p. 275. Repeated *totidem verbis* in the same author's *The Crimea*, p. 474.
[2] *Edinburgh Review*, April 1863, p. 331.
[3] 28 March 1936.

the attention of his subjects from his action at home, and that he therefore
dragged us into the war. It would, I think, be worth while to get some facts
respecting his status in France at that time. If I am not mistaken, he was
in no trouble or danger at all ; for the nation had accepted him as a sort of
deliverer from the *rouges*.' [1] I have chosen this example of divergent
interpretation because it concerns not recondite or unpublished documents,
where the ordinary reader cannot judge between us, but a familiar passage
in print, where he easily can. For though Professor Temperley's use of it
was entirely novel, yet the passage itself, so far from being ' not usually
recognised,' had been reprinted repeatedly in the most widely-read of all
English text-books on the subject, Sir John Marriott's excellent *The Eastern
Question* (pp. 233, 234).

Clarendon's ultimate judgment on Stratford seems then, *pace* Professor
Temperley, to remain uncertain. His *contemporary* judgment is simply not
in doubt at all. To the passages cited in my text above (p. 235) I will add
here only the following quotations from his private letters to Cowley in 1853.
July 8. ' My fear is that he [Stratford] will never consent to any arrangement that does not humiliate the Emperor of Russia.', And a few days
later : ' The humiliation of Russia has become a necessity of his nature.'
Of the Turkish rejection of the note he wrote in August : ' I cannot, I am
sorry to say, persuade myself that he is not at the bottom of the whole
difficulty.' And on September 13 he added : ' Stratford throughout has
been and will be our great stumbling-block. His course in exciting the
Turks has been bad, but the course he pursues towards his colleagues is
worse.' [2]

To take one's stand upon contemporary opinion is not, perhaps, a posture
that commonly commends itself to the historian. For to revise, or even
to reverse, contemporary judgments is for the historian a natural, and
within limits a legitimate, outcome of the desire to magnify his office. And
this desire has led, and will yet lead, to much valuable reinterpretation of the
past. Nevertheless there is a sense in which great reverence is owed to the
opinion of contemporaries. For those who saw with their eyes, and heard
with their ears, the men of whom we write had, without labour, immediate
sources of judgment which all our toil upon their letters and despatches,
all our careful collation of their recorded utterances, cannot even remotely
approach. And to that advantage itself must be added another, and perhaps
a greater still. The contemporary alone, provided he truly *is* contemporary,
has his judgment unclouded by the knowledge of the event : that blinding
knowledge which for the historian is for ever turning into statesmanship the
policy that succeeded, and into folly the policy that failed. Only those
who did not know whether it *would* succeed or fail could, *until* they knew,
give verdicts free from that most fatal bias. Both by what he cannot have,
and by what he cannot help having ; by the knowledge of their persons
with which no effort can endow him, and by the knowledge of their fate of
which no effort can divest him, the historian is doubly disabled from judging
the dead in comparison with those untutored contemporaries who walked
and talked with them alive. And for this reason I am content to share the
common belief of those who knew Stratford in the flesh ; even if to do so is
to part company with what is still, although 'the abhorred shears ' denied
it completion, the ablest and most learned of all later reconstructions of
his career.

[1] 25 Feb. 1863. *Laughton* II, 89.
[2] For these and other letters to the same effect see the papers of Earl Cowley
edited by his son, entitled *The Paris Embassy during the Second Empire.*
1928.

INDEX

Abd-ul-Medjid, Sultan (1823–1861), 234 n.

Aberdeen, S. H. S., Earl of (1784–1860), 220, 227, 235, 236, 242, 282.

Åland Islands, 256.

Albert, Prince (1819–1861), on Louis Napoleon, 238 ; agitation against, 241, 242 ; visits Louis Napoleon at Boulogne, 266 sq.; urges conscription, 273 ; meets Louis Napoleon at Dover, 289 ; at Paris, 324 sq.: on the Turks, 364 ; mentioned, 217, 236.

Alexander I, Emperor of Russia (1777–1825), 222, 355, 371.

Alexander II, Emperor of Russia (1818–1881), 286, 337, 347, 371.

Algeria, 186, 189 n.

Allais, M., 109.

Alma, battle of the, 258, 259, 274.

Alsace, 100, 104.

Alva, Duchess of (1825–1860), 206.

Ancona, 66.

Antonelli, Cardinal (1806–1876), 62, 65.

Arese, Count Francesco (1805–1881), 47 n., 61, 86 n., 178.

Arnaud, Marshal. See Saint-Arnaud.

Austria, occupies Ferrara, 51 ; and the Roman Republic, 59 sq.; on the coup d'état, 163 ; supports allied demands from Nicholas, 248 ; and the Crimean War, 250 sq.; and the Peace of Paris, 344 sq.

Auvergne, 159.

Avignon, 375 n.

Azof, Sea of, 341, 344.

Bagehot, Walter (1826–1877), letter of, quoted, 148–150; on the coup d'état, 171.

Balaclava, 274, 278.

Balaclava, battle of, 277.

Balmoral, 266.

Baltic, naval operations in, 256.

Barrot, Ferdinand (1806–1883), 84.

Barrot, Odilon (1791–1873), Louis Napoleon's first premier, 28, 81, 82, 83.

Bassanelli, V., 69 n.

Bastide, Jules (1800–1879), 55 n.

Baudin, J. B. A. V. (1801–1851), 147, 148.

Bavaria, 338.

Bayonne, Napoleon III at, 264, 266

Belgiojoso, Christine di Trivulzio, Princess (1808–1871), 85 n.

Belgium, 50, 266.

Bernstorff, Anna, Countess von, 201 n.

Berryer, P. A. (1790–1868), 79, 93, 116, 141 sq.

Bessarabia, 340, 355, 356.

Béville, Colonel, 129, 130.

Biarritz, 264, 266.

Billault, Auguste (1805–1863), 168 n.

Bismarck, Count Otto von (1815–1898), 353.

Blanc, Louis (1811–1882), 97.

Bologna, 65.

Bomba. See Ferdinand II.

Bonne-Nouvelle, Boulevard, massacre in, 153.

Bordeaux, Louis Napoleon's speech at, 194 sq.

Bosquet, General P. F. J. (1810–1861), 365 n.

Boulogne, 266, 288, 324, 327.

Bright, John (1811–1889), 180, 341 n.

Broglie, Duc de (1785–1870), 19 n., 93, 162.

Browning, E. B. (1806–1861), 156 n.

Bugeaud, Marshal T. R. (1784–1849), 67 n.

Bulgaria, 220, 221 n.

Bulwer-Lytton (1801–1871), 5.